MOSQUITO
MENACING THE REICH

MOSQUITO
MENACING THE REICH

Combat Action in the Twin-engine
Wooden Wonder of World War II

MARTIN W BOWMAN

Pen & Sword
AVIATION

First published in Great Britain in 2008 by
Pen & Sword Aviation
An imprint of
Pen & Sword Books Ltd
47 Church Street
Barnsley
South Yorkshire
S70 2AS

ISBN 978 1 84415 823 2

A CIP catalogue record for this book is
available from the British Library

Printed and bound in England
by CPI Group (UK) Ltd, Croydon, CR0 4YY

Pen & Sword Books Ltd incorporates the imprints of
Pen & Sword Aviation, Pen & Sword Maritime, Pen & Sword Military,
Wharncliffe Local History, Pen & Sword Select,
Pen & Sword Military Classics and Leo Cooper.

For a complete list of Pen & Sword titles please contact
PEN & SWORD BOOKS LIMITED
47 Church Street, Barnsley, South Yorkshire, S70 2AS, England
E-mail: enquiries@pen-and-sword.co.uk
Website: www.pen-and-sword.co.uk

Contents

'...For those of us who flew the Mosquitoes the memory of their versatility and their achievements will always remain. It would be impossible to forget such an experience as the thunderous din of twenty aircraft sweeping across the hangars as low as possible, setting course like bullets in tight formation for the enemy coast. The whole station would be out watching and each leader would vie for the honour of bringing his formation lower across the aerodrome than anyone else. Nor would it be possible to forget the sensation of looking back over enemy territory and seeing your formation behind you, their racing shadows moving only a few feet below them across the earth's surface; or that feeling of sudden exhilaration when the target was definitely located and the whole pack were following you on to it with their bomb doors open while people below scattered in every direction and the long streams of flak came swinging up; or the sudden jerk of consternation of the German soldiers lounging on the coast, their moment of indecision, and then their mad scramble for the guns; or the memory of racing across The Hague at midday on a bright spring morning, while the Dutchmen below hurled their hats in the air and beat each other over the back. All these are unforgettable memories. Many of them will be recalled also by the peoples of Europe long after peace has been declared, for to them the Mosquito came to be an ambassador during their darkest hours...'

Wing Commander John de Lacy Wooldridge DSO DFC* DFM,
author of *Low Attack*

CHAPTER ONE

Down Low

Dark clouds covered eastern England on 15 November 1941 when Blenheim aircrews of 105 Squadron braved the raw wind to gather near the hangars at the No.2 (Fighter Bomber) Group grass airfield at Swanton Morley, Norfolk to see a grey and green shape approach the aerodrome from the north-west. First it flew over at about 500ft, at a speed of 300 mph. Then it approached the Watch Office and hangar from the west and went into a vertical bank at a height of 2-3,000ft before turning a circle so tight and at such a speed that vapour trails streamed from his wing-tips. This was followed by a normal circuit and landing. It seemed that the rumours were true. For some time now the Squadron observers had attended conversion training on a new W/T and the gunners had started navigation courses, all amid speculation that they would be receiving a revolutionary type of aircraft built largely of wood to replace their outdated Blenheim IVs. Compared to the Blenheim IVs 105 Squadron was used to this performance was quite breathtaking. The tall frame of Company Chief Test Pilot Geoffrey de Havilland Jr. emerged from the tiny cockpit of the 'Wooden Wonder'. He climbed down the ladder to be received like a conquering hero by Group Captain Battle OBE DFC, the station commander, and Wing Commander Peter H.A. Simmons DFC. Simmons' air and ground crews were equally ecstatic. During September and October 105 Squadron had flown anti-shipping operations from Malta and losses were high. Returning to Swanton Morley, the surviving crews were due for a rest and in need of a morale boost. The arrival of the Mosquito provided it.

Sergeant (later Flight Lieutenant DFC) Mike Carreck was an observer in one of the newest Blenheim crews fresh from No.17 OTU Upwood, 2 Group's finishing school. He and Pilot Officer Ronald Onley, first violinist in the London Philharmonic, were one of the half dozen or so crews posted to 105 Squadron at Swanton Morley: 'a hellspot only 15 miles from Norwich but which might have been in deepest Siberia', as Mike Carreck recalls:[1]

> Waiting there for us were just a few survivors from 105's bloodbath in Malta where fourteen days was the lifetime of a Blenheim squadron. We rightly regarded these battle-scarred veterans with the deepest respect but they made us welcome. Life at Swanton Morley began sedately enough.

Now and then we did a Blenheim cross-country, as I handed my pilot the course, compass heading and ETAs [Estimated Time of Arrival]. Sometimes we ventured as far away as Lincoln. We flew to the range and dropped teeny-weeny bombs and once, a special treat and with much trepidation, a 250-pounder. Dullish days but nights were duller still, as for recreation, romance and merriment one had to rely on nearby East Dereham where mothers locked away their daughters after tea and every door slammed tight shut on the dot of 18.00 hours. Nothing to do but go shivering to our beds in our freezing Nissen huts. Excitement was somewhat lacking; except for a nonsense of a rumour going the rounds that we were to be re-equipped with a fabulous new aircraft, the fastest in the world, a day bomber that could out-fly any fighter and leave it wondering where we'd gone, that could fly 5 miles high into the stratosphere and had an incredible range of 1,200 miles. We shrugged our shoulders; we'd believe it when we saw it, which we very soon did.

On 15 November it came suddenly out of nowhere, inches above the hangars with a crackling thunderclap of twin Merlins. As we watched, bewitched, it was flung about the sky in a beyond belief display for a bomber that could out perform any fighter. After a well-bred whisper of a touch down, a door opened and down the ladder came suede shoes, yellow socks and the rest of Geoffrey de Havilland. We pushed and shoved around this impossible dream of an aircraft. No other word for it, it was beautiful. An arrogant beauty with a 'job-to-do, get out of my way', slim, sleek fuselage, high cocked 'to-hell-with-you' tail. It had awesome power on the leash in those huge engines and was eager on its undercarriage like a sprinter on the starting blocks who couldn't wait to leap up and away.

Called a Mosquito, they told us. It was Mosquito W4064 and it was to be shot down six months later on the squadron's first operation.[2] During those six months only seven more Mosquitoes joined W4064 on the squadron so flights were few and far between; indeed we new boys had to wait weeks for our first. For us, it was back to Blenheims and Arctic nights, not counting a Station exercise when it was pretended that German paratroopers had landed and a batch of us were sent to guard the Sergeants' Mess. We stretched out on the carpet; blissfully warm at last until somebody came in to wake us with the astounding news that the Japanese had bombed Pearl Harbor. We turned over to sleep our best night ever, the war was won...'Three to a crew in a Blenheim, only two in a Mosquito so sadly some of our navs and WoPs were surplus to requirements. Sadder still they were posted to Blenheim squadrons flying in the Sea of Carnage, attacks on North Sea convoys whose escorting flak-ships didn't bother to aim, just fired splash into the sea, a curtain of exploding steel through which the doomed Blenheim crews flew with unmatchable courage.

Among the throng of seasoned pilots and their navigators at Swanton Morley on 15 November gathered to admire the Mosquito's 'beautiful shape' was Flight Lieutenant D.A.G. 'George' Parry, who like his CO, was a veteran of two tours on Blenheims. He was always known as 'George' because, like the autopilot of the same name, he always came home! Parry had recently completed two tours and was 'resting' at 13 OTU at Bicester when he just happened to pick up the telephone and receive a call from Pete Simmons who had been his 'A' Flight commander in 110 Squadron at Wattisham. Simmons had rung to enquire when he was getting some more pilots, adding, 'by the way George, I'm getting some fast aircraft. Do you want to come?' Parry quickly turned down a posting to a squadron equipped with Bisleys going to North Africa and joined Simmons at Swanton Morley. The CO's promise of 'fast aircraft' had come true, although W4064 left almost as fast as it arrived. After lunch, Geoffrey de Havilland Jr. climbed back into the sleek Mosquito B.IV and was joined by Simmons, who took the right-hand seat for a joyride with a difference. De Havilland Jr. treated his passenger and the watching crews to an exhilarating display of aerobatics. When they landed, Simmons was reported to be '...looking a bit green around the gills, but it did not stop him talking about it in the Officers' Mess during lunch!'[3] The sleek new bomber had to return next day to Hatfield, where the first of a paltry ten B.IV bombers was coming off the production lines, for adjustments. Not until July 1941 had it been decided to build Mosquitoes as bombers and even then only converted photo-reconnaissance airframes.[4]

Meanwhile, 105 Squadron, now stationed at Horsham St. Faith near Norwich after Swanton Morley proved unsuitable for operations, had received only eight Mosquitoes by mid-May 1942, but 2 Group was anxious to despatch its new wonder aircraft on the first op as soon as possible. On 27 May it issued orders for 105 Squadron to prepare four Mosquitoes with bombs and cameras to harass and obtain photographic evidence in the wake of the 'Thousand Bomber' raid on Cologne, scheduled for the night of 30/31 May. Squadron Leader Alan R. 'Jesse' Oakeshott DFC, commander of 'A' Flight and his navigator Flying Officer Charles Hayden, set off first. Well over 6ft tall and a regular officer, Oakeshott cut an imposing figure. He had won the DFC flying as a bomber pilot on a Wellington squadron earlier in the war. They were followed later by Pilot Officer William D. Kennard and Pilot Officer Eric R. Johnson who took off from Horsham before the 'heavies' had returned. Pilot Officer Edgar A. Costello-Bowen and Warrant Officer Tommy Broom; Flight Lieutenant Jack E. Houlston and Flight Sergeant James L. Armitage followed them shortly before lunchtime the following day. Oakeshott and Hayden flew at 24,000ft over the battered and blasted city and added four 500lb bombs to the devastation; but with smoke reaching to 14,000ft, their F24 camera was rendered useless. Kennard and Johnson failed to return, their aircraft being hit by anti-aircraft fire. Costello-Bowen and Houlston dropped their bombs from high-level into the smouldering and smoking ruins to prolong the night of misery for the inhabitants and bomb disposal teams and headed back to Norfolk. In the late afternoon Squadron Leader Peter J. Channer, who as a Blenheim pilot on 18 Squadron had received the DFC for the attack on the Knapsack power station at Cologne, took off from Horsham and flew in thick cloud to within 60 miles of the city. Then he dived down at almost 380 mph to low-level to take photographs of the damage. Channer quickly realized that this highly successful approach would be particularly effective for future Mosquito bombing operations.

On the evening of 1 June, two Mosquitoes returned to Cologne to bomb and reconnoitre the city. One of the aircraft failed to return. Then, just before dawn on 2 June, 18 hours after a 'Thousand Bomber' raid on Essen, George Parry and his navigator, Flying Officer Victor Robson, flew a lone 2 hours 5 minutes round-trip to Cologne. They carried four 500-pounders to stoke up the fires and a camera to observe the damage. However, thick smoke made the latter task impossible. The Mosquitoes of 105 Squadron continued their lone reconnaissance missions over Germany and on 8 June, 139 Squadron was formed at Horsham St. Faith under the command of Wing Commander William Peter Shand DFC using crews and a few B.IVs from 105 Squadron. One of the pilots transferred to 139 was Jack Houlston AFC who was promoted to Squadron Leader. Houlston flew 139 Squadron's first operation on 25/26 June, a low-level raid on the airfield at Stade, near Wilhelmshaven and returned after dark just as bombers for the third in the series of 'Thousand Bomber' raids were taking off for Bremen. Two of 105 Squadron's Mosquitoes flew reconnaissance over the city after the raid and four more went to reconnoitre other German cities to assess damage and bring back photographs.

On 2 July the first joint attack by 105 and 139 Squadron Mosquitoes took place when four aircraft from 105 Squadron carried out a low-level attack on the submarine yards at Flensburg and two Mosquitoes in 139 Squadron also bombed from high level. Group Captain J.C. MacDonald DFC AFC the Station Commander and his observer, Flight Lieutenant Skelton were last seen flying slowly across the coast on the return leg, off Pellworm Island. They did not return to Marham and were later found to be PoWs. 'Jesse' Oakeshott DFC, who was now a Wing Commander, and his observer, Flying Officer Vernon F.E. 'Titch' Treherne DFM, were intercepted by an Fw 190 and they were shot down and killed 9 miles NNE of Husum, at Sönnebüll, Germany. Jack Houlston came off the target pursued by three Fw 190As but he and his observer made it back. Two more fighters chased Flight Lieutenant George Pryce Hughes MiD RCAF, who despite his name was an Argentinian, after he had been hit by flak over the target. Both pilots made their exits hugging the wave tops and by applying plus 12½ lb of boost, they easily outpaced their pursuers. (The Mosquito was only just faster than an Fw 190 under certain conditions. It all depended on the rating of the Merlin 21 engines. If they were rated to give maximum performance at either low or high level, the Mosquito could just outdistance the Fw 190A. However, the average Merlin 21s fell somewhere in the middle range of rating, which meant that they although they were just fast enough at low level, they were certainly not at high level).

On 11 July the Mosquitoes bombed Flensburg again, as a diversion for the heavies that were hitting Danzig. Pilot Officer Laston made it home with part of his fin blown away by flak, but Flight Lieutenant George Pryce-Hughes and his navigator, Flying Officer Thomas A. Gabe were killed when their Mosquito was shot down by *Unteroffizier* Herbert Biermann of 2nd *Staffel* JG1. Sergeant Peter W.R. Rowland, in DK296, borrowed from George Parry, flew so low that he hit a roof and returned to Horsham with pieces of chimney pot lodged in the nose. After he had landed Parry barked at Rowland, 'I'm not lending you my aircraft again!' High-level raids in clear skies were the order of the day during July and the first of twenty-nine 'Siren Raids' were flown. These involved high-level dog-leg routes across Germany at night and were designed to disrupt the war workers and their families and ensure that they lost at least two hours' sleep before their shifts the following day. Flying Officer Frank Weekes RAAF and Pilot Officer Frank Hurley of 105 Squadron failed to return from a sortie to Essen on 28 July: they were shot down over Mönchengladbach by *Unteroffizier* Karl Bugaj in a Bf 109F for 11th *Staffel* JG1's first victory. While the Mosquito could outpace the Bf 109 in a straight chase, when in a dive the Bf 109 had all the speed it wanted to engage a Mosquito. Bugaj's kill was made all the easier by *Hauptmann* Fritz Losigkeit, who controlled the interception.[5] For the first time he had the use of the recently introduced Freya early warning radar. Losigkeit decided to track the intruder only as it was flying a straight course, and give radio instructions to Bugaj, which resulted in him intercepting the Mosquito when he had a height advantage, so that he could gain speed by diving.[6]

On 1 August Wing Commander Hughie Idwal Edwards VC DFC, an Australian of Welsh ancestry from Freemantle, took command of 105 Squadron for the second time. Edwards had been CO of 139 Squadron when he took command of 105 Squadron in May 1941 when the two squadrons were flying Blenheims on suicidal anti-shipping strikes in the North Sea.[7]

On 25 August Flight Lieutenant D.A.G. 'George' Parry and Flight Lieutenant Victor G. 'Robbie' Robson and Flight Lieutenant Joseph Roy George Ralston DFM and Flying Officer Sydney Clayton DFM, were detailed to raid two electric power stations. Ralston and Clayton had both been posted to the squadron in May 1942 after flying Blenheim IVs in 107 Squadron. Ralston, a Mancunian from Moss side, had enlisted in the RAF in 1930 as a technical tradesman. By 1938 he had progressed to become a sergeant pilot on 108 Squadron flying Hawker Hinds and Blenheims. Flight Lieutenant Edgar A. Costello-Bowen and Warrant Officer Tommy J. Broom were given a switching station at Brauweiler near Cologne but they hit a pylon and crashed at Paaltjesdreef Wood at Westmalle in the Belgian hamlet of Blauwhoeve *en route*. Incredibly, both men survived and with the help of the Underground movement they evaded capture and were sent along the escape route to Spain. In October they returned to England aboard the battleship HMS *Malaya*.[8]

On 13 September 105 and 139 Squadrons received orders to vacate Horsham St. Faith by 28 September, as the Americans were due to arrive to base medium bombers there and in November the 2nd Bomb Wing would assume control of the airfield for P-47 and later Liberator operations. The Mosquitoes were to move to RAF Marham 9 miles south-east of King's Lynn where they would replace 115 and 218 Squadrons of 3 Group. Amid the changeover, on 19 September, six crews in 105 Squadron attempted the first daylight Mosquito raid on Berlin. Two pilots Sergeant Norman Booth[9] and Flight Sergeant K.L. Monaghan were both forced to return early. Flight Lieutenant Roy Ralston and Flying Officer Sydney Clayton bombed Hamburg after finding Berlin covered by cloud. George Parry and 'Robbie' Robson were intercepted on two occasions by Fw 190s but managed to evade them. Parry jettisoned his bombs near Hamburg and turned for home, heading back across the north coast of Germany and into Holland. At 1,000ft, just off the Dutch coast, two 109s attacked but although one of them scored hits, Parry dived down to sea level and soon outran them. Squadron Leader Norman Henry Edward Messervy DFC, an Australian from Point Cook, and his navigator Pilot Officer Frank Holland in M-Mother were shot down by an Fw 190 piloted by *Schwarmführer Oberfeldwebel* Anton-Rudolf 'Toni' Piffer of 2nd *Staffel*/JG1.[10] The Mosquito crashed 30 kilometres NNW of Osnabrück with the loss of both crew. Messervy was a second tour man having flown sixty-eight operations on Blenheims and PR Spitfires on 3 PRU in 1941. Only Warrant Officer Charles R. K. Bools MiD and Sergeant George Jackson succeeded in bombing the 'Big City'.

A few days later the expert low-level raiders in 105 Squadron were told to prepare for a long overwater operation, which would be flown at heights of just 50-100ft. George Parry, now a squadron leader, would lead, with 'Robbie' Robson as his navigator. The three other crews were Pilot Officer Pete W.T. Rowland and Pilot Officer Richard 'Dick' Reilly, Parry's No 2; Flying Officer Alec Bristow and Pilot Officer Bernard Marshall; and Flight Sergeant Gordon K. Carter and Sergeant William S. Young. Their target was the *Gestapo* HQ in Oslo. The Norwegian Government-in-Exile in London had been made aware by reports from the Norwegian Underground that morale in their *Nazi*-subjugated homeland was at a low ebb. They also learned that a rally of *Hirdsmen* (Norwegian Fascists) and Quislings would take place in the Norwegian capital between 25-27 September and it therefore seemed an ideal opportunity for the Mosquitoes to help restore national pride. As well as disrupting the parade, they were to bomb the *Gestapo* HQ between the Town Hall and the Royal Palace, which stands on a hill.

On 25 September the four Mosquitoes, their bomb bays empty, taxied out at Marham and took off for Leuchars in Scotland, where the operation came under the control of Wing Commander Hughie Edwards VC DFC. The raid involved a round-trip of 1,100 miles with an air time of 4 hours 45 minutes, the longest Mosquito mission thus far, the crews using dead reckoning along the entire route. The Mosquitoes were refuelled and bombed-up with four 11-second delayed-action 500lb bombs and they set off at low-level, 50ft all the way, to Norway. They went through the Skaggerak, made landfall at the southern end of Oslo Fjord and flew up the eastern side. As they flew up to a police radio station perched on a hill Parry hit the flexible 45ft-high radio antenna, although it did no damage to his Mosquito. Crews had been briefed that there would be 10/10ths cloud at 2,000ft over Oslo but it was a lovely day with blue sky. They had also been told that there were no fighters to worry about, but the Germans had brought some Fw 190s south from Stavanger for a flypast during the parade. They had landed at Fornebu and had only been on the ground a short time when, at 15.00 hours, the Mosquitoes swooped out of brilliant autumn sunshine over the centre of Oslo. A lookout at the southern end of Oslo Fjord reported the bombers and two Focke Wulfs got into the action although, fortunately, the rest did not get off in time. The pilot of the leading fighter was 22-year-old *Unteroffizier* Rudolf 'Rudi' Fenten, who had temporarily left his unit to train on and pick up the new Fw 190 at Sola/Stavanger. Flying the other Fw 190 was 24-year-old *Feldwebel* Erich Klein of 3./JG5 based at Herdla near Bergen. Both pilots were very experienced. Fenten had been in the *Luftwaffe* since 1940, while Klein had joined it in 1937. Fenten at first thought that the twin-engined aircraft flying ahead of him in two pairs were part of the flypast. (The Mosquito was still top-secret and largely unknown to the German units.)[11] Then he realized they were too low and he chased after Carter's Mosquito whose port engine was set on fire. Fenten followed until the Mosquito exploded in front of him and crashed into Lake Engervannet near Sandvika.

Parry meanwhile, was concentrating on 'buzzing' the parade and taking a line south-west over the centre of Oslo for the bomb run. Pinpointing the town hall near the harbour with the old Akerhus fortress, the Royal palace, at one end of the main street and the high dome of the building housing the *Gestapo* headquarters was simple enough. Parry was flying at 280-300 mph when he dropped his bombs. Erich Klein, meanwhile, went after Pete Rowland and Dick Reilly. The two aircraft chased around the fir trees north of Oslo for many minutes until Klein struck a tree with his wing and he was forced to return to Fornebu.[12] Some of the Mosquitoes' bombs did not explode but everyone thought that it was a remarkably successful raid especially because it was the first long-distance raid the Mosquitoes had carried out. All three crews were debriefed and they flew back to Norfolk the next morning to rejoin the squadron at Marham. The post-mortem and camera pictures taken on the raid revealed that at least four bombs had entered the roof of the *Gestapo* HQ; one had remained inside and failed to detonate and the other three had crashed through the opposite wall before exploding.

On 26 September George Parry flew down to Hendon to travel into London to Broadcasting House where that night he broadcast the story of the raid on the

BBC Home Service. Listeners heard that a new aircraft, the Mosquito, had been revealed officially for the first time by the RAF and that four had made a daring roof-top raid on Oslo. Parry recalled that the Air Ministry had 'cooked up' a script but he felt that it was not true but they said, 'Don't worry old boy, it's for the public. They'll lap it up'. Parry however changed it and the broadcast was very different to the handout he had been given by the Air Ministry. 'On Friday afternoon Quisling and I had an appointment in the same town. Quisling had a big crowd with him, I believe it was one of his party rallies. I only had a little crowd and we were in four Mosquitoes and they gave us very short notice. But we were punctual.' The BBC paid George Parry five guineas, which he gave to the RAF Benevolent Fund.

On 30 September Parry flew to Newmarket in a Mosquito with Flying Officer Thomas, to meet the people from the Norwegian Embassy. Parry landed on the racecourse runway and was soon in animated conversation with the four Norwegians in a large hotel in the centre of Newmarket. They had been very pleased with the raid and its outcome.

October was a mix of low-level shallow-dive raids at dusk on targets in Belgium and Holland and high-level attacks on German cities. It was also a month when several crews were lost to the 'Butcher Birds' of JG1 and JG 26. On 9 October Wing Commander Edwards and 'Tubby' Cairns and another Mosquito crewed by Warrant Officer Charles R.K. Bools MiD and Sergeant George Jackson set out to bomb Duisburg. *Feldwebel* Fritz Timm of 12./JG1 shot down Bools and Jackson over Belgium.[13] At dusk on Sunday, 11 October three pairs of Mosquitoes were despatched to bomb Hanover but two of the Mosquitoes were intercepted by Fw 190As of II./JG26 while *en route* over Holland. *Unteroffizier* Günter Kirchner of the 5th Staffel took off from Katwijk and intercepted Pilot Officer Jim Lang and Flying Officer Robin P. 'Tommy' Thomas 2 kilometres from Utrecht and shot them down. *Unteroffizier* Kolschek of the 4th Staffel was credited with shooting down Squadron Leader James G.L. 'Jimmy' Knowles DFC and Flight Sergeant Charles Gartside. Lang and Thomas survived to be taken prisoner but no trace was ever found of Knowles and Gartside who had flown a tour on Blenheims and had only just returned from a 'rest' at 13 OTU Bicester before they were posted to 139 Squadron on 3 August. It was Kolschek's second Mosquito victory as he had been credited with having shot down and killed Pilot Officer Geoffrey Downe RAAF and Pilot Officer Alfred Groves DFM on 15 August near Ghent-Mariakerke in Belgium during the operation to Mainz.[14]

Night Intruder operations were flown against targets on the continent. On 30 October Sergeant Reginald Levy and Sergeant Les Hogan and Flying Officer William 'Bill' Blessing RAAF and Sergeant J. Lawson in 105 Squadron attacked the *Luftwaffe* night-fighter aerodrome at Leeuwarden in Holland. Levy was born in Portsmouth and had lived in Lancashire for most of his youth before beginning pilot training in the USA with the first class of UK cadets in the 'Arnold Scheme'.

By the time he was sent to 17 OTU for conversion to Blenheims he had 200 hours, an enormous figure by the standards of the day. His instructor had 63 hours! One day he was at dispersal when the aerodrome was well and truly 'beaten up' by an aeroplane the like of which he and his fellow pilot's had never seen before. It finished the 'beat up' by feathering an engine and departed in an upward roll. It was June 1942 and this was Levy's first sight of the Mosquito. From then on there was no other aeroplane for him. Levy, who thought that he was fortunate to be one of the two crews selected for posting to 105 Squadron, remembers:

> We attacked Leeuwarden successfully but I was hit by flak from the ground defences coming across the boundary of the airfield. The port engine was set on fire and the instrument panel and windscreen disappeared with the nose of the aircraft. I was hit in the leg, although I didn't feel it at the time and my observer, Les Hogan, was hit in the arm. At 40ft or so control was tricky. So I called Les to press the extinguisher button on the port engine, which I had feathered. He promptly pushed the starboard one! The good engine was filled with foam, coughed once or twice and then, miraculously, the good old Merlin caught again and we snaked along almost sideways at about 160 mph. I had to jam my foot under the rudder bar to keep it straight as the rudder-trim handle had been shot away. We went out over the aptly named Friesian Island of Overflakee, straight between two German ships, which opened up on us. Luckily we were so low that they could not get their guns to bear down on us and the ship on the port side hit the ship on the starboard side, starting a fire in the bows. During the return flight over the sea Les wound down the trailing aerial to try and signal base. The aerial hit the sea and Les yelled that he had been hit again, but it was the handle whizzing round which had banged him in his seat. We managed to get back to Marham, but I couldn't go into cloud as we had no instruments and we were actually in the circuit when our long-suffering Merlin packed up. We went down into a nearby wood, skating along the tops of the trees, demolishing about thirty (according to the farmer who claimed compensation) before we came to a standstill and promptly blew up. My feet had gone through the side of the fuselage and I was helpless. Les Hogan stepped out of the front (there was no nose, it was in Leeuwarden), took off my boot and we ran like mad despite the wound in my leg, which was now making itself felt. We didn't have a scratch on us from the crash, which had completely demolished the Mosquito. Had the Mosquito been a metal aircraft I am sure that my foot would have been severed and I am sure that we were saved by the complete break-up of the aeroplane. After three weeks in Ely hospital we were back at Marham and operating again.[15]

On 7 November Squadron Leader Roy Ralston led six Mosquitoes at wave-top height across the Bay of Biscay to attack two large German blockade-running motor vessels in the Gironde estuary. The operation had been mounted at short notice and preparation had been minimal. The ships' crews were taken completely by surprise as the 500lb bombs fell full on them and things only got hectic afterwards, but no one stayed around for long. The Mosquito flown by Flight Lieutenant Alec Bristow and Pilot Officer Bernard Marshall was shot down by flak and they survived to be taken prisoner. Ralston was to become one of the most accomplished and skilful low-level bomber pilots of the war. A raid on 9 December demonstrates his quick thinking and rapid response to a given situation. He spotted a German troop train about to enter a tunnel on the Paris to Soissons railway line and immediately decided on a plan of action. Unlike the more conventional thinking of the 'average' pilot he did not attack the train itself but decided to create more havoc with an unconventional attack. He dropped down to tree-top height behind the train and dropped a bomb into the mouth of the tunnel. He then quickly orbited the tunnel and bombed it at the other end before it emerged, thus effectively entombing the train, its crew and cargo in the tunnel.

Meanwhile, plans were well advanced for mounting 2 Group's biggest operation of the war, an attack on the Philips works in Eindhoven, Holland from low-level. Although some industrial processes had been dispersed to other sites, Eindhoven was still the main centre, especially for research into electronic counter-measures and radar. Preparations for Operation Oyster, the most ambitious daylight raid conceived by 2 Group, had been given the green light on 9 November. Originally plans called for the Strijp Group main works to be bombed by twenty-four Venturas, twelve Mitchells and twelve Mosquitoes, while twelve Venturas and thirty-six Bostons would at the same time attack the Emmasingel Lamp and valve works half a mile to the east. The slower Venturas would lead the way at low level with HE and 30lb incendiaries before surprise was lost. On 17 November a full-scale practice was held on a route similar to the one to be used, with the St. Neots power station as the 'target'. Many basic lessons were learned, while other problems associated with a mixed force, such as the differences in bombing techniques and cruising speeds, were exposed. The Mitchells fared particularly badly on this first practice but even worse were the Venturas. Next day thirty of their crews tried again on their own on the same route and a vast improvement was recorded. On 20 November on the third practice, all four aircraft types took part. The aircraft flew east beyond the English coast then turned north. The tightly packed formation of Venturas was at almost nought feet but the 'tailgating' effect meant that they were flying in each other's slipstream and this caused aircraft to twist and yaw with the fearsome danger of hitting the water or another aircraft. At Flamborough Head, where they turned inland to the supposed 'target', the Venturas became entangled with Bostons and Mosquitoes 'in a frightening shambles', exacerbated by a simulated attack by Spitfires, which dived amongst them 'with amazing daring'. Surprisingly, there were no collisions, even though more than 100 aircraft were involved. Next day a frank post-mortem took place and then came the announcement: the target was Philips' Radio Factory at Eindhoven. The Bostons were to go in first and bomb from a medium height, followed by Venturas carrying a mixture of incendiaries and delayed-action bombs and finally the Mosquitoes would sweep in to distract the fire fighters. To bluff enemy defences, fighters would make three diversionary sweeps and there would be top cover as well.

On 6 December ninety-three light bombers prepared to take off to attack the Philips works. At Marham the briefings were carried out by Wing Commander Hughie Edwards VC DFC accompanied as usual by his white bulldog 'Sallie'. If she was late Edwards would halt proceedings until she had settled down![16] Edwards and Flight Lieutenant Charles Patterson, who had a black spaniel by the name of 'Jamie', often took their pet dogs aloft in a Mosquito during practice flights. Patterson, who had flown a tour on Blenheims in 114 Squadron, flew the Eindhoven operation with Flying Officer Jimmy Hill ('armed' with a cine camera) in O-Orange in the second formation of four Mosquitoes. Patterson recalls:

> Mosquito operations were far more ambitious than Blenheim ops but casualties were lower. For a period from about July-September 1942 the casualties were as high as the low-level daylights in Blenheims a year before. There was even talk of the Mosquito having to be written off after all. In some way we still had such enormous faith in this aeroplane so we just could not believe that it could not be made to operate successfully at an acceptable rate of casualties. Operationally, the Philips works from a Mosquito point of view was regarded as a comparatively straightforward target, nothing to get terribly frightened of. Something we would have taken in our stride as part of routine operations.

Eight Mosquitoes of 105 Squadron and two of 139 Squadron, crewed by Flight Lieutenant Mike Wayman and Flight Lieutenant Charles Hayden and Pilot Officer John Earl 'Junior' O'Grady and Sergeant George Lewis, led by Edwards would rendezvous with the other bombers at a point over the North Sea. Then they would trail the Bostons and Venturas to the target despite the Mosquitoes' cruising speed of 270-mph, about 100-mph faster. The Mosquitoes were to make a shallow diving attack on the Strijp works, while the other bombers bombed from low level. Unfortunately, the timings went wrong and instead of being 60 miles behind, the Mosquitoes caught up with the other bombers. As the Mosquitoes flew in over the Scheldt at 50ft they began to 'wobble' flying along at 160 mph, trying to maintain the speed of the leading bombers. They flew through a flock of ducks and one went through George Parry's windscreen, split his leather flying-helmet and cut his head. He did not feel a thing but his head went ice-cold. Robbie Robson was cut by flying glass and thinking his pilot was 'out' grabbed the stick. Parry recovered and headed inland. Fw 190 fighters came up and Parry and Flight

Lieutenant Bill Blessing, his No.2, broke away to decoy them away from the Venturas coming in over the coast behind. Parry went underneath an Fw 190 whose pilot did not see him and he and Blessing deliberately drew the 190s on themselves, then led them in a chase as they opened the throttles to full speed. The Mosquito IV was not quite as fast as the 190 at 20,000ft, but at deck level it was about 5 mph faster. Later, Parry was able to rejoin the formation. Blessing, who turned into the fighter attacks and circled for 10 minutes at 50ft decided to abandon the flight and made for home chased by the Fw 190, which only abandoned the pursuit about 8 miles east of Vlissingen. Pilot Officers Jimmy Bruce DFM and Mike Carreck had an equally close encounter with another Fw 190 until the enemy fighter ran out of ammunition and they also headed back to Marham after first jettisoning their bombs.[17]

Rain was falling in East Anglia on the morning of Sunday, 6 December 1942 but near the outskirts of Eindhoven, 60 miles from the coast of Holland, the weather was clear. Frits Philips and his wife, along with his brother-in-law van Riemsdijk and sister Jetty were visiting a niece who had christened a child. Philips was director-general of the Philips electro-chemical factories in Eindhoven, a built-up area of Holland only 50 miles from the Ruhr. Philips was the largest manufacturer of its type in Europe, thought to produce over one-third of the German supply of valves and certain radar equipment. Although some industrial processes had been dispersed to other sites, Eindhoven was still the main centre, especially for research into electronic countermeasures and radar. Production was centred in two factories, the Strijp Group main works and the Emmasingel valve and lamp factory, both in built-up areas within the town. Their destruction, which demanded precision bombing from a very low level to minimize the danger to the local people, was considered by London to be of vital importance. In Philips opinion however, his factory produced only a tiny amount of material for the Germans, a view shared by the Philips family and staff in America. But, in order to satisfy the German commission from Berlin, Philips always prepared graphs showing that production totals were better than they were so that the Germans could return home satisfied. These graphs were seen by a number of employees, some of who were members of the local resistance but Philips' efforts to look less productive were not forwarded to the Allies so readily. After the church service Philips, his wife, brother-in-law and sister were drinking the usual cups of coffee, when suddenly they saw a formation of low-flying aircraft approaching in the distance. Their suspicion was that it had to be British machines. Philips' first reaction was, 'Are they going to bomb the Eindhoven railway station?' At the same moment they saw the first bombs being dropped and heard the crashing of the impact. With a feeling of deprivation they realized that their town was being bombed! As fast as they could Philips and his brother-in-law cycled to the De Laak, where fortunately nobody was harmed. At some distance they saw the Demer, the most important shopping-street in Eindhoven, which was already ablaze.

Only now did Frits Philips realize that it had been his factories that were the target of the bombardment. There was a momentary silence and he thought that the bombardment had finished but cycling to the Emmasingel yet another wave of bombers rushed in to the attack and he had hurriedly to seek shelter in a cycle-shop. Meanwhile, he noticed that the office building had been hit several times and it was on fire. Despite this Frits wanted to rescue two portraits of his father and Uncle Gerard, which had been painted by Jan Veth in 1916 at the occasion of the 25th anniversary of the company. Fortunately all the other portraits and valuables had been stowed safely away long ago. The portraits were hanging in the commissioners-room at ground level. Frits climbed in through a window and he was able to rescue a silver cigar-box, which had been left by his father, from his desk. He distributed a box of good cigars amongst the fire brigade who had joined him. Philips went into the commissioners-room, opened the door and at that same moment a large piece of ceiling came crashing down. The firemen would not let him enter the room and so sadly he had to leave the portraits to the fire. The building burned out completely.

The Mosquito flown by Pilot Officer John Earl O'Grady, who was on his first trip, was hit by flak and streamed smoke as they left the target area. O'Grady and his navigator Sergeant George Lewis died when their aircraft hit the sea. Nine Venturas and four Bostons also failed to return. The Philips works was devastated, essential supplies destroyed and the rail network disrupted. Frits Philips concludes:

> The destruction was enormous. The time of the bombardment, on a Sunday morning, was chosen because the factories were closed but the death toll was over one hundred civilians. The hospitals were crowded with injured people and part of Eindhoven was destroyed by fire. My wife and my sister Jetty visited the wounded. They told us that not one of them blamed the Allies! There was one man who had lost his wife and three of his seven children. Still no complaints could be heard from him. The morale of the population during that bombardment had been exemplary. Personally the bombardment caused very deep emotions. To see the factories, that had been erected which such devotion and offered jobs to thousands of people, going up in flames was a terrible reality of war, though I realized that this war against the Germans had to be fought hard if they were to be conquered. This thought reconciled me to this hellish scene. The following morning I had visitors from The Hague. Our commissioner Mr. Woltersom, Mr. Hirschfeld and Dr. Ringers, the government commissioner for reconstruction, came to see the results of the bombardment themselves. Ringers and myself were on good terms and it was his help we needed the most. He did not disappoint us. My immediate concern was to commence repairs of our factories on short term, utilising all our personnel to prevent them being deported to Germany. In the first months all the effort went into

clearing away the debris. There was no way to make good the production capacity but it might have been worse. The heavy machinery could be repaired. Despite the never ending Allied bombardment, the German war industry had suffered less then expected but the damage was substantial.

On Christmas Day 1942, Sir Archibald Sinclair, Secretary of State for Air in Winston Churchill's wartime cabinet, wrote his Christmas message from the Air Ministry to the AOC-in-C [Air Officer Commander-in-Chief] Bomber Command at RAF High Wycombe, ACM Sir Arthur Harris:

> The Dutch Minister came to see me yesterday in order to express on behalf of his Government the admiration which they felt for the skill with which the attack on the Philips Works at Eindhoven was planned and executed. The admiration of the gallantry of the attacking crews was only equalled by their gratitude for the accuracy of their aim and for the consequent avoidance of unnecessary injury and suffering to the civilian population.[18]

After Eindhoven (among the awards was a DSO for Wing Commander Edwards and a DFC for his navigator, Tubby Cairns) the Mosquitoes' targets were small in a number of raids on railway lines and yards in France, Belgium and Germany. On 20 December eleven Mosquitoes of 105 and 139 Squadrons led by Squadron Leader (later Wing Commander) Reggie W. Reynolds DFC with Pilot Officer (later Air Commodore) E.B. 'Ted' Sismore attacked railway targets in the Oldenburg-Bremen area in north-west Germany. Reynolds, who was from Cheltenham, had flown a tour on Hampdens and a tour on Manchesters. Sismore, who hailed from Kettering, had flown on Blenheims on 110 Squadron in Malta. He had been wounded and was later evacuated by Sunderland to Gibraltar where he heard about the new 'wooden wonder'. (At Blenheim OTU at Bicester and the Whitley OTU at Honeybourne where he flew on two of the 1,000-bomber raids, Sismore teamed up with Reynolds and off they had gone to Marham). One Mosquito came down so low that the crew read the name Fritz on a river-tug. The bombers swept over men working on a new barracks and one pilot reported later that 'They were near the end of the work and we finished it off for them'. Near Delmenhorst Reynolds diverted to attack a gasholder and his four 500lb GP bombs set the gasometer on fire. The Mosquito took a 40mm cannon shell in the port engine, which made the aircraft lurch drunkenly but Reynolds managed to get the Mosquito on an even keel again. However, the anti-freeze mixture was pouring from the radiator and the cockpit filled with cordite fumes. His No.2, Warrant Officer Arthur Raymond Noesda, moved in closer to Reynolds. The pilot from Western Australia and his CO recrossed the German coast over Wilhelmshaven Bay. Coastal batteries opened up on them and the guns of a warship joined in. Fountains of water rose on each side of the aircraft which were down on the deck but Reynolds got his crippled Mosquito back to Marham where he landed wheels up. Squadron Leader Jack Houlston DFC AFC and his observer, Warrant Officer James Lloyd Armitage

DFC failed to return. They were buried in the Reichswald Forest war cemetery. Luck finally ran out for Noseda, who had flown Blenheims on suicidal anti-shipping strikes from Malta and his observer, Sergeant John Watson Urquhart, on 3 January when they were hit and killed by anti-aircraft fire in the attack on engine sheds at Rouen.

In January 1943 attacks were maintained on rail targets on the continent. With no armament the Mosquitoes had to rely on speed and hedgehopping tactics. Sergeant Reginald Levy recalls that:

At that time the Focke Wulf 190 was appearing and they could get in one attack on us if they saw us first. The main casualties came from flying into the ground or sea, bird strikes and even from our own bombs. These were fitted with an 11-second delay but sometimes this didn't work or else you were unlucky enough to get the blast from someone else's bomb. Whilst attacking the marshalling yards at Terquier, France on 3 January I watched with apprehension, a bomb, from the machine in front of me, bounce high over my wing. Just before that, on New Year's Eve 1942, I had been on another marshalling yard attack to Mouceau-sur-Chambres in Belgium. It was dusk and we ran into a snow storm and I flew between two huge slag heaps, only seeing them as they flashed past high above each wing. We then hit a bird, which smashed through the windscreen, covering my observer, Les Hogan and myself with feathers and blood. It was bitterly cold all the way back and although we bathed and scrubbed again the bird smell hung around and we were not the most popular partners at the New Year's dance.[19]

Then on 27 January Wing Commander Hughie Edwards VC DSO DFC and Flying Officer 'Tubby' Cairns DFC led nine Mosquitoes of 105 and 139 Squadrons in a round trip of more than 1,200 miles to Copenhagen in occupied Denmark. Their target was the Burmeister and Wain diesel engine works. In war paint of dull silvery grey and green on the wings the Mosquitoes blended well with the cold, grey-green wave-tops and Danish countryside as they flew at low level in close formation to avoid attacks from enemy fighters. If it had been summer visibility would have been impaired by dust and squashed insects splattering their windscreens but Edwards' only concern was that they were too far south and fuel consumption was a vital consideration. Near the coast light flak from ships opened up on the formation and Flight Lieutenant John 'Flash' Gordon and Flying Officer Ralph Gamble Hayes thought their aircraft had been hit when the trailing edge of the starboard wing became enveloped in puffs of blue smoke. Thinking he had been hit by flak Gordon carried out evasive action but he had caught the port wing in telegraph wires and damaged the aileron. This together with the fact that the rest of the formation had gained a considerable lead caused Gordon to decide to abandon and he jettisoned his bombs at 16.09 hours and headed home. Edwards and Cairns found the target only at the last moment and were on the point of returning but bombed the target and then broke for the sea and home. Light flak at the target was intense and accurate and Edwards' Mosquito received two holes in the starboard nacelle.

Sergeant pilot H.C. 'Gary' Herbert RAAF in 105 Squadron, whose navigator was Sergeant C. 'Jakey' Jacques, wrote:[20]

Quite a long trip. The leader got lost on the way out and led us around Denmark for over half an hour before we found the target. We went past a small coastal ship and it plastered us with tracer but didn't hit anybody. When we eventually found the target it was getting dark but we hit it good and proper. We attacked between two big chimneys and hit the machine shops and power station. Our bombs were delayed half-hour, three hours, 6 hours and 36 hours to disorganise the place for a while. Other kites had 11-second delay bombs as well as long delay. We got quite a lot of light flak as we left the target but kept on the housetops and nobody was hit. When we got well away it was pretty dark and one of the kites was hit by flak and exploded on the ground at 17.13 hours. The two sergeants in it [James G. Dawson and Ronald H. Cox] were damn good chaps too. Petrol was getting short so we throttled back to 230 mph and as we passed the last island on the west of Denmark we went straight over a machine-gun post at 200ft. It threw up a lot of flak but I jinked and dodged it OK. We came back quietly and landed in the dark at 8 pm.

One kite ran out of juice and crashed about 20 miles away [killing Sergeant Richard Clare and Flying Officer Edward Doyle of 139 Squadron, who hit a balloon cable and tree at East Dereham after the starboard engine failed]. We flew number two to Wing Commander Edwards vc. However, we had a scare on the way back when we were struck by lightning twice and each time a ball of fire appeared on the wing and gradually died out. I looked at the wing but there wasn't a mark on it. Seems queer to me but the weather man said it had happened before so I couldn't have had the DTs. [Edwards landed with only fifteen gallons of fuel in his tanks; enough for about another six and a half miles]. Invited the Officers over to the mess in the evening to have a few drinks and fight the battle again. Nice evening. At the time for the bombs to go off we drank a toast to them. On Friday 30th some news came in from Sweden of our raid on Copenhagen. Apparently it was a huge success and the Diesel works were flattened. A sugar factory and another six-storey building burned to the ground. They thought our delay bombs were duds but they all went off OK on time.

On 30 January there was some trepidation among Mosquito crews at Marham who were due to raid Berlin to disrupt speeches in the city's main broadcasting station on what was the tenth anniversary of Hitler's seizure of power. Three crews in 105 Squadron led by Squadron Leader 'Reggie' W. Reynolds DFC and Pilot Officer E.

B. 'Ted' Sismore would bomb Berlin that morning when *Reichsmarschall* Hermann Göring was due to speak. In the afternoon three Mosquitoes of 139 Squadron would arrive over Berlin at the time Dr. Joseph Göbbels, Hitler's propaganda minister, was due to address the German nation at the Sports Palast. Most of the pilots and navigators could not face breakfast. An exception was Flying Officer A.T. 'Tony' Wickham one of the three pilots in 105 Squadron who was taking part (with his navigator, Pilot Officer W.E.D. Makin). Wickham heartily drank three tins of orange juice and polished off half a dozen fried eggs. A month earlier, as a young pilot officer going on his first trip, a high level dawn raid on cities in the Ruhr (when casualties were particularly heavy), his reaction during a gloomy five o'clock breakfast had been quite different. Wickham suddenly burst out and said, 'I suppose this is a death or glory effort?' Hughie Edwards lent forward, looked at him and said, 'There is no glory in it and that's what makes it so worthwhile.' Flight Lieutenant John 'Flash' Gordon DFC and Flying Officer Ralph G. Hayes DFC who three days earlier had returned with a damaged port wing, completed the trio of aircraft due in Berlin for 'elevenses'

The three Mosquitoes arrived over Berlin at exactly 11.00 hours and the explosion of their bombs severely disrupted the *Reichsmarschall*'s speech. Listeners heard a few muffled words followed by confusion of many voices, then another shout or bang after which, the microphone was apparently switched off and martial music played. It was then announced that Göring's speech would be delayed for a few moments. But after three-quarters of an hour, martial music was still being played! That afternoon the three Mosquitoes of 139 Squadron flown by Squadron Leader Donald F.W. Darling DFC and Flying Officer William Wright, Flight Sergeant Peter John Dixon McGeehan and Flying Officer Reginald Charles Morris and Sergeants Joe Massey and 'Lofty' Fletcher arrived over Berlin at the time Göbbels was due to speak. They dropped their bombs right on cue. However, the earlier raid alerted the defences and flak brought down the Mosquito flown by Darling and Wright. Both were buried in Berlin's 1939-45 war cemetery. That night 'Tony' Wickham treated British listeners to the BBC's 9 o'clock news to an account of the action. 'Lord Haw Haw' trying to sound convincing in a German broadcast to any who cared to listen, announced that, 'Thanks to the U-boat campaign Britain is so starved of materials that she has been compelled to build her bombers of wood.' Reynolds was awarded the DSO while all the other officers received the DFC and the sergeants, DFMs.[21] The Berlin performance brought the following message from Sir Arthur Harris to the air officer commanding 2 Group:

> Please convey to all concerned and particularly to the crews of the aircraft, my warmest congratulations on the magnificent daylight attack carried out on Berlin by your Mosquitoes. Their bombs coincided with an attempt by Göring to broadcast to the German people on the tenth anniversary of Hitler's usurpation of power and cannot have failed to cause consternation in Germany and encouragement to the oppressed peoples of Europe.

23

On the afternoon of 14 February, in what became known as the 'Great Tours Derby' six Mosquitoes of 139 Squadron attacked the engine sheds in the French city from low level. The following evening, twelve Mosquitoes of 105 Squadron attacked the goods depot from low-level and on the 18th, twelve Mosquitoes made a shallow dive attack, two aborted and one aircraft failed to return. On 14 February Hughie Edwards, who had been promoted Group Captain four days earlier, left 105 Squadron to take up a post at HQ Bomber Command prior to taking command of RAF Binbrook on the 18th.[22] Edwards' successor was Wing Commander Geoffrey P. Longfield who on 26 February led an attack by twenty Mosquitoes of 105 and 139 Squadrons on the Rennes Naval Arsenal.

Ten aircraft were to go in at low level led by Longfield and ten Mosquitoes of 139 Squadron were to follow just behind, climb to 2,000ft and dive bomb behind the first wave. Longfield's navigator Flight Lieutenant Roderick Milne lost his bearings on the final run up to the target, which took the Mosquitoes to an airfield 6 miles south of the target. The airfield defences sent up a hail of light flak as the Mosquitoes turned towards the target. On low-level attacks the Mosquitoes had always flown in echelon starboard and any left-hand turns created no problems as all members of the formation could keep the aircraft on his left in sight. However, Longfield, who had turned too far to the left, suddenly turned right again. In a sharp turn to the right as each pilot lifted his left wing to turn right his wing obscured the aircraft to his left because he could not drop down as in higher altitudes. Canadian Flying Officers Spencer Kimmel and Harry Kirkland who were formatting on Longfield, sliced into their leader's tail and Longfield went up into a loop and dived straight into the ground west of Rennes St. Jacques. Kimmel lost height and disappeared below the trees at 300-mph. Longfield and Milne and Kimmel and Kirkland all died. (On the way home a 139 Squadron Mosquito flown by Lieutenant T.D.C. Moe and his observer 2nd Lieutenant O. Smedsaas, both RNAF, crashed and the two Dutchmen were killed).

By the time the others reached the target Warrant Officer 'Gary' Herbert, who before the operation had agreed to change positions with Kimmel, could see the dive-bombers already starting their dive. The Australian pilot knew his formation would be blown up by the 11-second delayed action 500lb bombs carried by some of the Mosquitoes if they went in. He therefore turned violently to the west and climbed to about 700ft and dived below the other formation and got his bombs on the target. Others in his formation bombed alternative targets. Pilot Officer G. W. 'Mac' McCormick, a young officer on only his fourth operation did not see the dive-bombers until it was too late and he went in at low level [139 Squadron were dropping 500lb MC (medium capacity) bombs with instantaneous fuses]. Herbert said, 'God knows how he got through because photographs showed him right in the middle of the bursts. He came back with his radiators full of flock from bombed bedding stores. He used up a lot of luck today.' Next day 'Mac' McCormick and visiting Wing Commander John W. Deacon were killed on a training flight when they failed to pull out of a dive from 30,000ft and crashed a mile to the south-east of Marham at Brick Kiln Plantation.

On Sunday, 28 February six of 105 Squadron's Mosquitoes led by Wing Commander Roy Ralston went to the John Cockerill Steel works at Liège. Four more led by Pilot Officer Onslow Thompson DFM RNZAF and Pilot Officer Wallace J. Horne DFC went to the Stork Diesel Engine Works at Hengelo, in what was the eighth raid on the Dutch town by Mosquitoes. At Liège the Mosquitoes bombed at about 200ft and results were 'good' but at Hengelo things were different. Teenager Henk F. van Baaren, whose father owned a shop in the Brinkstraat, saw at first hand the repeated bombing of his town, the first by RAF heavies on the night of 24 June 1940. This experience made a big impression on the young Dutchman. A single aircraft dropped bombs, which fell in the centre of town at the corner of the Brinkstraat, a street with shops whose shopkeepers, like his father, lived with their families on the first and second floors above. The bombs fell on a shoe-shop and a pub killing two adults and two children. Many of the inhabitants moved to the safety of the outskirts of town or in neighbouring villages The van Baarens moved to Enschede, 6 miles away and stayed there at night for six weeks with his grandparents, cycling back and forth to their shop during the day. Henk witnessed the first Mosquito raid on Hengelo, by 105 Squadron on 6 October 1942 and eleven more Mosquito raids on Hengelo thereafter including the one by 105 Squadron on 28 February. Although there was a war going on the Dutch still had their football matches. Tubantia, one of the local clubs was playing on the field situated between the Stork works and the Hazemeyer factory, which produced AA predictor and telecommunications equipment. After the match, at just after 18.00 hours local time, when all the supporters had left the area, the formation attack began. Thompson and Horne bombed from 550ft.[23] Then Flying Officer David Polgase RNZAF and Sergeant Leslie Lampen bombed from a height of only 150ft. Afterwards they saw a column of smoke rising 300ft into the air over the target. Another crew bombed from 100ft. The debriefing reports suggested that the bombing had been accurate. However very little damage was done to the factories and some large houses opposite the football field were hit. Elsewhere in the town more houses were damaged. Ten people were killed, including seven members of one family. One crew bombed Borne hitting several houses. Three people were killed and several were injured.[24]

On 3 March Wing Commander Peter Shand DFC led ten Mosquitoes of 139 Squadron to the molybdenum mines at Knaben in South Norway. Bomb bursts accompanied by orange flashes and a red glow were seen on and around the target, which resulted in the plant being enveloped in clouds of white and brown smoke and debris being blown to a height of 1,000ft. Four Fw 190s intercepted the Mosquitoes on the homeward journey and Flying Officer A.N. Bulpitt and his navigator, Sergeant K.A. Amond were last seen being pursued by two Fw 190s and crashed into the sea. Flying Officer J.H. Brown's Mosquito was hit and badly damaged but he made a successful crash-landing at Leuchars despite the loss of his hydraulics to operate the undercarriage and with no air speed indicator, rudder controls or elevator trim.[25] AOC Air Vice Marshal J.H. d'Albiac sent his congratulations for a 'well planned and splendidly executed attack... Mosquito stings judiciously placed are very painful.'

On 4 March Squadron Leader Reggie Reynolds DSO DFC led a successful attack by six Mosquitoes at low level from 50-200ft on engine sheds and repair workshops at Le Mans. Bad weather prevented any further operations until 8 March when three Mosquitoes bombed rail targets at Tergnier, 12 miles south of St. Quentin in France, from low-level and Flight Lieutenant Gordon led another pair of Mosquitoes in an attack on the railway shops at Lingen in Germany. The Mosquito flown by Sergeant W.W. Austin and Pilot Officer P.E. Thomas was hit by flak and crashed on the return trip at Den Ham in Holland. Both men survived and they were taken prisoner. Jean Hallade, a member of *Samson Reseau* (network) in the French Resistance witnessed some of the low-level raids by Mosquitoes over France. He recounts:

> I watched Mossies make shallow dive attacks on Aisne's marshalling yards, to slow and disturb the Germans' supplies into France of material such as food, steel, trucks, oil, chemical, coal, alcohol and aircraft built and manufactured in France for the Third Reich under Vichy's laws. French railways using strategic marshalling yards such as Tergnier, Laon, Hirson and St. Quentin transported all these materials. Rivers and canals were also used. Underground sources were to transmit to London numbers of convoys, loads carried, tonnage and destinations when we were alerted by abnormal quantities of concrete, wood, aggregates, tools, de Cauville compressors, cranes, Renault lorries and trains etc going to the St. Omer area, Arras, St. Pol-sur-Ternoise and Watten. Each of these sites took around fourteen trains per day. Resistance, as with *Samson*'s OCM played a part to slow down these activities by a week, waiting for the RAF's raid. February had been a quiet month as the weather for the most part was a mess for low level and poor visibility with snowstorms. Monday, 8 March however had ideal weather, which people called 'an air show sky'; ideal for aircraft missions. At 18.30 hours some friends and I of *Samson Reseau* saw, arriving from the west at around 400ft above the Oise River, three Mosquitoes flying aligned as in a parade.[26] They flew in line astern going straight to Tergnier marshalling yards. Bombs were dropped at 18.41 hours. The population and I heard it and we all felt the blast. We then saw much smoke and fire with the Mossies, at chimney level, on their way back home. They landed at 20.15 hours without any trouble. Twelve 500lb HE bombs were dropped, most on the loco depots and hangar repair shops, destroying several wagons and repair material, spares etc. The eight other bombs fell on railroads pulverising nine of them plus igniting a large

number of wagons, causing total confusion and panic. Traffic was reduced to a single railroad for several days. These 'insect stings' considerably confused and slowed down railroad traffic to the Littoral and V weapon sites. Several supplies were 'lost'. They were finally found a couple of weeks later in south Germany. A fresh-bread convoy destined for XV Army took a week to arrive at its final destination with its absolutely rotten freight. The confusion of the raids was a nice opportunity for sabotage. Several techniques were implemented to increase the German disaster!

On 9 March the Renault works at Le Mans was bombed by fifteen Mosquitoes of 105 and 139 Squadrons, which were met by a hail of flak that severely damaged one aircraft that nevertheless made it back to crash land at Marham. Another Mosquito flown by Squadron Leader Robert Beck 'Bob' Bagguley DFC and Flight Lieutenant Charles Hayden DFC of 139 Squadron failed to return. No trace of the crew was ever found.

On 12 March twelve Mosquitoes of 105 and 139 Squadrons led by Squadron Leader 'Reggie' Reynolds and Pilot Officer 'Ted' Sismore were briefed to attack the John Cockerill steel and armament works in the centre of Liège. At briefing, which lasted two and half-hours, the briefing officer stated that two crack fighter units had recently been moved to Woensdrecht, south of Rotterdam and that they had recently been re-equipped with Fw 190s. (II./JG1 at Woensdrecht was equipped with thirty-five Fw 190A-4s of which twenty were serviceable). Allowing for several dog-legs, flight time to target was between 2 and $2^1/2$ hours. Attacks of this nature were normally planned for dusk or just before dark so that the Mosquitoes could return to England individually under the cover of half-light or darkness. Bombing had to be carried out very accurately indeed to keep losses to a minimum and this task was given to the shallow dive section led by Squadron Leader John V. Berggren of 139 Squadron with his observer Peter Wright. Berggren had by now completed almost sixty operations. In peacetime Wright was a 'serious minded' schoolmaster.

At 15.30 hours all twelve Mosquitoes taxied out onto Marham's huge expanse of grass and after warming up their engines took off 10 minutes later. They headed south to Romney Marsh and Dungeness before flying across the Channel to France and up and over the cliffs to the west of Cap Gris Nez then on across the heavily defended Pas de Calais at nought feet. Finally, the Mosquitoes, seldom flying at more than 100ft and keeping echelon formation on the leader, picked up the River Meuse which led straight in to the target. At around 5 miles from the target the Mosquitoes of 105 Squadron split from the rest of the formation and each aircraft went straight in at low level to drop their four 500lb, 11-second delayed action bombs. These burst in the target area as Bergrren and his six Mosquitoes hurriedly climbed to 3,000ft and then dived onto the target to release their four 500lb bombs with instantaneous fuses. The Mosquitoes were buffeted by the concussion from the bombs and hit by flying debris, bricks and mortar but every aircraft made it through. Turning away to the north the crews could see a huge mushroom of smoke building up over the main target area. Leaving the target the formation broke into individual aircraft and raced for the Scheldt Estuary at 280 mph in gathering dusk. The Mosquitoes had to climb to 200ft to avoid HT cables, which criss-crossed Belgium and France. Bergrren and another 139 Squadron Mosquito flown by Sergeant Robert McMurray Pace and Pilot Officer George Cook overflew Woensdrecht and were fired on by anti-aircraft guns. Bergrren evaded by squeezing every last modicum of power from his Merlins by pushing the RPM control into the fully forward position, opening the throttle fully and pulling the 'panic valve', a lever which when pulled produced full supercharger pressure on both Merlins. Berggren glanced up and saw a flicker of flame emerge from the port engine of Pace and Cook's Mosquito that quickly became a flaming torch as the tanks in his port engine caught fire. In a long stream of bright light Pace crashed on the runway of Woensdrecht airfield and was smashed to smithereens on impact leaving a stream of burning debris in its wake. Berggren began counting the silhouettes of Fw 190s entering their circuit and was alarmed to see that there were twelve pairs of Focke Wulfs in the sky. Bergrren went even lower down to nought feet and exited the area at high speed with all the anti-aircraft guns that could be brought to bear firing at him. He did not return the 'panic valve' to its normal position for several minutes and he did not really relax until they were over the North Sea![27]

On 16 March sixteen Mosquitoes led by Bergrren made low level and shallow dive attacks on roundhouses and engine sheds at Paderborn. One Mosquito flown by Flight Sergeant Peter J.D. McGeehan DFM and Flying Officer Reginald C. Morris DFC was lost. On 17 March Acting Wing Commander John 'Jack' de Lacey Wooldridge DFC* DFM RAFVR took command of 105 Squadron. Wooldridge had joined the RAF in 1938 and flew two tours (seventy-three operations) on heavy bombers prior to taking command of 105 Squadron, including thirty-two ops on Manchesters. For the last three months he had been attached to the tri-service PWD [Political Warfare Department] working on the FIDO (Fog Installation Dispersal 01) system.[28]

On the 20th twelve Mosquitoes carried out low-level attacks on the engine sheds and repair shops at Louvain and another target at Malines in Belgium. The 139 Squadron leader was shot-up by flak over Blankenburg and crashed at Martlesham Heath with the loss of both crew. On 23 March ten Mosquitoes of 139 Squadron, led by Wing Commander Peter Shand DFC and five of 139 Squadron led by Flight Lieutenant Bill Blessing DFC attacked the Compagnie Générale de Construction des Locomotives Batigniolles-Chatillon at St. Joseph two miles north-east of Nantes at low level. The raid was timed to perfection as factory workers finished work. Next day, 24 March, three Mosquitoes of 105 Squadron were sent on a Rover operation to shallow dive-bomb trains and railway lines within specified areas in Germany. Sergeant H.C. 'Gary' Herbert RAAF in 105 Squadron had the line between Hamm and Bielefeld, a four-track line:

We got a bit of light flak on the way in at the coast and also east of Osnabrück but we weren't hit. When I reached the line I found plenty of trains and stooged up and down the line dropping one bomb at a time. Stopped two trains; I don't know whether they were derailed or not and blew about half a dozen trucks of another off the line and down the embankment. We carried a vertical camera and also a cine camera in the nose. Made six runs altogether and then went down to the deck to get photos with the cine. On the way back we passed over a small village and all hell broke loose. Tracer came from all directions. I slammed everything wide open and jinxed all over the sky but they were good gunners and hit us, plenty with cannon shells. Tore a hole a foot across in my port engine fairing. The starboard engine began vibrating badly and I shut it off. I tried it again later and it was OK. At the coast again small cannon and Bofors gave us a hot reception and we hand to jink plenty to dodge getting hit again. Got back to base and found that Squadron Leader Reynolds had done a belly landing on the flarepath, so I had to land at Swanton Morley. 'Groupie' [Group Captain Wallace H. 'Digger' Kyle DFC] was pleased with our effort.[29]

On 27 March 139 Squadron dispatched six aircraft on another low-level raid on the Stork Diesel Works at Hengelo. The bombing results at debriefing were described as being uncertain; though photographs showed many near misses. On this occasion serious damage was done to the primary target although nearby houses were hit once again. Henk F. van Baaren attended a funeral for the first time in his young life when a 17-year-old boy from his school and a member of the same gymnastic club that he attended, was killed.[30] On 28 March seven Mosquitoes led by Flight Lieutenant 'Flash' Gordon were despatched to attack the railway marshalling yards at Liège but rainstorms reduced the evening visibility to half a mile and instead he led the aircraft in an attack on a factory north of Valbengit Bridge at Liège. They were spotted by *Unteroffizier* Wilhelm Mayer of 6th *Staffel* JG26 heading towards Dunkirk at low level and *Oberfeldwebel* Adolf 'Addi' Glunz and three other Fw 190s of 4./JG26 were sent off from Vitry immediately. They intercepted the Mosquitoes after they had bombed and the Mosquito flown by Flying Officer George Bruce DFM and Flying Officer Dick Reilly about 18 miles east of Etaples and Sergeant George Leighton and Sergeant Thomas Chadwick. Glunz was credited with shooting down both the Mosquitoes south of Lille in the space of a minute. All four airmen were later buried in Lille Southern Cemetery. (Glunz finished the war with seventy-one confirmed victories).

On 30 March ten Mosquitoes of 139 Squadron led by Wing Commander Peter Shand DFC set off to bomb the Philips Works at Eindhoven which was about ready to begin full production again. The attackers switched back over Holland, dodging flocks of seagulls over the Zuider Zee and tearing over Eindhoven once more at zero feet. Pilot Officer T.M. Mitchell, who brought up the rear of the formation, saw the full effect of the strafing as he banked to turn for home. 'As we came in to attack I saw the Wing Commander's bombs, which were timed to go off a short time after impact, fall into the buildings as we skimmed over the roof-tops. Then I let our own bombs go right into the middle of the factory. As I circled after the attack I saw the whole building become enveloped in smoke with huge red flashes as the bombs exploded.' the Mosquitoes could only hit the corner of the factory. Pilot Officer Hay, a South African from Pretoria, saw V-signs flashing from Dutch homes in the failing light.

The next day, 1 April, six Mosquitoes of 105 Squadron led by Wing Commander Roy Ralston and four of 139 Squadron led by Squadron Leader John V. Bergrren, bombed a power station and railway yards at Trier and engine sheds at Ehrang respectively from 50-400ft. Bombs from the first formation were seen to fall in the middle of the railway workshops, throwing up large quantities of debris followed by showers of green sparks. Bomb bursts were also observed on the power station followed by a sheet of flame, which rose to a height of 100ft. The attack by the second formation on Ehrang resulted in a huge explosion and a red flash from a coal container. One bomb was seen to bounce off railway tracks into a house, which was blown to pieces. On leaving the target area smoke was seen rising to about 1,500ft. No aircraft were lost although a Mosquito of 139 Squadron, which was hit by blast from bomb bursts and also by flak returned on one engine with gyro artificial horizon and turn-and-bank indicator out of action and landed safely at Manston. Another 139 Squadron Mosquito, which was hit by flak on crossing the enemy coast lost its hydraulics and was unable to open its bomb-bay doors to bomb and abandoned the strike.

Two days later on Saturday 3 April, a warm spring day, Wing Commander Wooldridge led his first 105 Squadron operation and eight Mosquitoes carried out Rover attacks on railway targets in Belgium and France. All three of 105 Squadron's Mosquitoes returned safely from attacks on locomotive repair sheds shops at Malines and engine sheds at Namur but a Mosquito of 139 Squadron was lost. Flying Officer W.O. Peacock and his observer, Sergeant R.C. Saunders, were shot down by *Oberfeldwebel* Wilhelm Mackenstedt of 6./JG26 3 kilometres south of Beauvais for the German pilot's sixth and final victory.[31] Jean Hallade, a French Resistance leader, witnessed one of 139 Squadron's Mosquitoes flown by Canadian Flying Officer A.B. 'Smokey Joe' Stovel and Sergeant W.A. Nutter attack the Tergnier marshalling yards after a second aircraft had been forced to return shortly after take-off with faulty instruments. Hallade remembers:

It was 7.30pm and, while people were enjoying the cool of the evening, a twin-engine aircraft flying at low altitude and high speed suddenly appeared from the south of Chauny. It banked left over Chauny level with the poplars along the River Oise. The Mosquito made another vertical right-bank and returned at full speed. Confused by the darkness and the landscape the Mosquito crew missed Tergnier, which is 5 kilometres away from Chauny. Catching sight of tracks going in and out of some warehouses stacked with fertiliser, the Mosquito crew thought it was Tergnier's locomotive sheds. On his second pass they dropped four 500lb bombs. Two hit the chemical warehouse belonging to Saint-Gobain Cie but only one of them exploded, destroying one of the warehouse wings and creating a huge cloud of dust. The third fell into the silt of the River Oise and the fourth landed in a garden where it partially demolished a house a few metres away from the Saint-Quentin canal. There were no victims, although one of the bedrooms of the house belonging to the Arnoulds was damaged. Fortunately, a few minutes before the bombardment, Simone, their 20-year old daughter had left that room where she was having a rest, not feeling well that day. She could have been badly wounded. On 15 April the unexploded bomb was found in a heap of fertiliser, creating panic among the staff who were in charge of packing. The German Army Ordnance later defused the bomb. Four months later Simone Arnould married Jean Martin, who had been a bomber pilot in June 1940 when the defeat of France occurred.[32]

On 11 April four Mosquitoes of 105 Squadron led by Squadron Leader Bill Blessing DFC and his navigator Flight Sergeant A.J.W. 'Jock' Heggie ventured to Hengelo to bomb the Stork Works. This was the tenth and final low-level attack by 2 Group Mosquito IVs on the long-suffering town. Light was failing and visibility about 3 miles with 10/10ths cloud at 3,000ft when the formation was intercepted at 50ft by two formations of three Fw 190s before reaching the target. One section of Fw 190s fired a burst of two seconds and then they broke off to starboard to attack two of the Mosquitoes. Flying Officer Norman Hull RCAF and Sergeant Philip Brown, No.3 in the formation, were intercepted by four Fw 190s who came in from starboard and opened fire for about fifteen seconds at a range of 350 yards. The Mosquitoes carried out evasive action by turning into the attack, weaving and gaining and losing height between 150-200ft and increasing speed. After making one attack, the enemy aircraft broke off and wheeled round to attack Z-Zebra flown by Flying Officer David Polgase RNZAF and his observer Flight Sergeant Leslie Lampen. *Z-Zebra* was shot down by *Unteroffizier* Gerhard Wiegand of 2./JG1 and crashed in a wood near Bentheim, Germany with the loss of both crew. Flying Officer F.M. 'Bud' Fisher, an American pilot from Pennsylvania and Flight Sergeant Les Hogan were unable to bomb the primary target and attacked a train in the area instead. Blessing pressed home his attack from 50ft and he dropped his bomb load directly onto the Stork Works causing severe damage to the plant. The Resistance seems to have signalled London that the Stork and Dikkers factories should no longer be considered targets, as production of war machinery had stopped.[33]

On 19/20 April there were no Main Force operations and six Mosquitoes of 2

Group failed to locate rail workshops at Namur in bad visibility and returned without loss. On the night of 20/21 April nine Mosquitoes of 105 Squadron and two from 139 Squadron led by Wing Commander Peter Shand DSO DFC carried out a bombing attack on Berlin. This was a diversion for 339 heavy bombers attacking Stettin and eighty-six Stirlings bombing the Heinkel factory near Rostock. The Mosquito 'night nuisance' operations were also designed to 'celebrate' Hitler's birthday. Over Berlin it was cloudless with bright moonlight and the Mosquitoes dropped their bombs from 15,00-23,000ft. Flak was moderate and quite accurate but the biggest danger proved to be night-fighters. One of these was *Oberleutnant* Lothar Linke, *Staffelkapitän* 12./NJG1 who the night before had claimed to be the second *Nachtjagd* pilot to destroy a Mosquito whilst flying a standard Bf 110G.[34] Linke, again led by his night-fighter controller *Eisbär* ('Polar Bear'), overtook Shand's Mosquito at high altitude and at high speed in a power dive, shot the Mosquito down over the northern part of the Ijsselmeer at 02.10 hours. Shand and his navigator Pilot Officer Christopher D. Handley DFM were killed.[35]

Late on 27 May, 'a glorious, clear, hot but slightly misty late May evening' the final large-scale daylight raid by the Mosquito IVs of 2 Group took place when fourteen Mosquitoes were given two targets deep in Southern Germany. The briefing was very long and complicated. It meant flying at low level for well over three hours over enemy territory, of which a good two and a quarter would be in broad daylight. Six aircraft of 139 Squadron led by Wing Commander 'Reggie' W. Reynolds DSO DFC and Flight Lieutenant 'Ted' Sismore DFC set out to attack the Schott glassworks at Jena. A few miles further on eight Mosquitoes of 105 Squadron led by Squadron Leader Bill Blessing DFC and Flying Officer G.K. Muirhead were to bomb the Zeiss Optical factory, which at that time was almost entirely engaged on making periscopes for submarines. One of the 105 Squadron pilots taking part was Flight Lieutenant Charles Patterson, with the Film Unit cameraman Flight Sergeant Leigh Howard as his navigator. Patterson recalls:

> We saw the red ribbon running longer than we'd ever considered, right down into SE Germany near Leipzig and the target, the Zeiss optical lens works at Jena. It gave a great sense of anticipation and excitement that such a tremendously long trip was going to be undertaken but not undue alarm because it was so deep into Germany, an area that had never seen daylight flying aircraft before. We rather assumed that by going deep down not only could we achieve a great deal of surprise but there night be much light AA fire round this factory and what there was the gunners would be inexperienced.
>
> At seven o'clock all around the perimeter the engines started up and everybody taxied out. Forming up on these trips with a full muster of Mosquitoes was quite a lengthy business, the leader circling slowly round and round the airfield for everybody to get airborne and catch up. The two

formations swept across the hangars and the airfield at low level, an impressive sight and quite an exhilarating experience for the crews themselves. We settled down for the long flight right across to Jena in clear daylight as it was certainly a good 2½ hours before dusk. The Dutch coast was crossed with no difficulty but at the Zuider Zee we suddenly found ourselves flying slap into a vast fleet of little brown-sailed fishing vessels. In front of me the whole formation broke up and weaved in and around them, before we settled down again. On past the Ruhr and down near Kassel we went, then on into the Thuringian Mountains where the Möhne and Eder dams are. Even then we were only two-thirds of the way. You felt you were in a separate world, which has no end and will go on forever. On and on over the trees and the fields and the rising ground we went, mile after mile. Then suddenly, my navigator drew my attention to something. I looked across the starboard wing-tip and I had a clear view of Münster cathedral quite a few miles away, the interesting thing being that I was looking up at the towers, not down on them!

We carried on past Kassel then suddenly we came across all the floods of the Möhne dam raid which had taken place only ten days before. For 20 minutes there was nothing but floods. It was fascinating and confirmed in our minds what an enormous success the raid must have been. We flew between the Möhne and Eder dams and suddenly came over a mountain ridge and there was a dam [Helminghausen] beneath us. On the far side the front formation was just topping the far ridge when flak opened up. It didn't look very serious. An enormous ball of flame rolled down the mountainside, obviously an aircraft but it wasn't long after that I learnt that it was two Mosquitoes, which had collided. Whether one was hit by flak or whether it caused one of the pilots to take his eye off what he was doing and fly into the Mosquito next to him, nobody will ever know. But two had gone.[36]

We flew on over this mountainous country, over ridges and down long valleys with houses on both sides. On my starboard wing-tip we saw a man open his front door and look out to see these Mosquitoes flashing past. We saw the door slam in a flash of whipping past. Suddenly, the weather began to deteriorate and this had not been forecast. I think everybody was assuming that we'd soon fly out of it but it got worse and we were over mountains. We now began to fly right into clouds. Flying in formation in cloud and knowing you're right in the centre of Germany gives you a rather lonely feeling. Blessing put on his navigation lights to try and enable us to keep formation. Everybody put on navigation lights. I was very nervous flying on instruments in cloud and although I did my best to keep the next aircraft in view, I lost him.[37]

H.C. 'Gary' Herbert in the 105 Squadron formation adds.[38] 'A bit further on

33

another 139 kite [*B-Beer* flown by Reynolds and Flying Officer Ted Sismore] feathered his port airscrew and turned back. He got home OK.'

Ted Sismore recalled. 'As soon as we picked out the tall chimneys of the Schott factory the ground gunners began firing at us with all they had. We dropped our bombs on the factory building and almost at once three 20-mm shells hit us. A large piece was knocked out of our port airscrew and Reggie was hit in the left hand and knee.'

H.C. 'Gary' Herbert continues:

Just before we turned to make the last run up the valley to the target the clouds came right down to the deck and the formation had to break up. When the clouds broke I found the formation OK but three other kites were gone.[39] So six kites out of the formation went on to attack. Visibility was extremely bad and as we approached the target at nought feet we suddenly saw balloons over it. Then the fiercest cross fire of light flak I have ever seen opened up. I was last in the formation by this time. Free to go in how I liked I broke away and climbed up the mountain at the side of the town hoping to fox the gunners and dodge the balloons, which I expected would be spread across the valley. I didn't do either. As we went up the mountain they poured light flak down at us and we dived down the other side. The only thing to do was to weave straight in dodging the flak and praying not to hit a cable. We did that and as we screamed down the flak poured past us and splattered all over the town. They put a light flak barrage over the target hoping we would run into it but somehow we dodged it and put our bombs fairly in the glass grinding section: a sixteen storey building. We were hit in several places on the way out.

The heavy cross fire they put up over the glass grinding building (my target) was not directed at us but obviously to deter us from going through it. They don't know how close they were to succeeding! I was absolutely terrified and did not think anybody could get through that and survive and was sorely tempted to turn away and bomb and alternative target. The only thing that made me go through was the thought that I couldn't face men like Hughie Edwards, Roy Ralston, Reg Reynolds and say, 'I lost my guts and turned away. I now know that heroes are really cowards whose conscience would not let them hold their heads high in the presence of real brave men. Subsequent reports confirmed that I was not the only one who was tempted to turn away.[40] However, we managed to get away OK and only ran into one lot of flak on the homeward journey. We dodged it OK. When we got back we found that our hydraulics were out of action and had to put our wheels and flaps dawn by hand. The throttles wouldn't close and I had to cut the switches to get in. Made it OK. Two other kites crashed when they got back and both crews were killed.[41] Another kite was missing, making five crews los: our heaviest loss. It was certainly my stickiest operation and everybody else reckoned it was the stickiest too. There were so many aircraft pranged on the flarepath when we got back that we were ordered to go to an alternative aerodrome: Swanton Morley I think. We came back by car, which took many hours in the blackout. By that time all the Bigwigs from Headquarters, who were there to decide whether we should continue as a low level squadron or be switched to PFF [Path Finder Force] work, had left.[42]

On 4 June the Mosquito crews learned of a change in their role. They would do no more daylight ops. Instead the two squadrons joined Fighter Command and they were the first Mosquito units to join the specialist Pathfinder Force (later No.8 (PFF) Group), which had been formed from 3 Group using volunteer crews on 15 August 1942. At Marham 1655 Mosquito Training Unit (later relocated to Warboys) was tasked with training the specialist Pathfinder Force.[43] In 8 Group 105 Squadron became the second Oboe squadron and 139 Squadron high-level 'nuisance' raiders, flying B.IX Mosquitoes.

CHAPTER TWO

On High

In July 1940 the PRU (Photographic Reconnaissance Unit) was in desperate need of an aircraft not only capable of carrying multi-camera installations, but which was faster than the Blenheim and able to photograph areas beyond the range of a PR Spitfire. The answer lay in the development of the DH 98 Mosquito but the Air Ministry had taken some persuading. Ever since 1938, the de Havilland company at Hatfield had been trying, without success, to convince them that its unarmed bomber, which was to be mostly built of wood and had a crew of only two, could operate successfully in hostile skies without the need for defensive armament. The company argued that the DH 98's superior speed was its best defensive weapon against enemy fighters. Late in 1939 there was still strong opposition to any unarmed bomber version but the AOC-in-C, Bomber Command, conceded that there was a need for a fast, unarmed, reconnaissance aircraft, equipped with three F24 cameras. It was agreed that a two-man crew in any reconnaissance version put forward by de Havilland was acceptable (although at first the Air Ministry wanted them seated in tandem). On 1 March 1940 a contract was placed with de Havilland for fifty DH 98 aircraft, including nineteen PR versions.[44] On 21 June 1941 the Air Ministry decided that nine of these aircraft[45] should be converted to unarmed bombers and these came to be known as the PRU/Bomber Conversion Type, or B.IV Series I.

On 13 July 1941 W4051 was flown to Oxfordshire by Geoffrey de Havilland and handed over to 1 PRU at Benson, which was then commanded by Wing Commander G.W. Tuttle OBE DFC where it became the first Mosquito to be taken on charge by the RAF. By September 1 PRU had ten Mosquitoes on strength.[46] Until night photography using magnesium flares released through a tube in the cockpit floor were available in early 1943, all PR flights had to be made during daylight. They were restricted to times between first photographic light and last photographic light and these times varied with the seasons according to sunrise and sunset. Early camera installations were mounted to take oblique shots and they were used for mainly low-level sorties. Later 1 PRU switched to mostly high-level vertical photography. The cameras were fitted with a film magazine, loaded for either 250 or 500 exposures, mounted on top of the camera and the rolled film was advanced automatically after each exposure. A T.35 controller controlled the cameras and the photographers set the apertures and shutter speed before the flight according to weather forecasts. The time interval between exposures was controlled to provide a 60 per cent overlap, so that every object on the ground appeared on two photographs. These photos could be manipulated under a stereoscope to provide a magnified, three-dimensional image that provided much more detail than a single vertical print. The pilot could also take control and aim the oblique camera.

During tests on 16 September *Benedictine*'s[47] generator packed up over the Bay of Biscay and with no power to drive the cameras, 25-year old Squadron Leader Rupert Francis Henry Clerke (an old Etonian) and 32-year old Sergeant Sowerbutts (a pre-war Margate barber) were forced to abandon the sortie. They were pursued by three Bf 109s but the PR.I easily outpaced them at 23,000ft and returned safely. Clerke and Sowerbutts made the first successful Mosquito PR.I sortie the next day when they set out in *Benedictine* at 11.30 hours for a daylight photo reconnaissance of Brest, La Pallice and Bordeaux, before arriving back at Benson at 17.45 hours.[48]

On the 20th, Flight Lieutenant Alastair L. 'Ice' Taylor DFC and his navigator, Sergeant Sidney E. Horsfall successfully photographed Bordeaux, Pauillac, Le Verdon and La Pallice. Taylor was a brilliant PR Spitfire and Mosquito pilot who specialised in Dicing (low level PR of specific targets). The third flight was made when Taylor and Horsfall covered Heligoland and Sylt in *Benedictine*. After proving their worth over northern France, four of the PR Mosquitoes[49] were transferred to operate from Wick, in Scotland, with Squadron Leader Taylor in command. In October 1941 the PR.I Mosquitoes carried out sixteen successful sorties to Norway. On 4 December, Taylor, who by now was the first PR pilot to fly over 100 sorties, and Horsfall, flew *Benedictine* on a PR sortie to cover Trondheim and Bergen, but they failed to return. It is thought that after they were badly shot up by new German high-level anti-aircraft guns, Taylor put down in the sea to prevent the aircraft falling into enemy hands. After eighty-eight sorties, this was the first loss of a PR Mosquito. By December the unit had moved to Leuchars, near the Firth of Forth. The new base proved more suited to PR operations, greatly reducing the time taken to send photos to the Central Interpretation Unit at RAF Medmenham.

Unkindly referred to by pilots outside the unit as 'Pilots Rest Unit', No.1 PRU was anything but and its operational cycle was about to become even more far reaching. On 15 January 1942 Flight Lieutenant John R.H. Merrifield overflew Gdynia, in Poland and Danzig in eastern Germany in W4061 but his targets were obscured by cloud.[50] On 20 February W4051 was flown to the Franco-Spanish border and over marshalling yards and airfields at Toulouse, in southern France. On 22 February Flight Lieutenant Victor Ricketts and his navigator, Russian born Sergeant Boris Lukhmanoff, covered Cuxhaven and Kiel to take photos of the *Gneisenau* in dry dock there. On 2 March the same crew (in W4060) photographed the *Scharnhorst* undergoing repairs at Wilhelmshaven, whilst

W4059 photographed the *Gneisenau* again. W4060 and W4051 also photographed the French coast prior to the commando raid on St. Nazaire and on 3 March Flight Lieutenant John R.H. Merrifield successfully returned to the Danzig-Gdynia region as he recalls.

I took off from Leuchars at 10.25 hours with the intention of photographing Copenhagen, Danzig, Gdynia and possibly Königsberg (later Karliningrad) in Russian Lithuania. We set course for Copenhagen, climbing to 20,000ft over the North Sea and cruising at 280 mph. We sighted the Danish coast at Esbjerg, visible through patches of medium cloud and photographed the town and harbour. We then climbed to 23,000ft and flew towards Copenhagen. Medium and low cloud increased to 10/10ths and we were soon flying through a layer of cirrostratus. Copenhagen was not seen, so we altered course for Gdynia on ETA. Soon afterwards all low and medium cloud disappeared, though high cloud persisted, but we could see the Baltic Sea underneath us, covered with large patches of ice. We were making intermittent condensation trails in the cloud, so climbed to 24,000ft where the trails ceased. After 2 hours 50 minutes flying time we crossed the German coast at Leba and about 5 miles west of Gdynia the cirrostratus thinned and over the target disappeared altogether. We ran over Gdynia with cameras on, but while doing so noticed that a persistent trail was forming behind us, so descended to 23,000ft and did another run. We then proceeded to Danzig and photographed the town and harbour with Neufahrwasser from the same height. Königsberg was the next objective and it was photographed, with adjacent aerodromes, also from 23,000ft. From here we could see over 100 miles to the east, well into Lithuania. After 3½ hours flying we set course for Leuchars, encountering such a strong head wind that it was 15.25 hours before we passed Gdynia. Accordingly we descended to 18,000ft and cruised at 2,000 rpm in MS gear to economize in fuel. Fortunately as we flew west the wind decreased and we left the Danish coast at 16.30 hours, photographing Esbjerg again on our way out. After an uneventful trip across the sea we landed at Leuchars 18.10 hours.

Although the PRU's first priority remained that of keeping a watch on the *Kriegsmarine,* 1942 would see it being called upon to cover an increasing number of RAF Bomber Command targets. On 14 February the famous 'area bombing' directive was issued to Bomber Command and eight days later it became the responsibility of ACM Sir Arthur Harris, the new chief of Bomber Command, to carry it out. Harris immediately questioned the Admiralty's monopoly of PRU operations and felt that Bomber Command's need was now much greater. A full moon was predicted for the night of 3/4 March so Harris decided to send a mixed force of 235 aircraft, led by the most experienced crews in Bomber Command, to bomb the Renault factory at Boulogne-Billancourt just west of the centre of Paris. It was calculated that approximately 121 aircraft an hour had been concentrated over the factory and all except twelve aircraft claimed to have bombed. Photographic evidence was vital so even though the results of an RAF heavy raid had not been photographed before, a PRU Mosquito crew was ordered to make the flight. A deciding factor in the decision to go ahead was that PR Mosquitoes were equipped with a wireless, whereas most PRU aircraft were not. After talking things over with his observer, Victor Ricketts decided that he and Boris Lukhmanoff could probably get home safely using the wireless, so they offered to fly the sortie, in W4060. They took off from Benson at 11.15 hours in heavy rain and thick cloud. Ricketts recorded:[51]

At the time of leaving we could not see across the aerodrome. I thought, 'Are you a sucker to take this on?' But it was too late to turn back then, as we had lost sight of the ground. We did not see ground again until Boris, a very keen type, said, "Well, I think we are somewhere near Rouen, not very far from Paris and it is time we came down". We still could not see anything and it was raining like Hell and there were thick clouds.

We went down to 1,000ft. At 900ft we caught sight of the ground and he was reasonably happy. We found the River Seine and, as it was quite obvious that we could not navigate to Paris in that weather, we decided to fly along the twisting river. The only way we could do it was for Boris to lie on his stomach in the nose of the aeroplane, saying, "Turn right, now left etc.", as the river twisted. Very soon we found ourselves over the roofs of houses and saw people in the streets running for cover, thinking the bombers had come back again. We could not find the works now, so we went on and came out of clouds at 600ft to see people running like mad. Finally Boris said, "There it is" and I just caught a glimpse of roofs full of holes 500ft below. We had no time to take a picture, so Boris got his cameras ready and we hurried back, found the river and Boris said, "Here's the factory", started his cameras and said. "Oh! Boy Oh! Boy did they give that place the works!" We went over it once, across the middle and then it vanished into the mist again. We were very disappointed when we saw a golf course full of bomb holes. However, it had ruined a good golf course. We flew back over the factory, trying to get the other end of it. Boris said, "I don't want you to run into the Eiffel Tower, which is about 1,000ft high". We flew back up the river and had to come down to 400ft. We tried to do it a fourth time but lost it. Boris said we had been over for 34 minutes now. I thought we had been stooging around long enough and that the Huns would just about be bringing up their flak by then. He was very disappointed and I suggested he should stay if he wanted to, but he decided to come along too.

We went off flying blind all the time, up to 5,000ft thinking that the wily Hun would expect us to go back low as we had come in low. Back over the Channel we knew from the weather we had left that it would be very unlikely we could get home, so decided to try and come back very low down over the Channel and sit down on one of the coast aerodromes. I put the undercarriage down in case we hit the South Downs. We came lower and lower, until the clock registered 0ft. Then we managed to see the surface of the sea. The Mosquito is rather fast for that sort of weather. The beach suddenly flashed underneath the wheels and we gave up the idea of trying to land there. We shot up again into the clouds and called up the base by radio. Base said they could not see across the aerodrome, but gave us a bearing to come back. The whole country was blotted out so I wandered backwards, got south of the base with undercarriage lowered and speed as low as possible. Fortunately I just caught a glimpse through a tiny hole in the clouds of hangar roofs and a couple of aeroplanes parked. I thought where there are aeroplanes there's an aerodrome and where there's an aerodrome that's where we are landing. Boris got his nose down again, trying to see a clear way of getting down. We went round the aerodrome about six times and the sixth time we came out of cloud, narrowly missing a corner of the hangar and just sat down and stamped on the brakes. The Mosquito shuddered and finally came to rest. It was quite like old times on the Press, dashing to the telephone and getting in touch quickly with my place. I said, "We found the target. My boss said, "At 3,000ft?" and I said "No, 400ft". He said that none of the pictures would come out at that height, but I bet him that they would and later collected the dough.

The low-level obliques showed that 300 bombs had fallen on the factory, destroying 40 per cent of the buildings.[52] Ricketts was decorated with the DFC and in the weeks to come he and his Russian born observer made long-range sorties to Bavaria, Mulhouse and Stuttgart.

In March two of the longest photographic reconnaissance sorties were flown by Mosquitoes. On 11 March Flight Lieutenant John Merrifield covered Bødo and on the 25th Flight Lieutenant Victor Ricketts DFC and Boris Lukhmanoff covered Königsberg. On 30 March Flight Lieutenant Merrifield was flying W4061 over Trondheim at 18,000ft when he noticed a Bf 109 in his mirror about half a mile behind and 500ft above. He wrote:

It was making a trail of black smoke, presumably because it was at full throttle. I increased revs from 2,400 to 3,000, switched over from F.S. to M.S., pulled the cut-out and dived gently. My observer reported another 109 on our starboard quarter about the same distance behind. We levelled off at 14,000ft but did not seem to draw ahead. Observation of the enemy aircraft was difficult because they were dead astern and we were making a lot of black smoke ourselves. After a quarter of an hour they were no longer to be seen, so boost was reduced to 6lb and revs to 2,700. Shortly afterwards my observer reported one aircraft crossing our tail 400 yards astern but no fire was opened. Thereupon I opened up again and flew out to sea towards cloud, which was entered ten minutes later. I could not say what speed was reached during the dive but at 14,000ft the IAS was 320, which was afterwards computed to be 395. Engine temperature remained below 100C and oil temperature below 80C the whole time. The port engine had to be changed later because of an internal glycol leak.

Harris's night bombing offensive was gaining in intensity and the PRU, as a consequence had to fly an ever-increasing number of target acquisition and bomb damage assessment sorties. With attrition losses mounting[53] more long-range PR aircraft had to be found. Accordingly, between April and June 1942 four NF.IIs and two B.IV bomber variants[54] were diverted to the PRU as PR.IIs and PR.IVs, respectively. While the NF.IIs lacked long-range tanks, the B.IVs had bomb-bay tanks and two 50-gallon underwing slipper type drop tanks, to give the aircraft a range of 2,350 miles – enough to reach northern Norway and back. With three vertical camersa and one oblique camera installed, Flight Lieutenant Ricketts DFC and Sergeant Lukhmanoff performed the first operational sortie in a PR.IV on 29 April, in DK284, to overfly Augsburg, Stuttgart and Saarbrücken in a five-and-a-half-hour flight. On 24 April they used W4059 to take photos of the disastrous daylight raid by sixteen Lancasters of 44 and 97 Squadrons on the MAN[55] U-boat engine works at Augsburg on 17 April. On 7 May Ricketts and Lukhmanoff flew the deepest penetration over enemy territory thus far when they photographed Dresden, Pilsen and Regensburg, returning after six hours. On 14 May the unit's CO, Wing Commander Spencer Ring RCAF made the first operational flight in a PR.II when he piloted DD615 to photograph Alderney. On 25 May Ricketts and Lukhmanoff overflew Billancourt, Poissy and Le Bourget in this aircraft and on the 27th, Pilot Officer Gerry R. Wooll RCAF and Sergeant John Fielden crewed DD615 when they photographed Amiens. On 10 June Ricketts and Lukhmanoff flew a 7³/₄-hour sortie to Spezia, Lyons and Marseilles, but their luck finally ran out on 11 July when they were lost in W4089 overflying Strasbourg and Ingolstadt.

At Leuchars during May and June 1942 PRU Mosquitoes attempted to find and photograph the German battleships berthed in the Norwegian fjords. On 15 May the first PR sortie to the Narvik area was flown by Flying Officer Higson in one of the PR.IVs. Next day a photographic sortie over Trondheim by Flight Lieutenant John Merrifield brought back photographs of the *Prinz Eugen* heading south-west, apparently making for Kiel for repairs to damage inflicted by the submarine HMS *Trident*. On 17 May Flying Officer K.H. Bayley and Flight Sergeant Little took photographs of the *Prinz Eugen* and four destroyers still *en route* for Kiel despite attacks by two squadrons of Coastal Command Beauforts from Wick. Further coverage of Trondheim on 22 and 23 May revealed that the *Tirpitz, Admiral Hipper* and *Lützow* were all still berthed in fjords. On 23 June Pilot Officer Robin Sinclair who was the son of Sir Archibald Sinclair Bart and Pilot Officer Nelson (in W4060) used the new 36-inch F52 camera to photograph the *Graf Zeppelin*, Germany's only aircraft carrier, launched in 1938 and the battleship *Scharnhorst* in Gdynia. The *Graf Zeppelin* was last photographed at Swinemünde on 22 April but photographs taken on 5 May showed that the carrier had moved (it had put to sea for trials in the Baltic). Photographs taken on 23 June showed that *Graf Zeppelin* was berthed alongside the western edge of the Oder at Stettin. Subsequent photos showed no sign of activity and it was assumed, correctly as it turned out, that all work on the carrier's development had been abandoned.[56]

On 6 July 1942 the newly-promoted Flight Lieutenant Bayley and Pilot Officer Little took off from Leuchars in W4060 at 12.30 hours for Wick to top up their tanks before heading for Norway to photograph the *Tirpitz*. However, they were forced to return to base when the long-range immersed fuel pump failed to function. The starboard undercarriage leg collapsed on touch down at Leuchars but the crew emerged unscathed from their crash-landing.[57] PR.IV DK284 was prepared and at 21.30 hours Bayley and Little took off again for Wick. However, excessive temperature in the port engine forced the crew to return a second time and they landed at 23.05 hours. They took off for the third time at 05.30 hours on the 7th. A contemporary account of the sortie did not of course mention the setbacks and instead it painted a rosier picture for its readers.[58]

> The Mosquito was something the RAF was still keeping up its bright blue sleeve... But in July, to the ordinary man and woman in the street, the mosquito was still a summer pest with a horrid appetite for sensitive skins. One of those lowly and thoroughly noisome creatures an incomprehensible Providence had allowed to multiply alarmingly in an already over-crowded world. Certainly never to be accorded the dignity of a capital M! However, as two Coastal Command men[59] sat over their breakfast one bright July morning a twin-engined plane, clean-cut in line, sprouting cannon [sic], was warming up ready for a take-off. For those two excited and very proud men the only mosquito in the world was the one on the runway whose engines purred with the rhythm of power. They did not dally over the meal. The sun was beginning to find its real lustre when they climbed into the aircraft, settled themselves in their cockpits, checked quickly the instruments and radio and gave the ground staff the OK sign. The chocks were pulled away, the sleek length of the wooden frame shuddered slightly, and the Mosquito moved forward. It rose off the airfield, circled once and then headed east...the pilot knew his stuff. He headed straight out across the North Sea, making for the Norwegian coast. He kept high and thrilled at the effortless ease with which his Rolls-Royce Merlins pulled the

aircraft through the air. He kept glancing at the speed gauge, fascinated by what it revealed.

Making the Norwegian coast Bayley turned due north, still keeping very high. Fifteen minutes short of Narvik the oxygen supply failed. Little placed his finger over a hole that had appeared in the oxygen tube and Bayley put the Mosquito's nose down into a sharp dive at 450 mph to descend to 12,000ft. He pulled out of the dive suddenly and sent the Mosquito screaming away to the north-east. A glance below had revealed, spread over the surface of the sea at Arno in Langfjord, the German battle fleet and climbing to 14,000ft they photographed the battleships, *Tirpitz*, *Admiral Scheer* and *Hipper*, seven destroyers, two torpedo boats, three E- or R-boats and one *Altmark* tanker. They took an oblique photograph of a destroyer at Bogen and verticals of Bardufoss aerodrome and Tromsø before the 36-inch camera failed! Bayley and Little flew on to Vaenga in North East Russia where shortly before noon, they landed on the oiled sand-runway cut through a silver birch plantation, to refuel. According to a contemporary account:[60]

> ...the two Coastal Command men received a hearty welcome from the Russian airmen, who eyed the aircraft that had made the flight with keen, appreciative eyes. The British fliers were taken into the Russian mess for lunch, and a rare lunch it proved for men who had been on rations. There were mounds of pâté de foie gras, bottles of vodka, bortch, mountainous steaks of venison, piles of bright creamy butter and the samovars worked overtime producing cup after cup of what the pilot described as 'the most perfect tea I have ever drunk.' Lunch over and smoking cigarettes [Bayley and Little] were shown over the aerodrome and generally entertained by their hosts.[61] At three o'clock they were back at the Mosquito in flying-kit, ready to take off. Seven and a half-hours later [flying at 12,000ft for most of the way], with daylight still in the English sky, they dropped down over their own landing-field, [at 20.50 hours] having made an uneventful flight. 'We then had a late dinner' [Bayley] recounted later. 'Altogether we had been in the air 11 hours and 50 minutes. I was a bit cramped, since I couldn't leave my seat, and had to wriggle my body to avoid stiffness.'

On 13 August a small PRU Detachment embarked for Vaenga. (Initially three elderly Spitfire IVs were used until on 23 September Squadron Leader M.J.B. Young DFC landed in W49061 for photo-reconnaissance sorties over Norway).[62] Meanwhile, reconnaissance sorties were also made to Italy. On 24 August Flight Lieutenant Gerry R. Wooll RCAF and Sergeant John Fielden were dispatched in DK310 to confirm a report that Italian warships were putting to sea. They were to obtain photos of Venice, Trieste, Fiume and perhaps Pola, if conditions were right. DK310 took off from Benson and stopped at Ford to top-up its tanks before proceeding uneventfully to Venice. However, as Wooll departed the area the glycol pump on the starboard engine began malfunctioning. The shaft had become slightly elliptical and fluid began escaping. Within a few seconds, the engine seized. Wooll found the aircraft too heavy and unbalanced to attempt to continue on one engine and his problems were compounded a few minutes later when the port engine began overheating. Wooll headed for Switzerland and managed to put down safely at Belp airfield near Berne. After landing, Fielden tried unsuccessfully to set the aircraft on fire before the two men were marched off to a small village camp at Yen. After four months Wooll and Fielden were repatriated as part of an exchange deal which allowed two interned Bf 109 pilots to leave for Germany.[63]

On 19 October 1 PRU was re-formed at Benson as five PR squadrons.[64] No.540 Squadron's first operation was to Norway to photograph the *Tirpitz* and the *von Scheer* in Ofot Fjord. Shortly after, 'B' flight moved to Benson where Flight Lieutenant W.R. Alcott and Sergeant Leach photographed Le Creusot on the eastern side of the Massif Central, 200 miles south-east of Paris. The Schneider armaments factory had been bombed on the afternoon of 17 October by a force of ninety-four Lancasters of 5 Group[65] and the crews had claimed a successful attack. However, Alcott's and Leach's sortie brought back photographs, which revealed that damage to the factory was not extensive and that much of the bombing had fallen short and had struck the workers housing estate near the factory.[66] Flight Lieutenant W.R. Alcott and Sergeant Leach flew sorties to Milan, Genoa, Savona and Turin to obtain evidence of the results of heavy bombing raids during late October and November. Within days of being formed various 540 Squadron detachments were sent to Malta and Gibraltar to provide coverage for the 'Torch' landings in North Africa. Long and dangerous flights like these in unarmed Mosquitoes are often overlooked, while a contemporary wartime account added more than its fair share of romance. This flight was made by Sqn Ldr Rupert Clerke and his navigator:

> …Work like the truly remarkable flight to Malta by way of France and Italy made by another Coastal Command crew flying a Mosquito. Here are the navigator's own words, describing the journey: 'We took off from England in fog, and set course directly for Venice, climbing to 24,000ft. The Alps were a breathtaking sight and visibility was now good. At 11.45 hours we sighted Venice, and after reconnoitring the city, harbour and aerodrome and clearly seeing a large battleship and a passenger liner, we flew over the shipbuilding-yards at Monfalcone, and then headed for Trieste. There were a number of naval vessels in the harbour. We noted these, set course for Fiume, and flew over the small port of Pola, on the southern tip of the Istrian peninsula'. It sounds very much like a peacetime tourist itinerary. These Mosquito airmen, flying in daylight, apparently wandered Italian skies as they wished. There is something about the complete success of the flight that smacks of covert nose-thumbing, a quiet impertinence that is breath-taking. 'This job done,' the navigator continues, in the same rich

vein, 'we set course for Rome. The cloud thinned as we approached, and, clearly showing amid the modern and well-planned streets of this ancient city, we saw the Colosseum. Final course was now set for Malta, a distance of 420 miles, with Sicily to cross. Soon the island loomed ahead, with Mount Etna easily visible to port. Losing height gradually, we spotted Luqa and made a perfect landing, a little over six hours after leaving England'.

The weather, after their arrival, turned unfavourable for flying, so for twenty-four hours these intrepid 'tourists' stayed on the island, but at six o'clock on the following morning they were in the air again and the nose of their Mosquito turned south. They headed for the North African coastline. 'We then set course for Gibraltar,' the narrative continues, 'Malta to Gibraltar took just over 5 hours. Almost immediately after leaving Gibraltar we ran into heavy cloud and icing conditions, with the port engine missing occasionally, to keep us alive to the fact that we were not home yet'. But when they were over France the weather cleared, and they crossed the Breton coast somewhere just south of the U-boat base of Lorient. When one recalls the many squadrons of German fighters kept in that sector to deal with intrepid raiders, it almost seems as though the two men were throwing the enemy a dare. A dare, anyway, the Hun did not accept. They flew on and by radio pinpointed their exact position when well above heavy cloud once more. 'At the right moment,' the navigator concluded his account of the trip, 'we came below cloud, and there was our base, right where it should have been. Never was there a more welcome sight. We had covered nearly 4,000 miles since leaving England and had forgotten to eat our grapes!'[67]

On 1 October 1942 Pilot Officer Freddie 'Mac' McKay RNZAF made the first return trip to Malta, returning to Benson on the 4th. On 6 October a photographic reconnaissance of Upper Silesia by McKay revealed two oil plants at Blechhammer and one at Deschowitz, the existence of which was previously unknown. On 8 December 'Mac' and his navigator, Flight Sergeant Stan 'Paddy' Hope flew a long flight from Benson to Austria in a Mosquito PR.IV. Paddy Hope had flown operations on Blenheims and Beaufighters with Coastal Command before transferring to PRU Mosquitoes in May and he had completed twenty operations with 'Mac' McKay before this one. The starboard engine began to overheat and had to be feathered. 'Paddy' Hope set course for home but after a long, slow descent to about 5,000ft the port engine began to misfire from shortage of fuel. They only got as far as Enghien, south-west of Brussels in Belgium. Mac gave Stan Hope orders to bale out while he flew the stricken Mosquito a little further before he too baled out. Stan was able to evade capture but on 15 January 1943 he was caught at Urrugne near the Franco-Spanish border with the Comet Line [a Belgian underground organisation set up to help downed RAF airman escape back to Britain] leader, Andrée 'Dedeé' de Jongh, a 26-year old Belgian girl, and two other RAF evadees.[68] The *Gestapo* held the RAF airman for four months, who endured repeated questioning and two beatings, before being sent to a PoW camp in Germany. Meanwhile, Mac managed to set the aircraft on fire with an on-board incendiary device that was always carried. The New Zealander later attempted to board a train at night, which just happened to be carrying German troops. He was sent to *Stalag Luft III* at Sagan for the remainder of the war where he was involved in many attempts to escape.[69]

In the main, 540 Squadron photographed German capital ships in Baltic waters and in North German ports and carried out bomb damage assessment (BDA) and target reconnaissance. Serviceability of aircraft in the winter of 1942-43 was only 50 per cent at times because of water seepage into badly fitted No.7 bulkheads. Late in 1942 the first of five PR.VIIIs[70] began to reach 540 Squadron, this version being built to fill the gap until deliveries of the PR.IX and PR.XVI were made. The first PR.VIII sortie was flown on 19 February 1943 when Squadron Leader Gordon E. Hughes (later Wing Commander Hughes DSO DFC) and Sergeant H.W. Evans overflew La Rochelle and St. Nazaire. Unfortunately, they were unable to take any photos because the mud flap over the camera lens failed to open. The first successful PR.VIII sorties therefore took place on 27 February when Flight Lieutenant K. H. Bayley DFC flew to Frankfurt on a bomb damage assessment flight and another PRU Mosquito covered Emden and Bremen. On 8 March unit CO, Wing Commander M.J.B. Young, became the first Mosquito pilot to photograph Berlin.[71]

On 2 December 1942, 22-year old Canadian pilot Flight Lieutenant Bill White from Roland, Manitoba and his Mancunian navigator, 23-year-old Flight Lieutenant Ron Prescott flew their first operation (a short trip lasting 2 hours 30 minutes to Bergen) since joining 540 Squadron. Prior to this, they had had a close call during a training flight on 18 November when, at about 15,000ft, the starboard engine of their converted Mosquito F.II blew off a flame trap. When smoke began pouring from the rear of the engine White shut it down, feathered the prop and activated the fire extinguisher. This had little effect and by the time they were down to a few thousand feet over Mount Farm, flames were visibly issuing from the rear of the wing. Concerned that the fuel tanks might blow and by this time over the airfield, they decided to land rather than bale out. They crash landed at Mount Farm, where the right undercarriage leg fell off, but both men walked away virtually unscathed.

Two five-hour operations over Trondheim and the Norwegian coast followed in W4060 (which was the first long-range version of the PR.I). On 12 January 1943 they flew a 3 hour 55 minute flight in the same aircraft to an area of coast between Stattlandet to Lister in an attempt to locate the harbour where the *Scharnhorst* was at anchor but nothing was seen. On 24 January, again in W4060, they searched between Grimstadt Fjord-Bergen-Odda and Stavanger, where they were fired on by German flak, but again nothing was found. On the 26th in W4059, the original

PR.I, they searched from Sogne Fjord down to Stavanger, flying at 3,000ft, again without result! Two more flights were made on 2nd and 5th February, and on these sorties the search area was extended north from Stattlandet to Trondheim. Each flight lasted for over five hours and on the 5th they flew in 10/10ths cloud almost all the way. On 16 February the weather was not predicted accurately and Ron Prescott commented "X" is a bloody awful Met man'. Their flight, again to Norway, proved to be extremely hazardous and required great skill, as Bill White remembers.

> Since we preferred to stay just under the altitude at which we produced contrails, we did most of our flights between 20,000 and 30,000ft. In the belly of the aircraft we had two 36-inch cameras, which took line overlap pictures. These produced 3-D views of the areas being photographed, which were then examined by our intelligence people. Details as small as a golf ball were detectable. We also carried a smaller camera in the port side of the aircraft and with this we could take oblique pictures. Some of the trips involved low-level photography and this required flying at tree-top level.

More trips were made to Norway with occasional flights to other targets. On 9 February they flew over Copenhagen and Denmark during a 5 hour 5 minute reconnaissance flight and caused air raid sirens to be sounded from 13.14 to 14.10 hours. On 21 March they flew their longest flight so far, a six-hour round trip from Leuchars to Norway and back to Wick. On 22 April 1943, their 22nd sortie, Bill White and Ron Prescott completed one of the most memorable flights of their extensive operational careers. They were sent to photograph the railyards at Stettin, Germany's biggest Baltic port and which had been bombed two days before on the night of the full moon (20/21 April) by 339 'heavies', as well as the Politz oil refinery and Swinemunde on the Baltic coast. Twenty-four fires were still burning at Stettin when the PR aircraft flew over the target a day-and-a-half later; approximately 100 acres in the centre of the town having been devastated. On leaving Stettin they left their cameras running all down the north coast of Germany. After 5 hours and 20 minutes in the air they landed back and when the film was developed, it was found to contain pictures of Peenemünde. When they were developed, one of the prints showed an object 25ft long projecting from what was thought to be a service building, although it had mysteriously disappeared on the next frame! The interpreters of the CIU (Central Intelligence Unit) at Medmenham studied the photos brought back by the crew. From the type of buildings seen and the elliptical earthworks originally photographed in May 1942 by Flight Lieutenant D.W. Steventon in a PRU Spitfire, it was assumed that these were actual testing points. The interpreters concluded that Peenemünde must be an experimental centre, probably connected with explosives and propellants. A sortie flown on 14 May 1943 by Squadron Leader Gordon Hughes and Flight Sergeant John R. Chubb brought back more photos.

Bill White and Ron Prescott were unaware of these developments and on 15 May they had other things to think about, as Bill White recalls.

We were doing photo runs over Oslo when six Bf 109s jumped us. The 109 was faster than we were in a climb or a dive, but the Mosquito could out-turn them. With the excellent direction by Ron, we were able to do ever-decreasing turns and able to avoid their gunfire. We were also able to inch our way over to Sweden. The Swedes will never know how grateful we were to them as they opened up with every flak battery on their coast. The Ack-Ack was always behind us and I'll never know how many 109s they got. The return to Leuchars was just a normal flight from Sweden, with no problems from fighters.

Meanwhile, further investigation of the photos from the 22 April sortie at Peenemünde revealed that road vehicles and railway wagons near one of the earthworks were carrying cylindrical objects measuring about 38ft long. On 17 May it was concluded that German rocket development had not only probably been underway for some time, but was also 'far advanced'. A sixth sortie to Peenemünde on 2 June unearthed scant new information. Ten days later a sortie flown by Flight Lieutenant Reggie A. Lenton resulted in the first definite evidence that the previously unidentified objects were in fact V-2 rockets. One was photographed near to a building adjacent to one of the elliptical earthworks lying horizontally on a trailer. Also two objects were spotted, one described as being '35ft long and appears to have a blunt point. For 25ft of its length the diameter is about 8ft. The appearance...is not incompatible with it being a cylinder tapered at one end and provided with three radial fins at the other'; and the other as 'a thick vertical column about 40ft high and 4ft thick'. But initially they were not recognised as rockets.[72] On 23 June Flight Sergeant E.P.H. Peek brought back photos so clear that two rockets could be seen lying on road vehicles inside the elliptical earthwork known as Test Stand VII. The news was relayed immediately to Prime Minister Winston Churchill. PRU Mosquitoes photographed Peenemünde again on 27 June and 22 and 26 July. It was now almost certain that Hitler was preparing a rocket offensive against southern England and it had to be forestalled with all speed.

On 17/18 August 1943 596 Lancasters, Halifaxes and Stirlings set out to destroy the experimental rocket site. Although the German ground controllers were fooled into thinking the bombers were headed for Stettin and a further 'spoof' by Mosquitoes aiming for Berlin drew more fighters away from the Peenemünde force, forty Lancasters, Halifaxes and Stirlings (6.7 per cent of the force) were shot down. Altogether, 560 aircraft dropped almost 1,800 tons of bombs on Peenemünde. A daylight reconnaissance was flown 12 hours after the Peenemünde attack by Flying Officer R.A. Hosking of 540 Squadron and he returned to the area the following day. Photographs revealed twenty-seven buildings in the northern manufacturing area destroyed and forty huts in the living and sleeping quarters completely flattened. The foreign labour camp to the south suffered worst of all and 500-600 foreign workers, mostly Polish, were killed. The whole target area was covered in craters. The Peenemünde raid is adjudged to have set back the V-2 experimental programme by at least two months and to have reduced the scale of the eventual rocket attacks on Britain.[73] After the raid the Germans relocated development and production of V-2s to an underground facility at Traunsee near Saltzburg in Austria.

While PR never did reveal how the V-2s were launched (ground intelligence showed that they were to be launched vertically), during October 1944-March 1945 544 Squadron Mosquitoes and other PR aircraft, identified several launching sites in Holland. PR was much more successful in identifying the existence and launching sites of Germany's other secret weapons, however. It all began by chance on 28 November 1943 when a Mosquito from Leuchars, flown by Squadron Leader John Merrifield DSO DFC and Flying Officer W.N. Whalley, set out to photograph bomb damage in Berlin. They reached the German capital, but were unable to take any photographs because of the low cloud cover. Merrifield then turned north, back towards the Baltic coast, to cover secondary targets that he had been given at briefing. There were shipping targets at Stettin and Swinemünde, airfields and a suspected radar installation at Zinnovitz (Zempin) on an island, which is separated from the mainland by the River Peene. Merrifield covered each location in turn and realising that he still had film left, overflew Peenemünde airfield, before returning home. When the film was developed, the shots of Zinnovitz showed buildings that were similar in size and shape to those which had been photographed at Bois Carré, 10 miles north-east of Abbeville, on 28 October 1942 by Pilot Officer R.A. Hosking. This was the first V-1 flying bomb launching site in France to be analysed on photographs and the buildings shown were meant for storage of flying-bomb components. Frames of Peenemünde airfield revealed a ski-type ramp pointing out to sea, which were identical to examples photographed by PR Spitfires at sites in northern France. Merrifield's photographs of the ramp went one better, for they showed a 'tiny cruciform shape set exactly on the lower end of the inclined rails a midget aircraft actually in position for launching'.

The 'midget aircraft' was now revealed as a flying bomb and the curious ski-shaped ramps in France were to be the launch sites for a new reign of terror against London and southern England. The *Vergelrungswaffe* I (Revenge Weapon No 1) was a small, pilotless aircraft with a 1,870lb HE warhead that detonated on impact. On 5 December 1943 the bombing of the V-1, or *Noball* sites, became part of the Operation Crossbow offensive. PRU aircraft regularly photographed each V-1 site before and after an attack and by the end of the month, the Allies had overflown forty-two *Noball* sites, of which thirty-six were revealed as having been damaged; twenty-one of them seriously. By 12 June 1944, sixty weapons sites had been identified. Hitler's 'rocker blitz' began on 13 June when ten V-1s, or 'Doodlebugs' as they became known, were launched against London from sites in north-eastern France.

When the enemy began building new underground storage centres in caves and quarries, vertical photography was rendered almost useless, so PR Mosquitoes of 544 Squadron were fitted with forward-facing oblique cameras in the nose of their aircraft. Crews had to fly straight at the target at 200ft and they often had to brave heavy flak to obtain their photos. By the end of September 1944, when the Allied advance overran most of the sites, PRU aircraft had identified 133 V-1 installations. Only eight ever remained undiscovered by aerial reconnaissance.

Following a series of complaints from Air Chief Marshal Sir Arthur Harris, on 26 June 1943 1 PRU became 106(PR) Wing (and from 15 May 1944, 106 (PR) Group) at Benson. Also included in the new set up, which was commanded by Air Commodore John N. Bootham AFC of Schneider Trophy fame, was 309 Ferry Training and Despatch Unit and 8(PR) OTU at Dyce. On 29 May 1943 540 Squadron received the first two PR.IX Mosquitoes off the production lines.[74] The first sortie with the type was flown on 20 June, when Flying Officer T.M. Clutterbuck set out to cover Zeitz and Jena but he was forced to turn back after crossing the Dutch coast when smoke poured into the cockpit. Flying Officer R.A. Hosking, who had taken off soon after, had better luck and returned with photos of the airfields at Augsburg and Oberpfaffenhofen. On 3 August Flight Lieutenant Peter Hollick and Flight Lieutenant A.R. 'Ronnie' Knight, who had joined 540 Squadron a month earlier, photographed the whole of the Brenner Pass starting at Innsbruck and finishing at Verona. Ronnie Knight recalls.

> This was one the most interesting sorties I flew. As there was more than the usual amount of photography involved and the trip was going to the extent of the normal range of the Mossie we flew on and landed at La Merse. We returned via Gibraltar next day and the weather had closed in over the UK with cloud down to the deck so we had to make an emergency landing at Predannack in Cornwall. While searching for this airfield we were flying below the cliffs. When we landed we were told that the bad weather was due to a front moving west, which at that time was between Predannack and Benson. We were given the option of staying the night at Predannack or taking off immediately and get to Benson before the weather closed in there. We decided to get back to base over the top of the weather using the Gee to navigate. We had to go up to 30,000ft, which was very bumpy due to the Cu Nim in the cloud. We did a VHF descent through the cloud and landed at Benson, as it was getting dark. We had a similar experience on 30 October when we went to Leipzig. It went off OK but in the meantime the whole of the UK had become fog-bound. It was impossible to land at Benson and so we were diverted to Tangmere where we had to stay the night but the Fighter Boys made us very welcome in the bar of the Mess.

On 20 August meanwhile, Bill White and Ron Prescott, now back at Benson, were allocated PR.IX LR421 to fly their 39th operation, a sortie to Blechhammer on the Polish border. Bill White recalls.

Blechhammer's factories produced synthetic rubber, as Germany couldn't get a supply of natural rubber, so this was a very important target. The RAF wished to bring the wheels of the Germans to a stop due to a lack of rubber. Blechhammer was certainly well defended. The PRU had already flown six Mosquito ops against it and none had returned. We were to be the seventh to attempt this long trip. Ron and I took off from Benson and topped up with fuel at Coltishall. From there, we proceeded to Blechhammer, seeing nothing more than a bit of flak. The weather was clear over the target and we got excellent photos. On leaving the target we were intercepted by fighters and by using all our throttle power, we were able to escape from the enemy. However, when Ron calculated our fuel reserves, the strong headwinds on the route back to base meant that there was no way we would be able to make it. Our first plan was to go to Switzerland, but by conserving fuel and helped by favourable winds, we managed to get over Yugoslavia to Naples, in Italy, before eventually running out of fuel on the west coast of Sicily. There, we made a deadstick landing at Bo Rizzo. We were standing in front of our Mosquito when some of the 8th Army approached in an armoured vehicle to find out what had brought us here. Ron was about to say 'nothing' when he recalled that he had the *Daily Mail* from the morning in his flight bag. These soldiers completely gave up on us and all six were on the ground checking up on 'Jane' from the morning paper. When we finally got attention from our hosts we enquired about getting some 100 Octane fuel for our plane. The best they could do was automobile gas with which they had plenty. We got the engines started on this fuel but you never heard such knocking and weird noises in all your life that came from those Merlin engines. We managed to get off the ground and thumbed our way across the Mediterranean to Tunis. The fitters changed the spark plugs, flushed out the tanks and fuel lines and we were on the way home the next day. With refuelling at Maison Blanche, Algeria and Gibraltar we reached base after a trip lasting 14 hours 45 minutes.[75]

No. 544 Squadron borrowed LR431 from the Benson pool for its first PR.IX operation, a night sortie to Vannes on 13 September 1943, which was flown by Flight Lieutenant R. L. C. 'Dicky' Blythe. The unit received its first PR.IX on 22 October 1943, whilst the first PR.IX loss occurred four days later. PR Mosquitoes were now very much in demand, not just for RAF bombing operations, but also by the Americans. On 9 October 378 B-17s of the Eighth Air Force had been despatched on the day's operation, 115 to the Arado aircraft component plant at Anklam, near Peenemünde, as a diversion for 263 bombers sent to attack the

Polish port of Gdynia and the Focke-Wulf Fw 190 factory at Marienburg. Squadron Leader Reggie Lenton and Pilot Officer Heney of 540 Squadron supported the raid, taking off from Leuchars to photograph Marienburg, as well as also try for Gdynia and Danzig. Just before arriving over Danzig, two Bf 109s intercepted them, but the Mosquito was able to escape with ease and Lenton and Heney successfully photographed the Marienburg factory. The images they brought back showed that the aircraft factory had been demolished. Lenton was subsequently reported shot down over Sylt some weeks later.

On 18/19 November 1943 'Bomber' Harris began his nightly offensive against Berlin. This series of raids, which were to last until the end of January 1944, brought added demands for BDA. Flights over Germany were being made ever more difficult by enemy action, bad weather and other factors such as smoke from still burning factories and houses. It took no less than thirty-one PR Spitfire and six PR Mosquito sorties before the results of the bombing of Berlin on 18/19 November were obtained. BDA became such an issue with both the RAF and USAAF bomber commands that PR aircraft were required to cover targets within hours of a raid being carried out, sometimes even before the returning bombers had landed. While covering targets in the south of France on 20 January, Pilot Officer John R. Myles DFC RCAF and his navigator and fellow Canadian, Flying Officer Hugh R. Cawker had to feather the propeller on the port engine over Toulouse. (The cause was low oil pressure caused by a split in the 'banjo' union (oil pipe).) Myles recalls:

> We first thought of going to Corsica but we decided there was too much water to fly over and we were not sure where the aerodromes were, anyway. We next considered returning to base but I knew there was a lot of activity on the north French coast that day and I did not like the idea of coming out through it at 10,000ft on one engine. Besides, if anything did happen on the way it would mean walking all the way back again. Finally we decided to set course for Gibraltar. I did not know what our petrol consumption would be on one engine and I did not think we had enough to reach Gib but we figured we would fly as far as possible, then bale out and walk the rest of the way. After two hours on one engine we were getting a bit tired, but we had computed our petrol consumption again and it proved to be less than the first estimate. If only that engine would hold out! After three hours we found ourselves over the Pyrenees at 14,000ft with about one hour left. We flew over the mountains full of expectancy and we pinpointed ourselves on the coast at Malaga. There, silhouetted against the sinking sun was the Rock of Gibraltar. We circled the Rock at 10,000ft, descended to 2,000ft over the runway and fired off the colours of the day. I then made my first single engined landing in a Mosquito after spending 6 hours in the air, 3 hours of which, were on one engine over the Pyrenees and it did not even heat up.

Navigator G.W.E. 'Bill' Newby had teamed up at Dyce PR OCU in July 1943 with Flight Lieutenant William Hampson, a 6ft tall pilot who had flown a tour on Coastal Command Hudsons. On New Year's Eve 1943 Hampson and Newby flew a Mk.I to Norway and had to return to Dyce with engine trouble. On landing, using only the starboard engine, they lost their undercarriage and ran into a cottage just off the peri track. They were put to bed in the sick quarters but Newby awoke at about 9pm to find Hampson's bed empty. He had gone to find his current lady love in Aberdeen and Newby decided to join in the Hogmanay festivities at the best hotel in Aberdeen with other squadron members and the Royal Scots, who were having a party instead of guarding Balmoral. In January 1944 Hampson and Newby reported to 1 PRU at Benson.

Crews from Benson covered the Dams project, keeping an eye on how full they were in readiness for the raid, 16/17 May 1943 and photographing the after-damage and the chaos the Dambusters caused locally. Our job in 544 Squadron was to take photographs before and after air attacks by both RAF night- and USAAF day-bombers. (We high-tailed it back and overtook the USAAF on the way home). We photographed Wiener Neustadt, north of Vienna before the USAAF arrived, then we cleared off to Lake Constance to take the Zeppelin sheds at Friedrichshafen, before returning to take the after-damage shots. We also took strategic photos of the coastal defences prior to the invasion of Europe. And we photographed U-boat pens; pocket-battleships holed up in various French, German and Danish ports; oil-plants and aircraft factories deep in Germany; V-I launching sites in the Pas de Calais. We even photographed secret underground manufacturing sites in the Hartz mountains and fields etc, which were to he used for dropping zones in France for Special Operations Executive (SOE) agents. For all of this, the Mosquito was ideal.

Most PR flights, in cinematography terms, were very routine. Occasionally, they were spiced up with 'one offs'. Like rushing to Copenhagen late on Whit Sunday afternoon 1944 because one of our 'informers', sitting on a hillside in Sweden, was sure that the pocket-battleship *Deutschland* [renamed *Lützow*] had disappeared from its moorings overnight and was thought to be free in the North Sea. Bill Hampson and I did a square search up the Kattegat and Skagerrak but could find no trace. So with light fading, we swept low over the Tivoli gardens and Hans Christian Andersen's Mermaid to the dockyard, only to find that the ship had been moved to a new berth and was disguised overnight to look like a tanker. Other flights were more exciting. Long hauls up the Baltic as far as Gdynia, equally long trips to Austria and on over the Alps to Venice and Yugoslavia, stopping overnight at Foggia (San Severo). After the landings in Italy; returning via Ajaccio, Corsica, or Gibraltar, to refuel, on one occasion taking photographs of Vesuvius in eruption. Another operation, which took pride of place in the national press, was a visit to the Gnome-Rhône aircraft engine works at Limoges on the morning of 9 February 1944 after it had been a special target of Bomber Command the night before. The place had been utterly devastated and we could easily see the damage from 30,000ft but we had been authorized to go 'low-level', so we could not pass up the chance to scream across at tree-top height to take really close 'close-ups', which later appeared in the press.

Squadron Leader Bill Aston DFC of 544 PR Squadron also had an eventful PR career, sometimes flying Spitfires but more usually Mosquitoes with Flight Lieutenant Peter Fielding as his observer. In November and December of 1943 they ranged widely over Europe, going to Annecy and the Franco-Italian frontier; to Zurich and Bolzano on other trips (landing back at Benson with only 20 gallons of fuel left). In January, they fired six flash bombs on Abbeville, the same again on Cherbourg a few nights later and then to the Biarritz area. Flash bombs were very unstable and everyone was sceptical about their success rate. (Each photoflash weighed 60lb and each one could provide 120,000-candle power).

When Bill Aston took off in Mosquito PR.IX LR430 on 29 January 1944 on a night photographic sortie over France he had logged 1,934 hours and 50 minutes, many of them at night and in bad weather and it was his 175th operational sortie. While over France at 35,000ft a flash bomb exploded and both crew were thrown out of the Mosquito. Fielding had no time to clip on his observer-chute and he was killed. Aston, fortunately, was wearing a seat-type parachute and he free-fell from 35,000ft to about 500ft. He regained consciousness and frantically searched for the D-ring to open the parachute. Eventually he found the D-ring up by his left shoulder. It had obviously twisted in the harness. As Aston located the release and operated it he heard a bang as the parachute deployed and he hit the ground at the same time. Fortunately, it was dark and he was blind anyway from the explosion of the photo flash bombs, so he had no idea that the ground was so close. There had been considerable rain and he landed in the softest, muddiest field in France. His first thoughts were to escape so he got up and started to run, only to go flat on his face in the mud, as he still had his chute attached. Since it was pitch dark he did not realise that he was blind but he managed to pick up the chute with the idea of hiding it to avoid subsequent detection. By now Aston could not walk because his muscles had seized up. He crawled through the mud for about half-an-hour, still clutching the chute and eventually found a ditch and hid the chute under a pile of dead leaves. By now his teeth were chattering with the cold and the shock. Aston heard a dog barking in the distance and headed off towards it. After about an hour of slow and difficult crawling, he found a gravel path and started to shout, 'I am an English aviator' in his broken French. People came out but of course he could not see them. It was now about midnight. Aston was carried into a farmhouse and he discovered that he was with the Maquis. They asked him for his name, rank and serial number. He was informed that London would be notified that he was alive but later, the Maquis said that because of his injuries he would probably die without medical attention and that therefore he was a liability to their organisation. Unable to move, they said they had no alternative but to hand him over to the Germans and this they did. Aston received no medical attention of any kind for the next six months and was subjected to many beatings by the *Gestapo* in the process. Eventually he ended up in *Stalag Luft III* where it took him about six months to recover his sight.[76]

On 19 February 1944 a PR.XVI brought back photos of Berlin, despite the appearance of German fighters sighted at 42,000ft![77] 'Bill' Newby flew in the prototype PR.XVI,[78] the first aircraft in the world (apart from the pre-war Bristol Type 138A) to be fitted with a pressurised cabin. He recalls. 'I had the privilege of flying on cabin tests with my squadron commander, Wing Commander D.W. Steventon DSO DFC and Geoffrey de Havilland. We were having trouble with 'misting up' of windows and I was the smallest navigator on the two squadrons (my pilot Bill Hampson called me 'Tiny') so we flew '3-up' for short periods to carry out tests.'[79]

PR flights to southern France continued unabated in May 1944. Though crews were unaware the series of sorties were in preparation for Operation Dragoon, the Americans' southern invasion (which was due to begin on 15 August). On 15 May Flight Lieutenant Peter Farlow and Flight Lieutenant E.E.G. 'Dicky' Boyd, who had joined 540 Squadron in 1943, flew their 25th operation, to the south of France to cover about ten airfields. Although they did some night flying practice all of their ops were in daylight and 15 May was no exception. Dicky Boyd recalls:

> Whilst over the fourth target we were 'jumped' by a dozen Messerschmitts. We turned tail and headed off north going flat out and although we were able gradually to pull away from them, it was not before they had holed a fuel tank. Fortunately, there was no fire but on checking the gauge we found that we had very little juice left. It was streaming out like white smoke behind us. We had to find a suitable spot to put down on. Peter put her down, wheels up of course; a superb landing. The props were a tangled mess. There were a few splinters of wood and the perspex nose was shattered. Otherwise we were intact! As usual, the special detonator canister would not work but I was able to open a 'chute' in the nose and fire a Very light into it to 'get it going'. It was about midday so we beat it for cover in a nearby wood. We knew that before we came down that the nearest town was Châteauroux, an important railway junction in Central France. After a while we decided to move in a south-westerly direction towards Spain. Just as we were crossing a road a German motorcycle and sidecar unit came around a bend in the road. The occupants covered us with their rifles and thus put an end to our hopes of getting away. A week later we found ourselves in *Stalag Luft* III.

Just before D-Day 544 Squadron flew special rail sorties in daylight to France in an effort to detect any movement of Panzers towards the Normandy beachhead as early as possible. If any movement was observed, the crew had to land at Farnborough to give a verbal report to SHEAF HQ, who would then initiate interdiction bombing by 2nd TAF medium bombers. The first confirmation that the Messerschmitt Me 262 jet fighter was being operated by the *Luftwaffe* came on 25 July. A Mosquito of 544 Squadron flown by Flight Lieutenant A.E. Wall and his navigator, Flying Officer A.S. Lobban, was operating over Munich when it was intercepted and attacked by one of the German jets. The engagement lasted for 20 minutes until eventually Wall was able to evade his attacker by going into clouds over the Austrian Tyrol. He subsequently made an emergency landing at St. Fermo on the shores of the Adriatic. The usually low casualty rate in the PRU rose dramatically from 0.6 per cent in June 1944 to 2.9 per cent in September. Such an increase in losses could only have been caused by the Me 262, since 50 per cent of them occurred in the area where these jet fighters operated. In an effort to reduce casualties and combat the threat posed by the Me 262, from then on until early-1945 PR sorties over Germany were flown mainly by Spitfire PR.XIXs since their superior manoeuvrability and performance made them a better choice than the PR Mosquito.[80]

Flight Lieutenant Alan 'Joe' Morgan and Sergeant Frank 'Ginger' Baylis who flew forty-six PR Mosquito sorties on 544 Squadron from January to October 1944, were well aware of the dangers, as Joe Morgan recalls:

PR sorties were nearly always high level jobs, mostly without untoward incidents apart from the usual flak and occasional pursuit by fighters, which we could outpace if they were spotted in time for us to apply full power and accelerate to full speed. The Me 262 jet and the Me 163 rocket-powered fighter did not appear until about the end of our tour and we did not encounter either. The main threat arose during the actual photo runs when the navigator would be prone in the nose compartment, operating the cameras and directing the pilot, who would be concerned mainly with accurate flying concentrating on the flying instruments. The normal complement was two massive 36-inch focal length cameras, one 6-inch focal length camera for vertical photography at 6,000ft or below and forward and side-facing cameras for really low-level work. With all the film magazines and control gear, this was a really significant load. The rearward visibility from the pilot's station was not adequate, even from the perspex port-window adjacent to his seat. When we were *en route* in hostile skies, Frank would kneel on his seat, facing aft. He did not care for this but it proved a wise precaution. Although the Mosquito had the legs of the opposition, we could not afford the fuel to cruise on full power and thought that good look out astern was imperative for the early sighting of any pursuer. The aircraft was at its most vulnerable when making photo-runs, especially on the 'railway recces' in which the navigator was constrained to remain in the nose compartment for perhaps 28 minutes at a time.

Morgan and Baylis had flown the first of 544 Squadron 'rail recces' on 3 June 1944, as Baylis recalls.

We spent about an hour covering lines between Mont de Marsan and Bordeaux, which made Joe quite uncomfortable, as the last time he flew over Merignac in 1941, he'd had a pasting with accurate flak. Our most memorable 'railway recce' was on 6 August. We had been briefed to follow the railway from south of Paris to Lyon, then up towards Belfort. As we trundled towards Lyon, we saw this huge smoke cloud rising to 20,000ft from oil tanks south of the town. We could even see flames from our height of 28,000ft, conjecturing that 'it must be a raid by Fifteenth Air Force heavy bombers from Italy'. (There had been no information given at briefing). We cut across to the rail-line leading north-east to Belfort. As Joe turned quite steeply, I took an instant shot of the fire and towering smoke. We settled onto the railway and Joe asked me to have a last look around. Good job. I saw twelve fighters in three groups of four obviously in hot pursuit. Without any urging, Joe put the throttles through the 'gate' and we managed to avoid them, aided by some high thunderheads in which we played 'hide and seek' for ten minutes or so.

Morgan continues.

Our worst hazard arose from our life-preserving oxygen supply! It happened on our second trip. We were climbing outbound over the Channel when, at about 25,000ft I passed out. I later discovered that the oxygen supply had become disconnected from the face-piece of my mask. Frank told me later that he noticed we were flying erratically and he saw me 'hanging in the straps' as he put it. He pushed the stick forward and held the oxygen tube to my mask and I gradually came to. We were at 6,000ft in thick haze. The compass was swinging wildly, the engine temperatures were 'off the clock' and the gyro flying instruments had toppled. I felt dazed and ill and put out a Mayday call on VHF. Manston gave me a course to steer and I landed shakily. But after a couple of hours on oxygen I was able to fly back to Benson. All our oxygen masks were modified the next day so some good came of it.

We had two further jousts with oxygen! One was on our seventh trip when I began to feel 'woozy' again while we were being 'flakked' when photographing naval units in Oslo Fjord. Sure enough, the supply indicator was in the red sector. Having finished our task, we dived away out to sea and returned at low level. The third (and thankfully last) encounter came when crossing the North Sea *en route* to Berlin. I saw Frank had passed out. The bayonet fitting of the tube, which ran from his harness to the oxygen supply point had come adrift. I only had to get down from my seat and connect the pipe. He soon perked up and we completed the trip.

One of our most 'dodgy' encounters occurred on our tenth trip. We had just finished a long run in the Lyons area with Frank in the nose when we spotted a gaggle of fighters bearing down on us. We were at about 25,000ft with drop tanks still attached. It seemed a long time to shed these impediments and wind up to maximum power. Meantime, our pursuers were diving on us and gaining rapidly and opening fire. I put the nose hard down with full power and tried to jink to disturb their aim while we made for some scanty cloud cover far below. I feared for the integrity of the aircraft structure, but we reached the cloud unscathed. After some more hide-and-seek our pursuers gave up and we sneaked off home, duly chastened! I have since thought these were US fighters as there was a bombing raid in the area at about this time. I believe that a Mosquito of 540 Squadron went missing in this area at the time.

On 27 August one of the longest PR flights was flown by 540 Squadron's CO, Wing Commander John R.H. Merrifield DSO DFC in a PR.XVI. Taking off from Benson at 06.00 hours, he photographed Gdynia, Danzig, Königsberg in Russian Lithuania and Bromberg in Poland, Gleiwitz, in southeastern Germany and oil installations at Blechhammer, Bratislava and Zarsa on the Dalmatian coast before landing at San Severo, Italy, at 12.10 hours. After refuelling, the Mosquito took off again at 15.00 hours to make the return flight to Benson, where it landed at 19.00 hours, having photographed Pola, Trieste, Millsradr in the Tyrol and Le Havre on the return leg.

PR operations to northern Norway, meanwhile (especially those concerned with maintaining a watchful eye on the *Tirpitz*), were not being neglected, for the 544 Squadron detachment at Leuchars was kept constantly busy. In March 1944 *Tirpitz* had left its anchorage in Alten Fjord and later that month it was found in Kaa Fjord by a PRU Spitfire of 542 Squadron operating from Russia. On 3 April the ship was damaged in an attack by Royal Navy aircraft from *Victorious* and *Furious*, but to what extent, no one knew. On 9 July Flight Lieutenant Frank L. Dodd and Flight Sergeant Eric Hill in 544 Squadron were despatched to find[81] the *Tirpitz*. Eric Hill, born in Taunton and educated at Taunton School, where he showed considerable promise as a stylish batsman, recalls that:

In the course of fifty-three operational flights (we did all our ops together) I got to know Frank Leslie Dodd pretty well. We first flew together on 31 January 1944 from 8 OTU Dyce. The first thing I noticed about him was his calm, quiet, almost sleepy exterior and the second was that it covered a steely, inflexible determination to get things as right as he could possibly make them. The third was his modesty and indeed, when this profile was first mentioned, Frank demurred sharply. His reason was absolutely characteristic. He told me, 'A lot of people, especially in the early days, did a great deal more than we did in PRU'. Frank was immediately and obviously a chap of a thoughtful, observant, pacific nature with a sound family basis, centered completely on his splendid wife Joyce and a steadily growing family. Decidedly not the type to lead a riot in the Mess, or 'High Cockalorum' or the singing of 'Eskimo Nell', he would mingle, join in the fun and melt quietly into the background. This then, although it recounts a few things that happened to us in PRU with dear old 544 Squadron (one of the youngest and shortest-lived in the wartime RAF), is essentially a tribute to all the huge numbers of people. Most of them were unsung and unrewarded, who made PRU into the highly important arm of intelligence it became. This, in context, is to be taken as typical of some of the unusual things that happened to photographic reconnaissance crews all over the world, flying unarmed and unarmoured aircraft into the heart of enemy strongholds. Furthermore, this, we hope, will be taken as a memorial to the grievously large number who did not quite make it home.

Flying solitary missions over heavily defended enemy territory in unarmed, wooden aircraft, I suppose, needs special qualities. Having once watched a huge formation of Fortresses flying into and through heavy flak without budging, apart from the ones that were hit, I think PRU suited Frank and me. Like everyone else of any experience in PRU we had our moments and I think all of them reveal the cool calculation, coupled with the ability to make lightning decisions that made Frank the magnificent pilot he was and saved our lives quite a few times.

On 9 July the operational task was to carry out a visual and PR of the west coast of Norway, flying as far north as fuel permitted and certainly beyond the Lofoten Islands, paying attention to any fjords likely to provide suitable anchorage for the *Tirpitz*. Due to a rare gap in intelligence, there was great uncertainty as to her location and readiness for action. She was always a potential threat to Atlantic shipping and Murmansk-bound convoys. Not too many RAF crews have taken photographs of both sides of the superb German battleship *Tirpitz*. After the 'Bomber Boys' had put a Blockbuster down its funnel, it was a piece of cake for us to get some almost sentimental sea-level pictures of the upturned hull and poodle back to sun-soaked Sumburgh. Taking photos of the other side of it a long time before when its mere presence sent tremors through the Admiralty as a threat to all our sea connections and notably the Murmansk route, was a different matter. We had to operate with petrol overload (the numbing 100 gallon wing-tanks) at extreme range with the weather on return likely to clamp down irretrievably most of the Northern British airfields. There were other hazards, too, apart from the fact that in those days Sumburgh was a small 'drome, with one runway, usually crosswind and demanding a steepish turn to avoid a hill near the town. Frank handled this beautifully as always. We set off, with me still wondering why our dear allies, the Russians would not let us land at Murmansk to refuel, thus making the job about 400 per cent more likely to succeed. And what had happened to the glorious Norwegian underground, who were supposed to be keeping an eye on it?

Dodd and Hill carried out a search for the *Tirpitz* at heights ranging from between 6,000 and 24,000ft over the Norwegian shipping lanes from Stattlandet to the Lofoten Islands, including Narvik. Their Mosquito was hit by flak in the starboard wing whilst photographing Bødo at 15,000ft. Nevertheless, valuable photo-negative information was obtained from this sortie, the Mosquito having been airborne 7 hours 44 minutes when it landed back at Leuchars with less than 10 gallons of petrol remaining. On 12 July Dodd and Hill flew to Sumburgh to top up their tanks for another sortie in search of the *Tirpitz*. Hill recalls.

Fortunately, the weather for the first part of the sortie was reasonable and we were able to start the recce at 25,000ft without any apparent hostility. However, when 15 miles west of Bødo, we were greeted by a perfect box-barrage of flak at our precise height, which set the adrenaline flowing. This was just as well, because we needed all our wits about us shortly afterwards when the weather deteriorated, necessitating a blind Dead Reckoning descent through heavy cloud to regain visual contact, as we approached where we estimated the Lofoten Islands to be. Happily, the D/R navigation turned out to be correct and there were no hard centres to the clouds. Unfortunately, still no sign of the *Tirpitz,* so no alternative but to press on to Alten Fjord, which intelligence thought might be a possible lair.

We gentled up the coast and started to sneak into the many fjords past the Lofotens until we came to Alten. There it was 45,000 tons of *Tirpitz*, looking oddly menacing and peaceful at the same time. A bit of desultory flak (we were at an uncomfortable 8,000ft under the cloud, in an essentially high-level kite) down the fjord, persuaded Frank to steep turn on to a short photographic run on the ship. Almost immediately there was a huge explosion, maps, Q codes, escape kits, Horlicks tablets, hopes and fears flew wildly around the cabin and I remember thinking, 'God, these Germans are bloody good'. They weren't. The top of the cabin had just flown off into the fjord. We had no sunshine roof and no look out. Anxiously we checked that we were OK, then noted with surprised relief that so was the kite apart from the top.

We did the run, Frank calmly keeping me paying attention, then set off for a very long, chilly, anxious, noisy, frustrating 1,000 mile, four hour, trip back in a damaged aircraft, with a vast question mark over landing conditions. A petrol twitch and (what I was to find a lot later) the fact that nobody would talk to us on W/T or R/T because all the codes, which changed frequently, had gone out the top into the oggin of Alten Fjord. I put some outrageous priorities on my W/T requests for courses to steer and aerodromes to land at. I think I once told them our squadron, aircraft number and service numbers in order to establish who we were, but to no avail.

We discussed feathering one engine as the fuel situation was getting desperate (in our crippled condition we had to keep away from the enemy and having to fly at 15,000ft because of the fuel position, was just about our most vulnerable height). The sea, what we could see of it through generally 10/10 cloud looked unusually calm for the North Sea, suggesting that the light winds I had found on the way up, had, crucially, not changed much. At long, long last, we saw a gap in the cloud just after ETA, dived anxiously through it and saw land. Soon it became Wick, the most Northerly mainland 'drome there and with all fuel gauges reading zero, Frank made the most treasured landing of all. (It would have been a good one to me with 15 bounces, but it was not at all like that.) By the time we got back to Leuchars for a debriefing and a much appreciated operational meal (one revered egg), the bar had closed.

We had spent 9 hours 25 minutes in the air that day, with Frank's careful course keeping and cosseting of the engines a vital factor in our survival and in getting some useful gen. The closed bar, three days after my 21st birthday party, was a pity, but on my birthday, after a slightly shorter trip, my Sergeant's Mess friends had realised the position and laid on a vast supply of drinks for us 'after time'. Frank, then a Flight Lieutenant in deference to the occasion, came quietly in to share the celebrations. I remembered what one colleague had said when he heard we were going on that particular detachment to Leuchars, which incidentally cost us half our aircrew strength, the splendid crew of Bill Simonson and Jock Reid. 'Well', quoth Jimmy Clayton, who did a lot of good work with navigator Dicky Richards, 'I suppose we have to learn how to spell "posthumous".'[82]

Willard Harris DFC of 544 Squadron recalls a trip on 2 September 1944.

My excellent navigator Flying Officer Les Skingley and I were briefed to photograph the Experimental and Testing Establishment for the V-1 and V-2 bombs on the Peenemünde Peninsula. These were fired out to sea to land in the Baltic. Although our Mosquito MM246 was a long-range version with 100-gallon drop-tanks on each wingtip, it was considered that the very strong NW winds that day meant returning to the UK without much fuel reserves. So it was decided we would fly south from Peenemünde and land on the east coast of Italy at San Severo. There was a PRU unit there and they had film processing and printing facilities. The trip out was uneventful when we emptied our drop tanks and started on our main tanks. On high level trips the usual practice was to climb until you start making cloud trail at around 28,000ft in summer. As soon as we entered enemy territory Skingley would turn around and kneel on his seat looking backward. He would say when we started making trail and we would fly just below. In this way we could see any aircraft flying above and attacking from behind. Poor Skingley, he was on his knees at all times whenever over enemy territory except when in the nose operating the cameras.

We reached the southern end of the Peninsula and Skingley started filming. About half way up our run I spotted two Fw 190s just above and either side of me flying south. As the closing speed between us would be around 800 mph by the time they turned around and flew back there would be many miles between us, not a worry really.

We completed our run and turned round over the Baltic and started our run south for good measure in case we missed anything. Skingley came out of the nose and took his position looking backward and immediately said, 'someone on our tail and he's gaining on us!' Right, time to drop the wing tanks and gain a little speed. I pressed the release button and horror, only the port tank dropped! This called for hard left-rudder and aileron to keep the aircraft level and this was slowing us down. After several attempts on the release button and rocking the wings the tank finally dropped. So I pushed the stick gently forward and that's what a Mosquito likes! But Skingley said, 'he's still gaining. By this time we were over the city of Stettin and AA fire started coming up. Fortunately they miscalculated our speed and it was behind us and in front of the pursuing aircraft. Sensibly he turned away and left us in the clear. We then had a peaceful journey across Germany and Austria to land at San Severo. The ground staff there were very helpful. After lunch they took us through the village to the beach for a swim. My recollection of the village was of the trays of sliced tomatoes on either side of the road drying in the summer sun. The dusty road was unpaved and every vehicle raised clouds of dust, which settled on the tomatoes. Since then I've not been keen on Italian ketchup! We had a very refreshing dip in the Adriatic. Next day we flew our processed prints back to Benson.

Two days later on 4 September, Flight Lieutenant Kenneth W. Watson RAAF and his navigator Flying Officer Kenneth H. Pickup RAFVR of 540 Squadron were tasked to photograph the railway lines between Nürnburg and Munich and then fly on to San Severo. Ken Pickup recalls:

We were airborne at 09.25 hours and over Nürnburg at 29,000ft by 11.00 hours. By this time I was in the nose preparing to film when I spotted at

600 yards an He 280[83] approaching from starboard. I immediately alerted Ken Watson, who instantly took evasive action by making tight turns to port but the aircraft disappeared from view. Almost immediately its place was taken by an Me 262 500 yards to port. By now I had scrambled from the nose to my seat taking a kneeling position facing aft so that I could give a running commentary of the situation as I saw it. It was then that I sighted a second Me 262 about 1,000 yards to port and the jets attacked alternately. These attacks continued intermittently for 22 minutes. There was a lot of manoeuvring so that the actual aggressive attacking time would be a mere 15 minutes. We were still taking evasive action by very tight turns and losing height. We were soon at 3,000ft. At 11.36 hours one Me 262 broke off the attack and flew away. The other remained with us. As soon as I signalled this fact to Ken he dived to zero feet. The aircraft then followed us to about 1,500ft and stayed above us. We were now over farmland and approaching a belt of trees, which we climbed above skimming the tops. It was at this point that we hit the tip of the Bavarian pine, which shattered our nose perspex, filling the cockpit with pine needles and making it very uncomfortable, cold and draughty. It was at this juncture that the remaining Me 262 left us, but we still had to reach San Severo with our films. Since the aircraft was damaged there was only one course to be taken and that was through the Brenner Pass. So we did this and eventually touched down at San Severo at 13.05 hours covered in pine needles and looking like two blue hedgehogs!'[84]

On 11 September a 544 Squadron crew had a close encounter with Focke Wulf 190s. Flight Lieutenant Ronald Foster RNZAF and his navigator, Frank Moseley who came from Coventry, flew sixty-nine operations over Europe during the last 18 months of the war, five of them returning on one engine. Foster, who had interrupted a commerce degree course at Victoria University to volunteer for the RNZAF when he was aged 20, recalls:

Improvements were being made on a day-to-day basis. You might hear that the Fw 190 was faster at 26,000ft so we flew at 28,000ft. But the Mosquito was a thoroughbred. It took a bit of handling during evasive action but I always told myself that it was at least 5 mph faster than any of theirs. This claim was put to the test on 11 September over Berlin when Frank reported an Fw 190 closing on cross course to starboard. Normally he would be seated next to me and following maps plotting a course by dead reckoning to the target to be photographed. I decided the best option to and from the target was for Frank to kneel up behind us and to put his head up into the blister to keep an eye out to the rear while I navigated. I matched the Fw 190's course and then when Frank yelled that the fighter was opening fire I slammed the Mosquito back on the original course and he missed. I was teasing every ounce of speed out of her literally with my fingertips. Then Frank shouted that the 190 was out of ammunition. He invited me to have a look. I turned around and nearly had a heart attack. There, level with our tailplane was the 190. The German pilot gave me a wave and flew away. I did not wave back. I never realised they got that close. I forced the 3,500hp Rolls-Royce Merlin engines to maximum revolutions. This was only allowed in extreme emergencies and then only for two minutes before they over heated and stopped but I was a bit upset and gave poor Frank a hard time on the way home. Every day aircrew faced the possibility of not making the return journey. After one sortie over France our ground crew counted more than 200 holes in our Mosquito fuselage. I could visualise myself in a dinghy in the North Sea but that's as far as I thought.[85]

Another threat at this time was the *Tirpitz*, which would have to be put out of action once and for all by Lancasters of 5 Group. On 11 September thirty-eight Lancasters of 9 and 617 Squadrons, accompanied by Flight Lieutenant George Watson and Warrant Officer John McArthur in PR.XVI MM397 to provide up-to-date target information and weather report, flew to their forward base at Archangel, in northern Russia. The attack by twenty-seven Lancasters, twenty of which, were carrying 'Tallboys', the others, 400-500lb 'Johnny Walker mines', went ahead on 15 September and considerable damage was caused to the battleship. Subsequent PR revealed that although badly damaged, the *Tirpitz* was still afloat (albeit beyond practical repair, although this was not known at the time). On 16 September Frank Dodd and Eric Hill flew what Eric Hill considered perhaps the most harrowing trip they ever flew.

Having got what we hoped were some decent pictures of the oilworks at Magdeburg, we spotted two of the new twin-jet Me 262s and were chased around from whatnots to breakfast time for what seemed ages. When I gave the order to turn, Frank flung old NS639 into some violent turns and we got away. They had about 100-mph speed advantage and it was a bit unnerving to see them skidding by, unable to hold our turn. About eight times it happened, at one time Frank frightened the daylights out of them by lining up behind them for an imaginary squirt with our non-existent guns. Frank found some cloud, into which we gratefully disappeared. After a quiet spell trying to confuse the radar, we emerged, hoping to be able to head for home. Some nasty unkind flak came up a little off our port wing while the two jets were perched about 100 yards away on the starboard and above. This was nasty but we found some more cloud, played possum for long enough this time and trolleyed home, happy to hear Benson's call sign 'Gingerwine', welcoming us into the fold.

On 29 September Flight Lieutenant Ronnie Knight, now the 540 Squadron Navigation Officer, flew what he considered probably his most exciting trip. By now Peter Hollick, his first pilot, had completed his tour and Ronnie Knight flew with various other pilots including Wing Commander (later Sir) Alfred H.W. 'Freddie' Ball DSO DFC, who had taken command of the squadron that same month. Knight recalls:

> Our operational sorties were high level, usually at 30,000ft and 500ft below the condensation layer so that if we were attacked by German fighters we would see their con trails. However, the trip on 29 September, my first with the CO, was low level with forward facing cameras. The target was a dam on the River Rhine between Basle and Mulhouse and Wing Commander Ball decided we would do it. It was not an ideal trip as we were using a Mossie, which was used to high-level trips and the same heading system was still operating. To make things worse, our intercom and R/T went u/s. Despite this we carried on and we flew very low level [200ft!]. When we got to the Alps we were flying below them through passes. Quite a way before the target I took a look in the top blister and I saw four Fw 190s flying towards us. I shouted a warning to the pilot who heard me despite having no intercom. He pulled the Mossie up in the tightest turn I ever experienced. We then weaved our way down one of the passes. I thought, 'Thank God, we're going home.' However, we made three other attempts at photographing the dam but the flak and the fighters made it impossible so we had to give up. We landed at St. Dizier as we were running out of fuel. Due to the lack of R/T facilities we couldn't contact Benson so overdue procedures were being instigated when we got back.

At Benson on 13 October Flight Lieutenant Hubert C.S. 'Sandy' Powell, a pilot on 540 Squadron learned that his wife had given birth to a daughter, Jennifer Frances, in a nursing home at Edgware, London. On the 14th he sneaked off to hitch-hike home to see them both. Then on the 15th Powell and Flight Sergeant Joe Townshend, his navigator who was in his early twenties flew a PR sortie to east Germany. Light flak greeted them over Peenemünde and after photographing their final target, at Stettin, they returned after five hours in the air in the usual adrenaline-induced high-spirited exuberance. 'Sandy' Powell was three years older than his navigator and he tended to be absent minded and somewhat odd, taking most of any aggressive enemy action as an interesting experience, but not in a very serious manner. He had a tendency to sing parts of old ballads in an unusual monotone when gaps occurred in any action, which he felt needed filling. He was always mildly surprised when he found himself walking away from his aircraft completely unscathed after a complicated landing. The 16th passed quietly playing Mah Jong in the crew room at Benson. On the 17th Powell and Townshend and three other crews were transported to Scotland in a Hudson aircraft. Their orders called for an early start On 18 October and they were aroused at 04.45 hours. After breakfast they arrived in the Operations Room at 05.45 where a middle-aged Scottish intelligence officer briefed them that their job was to locate the *Tirpitz*. Information from the Norwegian resistance stated that the ship had left Kaa Fjord on its way south for Tromsø, where it was to be used as a heavy artillery battery. The *Tirpitz* lay stationary in Ofot Fjord restrained by tidal anchors wedged into the rocky seabed below. Around her for protection were floating booms hung with anti-submarine/torpedo next. These hung deep into the water down towards the seabed. The *Harald Haarfagre*, an anti-aircraft vessel stationed to the north-east, and several land-based anti-aircraft batteries provided protection against air attack. The position to be searched was beyond the usual range of the Mosquito so they were to refuel at Scatsta (now Sullom Voe) in the Shetland Islands opposite St. Magnus Bay. Met briefing, navigational planning and recognition signals data were completed and they reached the hangars at 06.50. After changing into flying gear they carried parachutes and other equipment to Mosquito PR.XVI NS641, which was fitted with drop-tanks and had a fuel load of 850 gallons. Townshend continues:

> We took off from Dyce on our 25th trip, at 07.46, climbed to 8,000ft and with a comfortable tail wind of 35 knots, 55 minutes later we landed at Scatsta in North Shetland in order to top-up with fuel. In the air again at 09.40, we set course for Norway. On switching from inner to outer tanks, we soon found that one of the 97-gallon drop tanks was not feeding, leaving 763 gallons for a flight of 1,600 miles over the sea. There would be little margin. We climbed to 25,000ft, first saw rocks at 11.30 and then followed the coast north, searching every fjord. We were over Bødo at 11.52 and at 12.30 we saw the *Tirpitz*, $3^3/4$ miles to the west of Tromsø, 215 miles inside the Arctic Circle. By this time we had come down to 15,000ft due to cloud and we made one photographic run over the ship at 15,000ft. There was some firing from the *Tirpitz* and the ground, but it was not accurate. We left for home immediately and on the return journey, heading into wind, Sandy was again intent on nursing the engines for maximum performance from minimum fuel consumption.

Sandy Powell had put the Mosquito into a medium turn to port while climbing away from the target, settling down on a westerly heading out over the sea with the Lofotens to port. When Townshend had finally settled back into his seat beside him Powell suggested that they should now make some decisions on future actions. It was agreed that the fuel left in the tanks severely limited flying time. There was a suggestion that they try for Sweden. But after discussing the options they decided to 'go for home'. Besides, Powell was sure that if his wife got to hear that they were living it up somewhere in Scandinavia with her and their new daughter languishing in food rationed Britain, he would probably never hear the last of it.

Townshend continues:

Wind lanes and 'white horses' on the sea indicated that the wind had changed little and at 13.55 I tried to get a long-range fix. The position given was ignored as it was well to the west of our course and it probably came from a German station in Norway. At 14.23 a QTE Sumburgh 03.20 confirmed we were on course. At 15.58 the white capped waves breaking around the outlying promontories and rocks north-east of Shetland could be seen. Eighteen minutes later two tired crew landed at Scatsta with 15 minutes' fuel left in the tanks. Sandy went to the control tower to telephone the intelligence officer at Dyce who had briefed them that morning. Using a scrambled line he said, 'Named Target spot on! Operation D.C.O! [Duty Carried Out] Return to base shortly.' We were back at Dyce in good time for dinner at 18.00 after 2,150 miles in an overall 8 hours 35 minutes flying. We went into Aberdeen that night for a drink to celebrate.

Even though the Mosquito completed this remarkable flight at reduced speed they had still managed to average almost 245 mph. Their outstanding feat earned Powell a DFC and Townshend the DFM. Teamwork, once again, had played a huge part in the success of these operations and twenty-five more together would follow. Sandy Powell recalls:

Joe Townshend's phlegmatic attitude to enemy belligerence, coupled with a keen intelligence and outstanding navigational abilities, was the driving force that enabled us to survive over fifty sorties. Imagine being in an aircraft, at 20-30,000ft centered in an open sky, in daylight, hundreds of miles inside enemy territory. You are aware of being fully exposed and know you've been detected by enemy radar since you crossed the coast and every mile since then. Around you, an implacable enemy watches, waits and could at any moment, range its mighty forces against you. You think of several targets you've been briefed to photograph and those leagues of hostile country that need to be traversed in order to carry out your mission. Then how long you must spend in hostile space before getting back home. If you can truly imagine all this, then you become aware of what it is like to feel truly lonely. Someone once said, 'PRU was the loneliest job in the world. There are rewards, however, when you return over the shores of the UK. Adrenaline charges through your being and you become a giant, ten feet tall.'[86]

Meanwhile, in addition to the detachment at Yagodnik, in the USSR covering the 5 Group operations against the *Tirpitz* a 540 Squadron detachment had also been established at Gibraltar in September in preparation for a survey of the Canary Islands. Further trips to the USSR commenced on 9 October with courier flights for Operation Frugal. No.544 Squadron's Mosquitoes transited to the Soviet Union, via Memel to Ramenskoye for eventual operations over eastern Germany and Poland. These flights lasted 6 hours and when Moscow (Vnukovo) was used they became 4 hour 30 minute trips for the crews involved. Others were flown to Yalta, via San Severn in Italy and Saki in the Crimea or via Malta and Cairo. In December some Mosquitoes were stripped of their cameras and used to carry diplomatic mail to Hassani, in Greece. This run, which was known as Operation Haycock was extended to Italy and Egypt in connection with the Cairo Conference. The PR Mosquitoes performed a similar service during the Potsdam Conference.

In October Flight Lieutenant Ronald Foster RNZAF and Frank Moseley (both of whom were awarded the DFC and French *Croix de Guerre*) were transferred to courier missions. They flew from Benson to Moscow in 4 hours 45 minutes, creating a new speed record for a flight from England to the Russian capital. In the courier bag were dispatches for Prime Minister Winston Churchill and a copy of the morning issue of the London Times. Foster adds:

> Mr Churchill was very pleased to get the newspaper but he was even more pleased that the Russians were impressed by the Mosquito's speed. Later I realised why we had been given an older version of the aircraft for the trip and why it had been stripped of all sensitive equipment. Soon after at Benson we were told that the Russians had completely disassembled it, photographed every part and put it back together in time for our return trip. They were none the wiser for their trouble. We were told on no account to allow the aircraft to fall into German or Russian hands and they meant it. We carried a bomb from which two wires were connected to a button on the instrument panel. In the event of capture we were told to press the button. The rest was left to the imagination. I don't know if I would have pressed that button. I never regretted flying Mosquitoes. You were left to use your own initiative and it was quality flying time. The down side was losing so many of my friends. The strength of our Mosquito squadron was supposed to be twenty two-man crews. We never reached that on 544 Squadron. I would meet people for a meal in the Mess and never see them again. During my 18 months on the Squadron twenty-six aircrew were missing or killed in action. Ridding the world of Hitler's Nazis was a worthy end but the price paid for a small country like New Zealand was high.

Late in 1944 Flight Sergeant Frank 'Ginger' Baylis crewed up with Flight Lieutenant O.M. 'Danny' Daniels on 54(M) PR Course at 8 PR OTU at Dyce. Baylis recalls:

> Danny was a gritty Canadian from Windsor, Ontario. A skilful pilot, you might say he was a born flyer. Good job. His ability was tested to the utmost on 5 December 1944 when we did a sortie from Dyce to Norway in a 'brand new' PR.XVI. We lost our hydraulic fluid on the starboard prop

and suffered an overspeeding engine at 28,000ft about 30 miles north of Bergen. We operated the Graviner, which put the fire out. Then the engine broke up and the resulting 12-inch diameter 'circle' stuck on the leading edge of the starboard wing rendered our aircraft quite unable to remain airworthy. By the time I was ready to bale out we were down to 7,000ft and Danny said he thought he could hold her before we reached the briny and would I like to stay? Not half. A dip in Norwegian coastal waters in mid-December did not appeal, so I returned to my seat. With both feet holding the rudder-bar at its fullest extension, Danny wrestled NS696 all the way back to Sumburgh, where he managed a good single-engined landing. Much relief all round. Danny had flown 1 hour 20 minutes at about 140 mph; just above stalling speed.[87]

On 23 December, 544 Squadron's Frank Dodd and Eric Hill experienced an eventful sortie, to Magdeburg, in PR.32 NS587.

Magdeburg, I can never hear the name without a shudder, was the start of another little 'tiswas'. We had the distrusted first XXXII; a very high flyer, but unreliable.[88] This time, we had 'done' a few targets plus the oilworks when suddenly a horrifying mixture of impedimenta poured out of the starboard engine, which Frank hastily feathered. Now being over the Third Reich two days before Christmas 1944 with a crippled, unarmed Mossie at 41,000ft making a huge, persistent contrail in a completely cloudless sky was decidedly suggesting a desire to end it all. I knocked out a course for the nearest bit of the North Sea, Frank went into a fastish dive and I was kneeling on the seat as usual looking anxiously backwards. In due course, somewhere near Emden, I reported, 'Fighter, my side, above, closing fast. (The word 'reported' distinctly fails to do justice to that sweaty, scary moment. 'Yelled frantically' might suit.) We knew that, provided you saw a fighter early enough and had a decent Mossie (they varied like cars), you could get away eventually by maintaining straight and level top speed. This despite the fact that the Fw 190 especially was far better in the climb, the dive and the turn and short speed-bursts than we were. We knew, too, that if you managed to lose a fighter once, the sky is a big enough space to give you a good chance of getting away. Once though, we found one hiding in our hated contrail, but managed to find a bit of cloud in time.

My world turned upside down. Frank flung that kite into a vertical dive, which clearly took the Fw 190 by surprise, as when I was able to examine his bit of sky again, he was diving disgustedly, earthwards. My joy at losing him soon evaporated. Frank's dive had started up the u/s engine, which now screamed and howled and shook the kite as if it was just going to depart and leave us in bits. Frank pulled her up into a near stall, rapidly pushed the feathering button and like me, I reckon, prayed. It worked, the engine stopped. We found a nice quiet bit of German coast and in a fast dive, worked our way home. The weather in England was poor, but when out of range of the German jammers, I was able to use the Gee set to get us right into dear old Benson on a brilliant system worked out by Flight Lieutenant Don 'Lofty' South. (He taught us how to tell pilots not only what course to steer, but when to change pitch, put down wheels and flaps and when to hold off. Lofty, a huge chap with a fine brain, was a London policeman. He sadly bought it in company with another great chap, Flight Lieutenant Doug 'Adco' Adcock, when they were trying to photograph a hotly defended rocket site at ground level.)[89] Hearing that we were coming back on one engine, half of Benson, all the aircrew, all the blood wagons and fire engines turned out to watch the fun. A perfect three-pointer on one engine was vintage Dodd.

Of course, like every PR Crew, especially when we were privileged to fly diplomatic mail to the 'Big Three' Conferences at Moscow, Athens, Yalta and Potsdam, there were plenty of other incidents to remember. (These included the three fighters near Moscow, who dropped a convincing pattern of tracer just in front of us, in order to dissuade us from having a look at the City Airport). And luck for which to be grateful. After all, I had the best luck of all. I had Frank Dodd as a pilot, whose brilliant airmanship, calm appreciations and simple courage got us through. Flying solitary sorties over heavily defended enemy territory in unarmed wooden aircraft I suppose needed special qualities. Perhaps many other navigators will say the same of their pilots and I hope that many who have forgotten the part PRU played in the victory, will perhaps pause and reconsider.'[90]

CHAPTER THREE

Finders, Markers and Light Night-Strikers

Originally formed from 3 Group, using volunteer crews, 8 Group had started as a specialist Pathfinder Force (PFF) on 15 August 1942 under the direction of Group Captain D.C.T. 'Don' Bennett and was headquartered at Wyton. On 13 January 1943 the PFF became 8 (PFF) Group and 'Don' Bennett was promoted Air Commodore (later Air Vice Marshal) to command it. The tough talking Australian ex-Imperial Airways and Atlantic Ferry pilot wanted Mosquitoes for PFF and target-marking duties. No.105 Squadron's few B.IX bombers, which were modified B.IVs with Oboe radar, which no one wanted, helped him achieve his objective.[91] Gee-H (from 1944, H₂S)-equipped B.IXs of 139 Squadron and Oboe II-equipped B.IXs of 105 Squadron spearheaded the Main Force bombing raids. Oboe had first been used on 20 December 1942. No. 139 Squadron went in with the target-marking Mosquitoes of 105 Squadron, sowing bundles of the thin metal strips called 'Window', which produced a 'clutter' of blips on German radar screens to give the impression of a large bomber force. They made diversionary attacks called Spoofs on other targets to attract enemy night fighters anything up to 50 miles away from the Main Force during the attack. Bennett's Mosquitoes were to prove so successful that ultimately, eleven Mosquito-equipped squadrons operated in 8 (PFF) Group (the other eight squadrons being equipped with Lancasters). In addition, 1409 (Met) Flight was established at Oakington on 1 April 1943 using Mosquitoes and crews from 521 Squadron, Coastal Command at Bircham Newton.

'Nuisance' raiding had begun in April 1943 and was so successful that by the summer a Light Night-Striking Force (LNSF) of Mosquitoes was established. Mosquitoes went in up to an hour before the main attack, descended slowly and released their Spoof cargoes of two 500lb bombs, two target indicators (TIs) or 'sky markers' (parachute flares to mark a spot in the sky if it was cloudy)[92] and bundles of Window. German fighter controllers sent up their night fighters, so that when the 'heavies' did arrive, the *Nachtjagdgeschwaders* were on the ground having to refuel. No.139 Squadron first tried Spoof raiding on the night of 18 November 1943 when flares and bombs were dropped on Frankfurt. Various plain colours with starbursts of the same or a different colour prevented the enemy from copying them. On 26 November three Mosquitoes of 139 Squadron, flying ahead of the Main Force, scattered Window on the approaches to Berlin and returned to drop bombs.

After having converted to the Mosquito at 1655 MTU at Marham, Flight Lieutenant Jack Richard 'Benny' Goodman[93] and his navigator, Flying Officer Arthur John Linzee 'Bill' Hickox (after 'Wild Bill Hickok' of American West fame) were posted in October 1943 to 139 Squadron at Wyton. Benny Goodman had completed a tour of thirty-seven operations and 1,300 hours on Wellingtons. Bill Hickox had also completed a first tour on Wimpys, although he had been shot down and had to walk back through the desert. Their first operational sortie in a Mosquito took place on 3 November 1943, the target being Cologne. Benny Goodman recalls:

> Marking was to be done by 105 and 109 Squadrons, using Oboe. Our bomb load was four 500lb HE bombs and the attack was to be an all-Mosquito affair. Out first operational take-off in DK313 was only marginally longer than out take-offs from Marham in Mosquitoes without bombs. The acceleration was rapid and in next to no time we were at the unstick speed of around 100 knots and climbing smoothly away. We climbed rapidly to 28,000ft, levelled out and settled down to an economical cruising speed of around 250 knots (true airspeed). As we neared Cologne the first of the Oboe-aimed target indicators began to cascade down ahead of us. Bill took his place at the bombing panel and began the time honoured verbal directions: 'Left, left, Steady...' and ultimately, 'Bombs gone.' We then turned for home, more bacon and eggs and bed. The post-flight interrogation was much the same as on any operational squadron in Bomber Command, with one important exception. 139's full title was 139 (Jamaica) Squadron and we were all offered a tot of rum on return from every operational sortie the rum being provided by the good people of Jamaica. When I was on 139 we had with us a Jamaican named Ulric Cross, a flight lieutenant navigator, highly efficient and well liked. Later he became Lord Chief Justice of Jamaica.

The best Oboe crews could place a bomb within a few yards of the aiming point from 28,000ft. However, since they had to fly straight and level for several minutes in the final run to the target they were vulnerable to flak and fighters. Moreover, they could only approach a given target from two directions; in the case of Ruhr targets, almost due north or south. The Germans quickly realized this and set up searchlight cones over the aiming point which they plastered with heavy flak. Another little trick was to position Ju 88s near the searchlight cones, at a higher level than the Mosquitoes. Thus, when coned, a Mosquito might first be blasted with heavy flak and then the barrage could suddenly cease. If the pilot wasn't in a position to react instantly, the next happening would be a highly unpleasant squirt of cannon fire from the night-fighter. The average time for a trip to the Ruhr was 2¹/₂ hours, while a run to Berlin took about 4¹/₂ hours. To carry out such sorties in a Wellington had taken something like 5¹/₂ hours and 8 hours respectively. For this reason alone, Mosquitoes were greatly to he preferred to Wellingtons, it is better to be shot at for a short time than for a long time!

At Wyton on 24 November 1943 'C' Flight in 139 Squadron and its B.IVs were used as the nucleus to form 627 Squadron at Oakington near Cambridge. Benny Goodman and Bill Hickox were among the crews posted to the new squadron as Bill Hickox recalls:

We went down to the flights after breakfast as usual. We were called in by the Flight Commander and told to go back and pack our bags, as we were to take an aircraft [DZ615] to Oakington, where we were posted to a new squadron being formed; 627. We duly arrived at Oakington, where we were told that we would be operating that same night. So without having time to unpack our bags, or go through the normal arrival procedures, we went to briefing, where we learned that we would be operating to Berlin along with two other crews. This was only my second trip to the 'Big City', but everything went well.

Benny Goodman adds:

It was a rule in Bomber Command that every new squadron became operational as soon as possible after it was formed and when we arrived, Bill and I found out that we were on the Battle Order for that night. The resident squadron at Oakington was No.7, a Lancaster squadron of the PFF force and on the day of 627's arrival, the station was a hive of industry. A Bomber Command maximum effort was in preparation and Lancasters were being made ready for ops that night. To the Oakington effort would now be added six Mosquitoes of 627 Squadron. As the day wore on it became apparent from reports from the Station met office that operations that night had become questionable; a warm front was spreading in from the south-west more quickly that had been expected. At tea time the Lancasters were stood down, but 627 remained on standby and after tea we were briefed for an all-Mosquito attack on Berlin in company with 139 Squadron. Early that evening Bill and I boarded DZ615 and set off for the 'Big City', a trip which turned out to be completely uneventful except that on returning to the airfield we were flying in thick cloud and pouring rain. We broke cloud at 500ft, still in heavy rain and approached and landed very carefully. On reporting to the Operations Room for debriefing, we were astounded to be told that DZ615 had been the only RAF aircraft over Germany that night. Ops had been cancelled by Bomber Command at a very late stage but two of us were already airborne and were left to get on with it. The other pilot had trouble with his aircraft and turned back, which left me on my own.

Bill Hickox has no doubts, as to what gave 627 its *Esprit de corps*

It seems to me that 627 had it from the very start. Mind you, we had everything in our favour. We were flying the finest aeroplane in the world (Ah, de Havilland) and lived in comfort in the pre-war messes of a permanent station near the beautiful city of Cambridge. Cambridge provided good entertainment for nights off, 'The Bun Shop', 'The Baron of Beef' and even 'Dorothy's Tea Rooms' being particularly memorable. Our CO, Roy Elliott, was the finest squadron commander I ever knew in a long RAF career.[94] His Navigation Leader, William M. 'Bill' de Boos DFC, was a splendid Aussie character and even the Adjutant was a good type, as were all the other air and ground crews. We were a small, close knit community, proud of being members of PFF and of being part of the Light Night-Striking Force operating practically every night, even when the Main Force were stood down. We didn't even mind being known as the 'Model Aeroplane Club'. On the rare occasions on which we were stood down, it was great to pile into the Hillman flight vans and blunder through the blackout until we came to the bank of a river. There we would pull ourselves across on a chain ferry to a delightful pub called the 'Pike and Eel'. How was it that it was always the Aussies who fell in on the return crossing?

Benny Goodman continues.

The winter of 1943-44 was famous, or infamous, depending on your point of view, because it saw the Bomber Command offensive against Berlin. Our C-in-C said that if we could lay waste the Big City the Germans would be brought to their knees.[95] Sixteen major attacks were mounted but Berlin was not destroyed. The truth is that the target area was too vast and the weather, which could often be worse than enemy action, was appalling. Bill Hickox and I took part in seven of these attacks against the German capital and also busied ourselves with spoof raids against other targets, for example Kiel and Leipzig. We knew only too well that we were engaged in a battle of attrition, as was the US 8th Air Force and the outcome could be defeat for the bombers.

During the Battle of Berlin we lost Squadron Leader 'Dinger' Bell, our Flight Commander. However, he and his navigator managed to bale out and became PoWs.[96] At this time, Bill and I began to wonder if the sands were also running out for us when, on the way home from the Big City, the oil pressure on the starboard engine suddenly began to drop and the oil and coolant temperatures increased. Eventually the readings reached their permitted limits and I throttled back the engine and feathered the propeller. Now we were in the cart with a vengeance, for we had to lose height and were eventually flying along at a height and speed comparable to that of our heavy brothers, but with no means of defending ourselves if attacked. Moreover, since the only generator on the Mosquito was on the starboard engine we had to turn off our internal lights, the Gee box and our VHF set. So we drove on through the darkness with our fingers and toes slightly crossed and feeling very tense. Wouldn't you?

Eventually our ETA at the Dutch coast came and Bill switched on the Gee. We were in luck. It worked and Bill quickly plotted a fix. So far, so good. Next we turned the Gee box off and I called up the VHF guardian angels on Channel 'C' – the distress frequency. At once there came that voice of reassurance, asking me to transmit for a little longer. She then gave us a course to steer and shortly afterwards said, 'Friends are with you.' Bill and I took a good look round and spied a Beaufighter, which stayed with us until we reached the English coast. We motored on eventually and got down fairly expertly which drew from the imperturbable Mr Hickox the comment, 'Good Show'. Praise indeed.

Shortly after this effort came another indication that Lady Luck was on our side. We were briefed for yet another trip to Berlin, but during the afternoon the raid was cancelled and a short-range attack on a Ruhr target was substituted. This was to be an all-Mosquito affair, led by 105 and 109 Squadrons. Our CO, Wing Commander Roy Elliott, decided that this was an opportunity for new crews to have a go and Bill Hickox and I were stood down in favour of two 'makey-learns'. We had air-tested the aircraft that morning and were satisfied that it was in all respects serviceable. Yet as the Mosquito lifted off at night and entered the area of blackness just beyond the upwind end of the flare path both engines failed and there came the dreadful sound of a crash as the aircraft hit the ground. Both crewmembers were killed. Would this have happened if Bill and I had been on board? We shall never know.

On the night of 2/3 December 627 Squadron lost its first Mosquito when Flight Sergeant Leslie 'Doggie' Simpson and Sergeant Peter Walker who were on their first operation since joining from 139 Squadron, failed to return from a raid on Berlin by 458 aircraft. Peter Walker recalls:

Before leaving the English coast it was found that the Gee set was unserviceable but it was decided to carry on using Dead Reckoning navigation with forecast winds. This proved to be highly dangerous as, instead of Southerly winds, it was later reported that the winds had veered to the North and strengthened. Apart from the occasional burst of flak nothing amiss happened until, 100 miles from Berlin, in the region of Magdeburg, a predicted burst of flak took out the starboard engine. Doggie Simpson decided to carry on to the target on one engine. At a much-reduced height and twenty minutes late on target Berlin was bombed and the aircraft turned for the journey home. Unfortunately there was no way of obtaining a visual pinpoint and those unreliable winds were used. At approximately 23.59 hours a terrific barrage of flak was encountered during which time the aircraft was continuously hit. The aircraft was then at a very low altitude with a considerable number of pieces missing from the airframe. After passing through this area, later presumed to be the Ruhr, we continued for a further 50 minutes when at 00.50 hours the aircraft was abandoned. 'F for Freddie' had flown 2 hours 10 minutes with both engines functioning and 4 hours 2 minutes on a single engine, a total of 6 hours 12 minutes. The approximate fuel consumption was 70 gallons per hour.[97]

Although it was a tight squeeze in the bomb bay, by early 1944 suitably modified B.IV Mosquitoes were capable, just, of carrying a 4,000lb Minol bomb, which went by the more familiar names of 'Cookie' or 'Blockbuster'. To accommodate this large piece of ordnance the bomb bay had been strengthened and the bomb doors were redesigned. Far from popular amongst ground and air crews, the bombs were unstable, prone to exploding if dropped accidentally while being loaded into aircraft. No.627 Squadron had experienced an incident when forming at Wyton with 139 Squadron. One lunchtime a Mitol bomb had been dropped accidentally at dispersal from an 83 Squadron Lancaster with tragic results.[98] Apart from this, the Mk.IV Mosquito was 'just' capable of a take-off on a main runway with favourable wind and once in the air the aircraft handled sluggishly until 'bomb gone' when the altimeter unwound itself at an alarming rate. At take-off time a fitter and rigger could be seen sheltering as soon as the aircraft taxied out for take-off.[99] Benny Goodman adds:

Our CO announced that we were to fly the 'Cookie-carrier' as much as possible and the most experienced crews were detailed to take her on normal operations. The night arrived when Bill Hickox and I were ordered to try our hand with this new machine on a target in the Ruhr. The aircraft looked like a pregnant lady, because its belly was markedly rotund. Take-off was not difficult, but quite definitely she was not a scalded cat. At 500ft, as her tail came up I pushed the throttles quickly forward to the gate (plus 9lb boost, 3,000 rpm) and then clenched my left hand over the gate catch releases and eased the throttles to the fully open position plus 12lb boost, 3,000 rpm). In 'G-George' this would have resulted in a glorious acceleration and a hop, skip and jump into the air. Not so with our pregnant lady. She waddled along and took most of the runway before she deigned to unstick. Moreover, the climb was a sedate affair and she took much longer to reach 25,000ft than with our usual steed; and when we arrived there she took a long time to settle to a steady cruise. However, we eventually sorted ourselves out and headed resolutely for the Ruhr.

In the target area I felt distinctly nervous. There we were, with the bomb doors open and Bill droning away with his 'Left, left...right...steady' and I just knew that every gunner in the Ruhr could see the enormous bomb we were carrying and was determined to explode it and blow us to smithereens. I looked at the bomb jettison handle in front of me, no delicate lever this; it was a solid bar of metal which, if moved, would manually release the massive catch holding the 'Cookie' and down the bomb would go. It the bomb doors had not been opened, that was hard luck, the 'Cookie' would still drop away and take the bomb doors with it! However, no such inglorious thing happened. Bill suddenly announced, 'Bomb gone' and as he did so the Mossie suddenly shot up like a lift. There was no delicate porpoising, as with four 500 pounders, the altimeter moved instantly through 500ft of altitude. I had never seen anything like this before. More importantly, as soon as I had closed the bomb doors our fat little lady became almost a normal Mosquito and accelerated to a fast cruising speed.

The B.XVI with its bulged bomb bay and more powerful two-stage 1,680-hp Merlin 72/76s or two 1,710-hp Merlin 73/77s, giving a top speed of 419 mph at 28,500ft, first flew operationally on 1/2 January 1944 when thirty-eight Mosquitoes attacked Hamburg, Witten, Duisburg, Bristillerie and Cologne. On this night Squadron 139 used H_2S for the first time, marking the target for a raid by twelve Mosquitoes on Berlin. At this time 139, which had pioneered the use of Canadian-built Mosquitoes, was operating a mix of B.IV, IX, XVI and XXs. Also, Mosquitoes dropped 'Blockbusters' for the first time on Düsseldorf on the night of 23/24 February.

No.692 Squadron was formed at Graveley on 1 January 1944. In the 12 months January-December 1944 five more Mosquito squadrons joined 8 Group.[100] Bennett wanted only experienced pilots with 1,000 hours total time for his squadrons. Group Captain T.G. 'Hamish' Mahaddie DSO DFC AFC, SASO (Senior Air Staff Officer) at Group HQ in Huntingdon, was tasked with recruiting volunteer aircrew from the Main Force bomber groups. Canadian pilot Terry Goodwin DFC DFM and his navigator Hugh Hay DFC on 692 Squadron had already completed two tours with Bomber Command. Terry Goodwin had flown a tour on Lancasters on 61 Squadron before completing a second, with 692. Hugh Hay had flown a first tour on Hampdens before converting to Manchesters and then Lancasters, flying sixty-three ops in all. This was at a time when loss rates were averaging 5 per cent so after ten trips you had used up 50 per cent of your chances. Twenty trips and they were all gone yet the tour was thirty. Incredibly, both men survived and they flew their first Mosquito operation on 8/9 February when the target for eleven Mosquitoes was Brunswick. Goodwin recalls:

We got to our cruising height of 28,000ft over the North Sea. There was no cloud at all and the full moon made it like daylight. Night-bomber crews like Hugh and me were not comfortable in such clear air. Gee was still working but could only give us a fix to a point because it operated on VHF, which meant line of sight. Our Gee set was behind the pilot and could be read by the navigator by turning to his left. Past the Dutch coast, cloud formed with tops to 10,000ft, which made the moonlight even brighter. On every trip Hugh had to do his navigation on a little clipboard on his knee. Suddenly ahead of us I saw a condensation trail from one then more of the other Mossies, which meant that we could be seen the same way. But there ahead at 2 o'clock was a thin white vapour-trail heading in towards those other Mossies. But then Jerry broke off to the left, 11 o'clock, 10 and then 9 as he turned back on reciprocal track to ours. Our throttles were full open at this altitude. As Jerry went past the wing-tip where he could judge our speed and turn in to attack from the rear I pushed the prop controls ahead to maximum continuous climb setting of 28,500ft. Hugh called, 'He's right behind us!' I pushed the rpms right up to take-off 3,000ft. The manifold pressure jumped because of the ram effect and the Mossie jumped like a scared rabbit. I still don't know how close Jerry had been, nor why he broke off; unless he had been beyond his control block.

Flying Officer Grenville Eaton, a 105 Squadron pilot, flew his first Mosquito operation, in A-Apple, an Oboe-equipped B.IV on 1/2 March 1944 when 557 aircraft of the Main Force went to Stuttgart. A-Apple was one of eighteen Mosquitoes that flew diversion operations to airfields in Holland. Eaton recalls:

Venlo, the target, was a German fighter aerodrome on the Dutch border near Aachen (The first few trips were usually to 'less difficult' targets, but they were certainly no less important in countering the threat of fighters). With a full load of bombs, four 500 pounders and of petrol, it took, perhaps, one hour following carefully planned and timed 'legs' all over East Anglia until setting course from Orfordness to the Dutch coast. Then, at the operational height of 28,000ft we flew towards the waiting point where the track to the target extended backwards for a further 5 minutes and there, at the precise appointed time in order to hear the call-in signal in Morse, we switched on Oboe.[101] I had to find the beam and keep on it for perhaps 10-15 minutes to the target. Thanks to Gee, Jack Fox's navigation was spot-on and we had a good run to target. His signals gave him our distance to target and finally, the bomb release signal, like the BBC time signal, five pips then the sixth, a dash, to press to release the bombs. We had a clear run. Holding steady for some seconds after bomb release to photograph the bomb explosions, we turned smartly on to the planned course home, keeping our eyes skinned for fighters, flak and searchlights, around 360° above and below. A gentle, slow dive at top speed and we arrived at the Dutch coast around 20,000ft and the English coast at 12,000ft. We landed at 0330 hours. So, Jack's 31st, and my first 'op', took 3 hours 25 minutes. A simmering feeling of incipient fear throughout had been kept in check by being fully occupied. Now, home, we felt a tremendous feeling of relief and achievement, especially when we were told at debriefing that we had achieved a 'Nil' target error on this, our first Oboe trip. Finally, a heavenly operational aircrew breakfast of bacon, eggs, toast, rum and coffee. Smashing!

Our second operation was on 7/8 March. The target was Aachen, an important road and rail junction just inside Germany. I was feeling more confident. Crossing Holland at 28,000ft with a clear sky, we could see the distant Zuider Zee. We switched on Oboe, found we were early, so guided by the navigator, I wasted a precise number of minutes and seconds until finding and settling into the beam towards the target, about 15 minutes' flying time away. We noticed we were leaving long white contrails behind us (frozen water-vapour crystals in the exhaust of each engine). Suddenly streams of cannon-shells and tracers enveloped us from the rear, hitting us in numerous places, but luckily missing Jack and me and the engines. I immediately dived to port, then up to starboard several times, then resumed height and regained the beam. The only protection was a sheet of steel behind my seat. Most instruments seemed to work, so we continued. Half a minute later, a second and noisier attack from the rear, so again I took evasive action, more violent and longer and again regained height and beam. Now there was considerable damage to dashboard, hydraulics and fuselage. Shells had missed us, truly by inches. However, engines and Oboe still worked, so being so near we had to continue to target, deliver the load and turn for home, changing course and height frequently and assessing the damage as far as we could. Certainly, hydraulics, flaps, brakes, ASI and various other instruments were smashed, but we were okay.

At Marham, landing in pitch darkness was a problem, but for safety I landed on the grass, by feel I suppose, at about 150 knots with no brakes. We hurtled across the aerodrome, just missing two huge armament dumps, straight on through hedges and violently into a ditch. Jack was out of the emergency exit like a flash. I could not move, could not undo the safety belt. Jack leapt back, released me and we scampered away to a safe distance in case of exploding petrol tanks but emergency services were quickly there. Debriefing was interesting, as not only was our run 'seen' on the CRT, but our bombing error was precisely calculated and we wondered whether all operations were to be like this one! Incidentally, we never saw the attacking fighter. Our aircraft was a write off.[102]

Mosquito bombers flew a series of operations to German cities in March. Flight Lieutenant John E.L. Gover DFC of 692 Squadron at Graveley, near Huntingdon, who flew thirteen operations to Berlin in 1944, flew his most unusual operation on 15/16 March, when the idea was for the Mosquito squadrons to attack Stuttgart after the four-engined heavy bombers had been there.

> Unfortunately my oxygen equipment was unserviceable and as we used to fly at 28,000ft I needed it. It took an hour to transfer the equipment from the reserve aircraft so my navigator and I were all on our own when we got to the target. This normally led to disaster, but luckily for us did not do so on this occasion. There was a sheet of low cloud over the target area and the heavies had bombed through it, but the heat from the fires that had been started had dissipated the cloud by the time we arrived. We had a grandstand view of two great holes in the cloud through which the fires could be seen burning. This was one of the few occasions on which I felt sorry for the enemy.

On some nights, including 18/19 and 22/23 March, when Frankfurt was raided by the heavies and Berlin on 24/25 March, the Mosquitoes acted as diversions for the Main Force effort with raids on German night-fighter airfields. The night of the 30th/31st fell during the moon stand-down period for the Main Force but the raid on Nürnburg, destination of 795 RAF heavy bombers and thirty-eight Mosquitoes, went ahead as planned. The Met forecast indicated that there would be protective high cloud on the outward route when the moon would be up. A Met Flight Mosquito carried out a reconnaissance and reported that the protective cloud was unlikely to be present and that there could be cloud over the target, which would prevent accurate ground marked bombing, but the raid went ahead. Flight Sergeant (later Pilot Officer) Jim Marshallsay in 627 Squadron at Oakington was aloft in a Mosquito this night as a 'Window Opener' for the heavies with navigator Sergeant (later Pilot Officer) Nigel 'Nick' Ranshaw by his side as usual. Nestling in the bomb bay were four 500lb bombs. By the time the two airmen had joined 627 Squadron in November 1943 they had flown fourteen LNSF trips on 139 Squadron, beginning with the big Hamburg raid of July 1943. Marshallsay recalls:

> Sometimes just a handful of Mossies would set out for the big German cities, usually in the 'moon period' when it was much too bright for the 'heavies'. If, on these trips, the weather was cloudy, it was possible to take off, climb into cloud, travel to Germany, bomb the target on ETA and return to base, having seen nothing but the runway lights at base on take-off and landing. If however the night was clear, with moonlight and stars, then you could get a hot reception from predicted flak and from the massive searchlight cones, especially at 'Whitebait', the code-name for Berlin. If you saw one of the attacking Mossies coned over the target, you took your chance, slipped in, bombed and slipped out again while the poor

unfortunate in the cone was dazzled and blasted. When you got back for interrogation, if you had been the one in the cone, you got no sympathy from the other crews, just a lot of banter like, 'Brave lads, taking the flak from us.'

The 30 March operation had started quite normally. We were airborne at 23.00 hours. 'Window Opening' meant that we had to be over the target before the first of the Marker aircraft and scatter Window to confuse the radar defences. The Lancs of 7 Squadron had taken off from Oakington about half an hour before us. The track to the target was past Brussels, then almost East between Koblenz and Bonn, on the so-called 'long leg', then south to Nuremberg. As we turned onto this long leg we realized that something was going badly wrong. The moon was much too bright for the heavies. The expected cloud cover was not there.[103] The Main Force was leaving persistent condensation trails, so there was a great white road in the air, leading into Germany. Combats soon broke out below us. As this was our 38th trip we knew what was happening to the heavies. First a long burst of tracer from the night fighter, then a ripple of flame from the wings of the Lanc or Halifax. A short interval, then a massive explosion and fire on the ground. Nick logged the first few crashes, but after we had seen sixteen go down in 6 minutes, he stopped, preferring to use his time and eyes searching for fighters. We later learned that over fifty heavies had gone down on the long leg.[104] Nuremberg, when we reached it, was covered in cloud.[105] We threw out our Window, dropped our bombs and circled to watch the attack develop, but little could be seen except for a few Wanganui flares. Nick said 'we're going straight home' and that is what we did. We turned the aircraft's nose towards Oakington and left at a great pace, landing at base at 03.17 hours, a trip of 4 hours 17 minutes. After interrogation we had our operational egg and as we left the mess to go to our beds, the first of the 7 Squadron Lancs were circling to land. The cloud base had lowered and there were flurries of snow in the air. Whereas we had taken the direct route to base from Nuremberg, the heavies were routed North of Paris, to Dieppe, Selsey Bill and home. The difference in flying times shows how fortunate we were to be operating in Mosquitoes.[106]

In April 1944 at 1655 MU at Warboys, Frank Diamond, a navigator who had flown a tour on Stirlings in 15 Squadron at Mildenhall, crewed up with Flight Sergeant Ron Hemming and they were posted to 571 Squadron at Oakington. Frank Diamond recalls:

As my pilot was not commissioned we did not share the same Mess. This was unfortunate but it did not interfere with our operational efficiency. We were destined to fly with the Pathfinders and operated alongside a Lancaster squadron with the role of providing some cover for the heavy bombers by creating diversionary trails and raids. Having in mind our wooden airframes, our friends on the Lancs dubbed us 'the model aeroplane club'. Our casualty rate was much lower than theirs. This was acknowledged later in our tour when it was suggested that we could extend it from thirty to fifty and this we agreed to do. However, predicted flak and radar controlled searchlights were a threat up to 30,000ft. We took Mosquito MM156 to Berlin and on our approach a master searchlight caught us. Escape was made impossible as others immediately backed it up and we were held for 12 minutes into and away from the target area. At first we were fearful of being taken by a fighter circling above us. Just after releasing our 4,000lb bomb and turning away there was a flak burst close to the tail. It had missed us. As we had now jettisoned our wing fuel-tanks and no longer had the bomb, we could increase speed and dash for home. Speaking of the experience the following day I said that as a true veteran of flak in a Stirling over the Ruhr, that it was a bit close but really nothing that bad. However, I agreed to go to the hangar and take a look at the damage. The holes in the tail unit were being repaired. The jagged holes in the skin were being trimmed with a fine toothed saw and inserts cut to fit and be glued in to place before taping with fabric and painting. I thought no more of it. We never flew that aircraft again but this was of little significance to my mind. The ground staff officer had taken a much closer look and found serious damage to the main structure in addition to the skin and he had ruled it unfit for further use. I now know that the Grim Reaper was denied our scalps by a very narrow margin indeed. If that shell burst had occurred at a mere fraction of a second earlier that would have been a direct hit. And, at age 22 I would not have lived to enjoy a further 60 years or more.

The C-in-C of Bomber Command, Sir Arthur Harris, was, I think, obsessed with attacking Berlin, recalled Flight Lieutenant John E.L. Gover DFC of 692 Squadron, and, I think, rightly so. It was considered, though, that such a target would be out of range, because we carried 600 gallons of petrol, which we burned at a rate of 120 gallons an hour, that is, a flying time of 5 hours. However, if it was possible to send a Mosquito with a 4,000lb bomb there and back in under 5 hours, it was far less risky than sending a four-engine heavy bomber, though with more bombs, which would take about 8 hours to get there and back. Therefore it was decided to send us to Berlin with each aircraft carrying a 4,000lb bomb. On 13 April we went there and back in four hours 15 minutes, showing it could be done. Subsequently, I made twelve further trips to Berlin but never in such a short time. Apart from the second trip on 18 April, when my radar was unserviceable and, far more important, so were my wing tanks carrying a total of 100 gallons of petrol. I just scraped in over the English coast and landed after 4 hours 5 minutes' flying time. On the first trip we had more or less gone straight there and straight back, so that it could be done in minimum time, but it would have been a disaster to have kept to the same route on every occasion. Other trips took from 4 hours 30 minutes to 4 hours 40 minutes, which left very little spare petrol.

Since the beginning of 1944 617 Squadron of 'Dam Buster' fame (now commanded by Wing Commander Leonard Cheshire, DSO* DFC) had successfully employed the tactic of marking and destroying small industrial targets at night using flares dropped by a Lancaster in a shallow dive at low level. Obviously the Lanc had limitations in this role, so Air Marshal the Honorable Ralph Cochrane, urged on by Cheshire, allocated a Mosquito to 617. The squadron's first Mosquito sortie was on 5/6 April when Cheshire and his navigator Flying Officer Pat Kelly marked an aircraft factory at Toulouse on his third pass with two red-spot flares from a height of 800-1,000ft. Cheshire used this aircraft (ML976/N) on 10/11 April to mark a signals depot at St. Cyr during a dive from 5,000 to 1,000ft. These successes led to 617 Squadron receiving four FB.VIs/XVIs for marking purposes. Benny Goodman recalls:

The brilliant AOC of 5 Group, Air Marshal the Hon Ralph Cochrane, was quick to appreciate that if a single aircraft could mark a target accurately for a squadron then it should be possible for a squadron of properly trained crews to mark targets with similar accuracy for the whole Group. The Lancaster was a splendid aircraft but it was vulnerable to light flak at low level; a more manoeuvrable aircraft was required for the operations Cochrane had in mind. Leonard Cheshire was aware of the limitations of the Lancaster and he had already decided that the best aircraft for low-level marking was the Mosquito. He briefed the AC on his ideas and this led to the meeting at Bomber Command HQ, which resulted in the redeployment of 627 Squadron from Oakington to Woodhall Spa and 83 and 97 Lancaster Squadrons from their respective Pathfinder bases to Coningsby. No.5 Group was about to receive its own PFF force and 8 Group was no longer to enjoy its hitherto unchallenged monopoly over pathfinder tactics. No hint of these momentous events reached the crews of 627 Squadron 'in the trenches' at Oakington. We had, of course, heard of Leonard Cheshire, but he belonged to 5 Group, the Independent Air Force, as it was known in Bomber Command. We were too busy attending to daily grind in 8 Group to concern ourselves unduly with what the glamour boys of a rival Group were doing.

Bill Hickox remembers:

My flying Log Book reveals in its cold and unremarkable way that in early April Bill Hickox and I went to Cologne, Essen, Hanover and, on 12/13

April, Osnabrück. The BBC had sent one of their top broadcasters, the Canadian, Stuart Macpherson, to cover the flight. He came to debriefing to meet the returning crews and the broadcast went something like this: 'Here are the crews just back from "Arznabruck". Here with me is the Squadron Commander, who wears the ribbons of the DSO and DFC, and his Navigator, who is an Australian'. Perhaps that is why soon afterwards several of us were awarded DFCs or DFMs. Sadly, all good things come to an end. After that last flight our complacency was rudely shattered when we were called to a meeting addressed by a somewhat emotional Don Bennett. He informed us that we were being taken from him, together with his two best Lancaster squadrons and sent up to 5 Group, where Leonard Cheshire had demonstrated a new technique of dive-bombing marking. We were to go to Woodhall Spa to do the marking for 5 Group, while the Lancs went to Coningsby as backers-up. Consequently, on 14 April we positioned our aircraft [DZ454 G-George] up to Woodhall Spa, where it soon became apparent that we were very much the poor relations of the famous Dambusters. While they lorded it in Petwood House in Woodhall we were relegated to a batch of Nissen huts on the far side of the airfield. There, the only amenity, apart from our own messes, was a tiny one-roomed ale house down the road: the beloved 'Bluebell Inn' run by a little old lady. We even had to go to Coningsby for briefing and debriefing.[107]

Benny Goodman continues:

After landing, we were formed into a single line and the Station Commander arrived with what I can best describe as a bevy of brass. It was the AOC with his principal staff officers. He moved along the line with Wing Commander Roy Elliott, our CO, who introduced us individually to the great man. Within a few minutes I found myself looking into the cold eyes of a tall, rather ascetic man, who abruptly welcomed me to 5 Group and moved on along the line. Why had he taken the trouble to meet us? Such a thing was unheard of in bomber circles. We all felt somewhat uneasy. Obviously, something was up and it promised to be bloody dangerous. Next day the whole squadron journeyed by bus to Coningsby and was directed to the station cinema. Here were assembled all crewmembers of 83 and 97 Lancaster PFF Squadrons, our own Squadron, the AOC and his entourage and Leonard Cheshire. The AOC opened the meeting by saying that 617 Squadron had made a number of successful attacks on important pinpoint targets and it was now intended to repeat these on a wider scale. The Lancaster pathfinder squadrons were to identify the target areas on H_2S [a terrain identifying radar] and were to lay a carpet of flares over a given target, under which 627 Squadron would locate and mark the precise aiming point. No.5 Group Lancaster bombers would then destroy the target. So that was it: we were to become low-level visual markers and it did sound dangerous.

Cheshire now took the stand and explained carefully how the low-level marking business was done. What the Lancasters had to do was lay a concentrated carpet of hooded flares, the light from which would be directed downwards onto the target, making it as bright as day. A small number of Mosquitoes, four or possibly six, would orbit, find the aiming point and then mark it in a shallow dive with 500lb spot-fires. Marker Leader would assess the position of the spot-fires in relation to the aiming point and would pass this information to a 'Master of Ceremonies' in one of the pathfinder Lancasters. The MC would then take over and direct the Main Force Lancasters in their attack on the target.

On returning to Woodhall, the CO called the Flight Commanders to his office and an intensive programme of dive-bombing at Wainfleet Bombing Range was worked out. Although Leonard Cheshire had said we must fly low for the best results it was decided to try dropping smoke bombs from various levels. Attempts were made to dive bomb from 15,000ft and, when this failed, from progressively lower heights. In the end we found it was as Cheshire had said. To get a smoke marker close to the target in the Wash we had to come down to around 2,000ft and then dive directly at the blob in the sea; down, down, until it was held in the middle of the windscreen. Then 'Bomb away'. This time however, it was not Master Hickox who did the releasing of the bomb. I had a button on the control column and merely had to press it with my right thumb when I judged that the correct moment had arrived. It was entirely a matter of practice and within a very short time the crews of 627 Squadron could plop their markers right alongside the Wainfleet target. The question now was, could we do this under battle conditions?

We did not know that the plans for the invasion of France, Operation Overlord, required the destruction of the French railway system leading to the landing area. The best way of doing this was by employing heavy bombers, but grave doubts existed at the highest level as to the accuracy with which this could be done. Winston Churchill was adamant that French lives must not be lost needlessly and eventually it was agreed that 5 Group should undertake a mass attack on a marshalling yard in the Paris area to prove the case one way or the other. Juvisy was selected as the target and the marshalling yard was attacked on the night of 18/19 April by 202 Lancasters led by Leonard Cheshire and a small force of Mosquitoes from 627 Squadron participating as 'makey-learns'. One of our pilots, Jim Marshallsay, was not detailed for the trip but thumbed a ride in a 617 Squadron Lancaster. The attack on Juvisy was a bombing classic. The railway yards were marked at each end with red spot-fires and the heavy bombers laid their cargoes between the target indicators. The bombing was concentrated, the yards were put out of action, few French lives were lost and all but one Lancaster returned safely to base. The railway yards were so badly damaged that they were not brought back into service until 1947.

The first major test for the new 5 Group marking method took place on the night of 20/21 April against a railway target at La Chapelle just north of Paris. It involved not only 617 Squadron's low-level Mosquito markers, three of which marked the target with phosphorous bombs and acted as backers-up, but also the three Pathfinder squadrons recently transferred from 8 Group as well. A few 8 Group Mosquitoes also dropped markers by Oboe to identify the target location prior to the main marking effort.[108] Six of the 247 attacking Lancasters were lost but despite a few difficulties with marking the bombing was extremely accurate and concentrated. Benny Goodman continues:

> The real test of the new tactics had still to be made against targets in Germany. No.5 Group was therefore unleashed against three of these targets in quick succession: Brunswick on 22/23 April, Munich two nights later; and Schweinfurt on 26/27 April.[109] Speaking for myself, I found the business of marking a German target no worse than marking anywhere else. The point was that enemy AA defences in Germany were almost exclusively of the heavy variety, for use against relatively high-flying aircraft. There was not much light flak; this was concentrated in France and the Low Countries. Consequently, when the Mosquitoes of 627 Squadron circled Brunswick on 22 April, there was not much opposition from the ground. The aiming point was a large park and we plonked our four spot-flares into it with the greatest of ease. So far as Brunswick and Munich were concerned, considerable damage was done.[110] In the case of Munich, 90 per cent of the bombs fell in the right place, doing more damage in one night that had been achieved by Bomber Command and the 8th Air Force in the preceding four years. The flexibility and superiority of the new system was clearly revealed.[111]

Bill Hickox DFC adds:[112]

> We were briefed to go to Brunswick 'Fire Watching', that is, arriving over the target about half an hour after the Main Force and reporting back on the results. It should be pointed out that, while at Oakington, our procedure had always been to climb straight up to 25,000ft and perform the whole flight at that level. Naturally we did the same on this night and on arrival over the target, which was burning nicely, we added our contribution to the flames and then returned to base. We obviously got back before the Main Force, as all the hierarchy were waiting for us at debriefing, including the AOC, Cochrane and the base Commander, 'Razor' Sharp, who asked how

it had gone. "Excellent," we said. "Massive fires everywhere." "What height did you come down to?" he asked. "25,000ft" replied 'Benny. I thought that for a moment the poor man would have apoplexy. "You mean you didn't come down?" he roared. "You'll do the same thing again and you won't go above 1,000ft all the way there and back" So it came to pass. The target was Munich and for some reason we operated out of Wyton. Anyway off we went, but being so low we rapidly ran out of Gee cover and so I was unable to get a very accurate wind. We could hardly miss the target, however and dropped our bombs and got away again without too much trouble, so that on our way home we thought that maybe this low-level operation wasn't so bad after all. Not being too certain of our position, I was vainly trying to detect a blip on the Gee screen through all the jamming, when suddenly all hell broke loose. We had obviously blundered into the Pas de Calais light-flak belt. Benny promptly shoved the stick forward and took us right down onto the deck. We were surrounded by multi-coloured tracers and searchlights were shining on us through the trees. At least it meant Benny could see any obstacles in the way! After what seemed an age, we finally managed to escape from this trap, apparently unscathed. However, some minutes later we hit the coast, slap over a port. My first thought was that it must be Dieppe, in which case we'd have no chance of getting through there alive! In the event we flashed through the harbour entrance without another shot being fired. It was several minutes later that I managed, at last, to obtain a Gee fix, which showed that the port must, in fact, have been Le Treport!

On our return we were once again met by the Base Commander, who greeted us with "Well, Goodman, what do you think of this low-level stuff then?" "Not much, Sir," was Benny's heartfelt reply. Nevertheless, from then on all our operational flying was at low level. A day or two later we were actually invited to visit Petwood to hear a lecture by Cheshire on Low Level Navigation at Night. "It's simple," he said, "You fly along, cross a river and get a pinpoint. Later on you cross another river, get another pinpoint, find the wind between the two and you've got it made". I couldn't help thinking it was not quite as simple as all that.

Operating from Lossiemouth on 28 April eight Mosquitoes of 627 Squadron crossed the North Sea to Norway to drop their markers on a factory target at Oslo-Kjeller airfield for fifty-one Lancasters of 5 Group. Visibility was clear and notably Flying Officer James Saint-Smith RAAF DFM and Flying Officer Geoffrey Heath RAAF DFM in O-Orange dropped their markers on the roof from 100ft.[113] The bombing was accurate and no aircraft were lost. On 29/30 April sixty-eight Lancasters and five Mosquito markers of 627 Squadron sortied to an explosives factory at St. Médard-en-Jalles near Bordeaux where 24 hours earlier only twenty-six of the eighty-eight Lancasters despatched had bombed because of haze and smoke started by fires in woods nearby. This time the Lancasters carried out concentrated bombing of the factory and all aircraft returned safely. Meanwhile, a further five Mosquitoes of 627 Squadron marked the Michelin tyre factory at Clermont Ferrand for fifty-four Lancasters of 5 Group who bombed accurately and again without loss.

On 1/2 May Bomber Command mounted six major attacks on rail and aviation targets in France and 627 Squadron provided twelve Mosquito markers for two of the raids. Two sets of four Mosquitoes each marked the aircraft assembly factory and an explosives factory at Toulouse for 131 Lancasters of 5 Group and four more Mosquitoes marked another target at Tours. Squadron Leader Norman McKenzie DFC, who with his navigator, Pilot Officer Norman Denholm, who led four Mosquitoes against the Tours assembly plant, recalls:[114]

> At Toulouse the Germans were using four large buildings (two pairs at right angles to each other) for the repair and overhaul of tank and aircraft engines, with much of Blagnac airfield having storage dumps dispersed around it. The aiming point for this raid was at the apex of lines drawn from the sides of the main buildings as they met at right angels. Intelligence briefing was 'Light flak in the area'. That must have been the understatement of the month! Or maybe they hadn't realised that German forces pulling out of Italy had to go somewhere. Certainly someone had decided that Toulouse was a good place to be at, particularly if you were a flak unit. Arriving over the target, flares from the heavy pathfinders burst over us, as arranged, illuminating the area in almost daylight conditions, to enable us to identify and mark the aiming point. But it also made it very easy for the defences to pick out our squadron aircraft going round in circles just above them. I had gone into the nose of the aircraft to help identify the marking point and, as was our normal practice, the first member of our team to spot the aiming point would call out, "Tally Ho" on VHF to indicate that he was going in to mark. On this occasion it was ourselves. Immediately after locating the target I pulled myself back into my seat, having fused the markers, then to call out the heights to Norman as we went down our dive. I had never experienced so much hostility before! The flak was coming at us from all directions, spiralling around us, when suddenly there was a great crash within the cockpit and within a second I could not see Norman for smoke. We were near the bottom of our dive by this time and before I could ask him if he was OK I could feel that we were pulling out. As we climbed and turned to go round I put my head into the 'blister' to see where the marker was for accuracy but it was nowhere to be found. "Norman, I can't see the marker", Norman replied, "We've still got it. I couldn't see for smoke to drop it. We'll have to go round again," said Norman. One hammering had been sufficient but we had to be gluttons for punishment, or so it seemed. This time we didn't have

to look for the aiming point, we knew where it was. Down we went, for a second time; 3,000ft, 2,500, 2,000, 1,500, 1,000, 900, 800, 700, 600, 500, marker gone! The treatment was as before, they obviously didn't like us one bit and were throwing everything up to prove it. This time the marker went down and was assessed for accuracy by another of our aircraft and reported to the controller, a pathfinder in the heavy force sitting above us.

The next stage in the procedure was for our squadron aircraft to circle the target during the bombing period in case the markers became covered up or extinguished, or in the event of the Germans lighting a spoof marker some way off. In either of these events, the target would have to be re-marked, or backed up. The bombing took some considerable time on this target, but eventually we were able to head for home. When we tried to set course on the repeater compass we discovered that it was totally u/s and we had to revert to the magnetic compass. Smoke was issuing from the rear of the fuselage with a strong electrical insulation odour about it, and we were to find out later that the master compass had received a direct hit, hence no joy from the repeater. Our intercom had also been put out of action. A shell had gone through the port wing between the inner and outer tanks, damaging a rib. Further damage had been done to the fin and various other parts of the aircraft, then when we got back to base we found that whatever had come in through the cockpit had struck the hydraulic control mounting block, severely bending it, and preventing us from lowering the flaps. Since this was a diecast aluminium block we decided that a little encouragement might persuade the control to operate. The axe was the nearest tool to a hammer on board and after a number of well placed strokes the lever started to go down, firstly giving us 15°, then full flap on the final approach. Touching down at Woodhall at 04.35 our flying time from the advance base at Tangmere had been 5 hours and 10 minutes, one of our longest trips.

Benny Goodman continues:

1 May was another first for Bill and me. The target was an engineering works outside Tours: the Usine Lictard works. We air-tested our faithful Wooden Wonder in the morning and then settled down to study maps of the Tours area and photographs of the target itself. The factory had been bombed a few days earlier by 8th Air Force B-17s, but the photographs showed that nearly all the bombs had fallen in the surrounding fields. To drop bombs a few hundred yards from the aiming point might be good enough on a large area, but on a pinpoint target like a factory the bombs had to be 'on the button'. We took off in the late evening and headed for France, climbing rapidly to 25,000ft. The PFF Lancasters of 83 and 97 Squadrons had taken off about an hour before us and were to drop a yellow

target indicator 10 miles from Tours, from which the four low-level marker aircraft would set course accurately for the target area. Having dropped the yellow indicator for us, the Lancasters would head directly to the target, identify it on H_2S and discharge hundreds of illuminating flares above it. As Bill and I approached the final turning point, losing height steadily, the yellow TI suddenly cascaded down ahead of us. So far, so good. We flew over the TI and headed for the target. Approaching Tours a great carpet of light suddenly spread out in front of us; we lost more height and soon we were under the marker at 1,500ft and it was as bright as day. If a fighter appeared now, we would be dead ducks and if there was light flak in the area we would certainly have a very tough time. Nothing happened. We circled around and suddenly I saw the factory close by. I immediately pressed the transmit button on my VHF and called "Pen-nib Three Seven, Tally Ho". This was the laid-down method of informing the other marker pilots that the target had been found; they now withdrew from the illuminated area to give me room to manoeuvre and make my dive onto the factory.

I circled around the works, losing speed and positioning the Mosquito for the dive, then opened the bomb doors and pressed the control column gently forward. Our speed increased and the target leapt up towards us, filling the windscreen. At about 500ft I pressed the bomb release button and there was a slight jerk as the four spot-fires left their slips. I continued in the dive for another couple of seconds, selected bomb doors closed and turned sharply to the left in order to cheek our results. There was a red glow among the factory buildings and in fact the spots had fallen through the glass roof of a machine shop. This was splendid from my point of view, I had marked the target accurately, but as the spot fires were inside the machine shop they could not be seen clearly by the Main Force crews, now trundling towards Tours. Marker Leader (Roy Elliott) flew over the works and called in the next marker pilot to lay his red indicators in the yard alongside the machine shop. This was done. Marker Leader then called the Controller and told him that the target had been marked successfully. The Controller broadcast to the Main Force on W/T and VHF to bomb the clump of red spots and this was done. The marking had taken less than five minutes, from my 'Tally Ho' to Roy Elliott's confirmation to the Controller that the target was ready for Main Force action. The low-level marking technique had been vindicated once more and the target was flattened.

During May-June Bomber Command was, apart from three major raids against German cities towards the end of May, fully committed to destroying the *Wehrmacht*'s infrastructure in France and bomber losses were relatively light. One exception, however, was on 3/4 May when Bomber Command attacked a Panzer depot and training centre at Mailly-le-Camp near Epernay to the east of Paris, about 50 miles south of Rheims, which was reported to house up to 10,000 Wehrmacht troops.[115] A total of 346 Lancasters and fourteen Mosquitoes of 1 and 5 Groups and two Pathfinder Mosquitoes of 617 Squadron (one flown by Wing Commander Leonard Cheshire, the 'Marker Leader') were despatched. Flight Lieutenant Benny Goodman DFC and Flight Lieutenant Bill Hickox DFC of 627 Squadron flew on the Mailly Le Camp operation. Goodman recalls:

Cheshire was to lead the low-level marker aircraft and eight Mosquitoes of 627 Squadron were to be at a slightly higher level and were to dive bomb the light-flak positions which were known to be around this depot. The raid was timed to begin at 0001 hours, when all good troops should be in bed. The Mosquito force arrived over Mailly, 5 minutes before zero hour as briefed. Although the target was marked accurately and Cheshire passed the order to bomb, confusion occurred. The first wave did not receive instructions and began to orbit the target. This was fatal and the German night-fighters moved in and began to shoot down the Lancasters. Eventually the situation was sorted out and bombs began to crash down unto the depot. From our worm's eye view, Bill and I could see bomber after bomber coming down in flames towards us. We had a scary time as we dived on the light-flak batteries, dropped our bombs singly on them, avoided light flak and burning Lancasters and contrived to keep ourselves out of harm's way. When our fourth bomb had gone I called Marker Leader and was told to go home. Bill gave me a course to steer for the French coast and I should have climbed to 25,000ft but because of the mayhem in the target area I stayed at low level. All went well for a few minutes and then a searchlight shone directly on us, followed immediately by two or three more. Light-flak batteries opened up and the pretty blue, red, green and white tracery associated with light AA fire came shooting up the beams and exploded all around us.

We were at 500ft and I did not dare to lose height, nor could I climb because this would have been a 'gift' to the German gunners. With Bill's exhortation 'watch your instruments' ringing in my ears I turned steeply to port through 30°, levelled out for a few seconds, then rolled into a steep turn to starboard and repeated the performance. Although we were in searchlights and flak for quite a long time, we were not being held by any one light or being shot at by any one gun for very long and we zig-zagged our way steadily towards the coast. It was a tense time for us and we did not speak. We could hear the explosions around us from light AA shells but incredibly, were not hit. Deliverance came eventually as we breasted a low hill and ahead of us lay the sea. Now we were treated to a rare sight. The final group of searchlights was shining through the trees on top of the hill we had just passed and the beams were actually above and lighting us on our way. We roared along a river estuary, below the level of the lighthouse at Le Treport and then were away over the 'drink' and climbing to safety, home and bed.

The Mosquito crew had been lucky. For the heavies it was a different story.[116]

On the night of 9/10 May bombing attacks were carried out on coastal gun batteries in the Pas de Calais area and a small ball-bearing factory at Annecy while fifty-six Lancasters and Mosquitoes of 5 Group attacked the Gnome & Rhône factory and another factory nearby at Gennevilliers in Paris. No.627 Squadron despatched four Mosquito markers on the Annecy operation and four more to Gennevilliers. Flying Officer James Saint-Smith RAAF DFM and Flying Officer Geoffrey Heath RAAF DFM in O-Orange dive bombed from 5,800ft to 1,000ft to release spot flares, which were assessed at 300 yards south of the aiming point. O-Orange returned with bricks from the works chimney embedded in the starboard wing-tip, much to the delight of the two Australians who claimed them as souvenirs, leaving the ground crew to replace the wingtip. A month later, on 29 June, O-Orange and Saint-Smith and Heath failed to return from the Squadron's first daylight operation, to Beauvoir. While flying over a V-1 site a newly launched V-1 exploded prematurely and destroyed the Mosquito.[117]

On 11/12 May 429 bombers of the Main Force made attacks on Bourg-Leopold, Hasselt and Louvain in Belgium. The target for 190 Lancasters and eight Mosquitoes of 5 Group was a former Belgian *Gendarmerie* barracks at Leopoldsburg (Flemish)/Bourg-Leopold (French), which was being used to accommodate 10,000 SS *Panzer* troops who awaited the Allied invasion forces. The weather was bad with low cloud and poor visibility and a serious error was made with the broadcast winds. As a result, the aircraft were late over the target area and consequently flare-dropping was scattered and provided no adequate illumination. An Oboe Mosquito flown by Flight Lieutenants Burt and Curtis of 109 Squadron dropped a yellow marker. The Mosquito marking force of 627 Squadron arrived late over the target with the result that the Oboe proximity marker was seen by only one of the marking aircraft and the proximity marker, unfortunately, seemed to burn out very quickly. Flare dropping was scattered and did not provide adequate illumination of the target. Haze and up to 3/10ths cloud conditions hampered the marking of the target. The 'Marking Leader' then asked the 'Master Bomber' if he could drop 'Red Spot Fires' as a guide for the flare force. The Master Bomber agreed and 'RSFs' went down at 00.24 hours in the estimated vicinity of the target. Unfortunately, the Main Force started to bomb this red spot fire immediately it went down and half of the Main Force bombed this. The result of this was that the five Mosquitoes of 627 Squadron returned to Woodhall Spa with their bombs and were unable to mark the target. Immediately the 'Master Bomber' ordered 'Stop Bombing', as he realised it was impossible to identify the target but VHF was very poor, particularly on Channel 'B' and the Germans had jammed Channel 'A'. Only half the Main Force received the 'Stop Bombing' instruction and ninety-four Lancasters bombed the target. At 00.34

hours a wireless message, 'Return to base' was sent out to all crews.

The following night, 12/13 May, while formations of the Main Force visited the railway yards at Louvain and Hasselt, twenty-two Mosquitoes of 8 Group attempted to block the Kiel Canal by laying mines from low level. Intelligence sources said that the flak defences on part of the canal had been removed. One of the 692 Squadron crews who took part was Canadian pilot Terry Goodwin DFC DFM and his navigator Hugh Hay DFC. Goodwin recalls:

First thing on 12 May we were told to do some low-level flying on the Great Ouse canal that was not too far away. We were told nothing else except we would be dropping something from 50ft. The briefing itself later in the day was from a high level. AVM Bennett was there as was his flak expert, the 'brown job' [British Soldier]. It was explained that Jerry kept his 'E' boats (fast motor torpedo boats armed with light flak) in the Baltic instead of the North Sea or the Channel so that they could not easily be attacked. They could create havoc amongst an invasion fleet. The Navy and the Air Force had mined all the coastal waters around the north Danish coast leaving only a small channel open. This had just been closed. The only route out of the Baltic to the North Sea was through the Kiel Canal. Our job was to drop anti-shipping mines in to the canal. The mines would fit into our large bomb bays. The proper time for attack was almanac dawn we were told. Flares would be dropped overhead and other Mossies with cannon (we had no guns on ours) would beat-up the gun positions. We would drop the mines from 50ft into the relatively narrow channel. The 'brown job' explained where the flak was, mostly at both ends of the canal, but also every so often along the canal itself. There was a gap, so he said, just east of the railway bridge. This was where we would drop. Privately I was not optimistic. The briefing was over. Things did not quite happen the way they were planed. Almanac dawn to a night bomber pilot is like being in Piccadilly Circus with your pants down. Then I questioned the 'brown job' (whom by now I really respected) about the position of the guns along the canal. It appeared they were every 200 metres or so. If nothing else, Jerry was methodical. There should be a gun right at the drop zone. 'Brown job' said they could not see it in the photos. I was dubious.

We took off to reach the coast at dawn as briefed. There were no markers and no flares (it was too bright for them to have done any good), no apparent action from anyone beating-up the flak positions. Our aircraft of course had no guns so we couldn't do it. We stepped down as briefed and then suddenly saw the railway bridge. I did not feel confident of making the run and swung to the right crossing the south end of the bridge. A light flak opened up. It was just pitiful. There was a balloon inflated but not up (no mention of this in the briefing). I swung south and then back north to the drop zone. It was daylight though the sun was not up yet. On the north side of the canal between the bridge and us was a ship, larger than a minesweeper, tied up in a passing bay. Although lightly armed, it did not fire at us; Live and let Live? I turned left in a large circle, came back to the canal and started the run. The first gun missed but the second one, the one that 'was not there' was sure putting out. From a distance light flak and its tracers look lazy and decorative. Up close, coming right at you, NO. And for every tracer there are likely to be six shells that you don't see. I acquired great respect for the army co-op pilots who looked down the throats of such cannon every day.

It seemed an eternity for Hugh Hay, the navigator/bomb aimer, to get rid of the mine, then a sharp turn left as more guns opened up on me. The 'not there' gun followed us and I shrank between the trees and hedgerows as its shots went overhead. We did get home. No.692 Squadron had sent out twelve aircraft, we got twelve back. The canal was closed for 2-3-weeks. There were three DSOs and ten DFCs awarded for this operation. Hugh got his well deserved DSO.[118] We heard later that twenty-one of Jerry's 'back room' boys had tried to salvage one of the mines and disarm it. They were not successful. It did its job and took all of them with it when it went off.

No.5 Group was now used exclusively in support of the bombing campaign against interdiction targets for Operation Overlord, as Flight Lieutenant Benny Goodman DFC recounts:

1 June 1944 was the same as any other day at Woodhall Spa. Bill and I walked to the Flights after breakfast, found that we were on the Battle Order and went to the dispersal and tested G-George. We then strolled to the Operations Room and were told that the target was to be the marshalling yard at Saumur. The day proceeded normally, with detailed briefing about the target and a close examination of maps and photographs. At the end of the afternoon we attended the AOC's broadcast link-up with the COs of all squadrons participating, then made ready to go. The operation was a copybook 5 Group attack, with no alarms and excursions. After landing, we switched off everything and climbed out as we had done so often before. G-George stood black and silent; the ground crew moved forward to ask if all was well; it was a lovely summer night. After debriefing we ate the usual bacon and eggs and went to bed. Maybe tomorrow there would be a stand-down for us. We did not know it, but in fact our tour was over. We had flown together against Fortress Europe thirty-eight times. Soon we would be instructors again and soon our work in 5 Group would be recognised by the award of a Bar to the DFC to each of us. Paradoxically, however, Bill and I would never fly together again.[119]

On the night of 4/5 June, while 243 heavies and sixteen Mosquitoes bombed coastal batteries in the Pas de Calais, six Mosquitoes went to Argentan and twenty more flew to Cologne. Flight Lieutenant John E.L. Gover DFC and Flying Officer Edward Talbot DFC of 692 Squadron were one of the crews that set out for Cologne and carried a 'Cookie' in the bomb bay. Gover recalls:

As was not uncommon, we were flying west to gain height before turning east. Pressures and temperatures were normal when, at about 5,000ft and somewhere near Oxford, my port engine stopped without warning. Then it came on again, stopped again, came on again and then finally stopped. Normally, with engine failure, one switched off the bad engine and feathered the prop so as to reduce drag. I did not want to do this, in case it came on again. If I feathered it, it could not possibly have come on again. I was praying devoutly that it would. The result was, I lost height more quickly than I would if I had feathered it. A Mosquito would fly quite happily on one engine; but not loaded with 600 gallons of petrol and a 4,000lb bomb. It was unsafe to jettison a blast bomb below 4,000ft. When my engine failed, I was high enough to have done it safely enough for myself but hardly safely enough for anybody who might be on the ground underneath. I turned east in the hope that I could make the coast and jettison the bomb into the sea. After a while I saw the lights of a flare path coming up [Warboys], so I decided to try and do a wheels-up landing. However, I had now lost too much height and, coming in on the approach at 155 mph, hit the ground. There was a half moon, which enabled me just to see the ground coming up. I switched off both engines and pulled back on the stick. The 4,000lb bomb was very dangerous in that it was all explosive with a very thin casing and it was liable to go off even if it was not fused. However, it didn't go off. All I remember was a most tremendous jolt and when I came to I was in a muddy field looking for my helmet, of all things! The aircraft had broken up and caught fire and, although I did not know it at the time, the 4,000lb bomb had just rolled away.

As a pilot, I had a Sutton harness which consisted of four straps coming up over one's legs and down over one's shoulders. If this equipment was locked, the pilot stayed with the aircraft. I did lock it, although I thought it was useless to do so; in fact it saved my life. Navigators only had a body belt, which meant my poor navigator's head went straight through the instrument panel and he was killed. This was hardly fair, as he was a married man with two children whereas I was single at the time. As a result of this accident, navigators were provided with Sutton harnesses in the same way as pilots, but it was too late to save poor Ted. I imagine the reason navigators were only provided with body belts before this accident was because they had to leave their seats to go to the nose of the aircraft to drop the bombs, but they could easily get out of a Sutton harness, so it seems a poor reason. Of course, there was an enquiry into the accident, but both engines were burnt out, so it was impossible to see what had caused the flow of petrol to stop. Subsequently, the same thing happened to somebody else on another squadron, but he jettisoned his bomb too low and blew himself up. The next time the same thing happened, it was to somebody in my own squadron, but he was only testing his aircraft by day with no bomb aboard. The result was that he made a successful single-engine landing, the fault was found and put right; and we had no further trouble. I had suffered second-degree burns and had to go to hospital and it wasn't until 10 August that I went back on operations. No prizes for guessing the target: Berlin!

In the run up to D-Day an 8 Group weather report by Pilot Officer Joe Patient and Pilot Officer Norry Gilroy, a 1409 Met Flight crew, delayed the Normandy invasion by one day and D-Day finally went ahead on 6 June. Four Mosquito crews in 627 Squadron at Woodhall Spa could pat themselves on the back for helping to remove one of the American objectives on D-Day, as Benny Goodman relates:

The Americans were nervous about the long-range heavy gun battery at St. Martin de Varreville behind what was to be Utah beach. This presented a threat to Allied shipping approaching Normandy and also to the troops landing on Utah beach. It was decided that 5 Group would attack this precision target, so on the night of 28/29 May, a force of sixty-four Lancasters, led by a flare force from 83 and 97 Lancaster Pathfinder Squadrons and four Mosquitoes of 627 Squadron, flew to St. Martin de Varreville. The flare force identified the gun battery on their H_2S sets and laid a carpet of flares over the target. At Zero Hour minus 5 minutes, the Mosquitoes roared in at 2,000ft and identified the gun battery visually. The first pilot to see the target called, "Tally Ho" on his VHF radio to warn his companions to keep out of the way and then proceeded to dive at the gun, releasing a red TI at the appropriate point in the dive. His companions followed suit, making individual dives on the battery and creating a box of red TIs around it.[120] The Master Bomber now called in the Main Force, with each aircraft carrying several 1,000lb armour-piercing bombs and the target was obliterated. On 6 June the 101st Airborne Division landed behind Utah beach as planned, but amid a certain amount of confusion. However, by 06.00 hours Major General Maxwell Taylor had mustered one sixth of his force and with this he captured the exits from Utah Beach. An element of the 502nd Regiment had orders to overrun the battery and to crush the garrison if necessary. Captain Frank Lilleyman, the first US soldier to land in Normandy on D-Day, reconnoitred the battery and discovered that it had been abandoned, as a result of the 5 Group bombing attack on 28/29 May. A document captured soon afterwards revealed that the Officer Commanding, *Heer Kust Artillerie Regiment 1261*, reported the

Flying Officer Bill
Clayton-Graham
DFC. (via Andy Bird)

Group Captain Max
Aitken DSO DFC, CO
Banff Wing. (G.A.B. Lord)

FB.XVIII HJ732/G armed with four .303 inch machine guns and the 57mm Molins gun in the nose.

PZ405 NE-A of 143 Squadron with 250lb RPs on rocket rails flown by Squadron Leader Pritchard DFC. (via Andy Bird)

143 Squadron FB.VIs led by Wing Commander C.N. Foxley-Norris DSO pulls up over the *Lysaker* at Tetgenaes on 23 March 1945. Two Mosquitoes were shot down. (via GMS)

At first RPs with 60lb semi-armour piercing heads of the type used in the Western Desert for tank busting were used on anti-shipping strikes. These did not penetrate shipping and caused little structural damage so they were soon replaced with the solid armour rockets. (via Andy Bird)

An armourer holds a 57mm armour-piercing HE shell in front of the Molins gun in the nose of a Banff Mosquito. The four .303 inch machine gun armament was later reduced to two guns to save weight and allow more fuel to be carried on anti-shipping strikes. (via GMS)

PR.XVI NS590/B with D-Day invasion stripes. (Ken Godfrey via George Sesler)

Lieutenant Walter D. Gernand (right), 654th Bomb Squadron, and his cameraman, Sergeant Ebbet C. Lynch, 8th CCU.
(via George Sesler)

1st Lieutenant Claude C. Moore, a navigator in the 654th Bomb Squadron. On 9 April 1945 1st Lieutenant John A. Pruis and Claude Moore flew a *Gray-Pea* mission with three other Mosquitoes on an escort for a long, maximum-effort mission by B-17s of the 1st Air Division to Oberpfaffenhofen in southeastern Germany. Their Mosquito was shot down by P-51s and Pruis was killed. Moore, who was very badly wounded, survived and spent the better part of two years in hospitals. Doctors concentrated on his broken back, a ruptured cartilage in his knee, an injured ankle and the shrapnel wounds in his arm. He was then transferred to two burn centers in England where his hand, face and scalp received skin grafts and other attention. Later, he was transferred to the States where he received attention at two more hospitals. When married years after the mission he was still wearing a body cast. Pruis is buried in Lorraine American Cemetery, France. (via George Sesler)

PR.XVI NS591/S of the 25th Bomb Group landing at Watton on 22 February 1945. (via Philip Birtles)

PR.XVI NS748 lost its tail and rear fuselage in this crash at Watton in April 1945. (via Ken Godfrey)

Lieutenant Raymond G. Spoerl (right) with a UK airman at Watton.

Lieutenant Dean Sanner at Watton on 8 April 1944.

On 18 September 1944 1st Lieutenant Robert A. Tunnel (pictured) in the 654th Bomb Squadron, with 19-year-old Staff Sergeant John 'Buddie' G. Cunney, 8th CCU cameraman failed to return from a PR mission to the Nijmegen-Eindhoven area where a supply drop was to be made by Liberators to the US Airborne. Tunnel was blinded by a searchlight, lost control and crashed on Plantlunne airfield. Both he and Cunney were killed and they are interred in the American war cemetery at Neuville en Condroz, Belgium. (via George Sesler)

PR.XVI NS553, still in its RAF PR blue scheme, suffered a starboard undercarriage failure after putting down in emergency at the 96th Bomb Group B-17 Flying Fortress base at Snetterton Heath in Norfolk. (via Dick Jeeves)

Len A. Erickson, a navigator in the 654th Bomb Squadron and Albert D. Rasmussen and two other officers playing cards at Watton. (Erickson)

H2X PR.XVI NS538/F with Photo Lab personnel, Carl J. Wanka and John W. Ripley. Mickey ships were fitted with modified B-17 H_2X sets for preparing photographic records of radar bombing approaches to high-priority targets deep inside Germany. The H_2X radar scanner was placed in a bulbous nose, the amplifiers and related equipment in the nose and bomb bay, and the radarscope in the rear fuselage. There was a tendency for the Mickey set to arc or even explode, when first turned on. The radar drew a heavier current than the Mosquito's electrical system. (via George Sesler)

Lieutenant Colonel Leon W. Gray, CO. 25th Bomb Group (23 September 1944-14 April 1945) (left); Major Albert S. Straff, Ground Executive; Lieutenant General James E. Doolittle, Major Alvin E. Podwojski, CO, 652nd Bomb Squadron, later Lieutenant Colonel, deputy Group CO and Colonel Elliott Roosevelt, Wing CO, at Watton. (via George Sesler)

PR.XVI MM386 was delivered to the USAAF at Burtonwood on 4 May 1944 and was assigned to the 653rd Bomb Squadron at Watton, where it was coded 'U'. Combat missions were usually signified on the nose, as here, by a cloud with a red lightning flash. Sometimes, a mosquito caricature with a telescope, a modified representation of the official 653rd Bomb Squadron badge, was used. (Jack Green via George Sesler)

2nd Lieutenant Vance J. Chipman (at the back with his pet monkey) a pilot in the 654th Squadron who flew *Chip's Chariot* was a former racetrack driver from Chicago who had joined the RCAF when war started in Europe. On 1 November 1944 2nd Lieutenant Vance J. 'Chip' Chipman and 1st Lieutenant William G. Cannon took off on a Mickey mission to take H$_2$X photos for a bombing run to Schweinfurt. They never returned.

Fifty miles from Schweinfurt the run was completed and on leaving the Mosquito received a direct AA hit. The right engine caught fire and Cannon was hit by shrapnel in his right leg and on the back of his head. Cannon was captured but Chipman tried to make his way toward France and during the journey he tried to steal a Bf 109 and fly it to England but a guard, using a one-inch rubber tubing, beat Chipman over the head until he was unconscious. When he recovered he was taken to the Dulag Luft in Frankfurt, interrogated, and finally taken to Stalag Luft III at Sagan. (via Ken Godfrey)

On 31 October 1944 25 FB.VIs of 21, 464 RAAF and 487 RNZAF Squadrons led by Group Captain Peter Wykeham-Barnes destroyed the Gestapo HQ at Aarhus University in Denmark with 11-second delayed action 500lb bombs. The buildings in the foreground are intact. (IWM)

Pilot Officer Maxwell N. Sparks (left) and his navigator. Pilot Officer Arthur C. Dunlap of 487 Squadron RNZAF who crewed HX982/EC-T on the Amiens raid. (Arthur Dunlap via John Rayner)

Amiens prison on fire after the raid. (via John Rayner)

Squadron leader 'Ted' Sismore DSO DFC* AFC was 'Bob' Bateson's navigator in FB.VI RS570 EG-X on the Shellhaus raid. (Derek Carter Coll)

On the Shellhaus raid three FB.VIs hit by flak had to ditch and all three crews perished. Flight Lieutenant Pattison and Flight Sergeant Pygram's FB.VI in 487 Squadron RNZAF was hit by the cruiser *Nurnberg* at anchor in Copenhagen harbour. Flying Officer Palmer and Squadron Leader Becker of 487 Squadron and Flying Officer R.G. 'Shorty' Dawson RAAF and Flying Officer Fergus Murray of 464 Squadron RAAF were the other two Mosquito crews lost. Dawson (left) and Murray (right) are seen here in Malta in 1943 when they were serving with 23 Squadron. (Tom Cushing Coll)

Mosquito pilot and navigator beside their FB.VI in the summer of 1944.

One of the 150 NF.IIs delivered to the RAF between April and October 1942 by de Havilland Hatfield, DD744 seen here with four guns fitted like the all-black NF.II behind, is in a high-visibility silver finish during its time with either No.1 or 301 Fighter Training Unit (FTU). Later converted to PR.II the fighter was flown to North Africa by the Overseas Aircraft Delivery Unit (OADU) and used by 60 Squadron SAAF on the unit's first sortie from Castel Benito, near Tripoli on 15 February 1943. (DH via Philip Birtles)

NF.XIII HK425/KP-D *Lonesome Polecat* of 409 'Nighthawk' Squadron RCAF on the unit's grass dispersal at Twente in Holland. On 6/7 October 1944 Flying Officer Al Webster and Flying Officer Ross H. Finlayson destroyed a Bf 110 in this aircraft, followed on 25/26 November 1944 with a claim for a Ju 88 by Flying Officer A.I.E. Britten RCAF and Flight Lieutenant L.E. Fownes over Rheindahlen. By the end of the war Britten and Fownes had destroyed five aircraft. *Lonesome Polecat's* final victory was on 18/19 December when Finlayson and Webster destroyed a Ju 88 in this aircraft. The nose art was inspired by a drunken Indian character from a very popular comic strip of the day, Finlayson having added the name to the aircraft and then asked his parents to send him a copy of the comic from Canada for copying. However, before the publication arrived, one of his groundcrew painted the skunk on the nose ahead of the titling, and it was considered to be so well done that Finlayson left it on. (Ross Finlayson)

Canadian built B.XXV KB471. (via GMS)

The bombed out barracks at Caserne des Dunes, Poitiers after the raid by twenty-four FB.VIs of 487 Squadron RNZAF and 21 Squadrons on 1 August 1944. (via Paul McCue)

HK425 of 409 ('Nighthawk') Squadron RCAF. (Ross Finlayson)

Air crews in 409 ('Nighthawk') Squadron RCAF in the winter of 1944. (Ross Finlayson)

FB.VI *Moonbeam McSwine* of 418 (City of Edmonton) Squadron RCAF was flown by Lieutenant Lou Luma (smoking his pipe) and navigator Flying Officer Finlayson (right). Wing Commander Howard Douglas 'Howie' Cleveland (far left) and his navigator Flight Sergeant Earl Boal (middle) are the remaining aircrew in this photo taken at Ford in April 1944. (Stephen M. Fochuk)

bombing attack had begun at 00.15 hours, parachute flares having been dropped first in great numbers. He said that the battery had been hit 'with uncanny accuracy', approximately 100 bombs of the heaviest calibre having been dropped in addition to several hundred smaller ones. Very large bombs had made several direct hits on the gun casement and it had burst open and collapsed. As a result of the destruction caused by the attack he had cleared the remainder of the battery out of the position into three farms in the Mesier area.

On the night of 8/9 June when 455 heavies and twenty-eight Mosquitoes attacked railways in France to prevent German reinforcements from the south reaching Normandy three Lancasters were lost. The first 12,00lb Tallboy bombs developed by Barnes Wallis were dropped by 617 Squadron on a railway tunnel near Saumur, 125 miles south of the battle area. During the first delivery of Tallboys to Woodhall Spa the M/T drivers pulled up alongside 627 Squadron's dispersals to enquire the way to the bomb dump. On seeing the Mosquitoes one of the drivers was heard to say, "I hope you don't think you can put these bloody great things in Mossies do you?" No.627 Squadron's targets were Pontaubault railway junction and Rennes marshalling yards. The Mosquito flown by 30-year old Flight Lieutenant Harry Steere DFM and Flying Officer K.W. 'Windy' Gale RAAF failed to return. 'Bill' Steere was a former 'Halton Brat' who had joined the RAF in 1930. By 1940 he was a flight sergeant flying Spitfires on 19 Squadron and he shared in the squadron's first victory on 11 May. In June he was awarded the DFM and he saw further action during the Battle of Britain. By late November he had been credited with a total of six German aircraft shot down and five shared destroyed as well as two probables. He was commissioned in 1941 and he joined 627 Squadron in November 1943 after a spell as an instructor. Steere was last heard telling his Australian navigator to "Get out of this as quickly as possible" after they were hit and on fire near St. Erblon. Both men died and they were buried at Orgeres. Steere's award of a DFC was gazetted later that month.

The German night fighter force was far from defeated and the *Nachtjagd* remained a constant threat.

CHAPTER FOUR

Berlin or Bust

Had it been introduced in quantity a new night-fighter, the He 219A-0, might have turned the tide for the German night-fighter force but like the Me 262 jet fighter in the day-fighter arm the *Uhu* ('Owl') was never available in sufficient numbers significantly to effect the course of the air war. Fast, manoeuvrable and with devastating firepower of six cannon the 'Owl' was equipped with SN-2 radar and the world's first operational nosewheel undercarriage and ejection seats operated by compressed air for the two crew. At Venlo, Holland, I./NJG1 had been equipped with the anti-Mosquito version of the *Uhu*, a modified version of the He 219A-2, which was lightened by the reduction in armament from six to four 20mm MG 151/20 cannon. It had FuG 2205-N26 airborne radar system, a service ceiling of 37,000ft and the installation of a nitrous oxide (better known as 'laughing gas') fuel injection system to its engines made it one of the few German night fighters fast enough to catch the Mosquito.[121] In late May 1944 the *Uhu* was abandoned in favour of the Ju 88G series, an aircraft that had sufficient performance to take on four-engined bombers but incapable of combating the 'Wooden Wonder'. A *Uhu* in the right hands was a different proposition. During the period 12 June 1943 to 2 July 1944, twenty *Uhu* pilots destroyed 111 Bomber Command aircraft including seven Mosquitoes.

On the night of 10/11 June *Oberleutnant* Josef Nabrich of 3./NJG1 began his patrol high above the Zuider Zee in a cleaned-up He 219 *Uhu* with the armour plating and four of the cannons removed especially for hunting Mosquitoes. Nabrich and his *Bordfunker, Unteroffizier* Fritz 'Pitt' Habicht were looking to add to the four bombers they had claimed destroyed during May, including two in one night (on 24 May). Suddenly, ground controllers reported the approach of a formation of Mosquitoes at a slightly lower altitude. Thirty-two of the Wooden Wonders were *en route* to Berlin. One of these was a 692 Squadron Mosquito B.IV[122] flown by Flying Officer I.S.H. MacDonald RAAF and Flying Officer E.B. Chatfield DFC. Habicht looked at his SN-2 radar display and directed Nabrich to reverse course towards the Mosquito flying east at high speed. Over Osnabrück the He 219 crew obtained visual contact and Nabrich closed to within firing range. He opened up with a short burst from the He 219's wing cannon. The starboard engine of MacDonald and Chatfield's Mosquito immediately burst into flames and started down in a spiral, out of control. Before Nabrich could attack again the Mosquito's bomb load exploded and the blast caused the *Uhu* to stall. Nabrich finally managed to recover just above the cloud layer. Only pieces of the Mosquito were found but MacDonald and Chatfield had baled out immediately after the first attack, convinced that a new anti-aircraft weapon and not a night-fighter had shot them down. Both men survived and they were taken prisoner.

Hauptmann Ernst-Wilhelm Modrow of I./NJG1, a pre-war Lufthansa pilot who joined the night-fighter arm in October 1943, was also airborne in an He 219 *Uhu* on the night of 22/23 April, when the target for 596 heavies was Düsseldorf. He had previously destroyed three *Viermots*, (four-engined heavy bombers) and now he was looking for his 19th victory. Modrow's *Bordfunker* scanned his SN-2 radar display and picked up a homeward bound aircraft, which was approaching the Dutch Coast at 27,000ft. Their quarry was a Mosquito B.XVI flown by Flight Lieutenant Joe Downey DFM and Pilot Officer Ronald Arthur Wellington of 571 Squadron, who were on their first Mosquito operation. Downey, who was approaching his 26th birthday, was like Modrow, something of an old hand too, having flown fifty-seven ops on bombers.[123] Arthur Wellington recalls:

> The attack on our aircraft consisted of a short burst of cannon fire, no more than five rounds. The starboard engine was hit and burst into flames. The aircraft immediately went into an uncontrolled dive and on receiving the order 'Bale Out' I made my exit from the normal escape hatch. At the time Joe was preparing to follow me. Very shortly after pulling the ripcord I saw the aircraft explode beneath me. It is therefore, very unlikely that Joe was alive when the remains of the aircraft crashed onto the dunes near Bergen, a small seaside town three miles north-west of Alkmaar.[124]

Airborne again in their He 219 *Uhu* on the night of 11/12 June *Oberleutnant* Josef Nabrich and *Unteroffizier* Fritz Habicht of 3./NJG1 sought more victories as the LNSF sent thirty-three Mosquitoes to Berlin and the heavies bombed rail targets in northern France. West of Salzwedel Habicht was able to pick up a Mosquito, so near that he could see it clearly without radar. Nabrich had difficulty getting into a firing position because the Mosquito pilot, Flight Lieutenant O.A. Armstrong DFM MiD RNZAF of 139 Squadron, was carrying out wild evasive action. Finally, Nabrich gave the B.IV two bursts of 20mm cannon and DZ609 went down vertically and exploded seconds later killing Armstrong and his navigator, Flying Officer G.L. Woolven. Now it was time for Nabrich to have concern. He had made his pursuit at full power and seconds after the Mosquito went down the port DB603 engine of his He 219 seized. He feathered the propeller and was able to make a single-engine landing at Perleberg. *Generalleutnant* Josef 'Beppo' Schmid sent Nabrich and Habicht a congratulatory telegram and a gift of several bottles.[125]

A second 139 Squadron Mosquito piloted by Scotsman, Flying Officer J.L. Cassels DFC and 30-year old Londoner Alan J.A. Woollard DFM failed to return to Upwood when their aircraft suffered engine trouble. Woollard had survived a Mosquito crash a month earlier while returning to Upwood on 10/11 May when a flare that had failed to release ignited. The Mosquito had crashed 8 miles NNE of Cambridge killing his pilot Flying Officer G.W. Lewis. The night of 11/12 June proved slightly less turbulent, as Woollard recalls:[126]

> We received a very rough reception. We were adopting the tactic of marking and then nosing down slightly to gain speed and get out the far side as fast as possible. As the tumult started to die down the port engine rad temperature went off the clock and my pilot had to feather it. As this engine supplied our heat (as well as powering the H_2S), we quickly frosted up inside and couldn't see out. We swung north, came down from 25,000ft to around 8,000ft and took stock. We were without radar, between Berlin and Stettin, flying slowly and with dawn fast approaching. Calculations showed that as things stood we were unlikely to make England with our stock of petrol and that it would be daylight before we reached the enemy coast. We decided to go to Sweden. The port engine was unfeathered several times to enable me to get the H_2S working and cross the Baltic at a quiet spot. We reached the Swedish coast OK but low cloud prevented us from flying north to Kristianstad where we understood there was a 'drome. We therefore crossed the Swedish coast near Ystad to the accompaniment of a furious shower of Bofors flak and after much searching for a field big enough to take us, had to land using three fields. This necessitated a 'wheels up' landing and we proceeded to leave bits of Mosquito in two hedges. It was also very noisy. Eventually the farmer arrived and took us to his farm for coffee, saying: "Welcome to Sweden."[127]

On 28/29 June 230 bombers hit the railway yards at Blainville and Metz for the loss of eighteen Halifaxes and two Lancasters (or 8.7 per cent of the force)[128] while thirty-three Mosquitoes of the LNSF went to Saarbrücken and another ten were despatched to drop 4,000lb 'Cookies' from 32,000ft on the Scholven/Buer oil plant in the Ruhr. All the Mosquitoes returned without loss but Flight Lieutenant David 'Russ' Russell and his navigator Flying Officer 'Barks' Barker of 109 Squadron, who had completed a tour on Stirlings and who were on their third Mosquito trip,[129] had a close shave after dropping their 'Cookie, as Russell recalls:

> Heading for home at 30,000ft it was clear and with bright moonlight. At almost one o'clock near Venlo on the German/Dutch border we were feeling relaxed and were trimmed for a gradual but fast moving descent with an hour or so return to base. Suddenly and without warning lines of orange coloured 'blobs' flashed past underneath, then gracefully and lazily fell away in the distance; quite fascinating. Shocked, we felt the dull thud of shells striking the Mossie. A fighter must have closed to within a hundred yards or so and attacked from below and dead astern. We must have been the perfect target, silhouetted against the light. Shells crashed between us, cold fluid from the compass got into my boots and poor Barker

kicked his legs in the air. I opened up to full power and went into a tearing, climbing turn to starboard toward the attack but with the Mossie shuddering it became more of a sluggish stall turn. Looking around for some cover I could see a few wisps of cloud below us but they were so sparse that the moon shone through in a watery way. After a few more violent turns and looking around hopelessly for any sign of our attacker, who must have overshot, I levelled out hoping that we had shaken him off but the thud and clatter of shell strikes began again. This time our attacker seemed closer. He really 'caned' us. I responded like a scalded cat, turning toward him with full power and varying my height at the same time. After what seemed an age I levelled out cautiously, weaved and looked around, wondering if our tormentor was standing off to have another go. I was frustrated at not being able to make out any sign of him. We were still at about 23,000ft and speed was now of the essence so I stuck the nose down and scarpered at about 400mph or so. Either he had run out of ammunition or thought we had 'had it' and left us to our fate.

I reduced speed and we assessed our damage. The radio and compass and the gyro were out of action and the port engine felt a little rough. There was the possibly that our fuel tanks were damaged but all the gauges seemed normal and all aircraft controls appeared OK. The intercom was still functioning. No physical damage to either of us but our real annoyance was, 'Why us?' I tried in vain to feather the port propeller so I decided to use the power for as long as possible. A windmilling or dead propeller may well have been the worst choice, particularly in view of the distance to cover. We set course for Woodbridge and hoped that the weather had improved. A feeling of calm after the storm now set in and with it reaction to the exertion of sheer survival against an unseen enemy. Poor Barks, he just had to sit there hoping and I'd like to think, trusting in me! The adrenaline uplift and feeling of elation and achievement in beating the odds loosened our tongues on the return home.

Crossing the Dutch coast at about 20,000ft we received a farewell gesture of light flak, the tracer rising slowly and then increasing in speed as it neared us before falling away. I reduced power slightly to ease the loading on the port engine and we had a good look around. Weather conditions and visibility were good with 3-4/10ths broken cloud to the South but complete cloud cover was forecast at base. I decided therefore to head for Manston airfield in Kent, which like Woodbridge had three very long runways and grass undershoot and overshoot areas for emergencies such as ours. With some relief we made a straight-in approach in a gentle descent but at 16,000ft flames started in the port engine cowling. Again feathering proved useless so I cut the fuel and the ignition off, reduced the revs and activated the fire extinguisher, all to no avail. Ditching was a possibility and so the roof panel was jettisoned but without radio and my own firm reluctance, I assured Barks that ditching was the last thing I intended. I was confident we would make the airfield and we could always bale out over land but the fire appeared to be gaining and spreading back over the wing and the inner wing tanks and control was beginning to fall off with a tendency to increase the rate of descent. Not trusting the hydraulics and with no flaps I advised Barker that we would land wheels-up to give us a better chance of getting out through the roof and away more quickly. At about 2,000ft I told him to fire off the colours of the day. Despite a marked increase in roughness on the closed down port engine I felt confident of hitting the threshold. At around 1,000ft and having crossed the coast we could see rooftops below from the glare of our burning aircraft. Final approach was made at about 500ft with elevator control virtually non-existent and maximum trim. It was with an almost casual feeling of anti-climax that we glided, or fell the remaining few feet at about 160/170.

We must have touched down on the grass undershoot area. Skidding and bumping along, our speed carried us to the threshold of the tarmac runway where the Mossie stopped suddenly, broke up and jack-knifed with the tail end of the fuselage folding forward, the tail-plane ending up against the trailing edge of the mainplane. Although my straps were secure they were not locked and I pitched forward, pranging my forehead on the screen frame. We appeared to be engulfed in fire and Barks left through the roof hatch. Dazed and my left foot jammed by the rudder, I thought about my new escape boots and was determined not to leave without them. Eventually I freed my foot and I clambered through the roof onto the starboard wing. It was hot and surrounded by glaring fire. I turned and escaped through a gap between the nose and the starboard engine. Jumping off the wing into darkness as the fire and ambulance crews ran toward me, all I could see behind was the huge bonfire of the poor old Mossie.'[130]

The Light Night-Striking Force of Mosquitoes raided Berlin 170 times, thirty-six of these on consecutive nights. On 10 July the Mosquitoes were on the 'Milk Run' again: Berlin or bust. Wing Commander Steven D. Watts DSO DFC MiD the CO of 692 Squadron, was shot down off Terschelling by Major Hans Karlowski of 2./NJG1. Watts and his observer, Pilot Officer A.A. Matheson DFM RNZAF were lost without trace.

The operational use of the Mosquito bomber had forced the *Nachtjagd* to reconsider the *Wilde Sau* (Wild Boar) method to hunt the high-performance aircraft at high altitude with Fw 190A-5s and A-6s and Bf 109Gs with *Neptun* AI radar and a long-range fuel-tank.[131] *Oberleutnant* Fritz Krause, a *Staffelkapitän* in the experimental I./NJGr10 at Berlin-Werneuchen commanded by *Hauptmann* Friedrich Karl Müller[132] whose main task this was, recalls:

The new Heinkel 219 two-motor night-hunter to combat the Mosquito was not quite ready while the jet-hunter, the Me 262, was not available in sufficient numbers. So the task of testing the new methods fell mainly to one *Staffel* of the *Wilde Sau*. We had to meet the two quite different uses of the Mosquito. Firstly, there was the nightly raid to bomb Berlin and secondly their use as pathfinders at high altitude in the Ruhr. Night after night, thirty to forty Mosquitoes flew to Berlin and dropped bombs and the psychological stress on the Berliners was considerable. Flak and searchlights were moved to Berlin without having any considerable or lasting effect. The Mosquitoes flew at altitudes above 30,000 ft and after crossing the Elbe lost height to fly over Berlin at the highest possible speed to avoid the concentrated flak. The direction of the flights across Berlin was different with each operation.

A number of different tactical methods using night-hunters was tested but the following method, which I used with success, was the most effective. When the first of the incoming Mosquitoes crossed the Rhine, five single-engined hunters took off from Werneuchen and climbed to orbiting positions at 35,000ft in the NE, NW, SE, SW and the centre of Berlin, each position being marked by a strong master searchlight. This made it possible for at least one night-hunter, irrespective of the direction from which the attack was coming, to spot the Mosquitoes before they flew across the city. (As the single-engined fighter's speed advantage over the Mosquito was only 60 kph there was only a short time available for hunting so a greater speed was required to catch the Mosquitoes and this was obtained by making a steep dive from the waiting position). Of course this method depended on good weather and visibility so that the searchlights could pick up the plane at high altitude. Up to 25,000ft the flak had a fire-free zone but the area above this limit was reserved for the hunters. The Mosquitoes usually entered Berlin at around 20,000ft and the problem now was that the hunters had to avoid their own flak. I often experienced shells exploding near me, disturbing me while hunting.[133]

On 8 July Krause took off at 00.40 hours in '*Weisse Elf*' ('White 11') a FuG 217 J2 (*Neptun*) equipped Fw 190A-5 and destroyed a Mosquito near Brandenburg, his only victory in this unit. Kruase describes his victory:

I was flying over Berlin at a height of 8,500 metres when I saw a twin-engined plane flying west caught in the searchlights. I closed in until I was 700 metres above, gave full throttle and dived. I went in too low and opened fire from approximately 200 metres from below and behind and kept firing as I closed. My first shots hit the right motor and an explosion followed. There was a burst of sparks and then a thick white trail of vapour. As I had overshot I had to stop the attack momentarily and found myself on the right, alongside the enemy aircraft, whose cockade and external fuel tanks I saw clearly and so was able to identify it without a doubt as a Mosquito. I fired ESN to draw the attention of the flak and the searchlight to my presence. The enemy 'corkscrewed' in an attempt to evade. Because of the thick 'white flag' of vapour I was able to follow him, although he had already left the searchlight zone in a north-westerly direction. Following the trail, I managed to attack twice more. At the third attack I noticed a further explosion on the right wing and an even stronger rain of sparks. At 2,000 metres he disappeared, turning at a flat gliding-angle under me. I did not see the impact on the ground as this was hidden from my angle of view.[134] On my return flight, passing Lake Koppeln I could estimate the crash-point as 60-70 kilometres north-west of Berlin. When I returned to base a report had already reached them about the crash of a burning enemy aircraft west of Kürytz. My own plane was covered in oil from the damaged Mosquito.[135]

On 18/19 July when twenty-two Mosquitoes were despatched to Berlin, 29 year old Squadron Leader Terry 'Doddy' Dodwell RAFVR DFC* and Pilot Officer George Cash, a 571 Squadron Mosquito team who had been on ops for nearly a year, were lost. They are believed to have been intercepted and shot down by *Hauptmann* Heinz Strüning of 3/NJG1, flying in a modified He 219 *Uhu* night fighter.[136] Dodwell was killed and Cash survived to be taken prisoner. Two nights later, on 20/21 July, during a LNSF raid on Hamburg by twenty-six Mosquitoes, Strüning shot down another 571 Squadron B.XVI crewed by Flight Lieutenants Thompson and Jack Calder RCAF. Thompson baled out but Calder was killed.

During the first week of August a series of heavy daylight bombing raids were made on V-1 flying bomb sites in the Pas de Calais and storage dumps at Bois de Cassan, Forêt de Nieppe and Trossy-St-Maxim. For photographic and marking purposes a lone Mosquito of 627 Squadron accompanied 5 Group's Lancasters. Flying Officer John Whitehead of 627 Squadron flew one of these photo sorties on 3 August. Whitehead recalls:

It was a wonderful sunny August day, marked forever in my mind: Woodhall Spa; flirting with girls around a swimming pool. But it was time to dress, to get into our Mossie and take off for France. I had a photographer aboard in place of my usual navigator, Johnny Watt. The idea was to cross one of our bomber streams that was on the way to bomb a V-1 dump, cross it diagonally, to get some of their fighter protection, then to descend steeply and mark a V-1 dump for the heavies. We were late off the ground and the poster that was displayed at all RAF stations during the war years: 'The Straggler is Lost!' came to mind and worried us. We crossed at the rear end of the 5 Group Lancaster stream, being turned nearly upside down a couple of times by the slipstream of one of them. Hundreds of them were silhouetted against the true blue sky, glistening here and there in that extraordinary day's sunlight. A stream of *Messerschmitts* appeared high up, not interested in us Mossies and some Spitfires streaked after them. We had two 500lb bombs aboard in addition to the markers and they also had to be delivered, in a second dive onto the same target. But the area had become somewhat of a wasps' nest. It seemed everybody was shooting down on us from the surrounding hills while we were, by now, hugging the ground at 300 knots awaiting a quiet stretch before I would dare to pull up sharply at full bore to gain height and get away. And there, an apparition, a scene, a happening! We whizzed by a tea party in the garden of a Chateau! I believe that I recognised the pattern of Sevre china and saw clearly the butler holding a silver tray. He was looking up frowning with disapproval. I am not quite sure whether the surprised people actually waved, but they certainly looked up. That's the least they could do, to express their support for my war effort? I was stunned for a moment by this dissonance of war and peace, those three seconds of it. Then we tried to get up to height, twisting and turning while the flak still followed us. Once it had thinned out we flew home happily to Woodhall Spa, hardly even looking back to France, confident and relaxed. Who would try to go after a lone Mosquito going home? The sun was still up, the sky still cloudless, when I returned to the swimming pool to continue my flirt with the girls. The number had shrunk to only one by now and she was somewhat sunburned. But she was there!

In August 692 Squadron at Graveley had a run of bad luck. On the 25th Squadron Leader W.D.W. Bird and Sergeant F.W. Hudson were killed when they crashed at Park Farm, Old Warden near Bedford. It was believed that the pilot misread his altimeter. On 27 August on a trip to Mannheim Flight Lieutenant T.H. Galloway DFM and Sergeant J. Murrell swung on take-off, caught fire and blew up. The 'Cookie' went off, but was not detonated, so it did not cause too much damage. Galloway and Murray got out when the Mosquito caught fire and ran to safety. Over the target Flying Officer S.G.A. Warner and Flying Officer W.K. McGregor RCAF were shot down and killed and the searchlights and flak followed them all the way down. On 10/11 September it was the old Milk Run again to Berlin. Terry Goodwin DFC DFM a 692 Squadron pilot at Graveley flew this operation, his last on the Mosquito and he had a rather anxious time, as he recounts:

After Hugh Hay had finished his tour I had several good navigators with nothing to worry about. However, when my last trip was coming up there was a new navigator posted in. He was a Warrant Officer with no trips in at all. I just could not figure that out when all crews at that time had a tour under their belts and knew what the score was. I took him for a cross-country, which was not satisfactory as he had trouble with the Gee. I did not know whether it was a 'short' or a 'long' trip: either the Ruhr or Berlin. It turned out to be the 'big city'.

The night was clear. The take-off with the 4,000lb 'Cookie' was good. The aircraft was singing right along with all gauges OK. The track was out over the North Sea towards Denmark then a sharp turn right south-east to a point just west of Berlin then straight east for the bombing run. When we were approaching this turning point it was clear with no moon. I could see the coast outline right from Denmark south. The tram trolleys of Hamburg were still making their blue sparks and then shut down fully. Then the sprog navigator said to me, "I don't know where we are!" I told him to get the course from the turning point and I would tell him when to start all over again. He did and got us just west of Berlin on time or at least I thought we were on time. I told him to log the time, then go and dump the Window down the chute. There was no action outside as we ran up looking for the 'TIs'. Jerry was playing it very careful giving nothing away. Where was that PFF type? The TIs should be going down! Then all hell broke loose. Every searchlight in the city came on right on us and the flak was too damn close. I turned sharp right and dived 2,000ft, straightened out back on course, held it, turned left and climbed and got more flak but further away. And this kept on and on. Finally the lights were bending east so I thought we should be through the city. I turned back west and still no PFF. I told the navigator to drop the 'Cookie' (I don't think we got a proper picture) because the flak was hard at us again. Then the TIs went down right ahead of us so we were pretty close. But the flak kept on and I twisted and dived and climbed and kept that up. I knew we were down to about 17,000ft when I suddenly saw the light flak opening up. You knew it was pretty if it was not so damn serious. I turned and climbed out on the west side of Berlin. I told the navigator to log the time. We had been in it for 11 minutes with Jerry's undivided attention. Were there any fighters? Not that I saw, maybe I was just too busy. It would not have been a safe place for them with all that flak around. We did get home and logged 4 hours and 30 minutes. The next morning the Flight Sergeant found me and then showed me the aircraft. It was full of flak; the main spar of the tail plane was getting an 18-inch splice. He dug a piece of flak out for me. One piece had just nicked the intercooler rad, then the fairing for the main rad. but not the tubes, but was spent as it bounced around the engine.

Berlin at this time was the 'favourite' destination for the Mosquitoes. 'A' and 'B' Flights at 8 (PFF) Group stations were routed to the Big City over towns and cities whose air raid sirens would announce their arrival overhead, although they were not the targets for the Mosquitoes' bombs. Depriving the Germans of much needed sleep and comfort was a very effective nuisance weapon, while a 4,000-pounder nestling in the bomb bay was a more tangible 'calling card'. The 'night postmen' had two rounds: After take-off crews immediately climbed to height, departed Cromer and flew the dog-leg route Heligoland-Bremen-Hamburg. The second route saw departure over Woodbridge and went to The Ruhr-Hannover-Munich. Two Mosquito bombers, which failed to return from the attack on Berlin on 13/14 September, were claimed shot down south-east of the capital by *Oberfeldwebel* Egbert Jaacks of I./NJG10 and at Braunschweig by *Leutnant* Karl Mitterdorfer of 10./JG300.[137]

Berlin was all too familiar for Flight Lieutenant Chas Lockyer DFC who had flown a tour on Hampdens on 106 Squadron at Coningsby in 1941 before beginning his second tour of operations as pilot of a Mosquito B.XX in 608 Squadron at Downham Market. His navigator, Flying Officer Bart 'Jock' Sherry DFC*, another second tour man, was a big cheerful Glaswegian with a laugh that could stop a bus at twenty paces. He had completed a tour on Lancasters in 1943. Lockyer recalls:

> Naturally enough, with 635 Lancaster Squadron and 608 Mosquito Squadron sharing the same airfield at Downham Market there was a lot of good-humoured rivalry and banter between the respective aircrews. Our cause wasn't helped by some idiot naming the Mosquito squadrons of 8 Group, 'The Light Night-Striking Force', which left us wide open to sarcastic suggestions that the qualification for service on a Mosquito squadron was presumably an inability to see in the dark! It was later changed to 'The Fast Night-Striking Force'; equally clumsy but less ambiguous.
>
> We were fortunate at Downham in having a FIDO installation: the fog dispersal system consisting of a double line of burners running parallel to either side of the runway, which burned large quantities of petrol on the Primus stove principle. The intense heat so generated burned off the fog and thereby enabled the airfield to remain operational when the test of the area was blanketed in fog. Coming in to land when FIDO was operating was rather like descending into the jaws of hell and proved a very useful incentive to keeping straight after touch-down!
>
> The Mossies were given a wide variety of tasks including such niceties as dropping route markers and target indicators over a false target while the Main Force pressed on elsewhere. With the introduction of the 'pregnant' Mosquito version adapted to carry a 'Cookie' we became a reasonably lethal bombing force in our own right, particularly as we could operate in weather conditions that grounded the heavies. The inhabitants of Berlin would be the first to acknowledge that 100 Mosquitoes each carrying a 'Cookie' weren't the most welcome visitors night after night. When bad weather grounded the Main Force, small groups of Mosquitoes could be sent to a wide variety of targets in the Reich. Their objective was to get a large part of Germany out of bed and into the shelter so there were very few nights when the sirens were silent.
>
> Our first operational trip in a Mosquito was to Berlin on 15/16

September, when twenty-seven Mosquitoes of the LNSF were despatched to raid Berlin, nine others going to Lübeck and eight to Rheine airfield. One aircraft of 608 Squadron failed to return.[138] We'd just released the bombs and had completed the requisite straight and level run for the benefit of the camera when a master searchlight switched straight on to us and we were immediately coned as its satellites joined in the fun. At the same moment Jock, who had scrambled back from the bomb-aiming position in the nose, spotted an Fw 190 closing in on us but slightly high. The pilot obviously hadn't seen us yet or his cannon shells would have blown us out of the sky by now and we were apparently in the blind spot created by the 190's large radial engine. This situation posed a bit of a problem as any sort of diving turn on our part would undoubtedly bring us into his line of vision and a highly probable early end of our tour. The only alternative seemed to be to try to stay in his blind spot. I throttled back slightly until he was immediately above us. For about the next ten minutes we performed a graceful *pas de deux* over the city; watching him like a hawk and responding as soon as we saw his wing dip as he searched left and right for his prey. Finally, and to our profound relief he gave up and turned steeply to starboard while we turned equally steeply to port and high-tailed it for home. We had a few chuckles on the way back trying to guess the gist of the conversation, which must have gone on between the 190 pilot and his ground controller. The latter probably asked what sort of short-sighted *dumkopfs* the *Luftwaffe* were recruiting these days, the pilot responding by asking the controller kindly to clean his screen as he didn't want to spend the rest of the night being vectored on to fly dirt.

After this initiation our second trip, to Bremen on 17/18 September, when forty-two Mosquitoes of the LNSF raided Bremen, and six others Dortmund, all without loss, promised to be a bit of an anti-climax. The Intelligence Officer at briefing assured us that women and old men were now manning the anti-aircraft guns at Bremen owing to the demand for manpower to stem the Allied and Russian advance. We'd just completed our bombing and camera run over Bremen when all hell broke out around us as we were introduced to one of the problems of ops in Mossies. We were often used on diversionary raids, involving extensive use of Window, which produced a blip on radar screens similar to that produced by an aircraft. This could be used in a variety of permutations to confuse the enemy and give the controllers problems as to where to send up their fighters. One popular ploy was for the Mosquitoes to overfly the main force of heavies and heave out masses of these strips as the Main Force either continued or diverted to its target. Meanwhile the Mossies carried on to an alternative target, leaving the Germans to decide which was the Main Force. Sometimes they got it right and sometimes they didn't. But the net result as far as we were concerned was that only a limited number of us would finally bomb our particular target and Jerry was able to dispense with his usual box barrage and concentrate on one aircraft at a time. What was happening at Bremen left us in no doubt that we'd drawn the short straw.

Climb and dive, twist and turn as we might, the flak was deadly accurate and it was only a matter of time before the flying shrapnel found a vulnerable spot. That spot turned out to be the cooling jacket around the starboard engine and a violent juddering accompanied by belching smoke signified the imminent loss of interest of the engine in any further proceedings. Jock feathered the propeller while I throttled back and trimmed the aircraft for single-engine flight and his finger hovered anxiously over the fire extinguisher button as we watched the trailing smoke but there was no fire. The smoke ceased and we breathed again.

We were now faced with a further problem. As returning Mossies would be tracked by German radar they would soon know our course for home. We would be spotted as a straggler at our reduced speed and fighters would be sent up to intercept. Some more accurate flak near Groningen convinced us it would be unwise to continue on this course and a hasty cockpit consultation resulted in our turning due North to get out to sea as quickly as possible. This wasn't going to get us any nearer home but it would help to throw off the tracking radar and also deter the German night fighters, who were always reluctant to venture too far out to the sea. The bright red 'Boozer' light receiver (tuned to the transmissions of the different types of German radar) in the cockpit soon turned to dull red and finally went out and we thankfully turned westward for home. On learning that we only had one engine, Downham control promptly diverted us to Coltishall on the well-worn principle, 'We're all right, Jack but if you're going to make a cobblers of your landing we'd rather you cluttered up someone else's flarepath rather than ours'. Welcome home!

On the night of 19/20 September the twin towns of Mönchengladbach/Rheydt were the targets for 227 Lancasters and ten Mosquitoes of 1 and 5 Groups. The designated Master Bomber was unavailable and Wing Commander Guy Gibson VC DSO* DFC*, the famous Dambusters' leader and navigator Squadron Leader J.B. Warwick DFC took off from Woodhall Spa in a 627 Squadron Mosquito [139] to act as Controller for the raid on Rheydt. It would appear that Gibson did not exactly endear himself to some of 627 Squadron's members but then 617 Squadron always engendered fierce rivalries. Squadron Leader Frank W. Boyle DFC* RAAF, a 627 Squadron navigator, encountered Gibson a few times at Woodhall. He reported that, 'he seemed a lost soul, particularly on the last occasion when he dropped in at the Mess. He was upset by the award of Cheshire's VC (and I would understand that after his own VC for the Dambusters raid), but he reckoned too forcibly and bluntly that, on the basis of Cheshire's citation, he would get a bar to his VC.' Fellow 627 Squadron navigator Wallace 'Johnno' Gaunt DFC recalled:

> Guy Gibson was a brave man and did a good job leading the Dambusters but he came back from the USA too full of his own importance. He walked into our mess one night and everybody was talking, playing liar-dice, drinking, etc, so he called out, 'Don't you know who I am?' He got very annoyed as he had expected everyone to stand up and cheer him. In the end he was de-bagged and put outside. He persuaded our CO to let him fly a Mosquito against his better judgement. A week or so later Peter Mallender and I were told that he wanted the aircraft we were due to operate that night. He did not return.[140] While returning over Walcheren both engines of Gibson's Mosquito cut (according to a Dutch farmer who witnessed the incident) and the aircraft crashed near the sea wall killing both crew. Gibson and his navigator are buried at Bergen-op-Zoom. The most likely theory for the incident is that the fuel transfer cocks were not operated in the correct sequence and the engines ran out of fuel.[141]

On 27/28 September 217 Lancasters of 1 Group and nine Mosquito markers of 5 Group carried out the only major raid by Bomber Command on Kaiserlautern. Over 900 tons of bombs were dropped and 36 per cent of the built-up area was destroyed. One Lancaster and a single Mosquito were lost. Squadron Leader Frank W. Boyle DFC RAAF, Flight Lieutenant Leo 'Pop' Devigne DFC's navigator on 627 Squadron, recalls:

> Leo was an outstanding pilot and we got on fine together. Physically strong and cool under fire but extrovert, e.g. his victory-roll over base on return from a successful trip. Our target, the railway workshops were on our port when 'Buzz' Brown called "Tally Ho" and dived to mark. He was hit by the flak crossfire and we saw him crash; ploughing along the ground with an awesome display of exploding coloured TIs. We followed him down and marked the target as he exploded. It was the only time that we were legitimately beaten to a target. (By 'legitimately' I mean not deliberately ignoring the flight plan, which was devised to confuse enemy defences as to the identity of our target, or deliberately to mark too early, which could initiate the defences before our Main Force were timed to bomb). I made it very clear at debriefing that if 'Buzz' had not been ahead of us we would have been the target of that crossfire.[142]
>
> Leo's physical strength was needed a month later when one engine was shot out of action by Walcheren gun positions that we were dive bombing in daylight. He had to fly the Mosquito back to Woodhall on the remaining engine and land. The ground crew showed us how the pressure from one finger easily broke off the wing from near the engine casing. That cured him of his victory rolls.[143] This was a daylight affair on 30 October when

eight Mosquitoes of 627 Squadron set out to mark four gun batteries for 102 Lancasters to bomb.[144] Marking proved difficult because the island was flooded and the only land above water was the sea wall and the beach. At high water only the sea wall was above the floodwater. Flying Officer 'Sandy' Saunders' first TI undershot and was just visible in the water. Flight Lieutenant Peter Mallender's Mosquito was hit by flak in the port flap but it did not stop him from beginning his first dive. Their first TI overshot but burned in shallow floodwater. The second TI undershot and went out quite quickly in deeper water. The Mosquito flown by Flight Lieutenant A.G. St. John RNZAF and Flying Officer L.J. Dick RCAF was lost after a TI exploded in the bomb bay of their aircraft. In the circumstances the Lancasters were told to bomb the gun emplacement target at the land end of a specific breakwater and they were accurate. This was the last operation by Bomber Command in support of the Walcheren campaign and the opening of the River Scheldt. Walcheren was attacked by ground troops the following day. Commandos sailed their landing craft through the breaches in the sea walls made by the Lancasters and the island finally fell after a week of fighting.

Despite the intensity of raids, 'Don' Bennett's LNSF Mosquito squadrons had the lowest losses in Bomber Command (one per 2,000 sorties). During October eleven Mosquitoes of the LNSF were lost on operations. New squadrons joined the force, with 142 Squadron re-forming at Gransden Lodge on 25 October and flying their first operation when their only two Mosquito B. XXVs were despatched to Cologne. That same day Flight Lieutenant A.P. 'Pat' O'Hara DFC* DFM of 109 Squadron at Little Staughton, who was on his second tour, found himself on ops as he recalls:

At this time I was flying with Wing Commander Peter Kleboe, O/C 'A' flight. Frank Griggs, who was also my pilot on my first tour on Stirlings on 214 Squadron, had been repatriated to Australia in December 1943. Peter Kleboe and I had been to Essen on the 23rd. I was under the impression that he had done his quota and I was about to depart for Bedford but I was mistaken. Pete called me in and said we were on a daylight to Essen. We were first on target with Red TIs for the heavy boys. Our ETA target was Zero-5 minutes. Turning on the bombing run, Oboe functioning, the flak was heavy at 30,000ft. I had just received 'C' when a voice on sixth sense said, 'Open the bomb doors'. I had never before on seventy-odd flights opened before 'D', which was the signal to be ready for the bombing signal. Anyway, I leaned forward and pressed the lever. As I did so there was a loud bang and a piece of flak came through the windscreen and took the epaulette off my battledress left shoulder and went out the back. The aircraft dived. I grabbed the stick and looked at Pete. His face was peppered with fragments of perspex but he said, "Wait for the bombing signal, which I did and we turned off. We descended to a reasonable level as we were icing up inside. During the flight home I worked out that if I hadn't leaned forward on hearing 'C' to open the bomb doors that piece of flak would have taken my head off instead of my epaulette. Although Pete was practically blinded we got back to Staughton. He said, "Tell me when we are crossing the hedge." Pete had been a BAT Flight instructor before joining 109 and he made a good landing. Pete recovered and the next time I bumped into him was at Melsbroek in March 1945 when he was CO of 21 Squadron. We had a chat and a little celebration and he asked me to join 21 Squadron. I said, "No thank you." I returned to Evere after a promise to meet up again.

On 6/7 November RAF Bomber Command sent out two major forces of bombers. Some 235 Lancasters of 5 Group, together with six Mosquitoes of 627 Squadron again attempted to cut the Mittelland Canal at its junction with the Dortmund-Ems Canal at Gravenhorst but crews were confronted with a cold front of exceptional violence and ice quickly froze on windscreens. Only thirty-one Lancasters bombed before the Master Bomber abandoned the raid due to low cloud. Ten Lancasters failed to return from the Mittelland debacle. (On 21/22 November 138 Lancasters and six Mosquitoes of 627 Squadron successfully attacked the canal banks of the Mittelland Canal at Gravenhorst and 123 Lancasters and five more Mosquitoes of 627 Squadron attacked the Dortmund-Ems Canal near Ladbergen and a breach was made in the only branch of the aqueduct which had been repaired since the last raid.)

Meanwhile, 128 Lancasters of 3 Group carried out a Gee-H night raid on Koblenz on 6/7 November. Eighteen Mosquitoes raided Hannover and eight more went to Herford, while forty-eight Mosquitoes of the LNSF carried out a Spoof raid on Gelsenkirchen to draw German night-fighters away from the two Main Force raids. The Gelsenkirchen raid began as planned, five minutes ahead of the two other attacks, at 19.25 hours. The city was still burning as a result of an afternoon raid that day by 738 RAF bombers. From their altitude of 25,000ft the Mosquitoes added their red and green TIs and high explosives to the fires. A few searchlights and only very light flak greeted the crews over the devastated city. On 25/26 November a force of sixty-eight Mosquitoes attacked Nuremberg.

After a couple of operations like their first two in September Flight Lieutenant Chas Lockyer DFC and Flying Officer Bart 'Jock' Sherry DFC* were thoughtful about their chance of doing another fifty-three to complete the tour. Lockyer noted that 'the good old Law of Averages prevailed and the next half a dozen ops were comparatively uneventful'. But on 3/4 November, whilst taking off for another Berlin raid, their aircraft had swung to the left due to the port engine suddenly losing power. Lockyer closed the throttles but he was unable to prevent the Mosquito from crashing into the radar hut at the other side of the perimeter track. Both men's top front teeth were knocked out but they were fit to fly again three weeks later, as Lockyer recounts:[145]

At the end of November there was a somewhat more unwelcome diversion in our flying programme when somebody at Command decided to try a daylight raid, employing the American pattern of flying in tight formation, led by two Oboe Mosquitoes and bombing in salvo. With no defensive armament we were inclined to think that this was carrying cockiness a bit too far, even though we were promised a fighter escort. [This operation took place on 29/30 November, with thirty Mosquitoes of 8 (PFF) Group attacking the *Gessellschaft Teerverwertung* tar and benzol plant in the Meiderich district of Duisburg]. At the appointed time and place the Mossies rendezvoused, but with no sign of the fighter escort, and since our time schedule didn't allow us to hang about waiting for them we pressed on. We were halfway along the straight and level run-up to the target when I spotted high above us a cluster of fighters. They had single engines and square wing tips, so they were probably Me 109s. If they were, then that famous 'corner of a foreign field' was going to accommodate twenty-four new permanent guests. It was with a tremendous sense of relief that we identified them as Mustangs, as they dived towards us. Just at that moment the flak started to burst among us and they retreated as quickly as they'd arrived and stood off nicely out of range, eyeing us, as Jock put it so succinctly, with morbid interest. They rejoined us when we were safely away from the target and we saw no sign of enemy fighters.[146]

We flew two more daylights after that but luckily never encountered any enemy fighter opposition, but on one of the raids I saw a Fortress going down over Rotterdam, and watching that great aircraft helplessly spiralling earthwards was one of my saddest moments of the War. After that we were thankful for the cover of darkness again, although Berlin appeared on the board at briefing more and more often until Jock knew its street geography better than he knew his native Glasgow. We got belted once more on a low-level attack on Erfurt and flak pierced our hydraulics, resulting in a flight home with the bomb doors open. Without flaps we opted for the emergency landing strip at Woodbridge in Suffolk and landed without any further problems, although Jock had to use the emergency system to pump down the undercarriage. And so our tour drew towards its end, but we completed it in style with nine of our last eleven trips to Berlin and we finally finished about three weeks before the German surrender.

On the night of 9/10 December *Feldwebel* Reichenbach of 4./NJG11 claimed a Mosquito near Berlin but the sixty Mosquitoes that attacked the 'Big City' returned without loss. One of them was a 139 Squadron Mosquito XX, one of five pathfinders airborne that night, crewed by Flight Lieutenant Mark Wallis and Flight Lieutenant Fred Crawley DFC. Crawley explains:

The programme detailing the names of crews to fly that night on operations usually appeared on the mess notice-board around mid-day. No matter how many operations one had under your belt, even the most experienced felt that tightening in the stomach that presaged night operations. The night-flying test in the afternoon, with its well-tried procedures and familiarity, coupled with the affection that exists between a particular crew and a particular aeroplane, restored the confidence. Later, at the crew briefing, when the target and route details were disclosed, nerves were well under control. The route was to be: Upwood to the coast. Then north-eastwards across the North Sea to the red rock island of Heligoland (there was a fighter airstrip on the nearby sand island of Dune). Then landfall north of the wide Elbe estuary the Great Lakes NW of Berlin – Berlin return on a straight line to the Zuider Zee and home to base. The bomb load was to be: Target Indicator (Green & Yellow) bursting at 9,800ft; Target Indicator (Green with Red drip) bursting at 8,000ft; Photo-flash Red and one 500lb HE bomb. Weather conditions were described as good for take-off and return at Upwood, with considerable cloud formations over most of Germany.

Upwood at 20.45 hours was a busy airfield, with the Lancasters of 156 Squadron and the Mosquitoes of 139 vying with one another on the perimeter track, anxious to get airborne. Rolling now, with a touch of rudder to correct swing, we got off at 20.46 hours and with wheels and flaps up, turned straight away on to the first course of 067, climbing at 160 knots to the English coast at Cromer. The 20 minutes' climb to 17,000ft at the coast found the navigator busy using Gee fixes to keep the aircraft on the planned track to the coast. (The calculation of wind speed and direction was not of much use because of the continual increase in height, but the noting of drift often gave indication of what to expect.) The coastline showed clearly on H2S and Cromer passed underneath at 21.09 when navigation lights and IFF were switched off. The two-stage booster was now put in to the engines and the next 24 minutes had the aircraft climbing to the operational height of 25,000ft. During this time the navigator fixed the aircraft's position every 3 minutes by Gee and calculated the wind velocity throughout the height bands. Accurate navigation throughout this stage was vital to the success of the operation when the aircraft could be flown with no interference from enemy action. On this operation, the calculated winds proved to be considerably stronger than forecast and about 10-15° to the southward of forecast. Navigation proceeded steadily until about 5° east, when enemy jamming of Gee rendered the equipment ineffective.

On DR navigation, we turned almost due east running towards Heligoland, a good H_2S target and very useful, where the next turning point, about 8 miles north of the island, would require a route marker to be fired off for the Main Force. Although I had never seen an aircraft shot down over the island, their anti-aircraft guns could make it pretty uncomfortable if you strayed too near. The island of Heligoland appeared on the H_2S screen and from the present track it was clear we were running too close to the island on the starboard side. An 'S' turn to port put this right and at 22.02 hours the route marker for the Main Force was fired to indicate the turning point north of Heligoland. It was bitterly cold, with the outside temperature gauge indicating -50° and the heating system could not prevent thick ice forming on the inside of the side-blisters.

Approaching the enemy coast, the coastline showed clearly on H_2S and once again we had drifted two to three miles south of track of the flight plan. Another route marker was fired crossing the enemy coast with the Main Force being informed on VHF that the marker was 3 miles south of track. Shortly afterwards two more flares went down on the port side. At 22.17 radar bearings on Hamburg and Harburg confirmed that the aircraft was still 4 miles south of track plan and at 22.25 hours an alteration to port was made to reach the Great Lakes at 22.37 hours. At the Great Lakes the reception committee awaited. The lakes showed up so well on radar (despite German attempts to cover them to spoil radar definition) that most operations were routed to the lakes, leaving only a 10-minute run-in to Berlin. The Germans knew this and therefore used the lakes area as a marshalling point for fighters. Usually with a height advantage and with all the Mosquitoes streaming contrails, the night-fighters had a chance to intercept on the run-in to Berlin, when the pathfinder aircraft had to fly straight and level. Heads down and sweat it out, was the order of the day.

On this occasion no night-fighters were seen but heavy ack-ack was predicted as always with remarkable accuracy and the ride was uncomfortable. The TIs were dropped at 22.45 hours, Main Force being advised as the drop took place; straight and level for the photograph and then a hard turn to starboard, nose down to reduce height to 22,000ft and the hard slog home against the wind. The home trek against a 65-knot headwind meant almost a full hour's flying to reach the enemy coast. Gee was ineffective and pulses would only start to appear through the jamming when approaching the Zuider Zee; the route chosen was well clear of all large towns and H_2S gave little or no hope for bearings. The moon was now well up and the cloud layer well below at around 12-15,000ft. Visibility was good and it was a question of DR navigation and wait for Gee and H_2S to come back on line nearing the coast. It was remarkable how lonely it was at 22,000ft late at night with only the presence of your partner and the occasional brief comment between you to break the loneliness. The aircraft was going well and thoughts of bacon and eggs started to intrude and yet....

About 10° east and north of Hanover began the feeling of unease. Nothing appeared to be wrong but the feeling persisted and indeed was getting stronger. A check of fuel, engine gauges, etc., showed nothing out of the ordinary and in desperation I told my pilot I was going to have a look backwards through the astrodome (the only way you could see aft in a Mosquito). Unlike daytime when you cannot see easily into sun, at night you cannot see easily down moon as this is the dark side of the sky. Also at night you usually do not see objects you look at directly, so the trick is to keep your head moving and hope to see from the periphery of your eyes. After a good look around and seeing nothing except our own contrails, I was about to sit down when suddenly my eye picked up something on the dark side to starboard. Once having seen something and just like radar, you can 'wash' it with your eyes and you can see it. And there it was, a single-engined aircraft, slightly down and off to the starboard side, converging slowly. As the distance between us decreased and with us aware, as the fighter turned towards us we made a steep diving turn to starboard, putting us now in the dark side of the sky. Tracer went over the top of the aircraft but no hits. The westerly course was resumed shortly afterwards and when the feeling of unease returned I needed no telling our friend was back, probably having carried out the same manoeuvre as us. This time, without waiting for a sighting, a second hard turn to starboard was made, flying on a reciprocal course back into Germany for 2 minutes before resuming our course homewards. No more unease and I was convinced he had given up. I have often wondered about this episode. When I do, I always remember how deeply superstitious most aircrew were, always wearing the same things and dressing in the same order and so on, before an operation; perhaps senses were more finely attuned during those difficult times. There were no more problems coming home. The Zuider Zee came up, Gee came back on stream and the gradual let-down over the North Sea to land at base at 01.15 hours. We were welcomed by the WAAF Officer in the debriefing room with hot tea laced with real Jamaica rum and bacon and egg in the mess. It was nice to be back.

Two nights later when eighty-nine Mosquitoes went to various city targets one of the aircraft that failed to return from the raid on Hamburg was claimed by *Oberleutnant* Kurt Welter of II./NJG11.[147] *Unteroffizier* Scherl of 8./NJG1 claimed a Mosquito east of Hagen on the night of 12/13 December when 540 aircraft attacked Essen and, although six Lancasters were lost, all twenty-eight Mosquitoes that attacked Essen and forty-nine others that raided Osnabrück returned safely.[148] Another daylight raid was despatched on 11 December when two waves drawn from 128 Squadron raided Hamborn. When 13 December broke it was under a very heavy frost and towards mid-morning thick fog enveloped stations in Norfolk and operations were scrubbed very early. That night fifty-two

Lancasters and seven Mosquitoes of 5 Group flew to Norway to attack the German cruiser *Köln* but by the time they reached Oslo Fjord, the ship had sailed so instead other ships were bombed. On 15/16 December 327 Lancasters and Mosquitoes of 1, 6 and 8 Groups raided Ludwigshafen and one Lancaster was lost.

On 18 December the size of 8 Group was increased when 162 Squadron re-formed at Bourn under the command of Wing Commander J.D. Bolton DFC. The squadron was operational in two days but crews were unable to complete night flying tests on their H₂S-equipped Mosquito B.XXVs because of the foggy weather. At Bourn on the afternoon of 21 December the crews were called to briefing for a Spoof raid on the important marshalling yards at Cologne/Nippes which the 'heavies' would bomb an hour or two later, the purpose being to help cut the jugular vein feeding the Ardennes offensive. Altogether, 136 aircraft sixty-seven Lancasters, fifty-four Halifaxes and fifteen Mosquitoes of 4, 6, and 8 Groups, were despatched and no aircraft were lost. Soon 162 Squadron was accompanying 139 Squadron on target-marking duties. In December some Mosquito Oboe aircrew were selected to fly a new technique, as Flight Lieutenant John D.S. Garratt, a navigator on 109 Squadron at Little Staughton explains:

From time to time many enterprising COs devised schemes (some cracked-brained) for improving bombing accuracy and results, or for meeting emergency calls. One such scheme which involved 109 Squadron in December 1944, was the Formation Daylight. The idea was for an Oboe equipped aircraft to act as Lead Ship (to borrow the American term) for a small force of Light Night Striker Mosquitoes, each carrying 4,000 pounders to attack small, vital targets in daylight, thus achieving, it was hoped, great precision. For some odd reason, two 582 Squadron Lancaster B.VIs, specially adapted for the leadership role, were at first allocated. The Lanc VI was good for 28,000ft, but its cruising speed was incompatible with the Mosquito IX or XVI. It was to carry an extra Oboe pilot and navigator of 109 Squadron to fly the specialized bombing run. This arrangement was not popular with the Oboe Mossie crews.

One of these was Flight Lieutenant Bob Jordan and Ronnie Plunkett of 105 Squadron at Bourn. Plunkett heard about the scheme on 9 December:

My pilot and myself were asked to operate the Oboe on the operation, which took place on 23 December. [To disrupt enemy reinforcements for the Battle of the Bulge, an attack on the Cologne/Gremberg railway marshalling yards would be made by twenty-seven Lancasters and three Mosquitoes, while fifty-two Mosquitoes were to attack the railyards at Limburg and forty more to Siegburg]. We were to lead the second formation of ten, while Squadron Leader R.A.M. Palmer DFC [from 109 Squadron] and his crew, would lead the first formation [in an Oboe-equipped Lancaster borrowed from 582 Squadron]. Having flown a couple of experimental exercises with Squadron Leader Hildyard on a Lancaster for the purpose of familiarization, we were considered to be capable of carrying out this duty. At Graveley (35 Squadron Lancasters) we were detailed to fly on PB272 'X for X-Ray' flown by Flying Officer E.J. Rigby and his usual crew. Bob Jordan and I were to take over the aircraft 60 miles out from the target to operate the Oboe. We were airborne at 10.38 with eleven 1,000lb MC on the racks. Our outward run was normal except that two Lancs touched wings and went down. When we took over, our aircraft came under predicted heavy flak and caught fire, which the crew were able to extinguish. Since we were not on the beam we did not get a release signal and had to jettison the load from 17,000ft. We had a clear view of Squadron Leader Palmer leading the first formation just ahead and his aircraft came under intense AA fire. Smoke billowed from the Lanc and I wondered why he did not bale out there and then because there seemed to be no hope for them. A German fighter then attacked them but they carried on and completed their bombing run. The Lanc then went over on the port side and went down. I cannot think what, other than sheer determination, kept him on the bombing run. He carried out his duty in textbook fashion.[149] After this we went down to 6,000ft and Rigby did a good job getting us all back to Manston.

The attacks on Siegburg and Limburg, meanwhile, were, after a change of heart, finally led by Oboe Mosquitoes, not Lancasters, as Flight Lieutenant John Garratt recalls:

After some bright spark suggested using an Oboe Mosquito as Lead Ship, the obvious choice in the first place, my pilot, Flight Lieutenant CM. Rostron DFC and I were detailed as Lead Ship crew! The target was a small installation at Siegburg in western Germany. Our bomb load was four 500lb MC (surprisingly!) and our kite, XVI MM123. We were to take twelve Night Light Strikers carrying 4,000 pounders. Most of East Anglia was fog-bound and the heavies were stood down, but we could land on FIDO at Graveley if we had to. We were to rendezvous with the strikers off Orfordness and proceed in a loose gaggle to the Turning-on-Point for the bombing run where the strikers would close in to a tight formation of Vics astern of the lead ship, with bomb bay doors to open 2 minutes before release point. (The bomb doors on the Mosquito were notoriously prone to creep and if not fully open when the 'Cookie' went, they went with it!) The striker's navigators were to release on visual cue from the lead ship, which I thought was the weak link in the scheme.

We took off at 14.55. Just enough time to reach the target in daylight. To my surprise we met the strikers on time and in position as planned and flew across Holland into Germany to the Turning-on-Point where the Oboe ground stations called us in and we began to transmit, creating the beam. The run down the beam went OK. There was little opposition and the striker-pilots' station keeping, I thought, remarkable, particularly since we had had no formation practice. Our timing was bang-on and the release signal came loud and clear. Immediately after bomb release we broke formation in an orderly manner (bearing in mind it was now getting dark, even at 30-odd thousand feet) and flew back to base singly. All kites returned safely. At debriefing we were told our error off AP was small and the timing spot on. Despite enquiries I never learned whether the operation was considered a success. The intelligence bods never told us much, safe in their ivory towers. However, we never flew another 'Formation Daylight'.

A successful daylight raid was carried out on 31 December against the Oslo Gestapo Headquarters, in Victoria Terrasse (last bombed by 105 Squadron Mosquitoes on 25 September 1942) by the low-level Mosquito diver specialists of 627 Squadron, as Flying Officer Robert G. 'Bob' Boyden RCAF recounts:

After nearly a year of constant practice, I was a confident pilot. The fabulous Mosquito had become a part of me. Our Squadron's accuracy had become so dependable that we grew from a 'toy airplane' to a lethal weapon. A quick, accurate placing of our target indicators and bombs would keep the damage centred on the main target and that is why we were chosen for the Oslo raid. We followed the same routine procedure, getting ready for the big one. Our target practices over the Wash increased a little and the aircraft we were slated to fly were checked out. My aircraft was DZ611 and I had flown her on a number of previous trips. We didn't get all excited about this target beforehand, as the crews knew nothing of what the upper ranks were planning. Our first information about the trip to Oslo was that we were to fly to Peterhead in the northern part of Scotland, which would be our advance base. Peterhead was an American base for B-17s and would cut off at least two hours flight time and give us a good start. The trip would be a long one, 4 to 5 hours, and that can be very tiring if weather conditions require continuous instrument flying or if there are a few unfriendly happenings along the way. Briefing told us that Oslo was the target, not target for tonight, as this would be a daylight raid, which we did not do very often. In fact, I believe I flew only three trips in daylight. It's quite different, as you feel you stand out like a sore thumb. At this time of our action against the enemy we flew to our destination at 28,000ft and around the target would descend to 3,000ft to look over the area for a pre-determined aiming point. We would then dive to 1,000ft or 500ft levels. After we had done our marking, we would climb back to 28,000ft and return to base. This time the target had flak positions and the German Navy

119

was in the Oslo Fjord. Wing Commander Curry was our new CO and would lead the group, which was made up of two flights of six Mosquitoes each. Squadron Leader Peter Mallender would lead the second wave. Flying Officer Joe Willis was my new replacement navigator and we hadn't done very many trips together. He had been Squadron Leader Ronnie Churcher's navigator and needed some more trips to wind up his tour of operations.[150] Warrant Officer Ralph Fenwick, who had flown a tour on Lancasters, had retired after another 30 flights in his second tour of operations and had left the Squadron.

I left Woodhall Spa with a full load of gasoline and two 1,000lb bombs. The two-hour flight to Peterhead was uneventful but the air was rough along the coastline as we came in to land and to my embarrassment I came in pretty heavily. Why is it that it seems everyone is watching at a time like that and no one ever seems to notice when you 'grease it in'? The Mosquito wasn't a nose wheel job so it had to be landed in a three-point position. We were up bright and early the following morning as our target arrival time was 11.00 hours. Much to my surprise Wing Commander Curry wanted us to take off in a V formation, three at a time. I was No.3 on his starboard side, behind and to the right of his wing-tip. I can only guess that he wanted to do this because the Americans were masters of formation flying and our Wing Commander had embellished our skills over a glass of black and tan the previous evening. I had flown formation in our early training days but hadn't done any for a long time. During the night 2 to 3 inches of snow had fallen leaving a nice light cover on the ground. When our leader opened up his throttles for take-off the resulting blizzard astonished even a good Canadian prairie boy like me. It was complete blackout and strictly instrument flying and as soon as we were airborne I pulled sharply to starboard. We waited for the other nine to take-off at least we had cleared the runway for them and form up into the echelon position. We climbed 12,000ft on a heading of 045° NE and started our trip to Oslo.

The North Sea is a long trip and we had been told that the water was so cold we would last only 2 minutes in it. I don't remember worrying too much about it on such a beautiful day. We relaxed and enjoyed the scene just below us: snow covered mountains and bright sunshine. Willis and I did not talk much, if at all. Each of us absorbed in our own thoughts, thinking of what could happen and Willis no doubt wondering what this bastard was going to do next. We cleared the Norwegian coast, with the Oslo Fjord to our right. The target was ahead of us but not in sight, lost in the haze. Suddenly bursts of flak came up, seemingly one for each aircraft and right on altitude. This was the first time that I had seen, heard and smelled flak all at the same time and we flew through the cloud. Wing Commander Curry called out for us to descend on target, probably with his usual 'Tally Ho'. He started to dive and we followed his movements. No.2 disappeared from my view and left a gap between the leader and myself. He told No.2 to close in and after a couple of instructions like that I realised I was the one he called No.2. I had already pushed up my throttles at the start of the dive to close the gap. I broke radio silence to tell him I was No.3 and closing fast. Everything happened so quickly. We had of course fooled the flak defences by our diving attack and at last: the target. Bomb doors open, wait for right moment, push the button and hold at 1,000ft. I felt two concussions that closely followed one another. There was no smoke, no dust. I then pushed lower over the city and I saw an open-air skating rink with people skating around, unaware of the chaos and explosions behind them.[151]

Suddenly No.4 was descending down on top of us. Once again I had to break silence and suddenly what seemed to be a mountain loomed up right in front of us and as we changed our straight and level to a steep climb, flak came off the mountain, then we were up and over. Curry ordered us to break up, every man for himself. I was doing a left-hand turn to head back when I saw a valley to our right. I slid down into the valley and kept at a low level. We passed over the coast and I began the climb back to our operational altitude of 28,000ft. There wasn't a cloud in the sky and no enemy aircraft were in the vicinity. I didn't know until years later that the second wave did not drop their bombs. All they saw was smoke and dust at the target site and would not risk killing Norwegians.[152]

Squadron Leader Peter Mallender in D-Dog was briefed to lead the second wave of six aircraft, which were ordered not to bomb unless they could see the target.[153] Mallender recalls:

I was instructed to follow our intrepid leader after an interval of 5 minutes. I did and the German naval gunners quickly learned how fast a Mosquito could travel in a dive. All the aircraft in my flight were hit.

Mallender's navigator was Flight Lieutenant Wallace 'Johnno' Gaunt DFC, who had been a forester and much later, a glider instructor who had also completed thirty-three operations on Wellingtons on 466 Squadron. Gaunt recounts:

We had been briefed to expect flak from the hillside of the fjord. In fact the *Prinz Eugen* with its flotilla of destroyers was just to starboard of our low-level mid-day attack and they were most unfriendly. We suffered massive damage and I got a cannon shell through my right leg, exposing but not breaking the bone. I later found a small arms bullet in the left-hand breast pocket of my battle dress. It had travelled through the tube of gentian violet and a field dressing.

Mallender continues:

It missed the back of my head and went out through the Perspex top. Another hit removed the whole of the curved part of the port leading edge outboard of the engine leaving the very flat and unstreamlined bare main spar to face the force of wind of a Mosquito in a dive. I did manage to regain control from the violent yaw to port by slapping the starboard Merlin right back. I called to my No.2 to take over and I flew through the smoke and dust still obscuring the target. I cleared flying low over the Royal Palace and poor old D-Dog received another load of shot from a machine-gun sited on the roof, just beside a huge Red Cross. D-Dog still wanted to make circles to port and I thought that perhaps I would have a little more control if I were to jettison the drop tanks. I tried that; the starboard tank dropped away but apparently the wiring to the port drop tank had been severed and that one stayed there. The yaw was exacerbated by this and my right leg was very cramped but pushing as hard as I could we sidled our way home to Scotland after I had jettisoned our bomb load after crossing the Norwegian coast near Stavanger.

'Johnno' Gaunt adds:

Peter was doubtful whether the aircraft would make it back to UK so flew north for several minutes debating whether to turn right and head for Sweden, but the engines kept going and we gained height slowly, so went west over the mountains.

Mallender takes up the story again:

I stuck John in the backside with the little tube of morphia that we carried. Even so he managed to remain conscious and helped me to get home until I told him that I could see the Scottish coast. I had managed to crawl up to 5,000ft whilst crossing the sea and thought that it was about time I found out if I was going to be able to land the old lady. I dropped 15° of flap and throttled back the port engine a bit but before I had time to ease back to reduce speed much she shook violently and I noted that we were still flying at 140 knots. All the other aircraft had got safely home so I had the runway to myself. Rather unwisely, I now admit, I put the undercarriage down and the pre-stall shaking began immediately. I put down about 15° of flap (previous experiments had taught me that this seemed logical), I jettisoned the top hatch and powered her over the boundary at something near 140 knots. She stayed down all right but was burning up runway much too fast. I touched the brakes and that did it. She spun round and around like a Dervish, collapsed the under-carriage and finally came to rest in what I thought was a heap of ply, balsa wood and aluminium. I was really quite pleased to see George Curry's grinning visage looking down through the open hatch. He helped me out and together we lifted from his seat a very comatose, if rather battered, navigator.

'Johnno' Gaunt, who was put into an ambulance and taken to a Naval Hospital just north of Aberdeen, concludes:

> They sewed me up in the last hours of 1944. Got a bar to the DFC for that escapade; notified by telegram whilst in hospital.[154]

Back to night operations again and on the night of 31 December 1944, seventy-seven Mosquitoes were despatched to Berlin and twelve to Ludwigshafen. One of them was Z-Zebra[155] of 128 Squadron, which was flown by Flight Lieutenant Leicester G. Smith RNZAF, who with his navigator Warrant Officer Bill Lane completed fifty-two operations on the Mosquito B.XVI from October 1944 to April 1945. Twenty of these were to Berlin. Smith recalls:

> The big 'Cookie-carrier' B.XVI was a wonderful aircraft to fly and although it had a pressurised cabin it was not used on operations in case of internal damage from flak. Take-off time was 16.15 hours. The flight plan kept our aircraft to 10,000ft to 6° East and an indicated airspeed of 215 knots at that height. It was a glorious evening for flying, as so many evenings were and mainly over 7/10ths cloud. The reason given was to miss the cumulonimbus cloud tops. We climbed to operational height and levelled out at 26,000ft. Flak was heavy between Lübeck and Hamburg (commonly called the Gap). Shrapnel was whistling around everywhere but our sympathy went out to one Mosquito crew who was coned by at least twenty searchlights. Flak was bursting all around them, at least 2,000ft above and below. I was about 2 miles north of this aircraft and he flew straight through it all. It was an unforgettable sight. Otherwise we had a comfortable run to the Big City. Over Berlin all was quiet as the target indicators, reds and green, went down. A warning was issued that fighters were in the area but none were seen. Bill reported contrails 2-3,000ft above. We put our 'Cookie' down on schedule, took the photo and had a relatively quiet flight back to England. We were coned by many searchlights over the Woodbridge area (must have been an army exercise), landing at Wyton from an operation of 5 hours airborne.

One of the 692 Squadron crews who were laid on, unexpectedly, for the operation to the 'Big City' was Pilot Officer Ron H.M 'Percy' Vere and his navigator, Flight Lieutenant (later Squadron Leader) John F.P. Archbold, who remembers that:

> The crew conference was at midday and navigation briefing at 13.15 so there was just time for a meal before getting ready. Our aircraft was K-King (MM224), Burbidge and Ramage's kite. Rumour had it that everyone who flew K-King except those two had something happen to them. We hoped that we were the exception! After the meal I went down to the billet to put on my old blue sweater, cheque scarf and flying boots and then biked to the crew room for briefing. Phil Earnshaw was doing the nav. briefing

and a hell of a route it was too! Tonight's op was a maximum effort with twelve kites on the Battle Order. There was something else in the air too. Wadsworth, Burbidge, Crow, Nairn and two others hung about as if waiting for a briefing after we came out. Ron had been out to the kite to ground run it and put in the kit. I didn't have the time.

The route out was via Cromer, over the North Sea, with a turn towards Heligoland, then north of Lübeck before turning SE to Berlin. The return route was south of Magdeburg, through the gap between Osnabrück and Münster before turning west for the English Coast. This was a route I did not like. We were going in north of Hamburg and the gunners there were pretty hot. They got bags of practice anyway so I hoped it was 10/10ths there. We plotted tracks, working out courses and times and recording them in the log, sorting out maps and charts. Then, after about three quarters of an hour we checked our work against the Master Log for any errors (on either side) and then sat back and waited for the main briefing to begin.

In came the Met man. He started drawing in his cloudscapes on his briefing board. It didn't look too good to me: 8/10ths Stratocumulus over the sea, clearing over the Third Reich. It looked as if we could be shot at! The drivers airframe [pilots] drifted in and sat down with their navs and the CO, Wing Commander 'Joe' Northrop DSO DFC AFC followed them. We got on with the main briefing. It was 14.15. First, Flying Control, Squadron Leader 'Lemnos' Hemming, a pioneer in photographic reconnaissance in 1940 with Sidney Cotton. We knew him as 'Popeye' because he wore an eyepatch. He told us the runway would be the long one; no obstructions. There were no other comments. Then Met gave his story. "Target will be clear; no cloud from the time you cross the coast in till you come out again. Base would be clear for the return. Forecast winds are up in the seventies and eighties." My guess was that they may well be a little stronger than he told us. Now Intelligence: "Usual place chaps; you've all been there before, so I can't tell you anything you don't already know. Target height, 17,000ft." The CO, in his slow methodical way told us the tactics and the type of the TIs to be dropped. We were to bomb the highest concentration of Red TIs, or failing that, the highest concentration of Greens, or on good DR. Finally the CO detailed take-off times for each aircraft. Ours was 16.08 and the full number of aircraft would set course at 16.17.

Well, it all seemed pretty straightforward so far. I caught Percy's eye and grinned. He was a bit cheesed off because his wife had come down for the New Year's Eve party and we were only put on this trip at the last minute. I could see us belting back tonight! Well, that was the end of the briefing. It was now about 14.45 and we all trooped out to the crew room where old Chiefy Tite had organised tea and sandwiches for us. Having munched these we went to the locker room and collected Mae Wests and navigation bag, signed for the escape kit pack and straggled out to the crew buses waiting to take us out to our aircraft. Our dispersals were at the east end of the airfield, south of the main runway. The bus duly deposited us at K-King. First thing to do was to stow the Window bundles in the nose while the skipper went to sign the F700; then cram the nav bag in on top. After this I had to check that the DR compass master unit was serviceable, that the oxygen cocks were turned on and the camera magazine was fitted; all this is in the rear hatch. Next I had to see that the navigation lights were working and that the safety pins had been taken out of the 'Cookie'; an awkward job. You had to use a torch and peer through a small circular hole at the lug. All done; time for a last smoke.

Percy was round the back having his operational pee, which he never missed. The usual curious hush had settled on the aerodrome just before the kites started up. There just wasn't a sound. A train whistled in the distance and then the silence descended again. I looked at my watch: 20 minutes to take off. Time to get in. I took a last drag at my cigarette. Ron was getting himself strapped in. It took him some time to do this. And I put on my parachute harness after slipping a piece of gum into my mouth and got in myself. "Have a good trip, Sir" said the rigger, as he stowed the ladder and shut the door. Good lads, our ground crews. Bill Brodie the duty CO came round to each kite in turn to see if everything was OK. We gave him a thumbs-up and he went to the next kite. We were eighth off, so it was about time we started-up. The first kite had already started-up so Ron ran up the engines and I checked the Gee and Loran to see if they were working. All were OK and I switched them off until we were airborne. The first kite taxied out in the dusk of this December afternoon. After a while we waddled forward, checked the brakes and moved slowly out on to the perimeter track and on in the queue to the take off point. A last check: petrol on outers, pitot head heater on, nav lights and oxygen on, radiator shutters open. We got a flashing green Aldis from the ACP's caravan and taxied on to the runway. We could see the tail light of the kite in front climbing away. Ron taxied forward a little to straighten the tail wheel and then said, "OK, boy, here we go." And we were off.

The next few moments were pretty tense. We had the maximum load of fuel and bomb aboard. You hoped she wouldn't swing or burst a tyre because you had a rather unpleasant companion about 6 inches underneath where we were sitting. Then the tail came up and we watched the airspeed creep up to 120 knots; full boost and 3,000 revs. The red light at the end of the runway came rushing up and the kite heaved herself off the deck. (You could almost hear her grunt). Then the skipper gave the word to raise the undercarriage. We listened anxiously to the engines. A misfire now would be decidedly unpleasant, but they didn't miss (we had a damn good groundcrew) and we climbed away to the delay pattern. We passed over Little Staughton, 10 miles from base at 1,500ft before turning back towards base, still climbing, to set course with the others.

We crossed the coast at Cromer and headed for Heligoland. At 17.12 we began climbing to 20,000ft. We were gaining a lot of time. The kite wouldn't go less than 190 knots at 10,000ft. That was 15 knots too fast and we now had 9 minutes in hand and had to lose some time. We decided to orbit to lose 4 minutes. We got back on course and 10 minutes later started to climb again to 27,000ft. During this time we transferred fuel from 100 gallon drop tanks to the outer tanks. This was done automatically and a red light came on when the drop tanks were empty and you switched off the transfer switch. Slap bang over Heligoland six rocket shells rose up on the starboard beam about 2 miles away and we altered course slightly to the north and pressed on. At 18.05 the Yellow route marker went down dead ahead and fairly close. Good, that meant that we were pretty well leading the stream behind the markers. Gee was no longer available now and I worked feverishly to average a wind velocity to apply to courses ahead. We crossed the German coast 25 miles NW of Brunsbüttel. All cockpit lights were out now; both of us keeping our eyes skinned for flak and searchlights. It was very dark now and the low cloud had completely dispersed. The kite was going like a bomb. Wizard! Aha, there were the first searchlights, ahead and to starboard and there was flak too, 88mm stuff and rockets. You could see the rockets coming up as little red points of light moving very slowly at first. Then they suddenly sped up to your level and burst with an angry red flame. Not near us though. The searchlights were coning over to starboard. They were too far off to see if they'd got someone but it looked like it.

At 18.14 we crossed the Kiel Canal and we were right in the searchlight belt. A master searchlight picked us up and three or four others swung over on to us immediately. The bright red lamp of the 'Boozer' came on, indicating that we were being tracked by radar-controlled flak. Ron stuck his head well down in the cockpit and did a corkscrew while I kept watch aft. Wow! Just as well we did, a burst of rockets came up just where we were a few seconds before. No sign of any fighters, touch wood. Hello, someone else was coned to starboard. It looked like a Mossie too. I'll bet they were twitching like we were a moment ago. We've lost the searchlights now, or they lost us. We seemed to be getting past the worst of it and the time was 18.20. Ahead and a little to port went the green route-markers. We seemed to have lost a bit of ground doing avoiding action. We still had to get past Lübeck. At 18.25 the marker leader broadcast a 'Zephyr' message: "Wind 345°/90 knots".

Lübeck was comparatively quiet, thank the Lord. Just past there, on course, someone yelled, "Snappers" (enemy fighters spotted). Another colossal corkscrew and bags of rubbernecking, but we saw nothing. We resumed course and tried to get some LORAN to check position but there were no signals visible, only grass. We expected the red route marker any minute now. When it came I'd switch on the bombsight which must be done at least 15 minutes from the target so that it could warm up. The reds went. It was 18.40 and we'd just crossed over 10/10ths cloud below, which looked like going all the way to the 'Big Town'. So much for the Met briefing but a bit of luck for us. I switched on the bombsight and got the Window ready to push out through the wooden Window chute down through the small hatch in the floor.

Our ground speed on this leg was about 338 knots (about 390 mph). We began Windowing with 8 minutes to go. The chute was on the floor between your feet and you had to bend almost double to drop the bundles. You could hear a crackle on the R/T as they opened up in the slipstream. Back breaking job, this and it made you sweat like blazes. Just 5 minutes to go. We should see the first TI in a minute. Out went the last Window bundle. I stretched up and had a look out. We were still over 10/10ths cloud. Good. The first TI was slightly over to port. I dived into the bombing position. 'Dive' is a misnomer. With all the kit I had on it was more like a wrestling match! I switched on the sighting head and put the final wind velocity on the computer box and waited for the TIs to come into view. All of the nose except for the optically flat, heated bombing window was frosted up so I couldn't see very far ahead. A couple of minutes to go now.

"More red and green TIs going down", said Ron. "Bomb doors open".

"Bomb doors open" I repeated and I heard the rumbling roar as they opened and the wind whistled in the bomb bay.

"I'm running up on a bunch of three", said Ron. "Can you see them yet?"

I craned my neck close to the window and looked ahead sideways. "Yep, I can just see them." I said. "OK now, left-left, left-left, steady. We're running up nicely. Keep weaving a bit, we've a minute or so to go yet". I got the TIs up on the centre line of the graticule and thumbed the release switch. I would press this when the markers reached the cross line. A couple of big white flashes under the cloud up ahead showed that the first two 'Cookies' had gone down. I noticed them almost subconsciously.

"A little bit of flak to starboard," said Ron.

"OK, keep going", I said. "Right, right a little steady now, steady... BOMB GONE!" and I pressed the tit. There was a thud underneath as the lug sprang back and released the bomb. The camera whirred and the red light on the selector box came on. We had to keep straight and level for 45 seconds to get a photo of our bomb burst in relation to the TIs so as to be able to plot the accuracy later. I scrambled back into my seat and looked down the window chute. The wait seemed endless.

"Bomb doors closed", said Ron.

The camera green light came on. "Hold it", I said. There was a great flash under the cloud. "There she goes; OK, lets get the hell out of here" and we turned south-west to get out of the target area. I turned off the bombsight and bomb selector switches and looked aft. Some flak was coming up now and some searchlights were on under the cloud. It must have been pretty thin, but they were quite ineffective. More bomb flashes appeared as the TIs drifted slowly down into the cloud tops. It looked like quite a concentrated effort. Just after turning we saw a kite (possibly a cats-eye fighter, a 190, or a 109) shoot over us in the opposite direction leaving a contrail. He didn't appear to have seen us but we kept a sharp look out just in case there were any more. Things being quieter now I entered the time, height and heading of when we bombed.

Ron said, "Check the petrol, will you?"

I did so and found that we had about 330 gallons left; a little less than we expected, but OK. At 19.19 I tried to get some LORAN but the signals were very weak and I discarded them. I would try again later. Just then the expected green route markers appeared ahead, so we were OK and pretty well on track. At 19.24 we altered course and we crossed the Dutch coast at 20.22, altering course slightly to the north for Woodbridge and still keeping our height above 23,000ft. We switched on the IFF and 'identify' on Channel D, making a VHF broadcast: "Lounger K King identifying, out". (This was for the Fighter Command plot so that we are not mistaken for an enemy aircraft). I got a string of fixes across the North Sea. The crossing always seemed to me to be one of the longest parts of the trip. The 'Scu' cloud that had reappeared over Holland near the coast was about 4-5/10ths but it dispersed completely before we got to Woodbridge, leaving a clear night. I worked out the ETA coast as 20.49 and Ron increased speed a little. At 20.38 he said he could see lights ahead and when I looked out for a minute or two later I could see the semi-circle of sodium lights which marked the Woodbridge circuit dead ahead. We coasted in at 20.46 and began to lose height slowly, switching on the navigation lights as we did so. We were really moving now, with a ground speed of 260 knots. ETA base was 21.00. I began to relax a little.

Ron changed frequency from Channel D to Channel A (base frequency) to listen out for other aircraft. All the way in from the coast was airfield after airfield, each with its Drem system of lights illuminated and one or two searchlights (called Sandra lights) over the top, forming a sort of canopy. Someone once said that airfields in East Anglia were as thick as fleas on a dog's back. He was right. We began to look for the base lights and I set up homing co-ordinates on the Gee. At 20.56 we sighted two Sandra lights in an inverted V with a flashing white light in between them (this was the Station identification letters GR in front of Flying Control; all Station idents were lit but ours was the only one in this area to have them flashing). As soon as we saw this, Ron prepared to call up Flying Control and I started packing up my kit. As we did this, two other kites called up almost simultaneously; Chandler and Ginger Wood in J-Johnny and another kite. We came tearing up behind them. As we arrived over the airfield, Chandler called, "J Johnny, funnels" and landed. The other kite called "downwind". We now called up: "Control from Lounger K-King over".

Control replied, "Lounger K-King, prepare to land, runway 270, QFE 1029, over".

We replied, "K-King preparing to land, out"; which meant that we acknowledged permission to land and were listening out. Someone else called up just behind us.

I switched on the downward identification light and opened the radiator shutters. We reduced height to 1,500ft and turned downwind. Ron lowered the undercart, put down some flap and called, "K-King downwind, out". This was not acknowledged by Control. Instead they called the next aircraft and told it to prepare to land. Now we were turning across wind and one-quarter flap was lowered. Two green lights showed that the undercart was down. The circuit lights were visible over the port wing tip and the funnel lead-in lights appeared, with the Station ident letters GR illuminated on the outer circle at their head. We turned into the funnels at 900ft and called "K-King, funnels, over".

Control replied, "K-King, land, out". Had the runway not been clear we would have been told to overshoot and come in again. The runway lights appeared now, narrowing into the distance. Two flashing lights either side of the threshold were the glide path indicators, or GPIs, which showed the correct glide path. Now Ron hunched himself over the stick, put down full flap and concentrated on his landing. We went sliding in at 125 knots. The runway lights came up quickly at the end. We gave the usual heave as Ron checked her and closed the throttles, touching down on the main wheels at about 95 knots and trundling down the runway to the accompaniment of the usual crackles and pops from the exhausts of those wonderful Merlins. We turned left at the end of the runway, pulled up the flaps and called, "King clear" and then taxied back to dispersal with the engines purring away as if they'd only just started up. At dispersal we were waved in by the groundcrew and we stopped and opened the bomb doors. (You got reproachful looks from the groundcrew if you forgot this, for they then had to pump them down by hand; a tedious exercise). Ron pulled the cut-outs and the engines rumbled to a stop. We switched everything off and climbed out stiffly with a mutual grin of congratulation at completing another trip safely. This was our 27th. We collected our kit and stalked over to the waiting crew-bus laden with parachutes and harness, nav bag, camera magazine and the rest and were driven back to the crew room for interrogation.

Back at the crew room we dumped our kit and went in to be interrogated. First, the CO had a word about the trip in general, then Intelligence. They wanted to know in detail about the bombing: how concentrated was it? Was there much opposition? What were the relative positions of the TIs you bombed? Draw a sketch of them as you saw them please, and a host of other details. While this was going on coffee and rum was brought in and the second cigarette lit. Boy, did the first one taste good! Following this the navigators had to hand in their maps, charts and logs and pass on details of radar coverage, Gee jamming, hand over signals flimsies and camera magazine, while the pilots signed the Form 700 and told the engineers about any snags. At last all was done and it was away to the Mess for bacon and eggs and the New Year's Eve party.[156]

CHAPTER FIVE

Fast Night-Striking Force

Quite late on New Year's Eve 1944, eighteen crews in 692, 571 and 128 Squadrons were called to a briefing for details of a raid starting at first light on New Year's Day. At Oakington, five crews in 571 Squadron were briefed, as Flying Officer Douglas Tucker DFC, one of the pilots, recalls:

Until we were called to the briefing room, everything had been very hush-hush. No one seemed to know anything definite or even if there was to be a raid at all. Because of the secrecy preceding the flight I did not take Sergeant Bert Cook, my own navigator (who had already completed twenty-four trips with me). Instead I took Flight Sergeant Fred David. We all soon knew what was in front of us. The German Army was hard pressed bringing equipment and men to the fighting front, mainly by rail. It was reasoned that if this rail traffic could be delayed even for a day or two, the confusion this could cause would be quite substantial. There was little point in bombing railway tracks because even if the rails were hit it was a relatively short time before the craters were filled in and new track laid. It was decided that if it were possible to bomb twenty-four strategic tunnels at precisely the same time, it would be bound to cause considerable confusion and inconvenience at the very least. How to achieve this was the next problem. Even using the latest bombsights, it would have been impossible to bomb from normal height and get the result, which was so essential. To fly across enemy territory in daylight would have been hazardous, especially when the desired effect would not be achieved. The decision was made to use Mosquito bombers, which were very fast and could out-pace most fighters.

Most of our aircraft were equipped with drop tanks; these were two torpedo-shaped tanks, one on each wing; which gave us greatly increased range. Although the tanks could be jettisoned at the press of a button, we were told not to drop them unless an extra-speed emergency that required a few extra knots. Our particular model of Mosquito carried no armour plating or armament. This saving of weight gave us an increase of speed, so we relied on this to keep us out of trouble, combined with our usual operational height in excess of 25,000ft, which was twice as high as most of the heavy bombers flew to drop their bombs. What type of bomb would be needed? We normally carried the one 4,000lb HE bomb, shaped like an oversize dustbin. Because of the relatively thin casing, they exploded on impact. On this operation, we were to drop our bomb as low as it was possible for us to fly in, aiming for 50 to 100ft above ground level. A 4,000lb bomb with orthodox casing was selected and fitted with a 30-second delay fuse. This would avert any possibility of us being blown apart by the blast. For some weeks, we had been practicing low-level bombing with small practice bombs. We were told that it was just a general exercise. In the event, this practice was of little use as the targets [in the Eifel and Ardennes area] were on a completely flat piece of ground and train tunnels are usually on the edge of hills, or hilly areas. To make a direct hit would require flying towards the mouth of the tunnel, dropping the bomb and hopefully pulling up at the last second to clear the hill.[157]

We had been flying low for some time before reaching the area of the tunnel, map reading frantically as the ground sped underneath us. We looked for landmarks such as railway lines, rivers, canals and villages etc. Suddenly, just ahead of us was the tunnel and just as quickly we had passed it. We were covering the ground at approximately 1 mile every 9 seconds. Two German soldiers had stopped their motorcycle and sidecar on a bend of a hill. One was astride the motorcycle and the other stood by his sidecar. It would have been difficult to have missed them, as they were less than 100ft away from me when I passed over them. They must have heard the roar of low flying aircraft and stopped just as I flew past. I throttled back, lowered the flaps slightly and turned to the left to complete a circle in the hope of locating the end of the tunnel again. After 360° we located the tunnel mouth. Now we would have to complete another circuit to make preparations for dropping the bomb. On the down leg I opened the bomb bay doors. This did nothing to improve the flying characteristics of the aircraft. At our normal bombing height of 5 miles this made little difference, except that it was more difficult to hold a steady course, but at ground level it was a different sensation altogether.

We came round for our third run towards the tunnel entrance. As we circled close to the hill we were suddenly confronted with a wood on a rise in the ground. Instinctively, I pushed both throttle controls forward hard and pulled the control column back equally hard. The aircraft continued towards the ground and the trees for what seemed a lifetime, until it wallowed, not flew, over the obstruction. Apart from shattering raw nerves, it also meant that we would have to do another circuit. So far we had met no opposition from either the air or the ground, but every second we spent in the locality increased the risk of attack. It would have been quite difficult for anyone to hit us, as we were in and out of trees and often below the top of the hill but there was always the chance that someone was just around the corner with a machine gun. It wasn't until the fifth time that we were at the correct height, position, speed etc and at last I was able to press the bomb release button. I pulled the aircraft up just clear of the surrounding land, closed the bomb-bay doors and then decided to do one more circuit to have a look at the result of our efforts. As we headed back towards the tunnel entrance the bomb exploded with a cloud of smoke earth and bricks.

We had hit the target.[158] Now our task was completed we realised that we had been in the area far too long. In actual time, the whole episode was only a matter of minutes, but whilst it was happening it seemed like an eternity. I decided to start back by flying at maximum speed in the general direction we had come-in, keeping fairly close to the ground. On our normal night-time raids we were given courses and heights and speed to fly at, both to and from the target and we were not allowed to deviate unless there was some exceptional reason. On this trip we were given a free hand on our return journey to decide what height and courses we should take depending on prevailing conditions based on weather, enemy opposition etc as long as we approached the English Coast within a certain corridor. Our route home took us back along the railway line from the tunnel we had bombed. Within a few minutes, we sighted a train steaming in the direction of the tunnel. They certainly would have a delay. We could take no action against the train, or anything else for that matter. We had dropped our one and only bomb and we carried no armaments except for our revolvers. I continued at low level. I didn't want to risk climbing and thus reducing our speed considerably. I waited until we reached what appeared to be a quiet patch of country and started a shallow climb, maintaining as high a forward speed as possible. Luck was still with us. We did not see any opposition, although it was quite likely that a ground barrage had opened up on us after we had gone past, but we saw nothing and suffered no damage, we considered in this case 'ignorance was bliss.'

Soon the North Sea was visible. So far we had been flying in the general direction of the East Coast. Now we could relax a little, we set course to cross the area allocated to us. As we approached England we discovered that a thick blanket of fog covered the land. There was no shortage of fuel but if we flew on to our base near Cambridge and then had to divert to another airfield there was a possibility of running low. A landing at Manston, an emergency airfield on the coast of Kent was the safest solution. The station was equipped with FIDO and if our reasoning was correct, it would be switched on in these conditions: it was. FIDO consisted of metal tubes similar to scaffolding drilled with many holes. This tubing was fixed to each side of the runway and petrol was pumped through the pipes at a rate of 1,000 gallons per minute and ignited. The whole system burned with a roar like a gigantic blowlamp. I had not seen FIDO in operation before and it proved to be a most amazing sight. It was just like looking down a giant map, which was covered by a sheet of cotton wool except for a square that had been cut out with scissors. The airfield was completely fog-free, with the sun shining on the runways. We landed without any problems and taxied to the far end of the runway, clear of the pipes. It was essential that the aircraft was not allowed to veer on landing. The heat was so intense that it could be felt through the cockpit windows with the plane in the middle of the runway.

On landing we contacted our squadron by phone to let them know we were back safely, then a visit to the mess for a hearty breakfast, the second that day. A further call to the squadron confirmed that all fog had cleared and with the aircraft refuelled, we took off and headed for Oakington. After debriefing I met Bert Cook, who was most upset to have missed the trip. He informed me that he would be flying that evening with another pilot. We were a small squadron with no surplus crews. He said that after the night's trip he and I would be back together again. Neither of us particularly liked flying but we had built up a certain affinity and closeness that can only be produced by working under conditions such as we had during our 24 operational flights. Unfortunately, we were never to fly together again. Bert Cook and his temporary pilot were both killed that night in a crash landing coming back from the raid.

One bomb, dropped by B.XVI ML963 K-King, crewed by Flight Lieutenant Norman J. Griffiths and Flying Officer W.R. 'Bill' Ball, totally destroyed a tunnel at Bitburg. Bill Ball wrote:

At 100ft the ground simply raced beneath us like lightning. From the big railway junction, dead on ETA the tunnel came up in a flash and we could just not position ourselves in time. We undershot the target and went around again and this time ran up, dead in line, astonished that the ack-ack batteries had not yet been alerted. We rapidly reached the target, dropped the 4,000lb bomb and soared almost vertically to get away from the blast and when we had gained height, we looked back and saw a great column of brown-black smoke and sizeable debris rumbling upwards. A mixture of bricks and shattered masonry rising and falling and scattering wide. Norman and I agreed that it would be some time before trains ran again on that line.

During January-May 1945 LNSF Mosquitoes or Fast Night-Striking Force (FNSF), as it had become known at Bennett's insistence, made almost 4,000 sorties over the dwindling Reich for the loss of fifty-seven 'Mossies' shot down or written off. The FNSF bombed Berlin on sixty-one consecutive nights. On 14/15 January eighty-three Mosquitoes raided Berlin.[159] On 25 January 163 Squadron re-formed at Wyton on B.XXVs under the command of Wing Commander Broom[160] who had instructions from Air Vice Marshal Bennett for 163 Squadron to become operational immediately. No.163 Squadron flew its first operation on the night of 28/29 January when four B.XXVs dropped Window at Mainz (a spoof raid for the attacks by 602 aircraft on Stuttgart).

On the night of 29/30 January fifty-nine Mosquitoes were despatched to Berlin and fifty reached and bombed the city without loss. Flying Officer Philip Back and 23-year-old Pilot Officer Derek Tom Newell Smith DFC in 692 Squadron flew their fortieth op, with their second operation to the 'Big City' in 48 hours, in K-King. Derek Smith had flown a first tour as a sergeant navigator on Lancasters on 61 Squadron. He recalls:

We returned to be greeted by the news that FIDO at Graveley was u/s and we were diverted to Bradwell Bay. Bradwell closed in and Coltishall advised that we should 'Get down where you can', which we did at Hethel, a USAF base [home to the 389th Bomb Group and B-24 Liberators] near Norwich. We were treated with the usual American hospitality but memory of the operational meal remains in both our minds: it was roast pork with gooseberry jam! Next morning our T-Tommy came up with a very bad mag drop so we were taken by jeep to Philip's home at Brundall for lunch and the weather closed in so we stayed the night. Next morning Philip's father took us by car to Norwich where we were picked up by American transport for a run-up of the now serviceable T-Tommy but we were at Hethel for another night due to continuing bad weather. On 1 February we woke to a sunny morning and after a good breakfast at Hethel, we were back at Graveley by 09.40 to find ourselves on the Battle Order for Berlin that night. Because of the problems at Hethel, T-Tommy had to be checked so we were in K-King, Burbidge and Ramage's aircraft, which had an indifferent reputation put about by them, I suspect, to keep it out of other hands!

The trip was fairly routine until we lost an engine near Hanover and again the weather was u/s with low cloud and snowstorms over East Anglia and the 8 Group area, so once more it was a matter of getting down where we could. The Mossie flew very well on one engine but it could be tricky to land especially at night and in the poor weather conditions, so we proceeded with care losing height gradually knowing we were over East Anglia. Eventually we saw a rocket come up through the low cloud and, losing more height, spotted a runway [Rougham near Bury St. Edmunds and home to the 94th Bomb Group] very well illuminated by wartime standards. Phil was quickly into the approach only to find a Fortress being landed; hence all the illumination. However, short of fuel, on one engine and in a snowstorm it was no place for the faint hearted. So Phil went in over the Fortress with rather too much height and speed so that we hit the runway past halfway but with hardly a bump. We shot off the end over a wide grassed area and ditch, to be brought to a halt at the perimeter by a row a tree stumps, one of which impacted with the starboard wing and slewed us around by 90°. Apart from two small cuts on my forehead neither of us were hurt. So we were very smartly out and taking off at speed in case of fire, only to be halted by the sound of voices behind us. We returned to find the aircraft was across a road with an Armstrong Siddeley car between the port engine and drop tank. We found four very lucky occupants, badly shocked but not too badly hurt, although one did need hospital treatment for a head wound requiring forty stitches. Then, almost immediately, we found ourselves surrounded by GIs brandishing rifles as they thought us to be a Messerschmitt 410 intruder. On this occasion we did not receive the usual American hospitality probably due to our unannounced arrival and were left to make our own way back to Cambridge by train to await being picked up by car. Of course we were lugging our flying gear and received some odd glances from other passengers. However, we made our way to the University Air Squadron and were lavished with their hospitality. Of course, we were not very popular with Burbidge and Ramage but everyone was pleased to see us in one piece, especially the Wing CO who put us in the Battle Order for the next two nights! However, they were Wiesbaden and Dortmund, rather easier than the six to Berlin up to that ending up at Rougham. This latter Philip described as being due to the bad judgement of a single engine approach. Many Mossie aircrew did not survive to tell the tale of single-engine landings. So in my view, as the only witness, to land from a steep approach at night in a snowstorm and to be able to walk away was a small miracle aided by airmanship of the highest order.[161]

In February the FNSF flew 1,662 sorties. The 1/2 February attack on Berlin was the largest Mosquito bombing attack on the Reich capital since the formation of the LNSF. In total 122 aircraft were dispatched in two waves to bomb Berlin. No aircraft were lost. On the night of 2/3 February while two other forces bombed Wiesbaden and Wanne-Eickel 250 Lancasters and eleven Mosquitoes of 5 Group attempted to bomb Karlsruhe. Cloud cover over the target caused the raid to be a complete failure and the Mosquito marker aircraft that dived over the city failed to establish the position of the target. To make matters worse, fourteen Lancasters were lost on the raid. German cities were continually bombed early in the month and all were marked by Mosquitoes of 8 and 5 Groups. On 5/6 February sixty-three Mosquitoes attacked Berlin. By way of a change, on 7/8 February 177 Lancasters and eleven Mosquitoes of 5 Group attacked a section of the Dortmund-Ems canal near Ladbergen with delayed action bombs but all missed their target. Meanwhile, thirty-eight Mosquitoes attacked Magdeburg, sixteen bombed Mainz and forty-one others attacked five different targets. On 8/9 February Mosquitoes of 5 and 8 Groups marked Pölitz oil refineries for 472 Lancasters, twelve of which were lost. The first wave's objective was marked by the 5 Group method. The Pathfinder Mosquitoes of 8 Group marked the second. The weather was clear and the bombing was extremely accurate and severe damage was caused. On 10/11

February eighty-two Mosquitoes bombed Hanover and another eleven raided Essen. The night following, 12/13 February, seventy-two Mosquitoes attacked Stuttgart and fifteen others hit Misburg and Würzburg.

At Woodhall Spa on 13 February Mancunian Flight Lieutenant William Worthington Topper RAFVR and his navigator Flying Officer Victor W. 'Garth' Davies went to the ops room to be told, 'It's Dresden tonight and Topper will lead'. A fair-haired giant of a man, Davies had teamed up with Topper in June 1944. Topper could see why he was called 'Garth'. He was straight out of the cartoon strip in the *Daily Mirror*. He noticed too that under his navigator's badge Davies wore the oak leaf of a 'Mention' [MiD, Mention in Despatches] and learned later from him that he was now on a second tour. In December 1943 while flying on 466 Squadron, Davies had been shot down over Belgium in a Halifax, picked up by the Resistance and had then walked back over the Pyrenees into Spain and back home via Gibraltar. He had never been far afield in his youth but he walked for miles and this and his mother's strict upbringing, which included senna pod tea every Friday, stood him in good stead in the five days and nights walk through the Pyrenees in continuous rain. While Garth was the country lad, Topper was the 'posh city gent' who owned an open top 3-litre Bentley Red Label that his dog 'Rostov' rode in standing erect in all his glory as the two aircrew motored over the Pennines. (The story was that Topper had bought the Bentley from a lady in Bournemouth for about £20). Topper and Garth Davies had their differences, settled many times over pints of beer and they became, like many Mosquito crews in wartime, almost inseparable. In addition to Topper and Davies there were seven other crews in the marking team.[162] Bill Topper remembers:

> We went into briefing where we heard that the defences were not known (the city had received attention once before, early in the war, but by common consent it had been considered a 'safe' one, full of art treasures and architecturally superb). There would probably be light flak from trains in the marshalling yards as the Germans were sending supplies up to the front, about 70 miles East. The Russians had asked for the target because of this. There were a lot of refugees moving West. If we got into difficulty, that is where we should head, West, in no circumstances force-land to the East. The problem was going to be a weather front with 10/10 cloud over the target – unless it cleared as we got there.

For most of the participating aircrew the Dresden raid would just be another bombing attack.[163] Dresden would be bombed in two RAF assaults 3 hours apart, the first by 244 Lancasters of 5 Group and the second by 529 Lancasters of 1, 3, 6 and 8 Groups. No. 5 Group was to attack at 22.15 hours, using its own pathfinder technique to mark the target. This was a combination of two Lancaster Squadrons; 83 and 97, to illuminate the target with Primary Blind Markers and parachute flares to light up the target and 627 Squadron whose Mosquitoes carried ten Red TIs, two yellow and eight *Wanganuis*, to mark visually the aiming point from low level. The first Mosquito marker had to identify and mark with Red TI to be assessed if accurate to be backed up by other Markers. If the Red TIs were more than 50 yards from the aiming point the Marker Leader would call for the 'Yellows' to be dropped alongside the inaccurate Reds and then the target would have to be marked by the other members of the team. The bomber crews knew that if they saw reds and yellows together they had to ignore them and concentrate on the Red TIs burning alone. If the marking point could not be marked the primary Greens were to be backed up with Reds. If the Greens were inaccurate, the aiming point was to be marked with Reds. At Dresden the aiming-point was to be a sports stadium in the centre of the city situated near the lines of railway and river, which would serve as a pointer to the Stadium for the Marker Force, especially since it was anticipated that visibility might not be too good. There were six such stadiums in the area so particular care had to be exercised. At 22.13 hours 244 Lancasters, controlled throughout by the Master Bomber, would begin their attack. A second raid was timed for 01.30 hours on the 14th by another 529 aircraft of Bomber Command.[164] Calculations were that a delay of 3 hours would allow the fires to get a grip on the sector (provided the first attack was successful) and fire brigades from other cities would concentrate fighting the fires. In this second attack target marking was to be carried out by 8 Pathfinder Group.

Bill Topper continues:

> We were operating at the limit of our fuel, which didn't allow a very good dog-leg to disguise the target.[165] We went towards Chemnitz and at the last minute altered course a few degrees and went down fairly rapidly from 30,000ft to 5,000ft at which point I called the Controller, who was Maurice Smith of 54 Base, to say I was clear of cloud cover. Garth said we would be there in one minute, packed all his navigational gear away, put the bag on his knees, his usual habit, with the Target map on top. This had concentric circles 100 yards apart surrounding the marking point, which was the centre of the middle stadium of a line of three across the city. In the event the bad weather front cleared as we got there and 5 Group Lancasters had no trouble in seeing the TIs. And then, as if by magic, the green flares were coming down from the two Lancaster Pathfinder Squadrons of 5 Group, which were flying at about 12,000ft. Down below was the city, as though in bright moonlight, with the river winding through it and there were the three sports stadiums. By now we were down to 3,000ft and Garth had selected the switches on the bomb panel. I called out, "Tally Ho!" and down we went, Garth calling out each 100ft as the altimeter unwound itself. At 700ft I pressed the button and away went a 1,000lb Red. Immediately there came a brilliant flash under the aircraft; the first photograph had been taken. We continued down to about 400ft where we levelled out, counting the flashes: six. Up with the nose and full power to regain height quickly, but there was no need: there was no flak;

the city was undefended. (The opposition started the next day, at home, at Westminster).[166] The Controller and one of the markers assessed the TI as 100 yards east and backing up was called for. One by one they called up, went in, cleared and climbed away while the red splash in the stadium widened and intensified.

Flight Lieutenant 'Mad Jock' Walker and his observer, Warrant Officer (later Flying Officer) Ken Oatley were Marker 2. Oatley recalls:

We had just about completed our turn when to my relief the illuminating flares started to fall about 5 miles away. Down we went like the clappers to 2,000ft and under the flares into the target area in no time at all. Jock immediately picked up the aiming point in the sports drome. With great excitement at the thought of being first man in for a change, he was just turning into his dive and about to press his R/T button for a 'Number 2 Tally Ho'. When up came Bill Topper, I might say as usual and stole his thunder for the umpteenth time. However, we held off and followed him in, marked and as we pulled away, went between the spires of the cathedral. Levelling out we then proceeded to do a low-level run around the city. It was quite eerie. The streets were deserted. It was like daylight down there. You could see quite clearly the beautiful old buildings. There was not a sign of life anywhere, nor was there any gunfire, but now the bombs had begun to fall. Jock asked me for a course for home, which I gave him from my pre-flight plan. Being true to his name and much to my horror, he flew straight over the target area with 4,000 pounders crumping underneath and goodness knows what else coming down around us, he set course as if we were on a cross-country.

Marker 8, Flying Officer Ronald Wingate Olsen and Flying Officer Frank Leslie 'Chipps' Chipperfleld, were last to mark, in Y-Yankee.[167] They had been together on Lancasters on 619 Squadron and had been awarded the DFC. Olsen was 24 years old and it seemed to him that Chipps was very old, though he was about 10 years older. Chipperfield was very musical and he often played the grand piano in the Mess at Woodhall Spa, but only when few members were about in case he got himself recruited for ENSA. They were in their bombing dive when the Master Bomber called, "Markers to clear the target area" followed by, "Main Force come in and bomb". Olsen recalls:

Having released my markers and while pulling out of my dive, two things caused consternation: first there, right in front of me were the spires and turrets of Dresden Cathedral; secondly, some of the Lancasters were a bit quick to drop their 'Cookies', much to my discomfort. The aircraft was rocked and buffeted just like a rowboat in a heavy sea. It was on this occasion that I learned why the safety height to fly when 4,000lb bombs were exploding was a minimum of 4,000ft. This was the only occasion

139

when I pushed the throttles through the gate to get extra power from the engines to get out of the area as quickly as possible. The return journey was uneventful after we had been given, "Markers go home", by the Marker Leader. On landing Chipps and I were tired. Debriefing, followed by a meal and back to the billet to get some much-needed sleep. Later we realised that this operation was the longest time we had been airborne in a Mosquito: 5 hours 40 minutes, close to the maximum fuel endurance.[168]

Topper concludes:

Controller asked for the area to be cleared; a few moments later the bombs started to erupt in patches over the still, to us, silent city. I asked permission to send the marking team home, got it and passed it over. One by one the markers acknowledged. Garth and I continued to fly round the city at about 1,500ft. It had attractive bridges across the river and many black and white buildings. The bombing intensified and we climbed higher and away. There was a brilliant blue flash, probably a power station, and I commented on this to the Controller. A little later he said I could go; I acknowledged. Garth gave me the course to steer. As we climbed up, the glow on the ground spread as we went into thin cloud, then disappeared as the cloud thickened. At 30,000ft there were stars overhead and three hours of flying to be done. We were airborne for 6 hours. No.5 Group's raid was at 21.00 hours and four groups of Bomber Command arrived at midnight to add to the flames already growing. The Americans followed up at 08.00 hours the next day to add to the destruction, which PRU photographs, taken later that day, showed to be very extensive. As an operation it was markedly successful. Nothing went wrong the marking went smoothly, the bombing was accurate and there were very few casualties in the bomber force. The Mosquitoes were aided by the newly installed LORAN sets, which enabled reliance on radar to be greatly extended as they went further east and out of Gee range. Navigation was excellent, spot on by all navigators, and the backing-up by all markers first rate. Little did we all think as we climbed down from our aircraft that the following days were going to see an outcry, which was to continue for months and years.[169]

So great were the conflagrations caused by the firestorms created in the great heat generated in the first attack that crews in the second attack reported the glow was visible 200 miles from the target. In a firestorm similar to that created in Hamburg on 27/28 July 1943, an estimated 50,000 Germans died in Dresden.

During February-March 1945 several major raids were carried out on the Dortmund-Ems canal and naval mines code-named Young Yams were dropped in the Kiel Canal. On 7 February 177 Lancasters and ten Mosquito markers of 627 Squadron attacked the Dortmund-Ems canal section near Ladbergen with delayed action bombs but the raid was unsuccessful. The bombs fell in nearby fields and three Lancasters were lost. Mosquitoes of 627 Squadron and 154 Lancasters of 5 Group returned to the Gravenhorst area again on the night of 20/21 February when 514 Lancasters and fourteen Mosquitoes of 1, 3, 6 and 8 Groups set out for Dortmund. Another 173 bombers raided Düsseldorf and 128 aircraft attacked Monheim. Wing Commander Brian R.W. 'Darkie' Hallows DFC, the new CO of 627 Squadron, led ten Mosquito markers to Gravenhorst.[170] One of his Mosquito crews was Flying Officer Sam Fletcher and 20-year old Sergeant William W. 'Bill' Burke of 627 Squadron. Bill Burke had ended his first tour of operations with 207 Squadron as a non-commissioned navigator on Lancaster Main Force bombers of 5 Group at Spilsby in January and in no way did he want to join 627 Squadron. He had been flying on operations continually since August 1944 and as he admits, 'was a shade flak happy. His hands had the typical 'Bomber Command Twitch' which sometimes called for an effort to light a cigarette. Even so, he liked life on an operational squadron and he wanted to stay there. Burke states:

> This may seem surprising, but my 21st birthday was still 5 months away and at that age one can crave excitement. Danger, like drugs can become habit forming and one wants a regular 'injection' of danger and the enormous elation, which one experiences when the danger is past and one is still unharmed. It was also a glamorous life. The contract was that you flew the RAF's aeroplanes with the statistical likelihood that you would be killed, wounded or taken prisoner. In return the RAF paid you well, gave you a great deal of freedom and time off, with leave every 6 weeks and extended to you a variety of privileges, which few enjoyed in war-time Britain. These included such things as aircrew meals of bacon and eggs, special sweet rations, petrol for use in private cars and sheets to sleep in. If you weren't required for flying you could do more or less what you liked; large numbers of air crew in 'Bomber Counties' such as Lincolnshire largely spent their spare time in pubs and dance halls, getting 'stoned' and chasing the ladies. Cities such as Nottingham were an air crew paradise and the White Hart in Lincoln was like a 5 Group Headquarters. To turn one's back on this sort of *Boys Own Paper* life and the conscious pride that goes with being a member of an acknowledged *corps d'elite* was unthinkable to me at the time. So I decided to volunteer for an immediate second tour of operations, but not with Bomber Command. I decided I would like to fly in Beaufighters in Scotland on anti-shipping strikes. I thought that would be exciting but my request was turned down out of hand. At the same time I was told that if I did want to continue operational flying I could be fixed up with a navigator's job on 627 and if I accepted I could have a commission, so the deal was done. (My promotion to Pilot Officer came through on 26 March).
>
> Having accepted the switch somewhat reluctantly and unenthusiastically my initial impressions, when I arrived at Woodhall Spa,

were not especially favourable. At Spilsby with two squadrons of Lancasters, each with seven to the crew, there was a very considerable number of air crew personnel to chum up with, whereas at Woodhall there was a single squadron (617 messed quite separately from 627 Squadron) with only two crew per aircraft. So the total number of aircraft with whom to make friends and associate was quite small. Having said that, it was obvious that, on average, the flying personnel were generally more battle-hardened and experienced than those of a normal Main Force bomber squadron. Shortly after my arrival I moved over to the Officers' Mess and soon found that although I had joined a smaller 'family' I was with excellent comrades for whom I quickly acquired considerable respect. One really did feel that one was a member of a 'crack' unit.

At first, flying in Mosquitoes proved a daunting experience for the 6ft tall Bill Burke, who was dismayed at the prospect of having to escape from a burning Mosquito through an opening the about the size of a 'large rabbit hutch door'. After a few familiarisation flights he soon thought to himself, 'My God what have I let myself in for?' And devoutly wished to be back aboard a Lancaster! Another problem was light, or the lack of it. In a Lancaster a navigator was able to flood the navigating table and instruments with light as curtains prevented light entering the cockpit. In a Mosquito he was expected to navigate with a small insignificant light playing on his chart. Burke wanted as much light as possible. Conversely, his pilot, concerned about attracting night fighters, wanted as little light as possible; indeed, if it had been feasible he would have preferred his navigator to work in the dark. Bill explains:

One way or another I was totally uneasy and lacking in confidence as I navigated us towards the Mittelland canal and then I had an extraordinary stroke of good fortune. At 'H-10' (ten minutes before H-Hour) I announced to Sam that by my calculations we were precisely over the target and precisely to time. Hardly had I spoken when the first batch of illuminating flares hit the sky and came cascading down around us. Never having seen them before I mistakenly supposed that they were parachutists and shouted out accordingly. To have been brought to the target with such exactitude in terms of time and position must have made Sam think that he had acquired one of the best navigators in Bomber Command. (A misapprehension, which I certainly put right on a later operation when I missed the target by 40-50 miles!) Be that as it may, the next ten minutes proved to be exciting to a degree, which I find difficult to put into words. The illuminating flares and searchlights made the whole area as bright as day or at least as bright as the brightest moonlight. The sky was a mass of exploding anti-aircraft shells and lazily moving streams of tracer amongst which we played a competitive game of 'who can find the target first?' Scudding above the ground at well below 1,000ft we heard one of the other markers shout,

"Tally Ho" and saw his marker strike the ground and burst into coloured fire. I listened as Marker Leader inspected the accuracy and gave us instructions for backing up the marker on the ground. As Sam and I dive bombed with our marker I could see the ground in almost minute detail. With our marker released and bomb doors closed we hurried off for home as fast as our two Merlins would take us. As we did so and still hyped up from the excitement of the attack, I thought of what we had done. I marvelled at the smooth organisation and knew that I would never do anything else in life, which could match the excitement and elation, which this form of flying offered. And I never have. It made the adrenaline run like a ten-minute 'white-knuckle' ride! (The operation against the Mittelland canal was repeated the following night and it proved equally exciting).

The Master Bomber ordered the 20/21 February raid to be abandoned because the area was covered by low cloud and it prevented anyone marking the target. The 5 Group force was diverted due to fog at their bases and 'Darkie' Hallows landed at RAF Coltishall. Hallows recalls:

On 21 February the raid was repeated and the Canal was well and truly marked and clobbered. I did not drop markers, as the aiming point was well marked and backing up was not required.[171]

Including diversionary and minor operations aircraft, 1,283 sorties were flown on the night of 20/21 February. Included in this grand total were sixty-six Mosquitoes of 8 Group that went to Berlin. One of these was B.XVI MM202 V-Victor, which was flown by Flight Lieutenant Leicester G. Smith RNZAF and his RAF navigator Warrant Officer Bill Lane who were flying their 31st operation on 128 Squadron. Smith recalls:

Our flight time was 4 hours 15 minutes. Many and varied are the experiences Bill and I shared over enemy territory, but that evening we certainly had our fair share. We were over the 'Big City' at 20.10 hours. We had quite a fire raging in the cockpit prior to the release of our 'Cookie' and on our bombing run. I didn't realise its importance as, at the time, my attention was on the controls, but seeing the flames a foot in length urgent action was required. At the time we were at 27,000ft, ahead of schedule by 3 minutes, so climbed the aircraft for the bombing run. Within a few seconds the cockpit was filled with black smoke following from the flames, which Bill thought at first was from the outside. My first action was to dive the aircraft, thinking incendiary bullets from an enemy fighter had hit us. The flames were out before Bill could use the fire extinguisher and with target indicators ahead, we dropped the 'Cookie'. The resulting dive found the aircraft at 22,000ft, so I turned onto 296° and on the way out an enemy fighter jumped us, as indicated by the white flashing

'Boozer' light in the cockpit. I took evasive action but as nothing happened I climbed back to operational height. All told a very busy 5 minutes. However, I am a little ahead with my story. It had been a wonderful night flying the German skies with, at times, cirrus cloud for protection, but on the whole quite clear. Flying in near Hanover the plotting became serious, as the contrails were plainly visible to the enemy. At 20.00 hours I switched over to the main fuel tanks, with V-Victor cruising at a steady 180 knots, while Bill computed his final course to Berlin. In the distance and at operational height, we could plainly see the lights of the advancing Russian Army approximately 50 miles away and east from Berlin. To the north the Germans had lit their Dummy City, so that before our ETA it was quite a pretty sight. However, with our own red and yellow target indicators clearly visible, on these we bombed Berlin.

It was during our bombing run that the fire started and so did the problems. In fact, who would feel secure at the thought of baling out over the 'Big City' with all the 'Cookies' bursting. But my chief concern was getting V-Victor back to good flying condition. We had lost 5,000ft in the dive. At a steady 200 knots and back at 26,000ft turned onto a course of 285°. Near Hanover the guns were opening up on the incoming wave of Mosquitoes, one of which nearly hit us. Seeing the black outline rushing towards our aircraft at an incredible speed, I just had time to ease the control column back and fly over the top of the other aircraft. Left to ourselves, the enemy plotting ceased and then was able to enjoy the glory of the German skies. With no navigational equipment serviceable, Bill pinpointed himself over the Dutch coast, the water shone in brilliance, giving perfect relief to the coastline. Over the North Sea we received a Vector from 'Largetype' [a codeword for the controller] to steer 305°, only 20° difference from Bill's original course. We returned to clear sky over England, landed at Wyton 21.53 hours, after circling base for 15 minutes. Because Gee and LORAN navigational aids went unserviceable at the same instant we assumed the fire was the cause. On return the aircraft was checked and no sign found of a fire from the motors. We were both very relieved and again our faithful friend, V-Victor, brought us safely home.

On 28 February/1 March when seventy-four Mosquitoes went to Berlin, five Mosquitoes of 627 Squadron dropped mines in the Kiel Canal. On the night of 2/3 March seven Mosquitoes of 627 Squadron were despatched to the Kiel Canal to lay mines. One of the Mosquito pilots who took part, Flying Officer Ron Olsen DFC, remembers:

Because of the strong coastal and river bank defences, mining in daylight was out. The raids had to be done at low level and at night. The moon being used as a means of illumination, it would have to be a full or almost full moon. The mine-dropping run would be towards the moon, as that gave best visibility and the best time would be before the moon had risen too high above the horizon, giving a better reflection from the water. The use of surprise was necessary so that the defences would not be alerted until the last possible moment. The mines themselves had to be dropped from a very low altitude as their individual arming systems, fusing and detonators would be damaged by too great an impact with the water. The placing of the mines to create the greatest amount of destruction to shipping required accuracy of timing and positioning. These were some of the factors considered in the planning of the operation. The Kiel Canal and Elbe River were both suitable targets for this method of laying naval mines and the Mosquito was well suited for this type of attack. The trips necessitated flying low over the North Sea to cross the enemy coast and find the appropriate river mouth, still at low level to keep up the element of surprise, flying through the defences along the route, picking out the identifying landmarks along the way to lead into the dropping point. It was very necessary to find the leading marks so that the mines could be dropped on the first run in, it being very hazardous missing the aiming point and having to line-up and run into the dropping zone a second time.

Flying Officer John Watt, Flight Lieutenant Johnny Whitehead's navigator on 627 Squadron, adds:

I was flat on the floor, looking down through the optical flat in the nose of the Mosquito, trying to map read along the canal in the moonlight and pretending we were not there. Flying at around 200ft I noticed a faint orange light reflected from the water. Having checked that we had not accidentally switched on any navigation lights I noticed that the reflection was not in quite the same place as before. On further close examination I discovered that I was looking through the perspex canopy of another Mosquito flying below and was seeing the dim orange light that the navigator used to illuminate his log and chart! After dropping, care had to be exercised as you climbed away for home as the flak ships at the entrance to the rivers and elsewhere were very active. Once over the sea and clear of the Islands it was possible to head for home without much worry as our speed would keep us clear of most troubles.[172]

On 5 March we flew in P-Peter to a synthetic-oil refinery target at Böhlen. Target marking was to be in the top corner of a quarry, backed up with green TIs. This was another long trip: we were airborne for 5 hours 20 minutes, landing back at Woodhall about 20 minutes past midnight.[173] During the month of March the squadron continued with various operations bearing in mind that the Allies were pressing forward across France and the Low countries and needing aerial support. Also, the Russian offensive was pushing westward and the destruction of targets now coming within our flying range would help the Russians. Strategic targets such as oil refineries at Harburg and the town of Wesel, which had become packed with troops behind the German lines, were bombed on several occasions. However, the laying of mines in the Elbe and canals continued.[174]

One of the most dramatic marking operations of the war occurred on 14 March when eight Oboe Mosquitoes of 105 and 109 Squadrons set out to mark for 5 Group Lancasters in attacks on the Bielefeld and Arnsberg viaducts. For filming purposes a 627 Squadron Mosquito at Woodhall Spa accompanied the Lancasters attacking the Bielefeld viaduct. Four Mosquitoes attempting to mark the Arnsberg viaduct for 9 Squadron failed in the attempt, with no damage to the viaduct. Three of the Oboe Mosquitoes were unable to mark the Bielefeld viaduct for 617 Squadron but Flying Officer G.W. Edwards of 105 Squadron succeeded in getting his markers on target and more than 100 yards of the Bielefeld viaduct collapsed under the explosions.[175] That same night 244 Lancasters and ten Mosquitoes of 5 Group attacked the Wintershall synthetic-oil refinery at Lützkendorf. For Bill Burke in 627 Squadron it was only the third time he had occasion to fly an operation on Mosquitoes since his first two against the Mittelland Canal in late February. If he expected the same excitement then he was bitterly disappointed as he explains:

> This time I was to be a Wind-Finder for the attack and not part of the marking team. To be frank, I hated the job. The purpose of wind finding was to establish an accurate measure of the wind speed and direction, at attack height in the target area, which could be fed into the bomb sight mechanism of the Main Force bombers. One flew to a predetermined point close to the target, a marker was put down on the ground and using the Mosquito's bombsight the navigator guided the pilot over the marker noting the precise time and air position. By repeating this operation 3 or 4 minutes later the navigator could make the required wind calculations. Three aircraft were used and by R/T the three navigators' assessments could be broadcast, with one navigator determining a mean. This would be relayed to the 'heavies' that would be closing in on the target. My reason for detesting the work was that I simply hated having to crawl into the nose of the aircraft to crouch over and use the bombsight in such a confined space and to slide back hurriedly into the cockpit; all in full flying kit. With my height I just found it physically difficult. Fortunately I was assigned to wind finding on only two other occasions: a repeat attack on the Lützkendorf oil plant on 8 April and an operation against the railway yards at Cham in the Sudetenland on 17 April. As a marker, I flew against Würzburg, Hamburg, Molbis near Leipzig and Komotau in Czechoslovakia during March and April. Additionally, I flew on the Gardening operation in the River Elbe on 22 March. For me that operation was so unusual that I

can still recall it clearly. The illuminating flares were hanging over the river as our attacking Mosquitoes skimmed over the water passing by a variety of ships at mast level before unloading our naval mines, then disappearing into the darkness homeward bound. The scene had an eerie unreal quality about it. In the bright but artificial light one was close enough to see the faces of individual sailors. Komotau marshalling yards on 18 April was my last operational foray before the European war ended and with the cessation of hostilities I expected to be able to hang up my navigators' kit like the proverbial cowboys' boots.[176]

The largest operation ever on Berlin occurred on the night of 21/22 March when 138 Mosquitoes attacked in two waves. Only one aircraft was lost. On 27/28 March three Mosquitoes of the Light Night-Striking Force were missing from a raid on Berlin.[177] It was also the night that 627 Squadron lost its last Mosquito on operations when F-Freddie flown by Flying Officer William A. 'Bill' Barnett RNZAF and 20-year old Flight Sergeant Johnny Day RAAF from Murrumbeena, Victoria, was lost on the 5 Group minelaying operation in the River Elbe. They had just dropped two mines from a height of 100ft and at 120 mph when they found a flak ship waiting which set the port engine on fire. Over the air the big towering New Zealander announced in his broad dialect, 'I lost an engine over the taaarget!' Nothing more was heard from them. The fire in F For Freddie's port engine went out and Barnett commenced to climb on course for home but at just over 600ft off Heligoland the starboard engine cut out. He set about for ditching the aircraft, as he recalls:

Fortunately it was full moon and I could see a moon path on the water, which I used as a landing path. This helped me to level off just above the water and raise the nose of the Mossie just before we hit. The tail of the aircraft struck first and we evidently bounced some 300-400 yards before hitting the water again. I was not aware of anything after feeling the tail section hit, until I regained consciousness in the cockpit, which was nose down about 60° to 70° and the water was up to my face. I must have swallowed some as I came to coughing and spluttering. I had trouble seeing until I realised that blood was in my eyes from what, I found later, were two large gashes in my forehead. My navigator had gone and the emergency hatch was out, so I started trying to get out but with parachute and dinghy attached it took some time. I eventually fell out only to sink with the weight of everything and I could not get my Mae West to inflate, but after several descents and surfacings I got the Mae West inflated. The next problem was removing the parachute and then to inflate the K-type dinghy. Eventually, after lots of panic, the dinghy inflated and I climbed in. The aircraft dinghy was not released due to the automatic release being disconnected some days previously and the manual control, by the time I tried to reach it, was 2ft under water and out of reach. Johnny had got out much earlier but had left his dinghy in the nose of the aircraft and he was sitting up on the trailing edge of the wing and engine nacelle when I managed to sort myself out. After some discussion I tried to support both of us on my dinghy but it was no use, so he got back onto the remains of the aircraft. He was feeling very cold but there was nothing we could do. At some time I must have lapsed into unconsciousness, as the next thing I knew it was daylight and I was in my dinghy, which was full of water and just buoyant, floating in a rough sea with nothing in sight.

The next days and nights passed without sight of anything, but the dinghy kept capsizing and filling with water. I opened my survival pack and wished that I had some water. The few biscuits in the pack were marvellous, even when soaked in salt water. I just drifted on, climbing back into the dinghy at frequent intervals, getting weaker each time and took to lying flat in the dinghy, but it filled with water too often and I swallowed some on a number of occasions; just as well, as I had no water. Then I awoke the fourth morning to find myself bouncing on a rock and close to a rock wall about 6 to 8ft high. I immediately tried to climb it but could not, so opened the survival pack and took a Benzadrine tablet. After this I felt a lot better so I had another go and, after considerable effort, reached the top of the wall, which was the level of the land. This turned out to be Hallig Hooge in the North Friesian Islands.[178]

One of the Berlin losses on 27/28 March was a Mosquito of 692 Squadron, which was lost without trace and the other two were involved in a collision. Flight Lieutenant Leicester G. Smith RNZAF and his RAF navigator Warrant Officer Bill Lane of 128 Squadron in Mosquito B.XVI MM202 V-Victor who were on their 44th op, were on the outward leg to Berlin over Holland at 25,200ft under a full moon when at about 20.00 hours they were involved in a collision with Mosquito RV326 of 571 Squadron. Smith recalls:

> We were waiting for the arrival of the Yellow Route Markers, which was but a couple of minutes away when the collision occurred. There was a sudden jolt, the sensation of which was like being bounced off a trampoline. The aircraft started to go into a spin to the right with the nose well down and for a time out of control.

RV326 spun in, crashing in a cornfield near the village of Zevenhuizen, or Seven Houses, near Groningen. Flying Officer Gordon D. 'Huddy' Hudson AFC RNZAF and his Canadian navigator Flying Officer Maurice G. Gant, who were on their 11th consecutive sortie to Berlin, were killed. They were later buried in a single coffin at the local cemetery of Leek.[179] Smith's starboard propeller had been torn away before it could be feathered and it cut a huge hole in the fuselage near the nose and splintered the cockpit windscreen. A small explosion followed and a fire broke out but Smith quickly extinguished it with the graviner and after falling to

16,000ft Smith was able to jettison his 'Cookie' and regain control. He nursed V-Victor back across the North Sea and put down safely at Woodbridge.

Throughout the attack on Berlin the searchlights were active across the city and a jet fighter was spotted in the area on the 128 Squadron bombing run. Flight Lieutenant Jim Dearlove and Sergeant Norman Jackson's Mosquito was coned on the bomb run and it was attacked by an Me 262 of 10./NJG11 just after they had dropped their 'Cookie'. He fired two short bursts of cannon fire, which missed the Mosquito and Dearlove was able to take evasive action and escape. Two other Mosquitoes, which failed to return were claimed shot down by Me 262 jet fighters. *Oberfeldwebel* Karl-Heinz Becker flew one of 10./NJG11's three Me 262A-1as this night and claimed his sixth victory. At 21.38 hours and flying at 27,600ft Becker clearly saw the RAF aircraft and opened fire at 150 metres whilst pulling up the nose of his aircraft. He hit the Mosquito squarely. Pulling away to the left Becker observed large burning parts of the Mosquito falling and scattering the ground near Nauen.[180]

On the night of 3/4 April ninety-five Mosquitoes went to Berlin, eight to Plauen and five to Magdeburg. A Mosquito of 139 Squadron flown by Canadian Squadron Leader Roy Dow DFC and Flt Lt J.S. Endersby was shot down on the raid on Magdeburg by an Me 262 of 10/NJG 11 for the only loss of the night. Roy Dow was on his 90th op. On 13/14 April twenty-nine Mosquitoes were despatched to bomb Berlin. One of the 608 Squadron Mosquito XVIs at Downham Market that took part was piloted by Flight Lieutenant George Nunn, who had flown a first tour on Wellingtons, his first being the 1,000-bomber raid on Cologne in May 1942. His navigator, Pilot Officer Harry S.T. Harris DFC, had flown a tour on Lancasters. Take-off was at 23.09 hours as Harry Harris recounts:

It was a warm spring night and the aircraft was reluctant to leave the ground as, apart from a full load of fuel, it carried a 'Cookie'. A minute later the aircraft staggered into the air and started the long, slow climb to 27,000ft As the roof of the crew compartment was perspex the view from both seats was very good. In addition there was a perspex blister on the side of the canopy next to the navigator. By putting his head in the blister he could see to the rear of the aircraft. The ability to see behind us was to play a vital part in just over two hours' time. The route was via Clacton, which was reached at 23.34 hours. Our height was then 17,000ft. From there we crossed the sea to reach the enemy coast at Westkapelle at 23.54 hours. At 23.59 hours the heading was changed to fly directly to Berlin. At 00.07 cruising level at 27,000ft was reached and we settled down to another hour's run to the target. It was black all around, although the stars shone brightly above. The navigational aid Gee was working well and fixes were obtained until 00.57. The route had taken us north of the Ruhr and then between Hanover and Magdeburg, avoiding the heavily defended areas of Germany. As we cruised at 310 mph we had no fear of enemy fighters as only jets could get at us and

149

we thought they were few and far between. And they would not bother us when the heavy four-engined bombers were attacking other targets that night, including Magdeburg. We passed 10 miles north of it at 13.00 hours. Although we knew there were Mosquitoes all around us heading for Berlin we saw none. On a previous trip one had crossed only about 30ft above us, the flames from his exhausts terrifyingly close.

George and I were no strangers to flak or fighters but there was always some apprehension as the target was approached. Mine came mainly from the thought that I might have made an error in navigation and that at the appointed time there would be no sign of the TIs by the Pathfinder Force going down on the target. Tonight they would illuminate at 01.11, 01.12, 01.13 and 01.14 hours. Green coloured markers at 5,000ft, red at 7,000ft and yellow at 10,000ft. The lower the markers the more accurate they ought to be. In the event the first TIs did not show until 01.16. At that time I was down in the nose ready to bomb. As we spotted the TIs a blue beam flashed across the sky and stayed on our aircraft. This was a master searchlight, controlled by radar and deadly accurate in picking out its victim. Within seconds ten or twelve white searchlight beams lit up our aircraft. For us this was not unusual. Nearly every time we went to Berlin we got coned. The good thing about it was that when I was down in the bombing position I didn't have to fumble around with a torch to set up the bombing instruments. With searchlights it was clearer than day. But that night they came too late to help me, as the bombing run had started. As the searchlights were positioned on the outer areas of Berlin they in no way affected the bombing run. At 01.18 I pressed the bomb release and the 'Cookie' slipped gently off the bomb rack and sped on its destructive way. The aircraft had to be flown straight and level for the next 42 seconds. This was the time for the 'Cookie' to reach the ground and explode, the aerial camera mounted in the aircraft hopefully photographing the point of impact. At 01.19 another group of TIs burst over the target, but by that time the 'Cookie' had exploded.

George Nunn continues:

The heavies were doing their stuff on Potsdam just outside Berlin. It was fairly spectacular; they seemed to have set fire to everything around. We were caught in the searchlights, having bombed on the markers and turned for home. The area illuminated by searchlights was too big to get out of. It was just a big pool of light made by perhaps fifteen searchlights, with you in the middle. No violent weaving, because that just kept you longer in the cone. Best to get out of the area as fast as you can. The nav. was watching behind us and I heard him call, "Fighter!"

Harry Harris continues:

We made a turn to the left, climbing steadily, until we were heading westwards for home. We did not even try to get out of the searchlight cone, as it would be quite impossible. The flak was below us and then it stopped. As we settled on course for home at 01.25 the searchlights suddenly went out. I looked through the blister to the rear of the aircraft and saw we were making extremely thick condensation trails. These are commonly seen today in the wake of high-flying jets and are caused by the heat from the engines condensing the water or ice crystals in the air into clouds, very white clouds, streaming out behind the aircraft. As I looked behind I saw a red and a green light just above our contrail. I said to George: "Some idiot is flying with his navigation lights on and is following behind us." As I said this I realised the lights were gaining on us very fast. I then knew it was not one of ours but the dreaded German jet. At that moment a white light appeared between the red and green lights from the nose of the aircraft. As it did I shouted, "Dive to starboard Go!" Simultaneously three things happened. The searchlights from the ground came on, bathing our aircraft in dazzling light. Secondly, George flung the Mosquito over to the right, pushing its nose hard down. And thirdly, a hail of coloured lights came across the top of the canopy. The fighter was firing and had just missed the cockpit, the cannon shells and tracer bullets missing us by inches. George said a rude word and pulled the aircraft over to the left. The change of attitude must have been sufficient for the light cone to flood the cockpit.

George Nunn recalls:

I got slightly blinded. The next thing I knew we were upside down. The nav. was not strapped in because he had been down in the nose, bombing. So, at that moment, he was up against the roof, all the gyros had toppled and so the instruments went berserk.

Harris adds:

As the aircraft was pushed around by George, I lost all sense of direction or attitude. I was forcibly shot out of my seat and crashed into the top of the perspex canopy. Then I was floating in the cockpit. Also floating was my parachute, which I grabbed and clipped on to my parachute harness. This harness was worn before entering the aircraft and the parachute itself was stowed in a special container in the bomb-aimer's position. The violent movements of the aircraft had dislodged it. It has two 'D' rings, which clip onto two hooks on the harness and the parachute was then in place on the chest; ready to jump. As I clipped on the parachute George said, very quietly: "I can't see. I've been blinded by the searchlights. Bale out, quickly." Having assured me that he would follow me out, I scrambled down to the nose, where the escape hatch was situated. It consisted of a square hole in the floor, with a door on the inside floor and another on the other side. This was the normal method of entry and exit. I found the handle, but I could not budge the door. Suddenly it was pitch black. The searchlight had gone out.

I cursed then, as I could not see and I could not open the escape hatch, possibly due to the twisting action of the aircraft or due to pressurisation. I gave it up and went back to George. He was still in his seat. As the aircraft turned over slowly, I saw fire through the top of the cockpit. I was looking down at the ground and the fires were the result of the heavy bomber attack on Potsdam. I asked George if he could see. He had closed his eyes to try to get his vision back. As several minutes had passed since he was blinded. I asked him if he would open his eyes and look for the fires. Fortune was with us as he saw the red light of the fires, now on his left side. Using the fires as reference, he slowly and carefully brought the aircraft on to a level keel. The instruments on the flight panel were useless. All the gyro-operated ones were spinning furiously, including the artificial horizon and compass. A careful reading of the altimeter, still moving erratically, showed the height as 20,000ft. Then, checking even more carefully, we found it to be 2,000ft; only 1,600ft above the ground. A check on my watch showed it was 15 minutes since evasive action had started. The Mosquito had descended at about 2,000ft per minute, so, luckily for us, it must have stayed level or even gained height at times.

Using burning Potsdam as a datum, I was able to give George a direction to go for England and then we climbed hurriedly away, shaken but undismayed. As the gyros settled we were able to resume normal flight and 110 minutes later were over base. An inspection of the aircraft on the ground showed a hole through the rudder and through the tail fin from a cannon shell. Following this line of sight, it missed the cockpit by an estimated 3 inches. There was no trace of any other hits. While on the staff of the RAF Flying College in 1955 I read a report by a German pilot of an Me 262. On 15 April 1945 he shot down a Mosquito just north of Berlin at 01.30 hours. Apparently he couldn't follow us down!

George Nunn commented:

I flew back on the Turn and Bank Indicator until the instruments recovered. We were minus half the tail, but this didn't affect the flying qualities of the aircraft.

Flight Lieutenant Mike Young and his navigator-observer Flying Officer Ted Jenner flew their first op on 142 Squadron on 11/12 April 1945 when 107 Mosquitoes attacked Berlin in three waves. According to Jenner the crew's arrival at Gransden Lodge on 6 April had been a chastening experience:

On arrival Mike and I were directed to a Nissen hut to dump our kit before seeing Wing Commander B.G.D. Nathan. We were greeted by; "Oh you'll be the replacements. Have these two beds; the bods who had them got the chop last night!"[181] Life, all of a sudden, seemed to become very precious! Watching the take-off with the Wingco later that evening, Lancasters of 405 RCAF at 19.30, Mosquitoes at 20.30, we were startled by a very large explosion nearby. A Mossie of 692 Squadron had felt obliged to jettison their 'Cookie' in the circuit! An evening or two later the crater was observed on a liberty run into Cambridge; impressive tribute to the power of the 4,000 pounder.

On our first operation the Navs. were issued with topographical maps of Northern Europe with over-printed Gee lattices. Somehow, we got to the target on time, dropped our 500lb bombs and turned for home. As a sprog Flying Officer I was fairly alarmed to find Gee so erratic, giving me impossible wind-speeds and ground speeds of over 600 mph. I knew that the Mossie was fast but thought, 'this can't be right!' We got back somehow on time but mentioned the hairy trip at debriefing. It turned out that the problem had arisen due to the Allies fast advance into Germany, with consequent movement of the mobile Gee transmitters. We had been issued with obsolete maps relating to previous positions. Thereafter, the WAAFs double checked the maps before issue and we had no further trouble. At breakfast the following morning one of the crews mentioned 'port engine running a bit rough on way home'. It transpired on a visit to dispersal later that an unexploded 20mm cannon shell was buried deep into their port engine boss, much to their surprise! At this time of the war, few of us ever saw an enemy aircraft, but some of them evidently saw us! On 19 April we took off for Berlin once more, returning to base after 45 minutes due to a faulty fuel pump and consequent non-functioning port engine. We knew the Mosquito could fly on one engine but the Gee had also gone U/S and it seemed pointless to press on to the enemy coast. Our debriefing was unpleasant: We had put up a real 'black', so we were told it was no eggs and bacon breakfast.

When the last attack on the Big City by Mosquitoes took place on the night of 20/21 April the progress by the Soviet forces converging on the Reich capital from the east was very plain to see. Tracer from field artillery could be seen going into Berlin itself when seventy-six Mosquitoes made six separate attacks on the Big City. Flying Officer A.C. Austin and Flying Officer P. Moorhead flying Mosquito XVI ML929 claimed the last bombs dropped on the 'Big City' when they released four 500 pounders at 14.14 hours British Time. All the aircraft returned safely. Two Mosquitoes were lost on 21/22 April when 107 Mosquitoes bombed Kiel. Another attack was flown against Kiel on 23/24 April by sixty Mosquitoes who returned without loss.

On Sunday, 25 April, 359 Lancasters and sixteen Mosquitoes set out to bomb Hitler's 'Eagle's Nest' chalet and fifty-five barracks at Berchetsgaden, deep in the Austrian Alps. Eight of the Mosquitoes were Oboe markers. One was crewed by Flight Lieutenant Derek James DFC and Flight Lieutenant John C. Sampson of 105 Squadron. Sampson recalls:

> We took off at 07.25 and the flight was 4 hours 15 minutes. We carried four red TIs to mark for the heavies. We flew at 36,000ft because of the Alps and, since Oboe signals went line of sight and did not follow the curvature of the earth, the further the target, the higher one needed to be. (Following the Normandy invasion, Oboe ground stations were located on the continent thus increasing the effective range of the system). I heard the first two dots of the release signal and then nothing more. We were unable to drop and brought the markers back to base. On investigation, it was established that a mountain peak between the ground station and the aircraft had blocked out the signal. No Oboe Mosquito was successful this day.

On 25/26 April twelve Mosquitoes dropped leaflets over PoW camps in Germany telling Allied prisoners the war was almost over. On 29 April flights to deliver food to the starving Dutch population in German-occupied Holland began. The operation, called Manna, took place using RAF and USAAF heavy bombers, their bomb bays filled with provisions instead of bombs, the food dropping areas being marked by the Oboe Mosquitoes. Meanwhile, it was feared that the enemy might stage a last stand in Norway when ships laden with troops began assembling at Kiel. Therefore, on the night of 2/3 May three final raids by 142 Mosquitoes of 8 Group (and thirty-seven Mosquitoes of 100 Group) were organised. In the first raid, a record 126 aircraft from 100 Group led by sixteen Oboe Mosquitoes attacked airfields in the Kiel area with Napalm and incendiaries. In the second and third attacks, one hour apart, 126 Mosquitoes of 8 Group bombed through thick cloud using H2X (the US development of H2S) and Oboe. It was the last Bomber Command raid of the war.

In the period January-May 1945, LNSF/FNSF Mosquitoes had flown almost 4,000 sorties. Altogether, 8 Group's Mosquito squadrons flew 27,239 operational sorties between May 1943 and 2/3 May 1945. (During these sorties, about ten thousand 4,000lb 'Cookies' were dropped on Germany). Yet they had the lowest losses in Bomber Command; just 108 (about one per 2,800 sorties). (A further eighty-eight Mosquitoes were written off on their return because of battle damage). This is an incredible achievement, even more remarkable when one considers that well over two-thirds of operations were flown on nights when the heavies were not operating.

CHAPTER SIX

The Banff Strike Wing

It was on 27 March 1943 that five crews from 235 Beaufighter Squadron were told that they were to be members of a new squadron that was to be formed. One of Coastal Command's tasks was to attack German capital ships, which lurked in the Norwegian fjords ready to break out for raids on the rich shipping lanes of the North Atlantic. One of the capital ships that posed the greatest threat to Allied shipping in 1943 was the *Tirpitz*, but sinking it with conventional weapons was out of the question. No.618 Squadron was formed at Skitten, a satellite airfield for Wick in Coastal Command, under strict secrecy on 1 April for the sole purpose of using Dr. Barnes Wallis' 'Highball' weapons against the *Tirpitz* and other capital ships at sea. (This was just one month before 617 Squadrons attack on the German dams on 16/17 May). The new 618 Squadron was made up of eight former Coastal Command Beaufighter crews including the CO, Wing Commander G.H.B. Hutchinson DFC and his navigator. Eleven other crews and their aircraft came from 105 and 139 Squadrons at RAF Marham. The Beaufighter crews joined the Mosquito crews at Marham on 30 March. When they had their first glimpse of a Mosquito Flying Officer A.H. 'Hilly' Hilliard and his navigator, Warrant Officer Jim Hoyle realised that their new squadron was to be equipped with these already legendary aircraft. Jim Hoyle recalled that Sergeant Joe Massey and his navigator Sergeant 'Lofty' Fletcher were from 139 Squadron. They had each been awarded a DFM for taking part in the first daylight raid on Berlin a month or so earlier. Jim continues:

I immediately remembered seeing them on a cinema newsreel, particularly 'Lofty' who responding in a very casual way to his interviewer, made the immortal remark that, "as we approached the target area there was a sudden break in the cloud and bless my soul, there was Berlin". Like me, Joe was from South Yorkshire and we quickly became firm friends. It was a sad irony that after such an adventure, he was later to lose his life in a road traffic accident whilst serving in the Far East.

Hilly and I made only one conversion flight in a Mosquito at Marham and for me it seemed a real treat to sit beside my pilot with a superb forward view, after previously being cooped up in splendid isolation, halfway down the fuselage of a Beaufighter. A day or so later we set off on the long rail journey to our new home at Skitten, north of Wick. Here we were very puzzled when our new Mosquitoes arrived as we immediately noticed a large gaping space under the fuselage from where the bomb doors had been removed. We were soon to learn that this space was to accommodate two bouncing bombs with the name of 'Highball' and that the squadron had been specially armed with these new weapons to attack the German battleship *Tirpitz*.[182] We did a lot of exciting low-level formation flying, up hill and down dale over the mountains of Northern Scotland, including mock attacks on an old French battleship, which had been moored very close to a hillside on Loch Cairnbawn in Sutherland. It all ended in anti-climax when the planned operation was aborted.[183]

Fortunately for us we were among four crews who were to regroup as 618 Squadron Special Detachment at Predannack under the leadership of Squadron Leader Charlie Rose DFC DFM. For pay and rations we were to be attached to 248 Beaufighter Squadron and later in 1944 at Portreath, when 248 also converted on to Mosquitoes we were to be absorbed as 'C' Flight on that squadron.[184] At a very quick briefing Charlie told us that our new Mosquitoes had been armed with yet another new weapon, a 57mm Molins gun, which fired 6 pounder shells and which was soon to be known as the 'Tsetse' after the fly which induced Sleeping Sickness in its victims.[185] The purpose of this heavy gun was for attacks on U boats, as they made their way into the ports of Lorient, St Nazaire and La Pallice etc on the western coast of France. At the time, we were told that information was being received from secret sources in France about the arrival of these U-boats, which had to make their final approach to the French coast on the surface because of underwater defences.

Hilly and I made our first flight in the new Mosquito on 18 October 1943 and we soon got down to some serious firing practice with our new gun. There was a hell of a bang when Hilly fired his first shot and although Charlie had warned us what to expect, it was still quite a severe shock to the nervous system. A flash eliminator had not yet been fitted and I noted with astonishment that a great tongue of flame, about 30ft in length, seemed to leap out of the front of the aircraft as each round was fired. I also observed that at the same time, the airspeed indicator went back to zero and such was the power of the recoil that it did in fact feel as though the plane had been literally stopped in its tracks. Although there had been some strengthening to the nose, it really was quite astonishing the amount of punishment that the Mosquito would take. No wonder it was later to become known as the Wooden Wonder.[186]

Sad to say the very first time that the gun was fired in anger, on 4 November, Charlie Rose was shot down by an armed trawler close to the French coast and he was killed.[187] For most of the time after that the Tsetse Flight was under the command of Flying Officer Doug Turner.[188]

By 1 January 1944 248 Squadron Mosquito Conversion Flight had mustered sixteen Tsetses and four FB.VIs available for anti-shipping operations. On 16 February, 248 and 618 Squadrons were moved to Portreath and the former would now provide fighter cover for the Tsetses for 618. On 20 February 248 Squadron flew its first interceptor and anti-shipping patrols in the Bay of Biscay. On 10 March four Mk.VIs, which escorted two XVIIIs to an area about 30 miles north of Gijon on the Spanish coast, got into a vicious dog-fight with eight to ten Ju 88s flying top cover for a German convoy of four destroyers and a U-boat. One of the Ju 88s immediately fell to a head-on attack by the four VIs and a second was shot down into the sea in flames shortly afterwards. The XVIIIs, meanwhile, went after the convoy. Squadron Leader Tony Phillips carried out four attacks on the U-boat and Flying Officer Doug Turner, two. They damaged a destroyer and Phillips blasted a Ju 88 out of the sky with four shots from his Molins gun. One of the shells literally tore an engine from the Ju 88 and it spiralled down into the sea.

On 25 March 1944 two Tsetses (one crewed by Flying Officer Doug Turner and Flying Officer Des Curtis and the other by Flying Officer A.H. 'Hilly' Hilliard and Warrant Officer Jimmy Hoyle) escorted by four Mk.VIs of 248 Squadron, came upon a formation of two armed minesweepers and a destroyer. In the middle of these escorts was U-976, a Type VIIC of 769 tons, commanded by *Oberleutnant zur see* Raimund Tiesler, which was returning to St Nazaire after being recalled from her second war cruise. The two pairs of escorting Mk.VIs dived on the escorting ships down sun and opened fire with cannon and machine guns. A heavy fusillade of fire from the ships came up to meet them. Doug Turner opened the attack on U-976 and got off five rounds with the Molins. Every burst was accompanied by recoil, which whipped the needle of the airspeed indicator back to zero. Turner made four attacks in all and fired off all his twenty-four rounds. One of the shells in the first diving attack destroyed one of the guns on the U-boat. Hilliard attacked U-976 on the waterline below the conning tower before breaking off. About ten hits were seen on the conning tower and on the forward deck near and below the waterline. After the attacks U-976 sank and Jimmy Hoyle saw an oil patch which he estimated to be 100 yards long and 30 yards wide. Survivors from the U-boat were picked up by the minesweepers. For this and earlier successful strikes, both Doug Turner and Des Curtis were awarded their DFCs.

On 27 March the same Tsetse crews, but with six FB.VIs of 248 Squadron, set out for the same area again. Intelligence had monitored the course taken by two Type VIIC U-boats, U-769 and U-960, which were due to arrive at La Pallice escorted by four 'M' Class minesweepers and two *Sperrbrechers* (merchantmen converted to flak ships). Jim Hoyle continues:

We set off with Doug Turner leading. In our pre-flight cockpit drill 'Hilly' and I discovered that neither the VHF nor intercom were working. This meant of course that we would not be able to make verbal contact with the other aircraft and that we would have to rely on sign language for our own internal communication, as the noise of the engines made normal conversation between pilot and navigator impossible. We took off at 07.00 hours and following the familiar route, we soon had the French Island of Ushant in sight. Carrying on round the Brest Peninsula and the Ile de Sein we flew on past the Ile de Croix, Belle Ile and the Ile de Noirmoutier. After rounding the Ile de Re and close to the mainland, we came across two U-boats escorted by four M-class minesweepers and half a dozen other ships. Some were *Sperrbrechers*, which had a rather fearsome reputation as they were armed to the teeth with anti-aircraft weaponry. Flak from these ships as well as from distant coastal batteries became intense and the sky seemed to be covered in flak bursts and tracer fire. I can still remember the odd, isolated feeling of being cut off from all verbal communication whilst watching the other Mosquitoes milling around the convoy without knowing precisely what was happening.

Suddenly Hilly peeled off and went into a headlong dive straight at one of the U-boats [U-960, commanded by *Oberleutnant zur see* Günther 'Heini' Heinrich][189] firing his Tsetse gun as he went in. Another Mosquito flown by Flight Lieutenant Jeffreys DFC had latched himself on to our port side to attack an adjacent escort ship whilst the remaining Mosquitoes were attacking other ships in the convoy. Meanwhile, I was busy with my heavy hand-held camera and one of my photographs was later to confirm a direct hit on the conning, tower. [The hit damaged U-960's periscope and inflicted shrapnel wounds to Heinrich and some of his crew].

'Hilly' Hilliard adds:

We had commenced our run-in and the formation began to climb from our low-level height and, as we did so, I counted about nine ships. On reaching 2,000ft I saw a U-boat at the rear end of the convoy, which was heading east. Behind the U-boat was a *Sperrbrecher*. The U-boat was in an ideal position, side-on, for a beam attack. I dipped my port wing to turn into it, as did the escort Mosquito on my left, so I dived for the U-boat and the escort went for the *Sperrbrecher*. Both of us had the sun behind us! At this time the rest of the formation was still climbing. As my R/T was u/s I was unaware of any orders being given regarding the attack on the shipping. During the attack there were plenty of black puffs from the anti-aircraft shells bursting all around us. The flak was everywhere. I saw spouts of water each end of the U-boat where my shells had hit the sea. I fired seven shells and I was sure that I hit my target. (As they were armour piercing shells, any contact would not show up like an explosive shell). I saw a green light fired from another ship, indicating that enemy aircraft were attacking the convoy. Just before I 'skimmed over' the U-boat at roof-top level I noticed the gunners near the conning tower pull their gun to the upright position. When we were slightly overhead that gun there was an almighty bang from underneath us.

Jim Hoyle continues:

After 'Hilly' had finished his attack he sped out to sea away from the coast. When I put my camera down. I saw to my consternation that the inspection cover doors over the machine guns had opened up and were now flapping madly in front of us. I realised that we must have been hit by flak and Hilly nodded grimly to acknowledge that he was already well aware of that fact. I had visions of one or both doors breaking off altogether as they continued to judder away on the long journey back and I wondered what effect it would have if either of the doors smashed through the cockpit window and landed in my lap. I decided that this could be safer than if they crashed into the tailplane. Either way, it wasn't a particularly happy prospect. When we finally landed at Portreath, we immediately spotted a large jagged shell hole, plumb in the centre of the nose cone at front of the fuselage with surrounding shrapnel damage caused by the resulting explosion. We were very fortunate that the Tsetse planes were among the very few Mosquitoes to carry armour protection in the nose section.

The brakes on the Mosquito failed and 'Hilly' Hilliard had to switch off the engines and come to a standstill at the end of the runway. He states:

Within minutes our groundcrew were towing us off with the maintenance tractor. We had been airborne for 4-hours and on checking the fuel gauge the port one was registering zero and starboard 10 gallons! On examining the aircraft the German 37mm shell from the U-boat had penetrated the circular inspection panel which on the underside of the Mosquito, dead centre of the nose. It had entered and exploded in the ammunition chamber, which housed the machine gun cartridges. Inside the chamber the cockpit was protected by armour plating, which was pitted with shrapnel, so we were lucky the shell did not set off any of the cartridges! If the shell from the U-boat had hit the Mosquito 3 to 4ft either side of the nose it would doubtless have hit a radiant cooler and thereby overheated an engine, putting it out of action. At debriefing we learned that five of the Mosquitoes sustained flak damage which caused one to crash land. My escort had a gun jam when he dived for the *Sperrbrecher* but he arrived back OK with no damage.[190]

On 11 April nine FB.VIs and two XVIIIs of 618 Detachment escorted by five FB.VIs from 248 Squadron and six from 151 Squadron at Predannack, took off on another coastal patrol from Portreath. One Mosquito crashed into a hill on take-off and one of the Tsetses returned early with mechanical problems. The others pressed on to St. Nazaire where they came upon a U-boat with a four-ship escort and an air umbrella of about a dozen Ju 88s. The FB.VIs attacked the escort ships and then turned their attention to the Ju 88s while Flight Lieutenant B.C. Roberts went after the U-boat. He saw spouts of water near the hull of the U-boat as he fired his Molins but could claim no definite hits. Flak was extremely heavy and Wing Commander O.J.M. Barron DFC, CO of 248 Squadron, and another Mosquito were shot down. Two of the Ju 88s were claimed destroyed. A third Mosquito was lost in a crash landing at Portreath. At the end of April 248 Squadron ground crews began fitting drop tanks in place of bombs below the wings of the Mosquitoes as the role of the squadron changed to land targets in support of the coming invasion of France. In May the 618 Squadron Special Detachment joined 248, the Tsetses now making attacks on surface vessels as well as U-boats. Their technique was to fire the armour-piercing shells through the wooden deck planking of the ships while rocket-firing Beaufighters went in at 500ft in a shallow dive.

On D-Day, 6 June, 248 Squadron flew five operations being employed on anti-shipping, escort and blockading sorties off the Normandy, Brittany and Biscay coasts, including one operation as escort for seventeen anti-flak Beaufighters of 144 Squadron and fourteen rocket-armed Beaufighters of 404 'Buffalo' Squadron RCAF. During one of these sorties, a 248 Squadron Mosquito shot down a Ju 188. On 7 June two Tsetses flown by Doug Turner and Des Curtis and Al Bonnett and 'Pickles' McNicol each made a run on a surfacing U-boat. A dozen 57mm shells were fired at U-212 but on his second run, Bonnett's cannon jammed and he only made a series of dummy runs on the U-boat, which crash-dived, leaving a pool of oil and a crewman on the surface.[191] Turner's Tsetse was hit by flak in the port wing and engine nacelle but he and Bonnett made it back to Cornwall safely. Two days later Bonnett and McNicol were killed following a search for survivors of a German destroyer in the Channel, when Wing Commander Tony Phillips DSO DFC, now CO of 248 Squadron, collided with their Mosquito while approaching the airfield. Phillips lost 6ft of his outer wing but landed safely.

On 10 June 248 Squadron Mosquitoes attacked U-821 near Ushant with such ferocity that the crew abandoned the submarine, which was then sunk by a Liberator of 206 Squadron. That afternoon Flight Lieutenant E.H. Jeffreys DFC and Pilot Officer D.A. Burden of 248 Squadron were shot down by a motor launch carrying the survivors of U-821. The other Mosquitoes promptly sank the launch. Attacks on U-boats were the order of the day throughout the summer of 1944, using wing-mounted 25lb Mk.XI depth charges for the first time on 22 June and also A.VIII mines, in addition to more conventional bombs, cannon and machine gun fire. One of the pilots on 248 Squadron who took part in the operation on 22 June was Les Doughty DFM MiD. He reports:

> As one of the crews listed we were warned to be ready for a possible pre-dawn take-off so Ron Grimes, my observer and myself retired very early just in case the show was on. We were woken at some ungodly hour in the

B.IVs DZ353/E and DZ367/J of 105 Squadron in formation. DZ353 flew its first operation in 105 Squadron on 23 October 1942 and later served with 139 and 627 Squadrons in 8 Group (PFF) before failing to return from a raid on the marshalling yards at Rennes on 8 June 1944. Flight Lieutenant Bill Steere DFM and Flying Officer 'Windy' Gale DFC RAAF were killed. (via Shuttleworth Coll)

B.Mk.IV Series ii DZ367/J of 139 Squadron is bombed up in preparation for a raid. (Note that the shrouded exhausts have scorched the cowlings). DZ367/J flew its first operation in 105 Squadron on 16 November 1942 and was one of the Squadron's eight Mosquitoes that took part in the Eindhoven raid on 6 December 1942 when it was flown by Flight Lieutenant Bill Blessing and Sergeant J. Lawson.

DZ367 failed to return from Berlin on 30 January 1943 when 105 and 139 Squadrons were the first to bomb Berlin, during an attempt to disrupt speeches by Goering and Nazi propaganda minister, Dr. Joseph Göebbels at Nazi rallies in the capital. Squadron Leader Donald F.W. Darling DFC and Flying Officer W. Wright were KIA. (via Shuttleworth Collection)

Flying Officer A.B. 'Smokey Joe' Stovel RCAF of 139 Squadron gets a light from his navigator Sergeant W. A. Nutter before setting off in B.IV DZ593/K on 27 May 1943 to bomb the Schott Glass Works at Jena with five other Mosquitoes. A few miles further on eight Mosquitoes of 105 Squadron bombed the Zeiss Optical factory. Stovel made it back and landed at 23.40 hrs. (via Peter Pereira)

Flying Officer William S.D. 'Jock' Sutherland, a Scot from Dollar, whose navigator was Flying Officer George Dean. Returning from Jena on 27 May 1943 they flew into high voltage overhead electric cables when attempting to land at RAF Coltishall and they crashed at Wroxham railway station. Both were killed. (RAF)

Squadron Leader Roy Ralston DSO DFM and Flight Lieutenant Syd Clayton DFC DFM of 105 Squadron on 9 December 1942 following a very successful bombing raid which saw them lead two other B.Mk.IVs in a 'skip bombing' raid on the mouth of a French railway tunnel. The attack was designed to cause damage to both the tunnel and the track on the other side, thus making it difficult for the Germans to effect repairs. (via Philip Birtles)

Flying Officer F.M. 'Bud' Fisher DFC, an American pilot from Pennsylvania, in front of his Mosquito DK337 GB-N *UNCLE SAM*. On 22/23 September 1943 Fisher and his navigator, Flight Sergeant Les Hogan DFM were one of twelve Oboe Mosquitoes that visited Emden as a diversion for the Main Force attacking Hanover. They crashed while flying Mk.IX LR506/E one mile north-west of RAF West Raynham and both men were killed. (RAF Marham)

Flying Officer Ralph Gamble Hayes DFM (left), navigator and (right) his pilot, Flight Lieutenant John 'Flash' Gordon DFC of 105 Squadron who were killed on the night of 5/6 November 1943 over Norfolk. They tried to land at Hardwick, an American B-24 Liberator base used by the 93rd Bomb Group, when at 21:10 hours, they crashed into a field at Road Green Farm, Hempnall, about 10 miles south of Norwich. (RAF Marham)

B.IVs of 105 Squadron taxi out at Marham. Left is DZ367 GB-J.

B.IV *POPEYE* veteran of 105 Squadron at RAF Marham.

139 Squadron at Marham. Wing Commander Peter Shand DSO DFC in white jacket stands before XD-G DZ421, which flew with the squadron from 31 December 1942 until it passed to 627 Squadron on 21 April 1944. It crashed at Wistow in Yorkshire on 25 July 1944 when it was being operated by 1655 MTU. Shand and his navigator Pilot Officer Christopher Handley DFM were shot down and killed over the Ijsselmeer on the night of 20/21 April 1943 by Oberleutnant Lothar Linke, Staffelkapitän 12./NJG1. DZ373 XD-B, next in the line, was hit by flak and caught fire before it crashed on the runway of Woensdrecht airfield and Sergeant Robert Pace and Pilot Officer George Cook were killed. Next in line are XD-T DZ423 and XD-K DZ428.

B.IV DZ476 XD-S for Scottie (note the dog and the black spinners) of 139 Squadron normally flown by Flying Officer G.S.W. Rennie RCAF and Pilot Officer W. Embry RCAF. The Canadian pairing flew DZ476 as one of the 'shallow diver' crews on raids to the railway engine sheds at Aulnoye on 4 March 1943 (a flak burst during this trip hit the fuselage and severed the rudder control cables), to the John Cockerill Steel and Armament Works at Liège on 12 March and to the engine sheds at Paderborn four days later. In April 1943 Rennie and Embry were one of eleven crews posted from Marham to Skitten to form 'A' Flight within the newly created 618 Squadron. They finished their tour and returned to Canada on 8 August 1944. DZ476 remained with 139 Squadron until on 1 April 1944 this Mosquito swung in a crosswind and suffered undercarriage collapse at Upwood.

Wing Commander Hughie Idwal Edwards VC DFC, an Australian of Welsh ancestry was 26 years old when he took command of 105 Squadron in August 1942. He was only the second Australian to receive the VC (the first had been awarded to Lieutenant F.H. McNamara of the RFC in WW1) for his leadership on 4 July 1941 when he led 9 Blenheims on the operation to Bremen. On 10 February 1943 Edwards was promoted Group Captain and he became station commander of Binbrook. By 1944 he had taken up an appointment in ACSEA, and held the rank of Senior Air Staff Officer until the end of 1945. Edwards was awarded the CBE in 1947 and in 1958 he was promoted to Air Commodore before retiring from the RAF in 1963. He returned to Australia, was knighted, and in 1974 became Governor of West Australia. (RAAF)

On 4 September 1944 Flight Lieutenant Ken W. Watson RAAF (right) and Flying Officer Ken Pickup RAFVR of 540 Squadron were flying PR.IX LR429 when they were attacked over Nurnberg at 29,000 feet by Me 262s. For 15 minutes they evaded them before escaping at 1500 feet but not before hitting the tip of a Bavarian pine tree which shattered the nose perspex and filled the cockpit with pine needles, making it very cold, uncomfortable and draughty. The crew flew on through the Brenner Pass to San Severo, Italy, where they safely recovered. After repairs LR429 was written off the next day in a crash-landing after the crew tried to return to Benson. Both men were unhurt and they completed their tours. On 3 June 1954 following a test flight to Cuxhaven Watson was killed landing an RAF Canberra when a Night Photo Flash bomb exploded in the bomb bay. (Pickup Coll)

On 11 September 38 Lancasters of 9 and 617 Squadrons, accompanied by a PR XVI Mosquito to provide up-to-date target information and weather report, flew to their forward base at Yagodnik on an island in the Dvina River near Archangel, in northern Russia to attack the *Tirpitz*. On 15 September the attack, by 28 Lancasters, 20 of which were carrying Tallboys and 6 or 7 others, twelve 500lb 'Johnny Walker' oscillating mines, went ahead and considerable damage was caused to the battleship. Subsequent PR revealed that although badly damaged, the *Tirpitz* was still afloat.

On 17 October a detachment of four PR Mosquitoes of 540 Squadron was dispatched to Dyce to keep watch on *Tirpitz*. Information from the Norwegian resistance stared that the ship had left Kaa Fjord on its way south for Tromsø Fjord, where it was to be used as a heavy artillery battery. On 29 October 37 Lancasters (18 Lancasters each from 9 and 617 Squadrons plus the photographic aircraft from 463 Squadron) attacked the *Tirpitz* in Tromsö Fjord. Though no direct hits were scored a Tallboy near-miss by the stern caused considerable damage, distorting the propeller shaft and rudder, which flooded the bilges over a 100 foot length of the ship's port side. The damage meant that the *Tirpitz* was no longer able to steam under her own power.

In the daylight reconnaissance 12 hours after the Peenemünde attack on 17/18 August 1943, photographs revealed 27 buildings in the northern manufacturing area destroyed and forty huts in the living and sleeping quarters completely flattened. The foreign labour camp to the south suffered worst of all and 500-600 foreign workers, mostly Polish, were killed. The whole target area was covered in craters. The raid is adjudged to have set back the V-2 experimental programme by at least two months and to have reduced the scale of the eventual rocket attack on Britain. (Australian National Archives)

Bombing up a Mosquito with a 'Cookie' for a night raid on Berlin.

Sergeant Derek Smith, an observer/navigator at 25 OTU, flew his first bombing operation in a Wellington on 10/11 September 1942 and completed his first tour with Pilot Officer Gordon Oldham's Lancaster crew on 61 Squadron. Promoted to Pilot Officer, Derek Smith flew a second tour, 1 September 1944-12 March 1945, as a navigator on Mosquitoes in 692 Squadron, 8 (PFF) Group. He was awarded a bar to his DFC. (Derek Smith Coll)

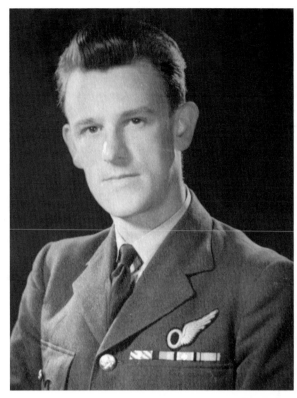

Canadian built B.XX KB326 *ACTON ONTARIO CANADA* was the first of two such aircraft to arrive at Hatfield on 12 August 1943. The B.XX was basically a Canadian-built B.IV. (via Jerry Scutts)

A 4,000lb Cookie being hoisted aboard a Mosquito.

Flight Lieutenant Alfred J. Cork DFM of 109 Squadron in January 1945, a month after being shot down, on 27 December 1944 during an Oboe marking operation to Rheydt during the Battle of the Bulge when 200 Lancasters and eleven Mosquitoes attacked the marshalling yards. Cork and his pilot, Flight Lieutenant Hodgson, took off from Little Staughton at about 1300 hours in ML961 T-Tommy. After takeoff it soon became apparent that the cabin heating was not working properly, if at all. Soon after crossing the coast the windows became completely frosted over and visibility was virtually nil but they pressed on. They completed the release run and Cork believes that he had already received the release signal and he released the first TI when a burst of machine gun (or cannon) fire hit them. He could still see nothing through the iced up perspex. 'Hodge' signalled to him that they were out of control and pointed to the escape hatch. At that moment, a second burst of gunfire hit them and the aircraft went into a dive. Cork got out. Sadly, Hodge didn't. Cork's parachute opened and one of his highly prized pre-war fleece-lined all-leather flying boots fell off. He was angry – those boots were a mark of seniority! (Latecomers had to make do with canvas legged boots!) Cork was picked up and transported back to England. (A.J. Cork DFM)

A 4,000lb bomb being released by B.XVI MM200/X of 128 Squadron. During the final months of the war, Mosquitoes of the Light Night Striking Force were the scourge of the battered German cities, especially the Reich capital. Berlin, suffered severely at the hands of 4,000lb Cookie-carrying LNSF Mosquitoes. These 'nuisance' raids culminated in a devastating series of 36 consecutive night visits against Berlin, beginning on 20/21 February 1945. Of 1,896 sorties flown, only 11 Mossies failed to return from the 'Big City'. MM200 overshot landing on one engine at RAF Valley, Wales on 27 August 1945. (Graham M. Simons)

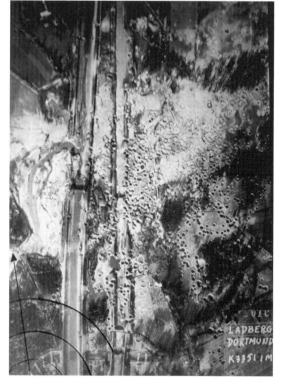

Aftermath of the raid on the Dortmund-Ems canal at Ladbergen on 4/5 November 1944. Three Lancasters from the 174 dispatched by 5 Group failed to return from the raid on the canal. On 6/7 November when 235 Lancasters and seven Mosquitoes of 5 Group again attempted to cut the Mittelland Canal at Gravenhorst, crews were confronted with a cold front of exceptional violence and ice quickly froze on windscreens. The marking force had difficulty in finding the target due to low cloud and the bombers were told to bomb at low level. Only 31 Lancasters bombed before the Master Bomber abandoned the raid due to low cloud. Forty-eight Mosquitoes dispatched to Gelsenkirchen on a 'spoof' raid to draw German night fighters away from the Mittelland attack and a 3 Group raid on Koblenz, had better luck. Gelsenkirchen was still burning as a result of that afternoon's raid by 738 RAF heavies. Ten Lancasters FTR from the Mittelland debacle.
(via Derek Patfield)

128 Squadron B.XVIs of the LNSF (Light Night Striking Force) taxi out at Wyton fitted with 50-gallon underwing drop tanks for another visit to Berlin. Mosquitoes flew so often to the 'Big City' that its raids were known as the Berlin Express and the different routes there and back, as platform one, two and three. LNSF Mosquitoes raided Berlin 170 times, 36 of these on consecutive nights. (via Jerry Scutts)

Flight Lieutenant D.W. Allan DFC, navigator and Flight Lieutenant T.P. Lawrenson, pilot, in front of B.IX LR503 GB-F of 105 Squadron on the occasion of its 203rd operation. LR503 eventually set a Bomber Command record of 213 sorties but was lost on 10 May 1945 along with the crew Flight Lieutenant Maurice Briggs and John Baker, when it crashed at Calgary during a goodwill tour of Canada. (via Norman Booth)

Flight Lieutenant Leicester G. Smith RNZAF, a B.XVI pilot in 128 Squadron at Wyton, who with his RAF navigator Warrant Officer Bill Lane completed 52 operations October 1944-April 1945. Twenty of these ops were to Berlin. (Leicester G. Smith)

B.Mk.XVI ML963 K-King. ML963 was assigned to 109 Squadron on 9 March 1944, transferring to 692 Squadron on 24 March, before becoming 8K-K in 571 Squadron on 12 April and which flew this Squadron's first sortie on 12/13 April 1944, to Osnabrück. On 1 January 1945 it was flown by Flight Lieutenant N.J. Griffiths and Flying Officer W.R. Ball on the precision raids against the railway tunnels in the Eiffel region during the Battle of the Bulge. Their 4,000lb delayed-action bomb totally destroyed a tunnel at Bitburg. On 20-24 March 1945, now coded 'F-Freddie', ML963 flew six consecutive ops to Berlin. On 10/11 April 1945, having flown 87 ops, ML963 failed to return from Berlin following an engine fire. The 'Cookie' was jettisoned and Flying Officer Richard Oliver and Flight Sergeant Max Young, who baled out near the Elbe, returned safely. (Charles E. Brown)

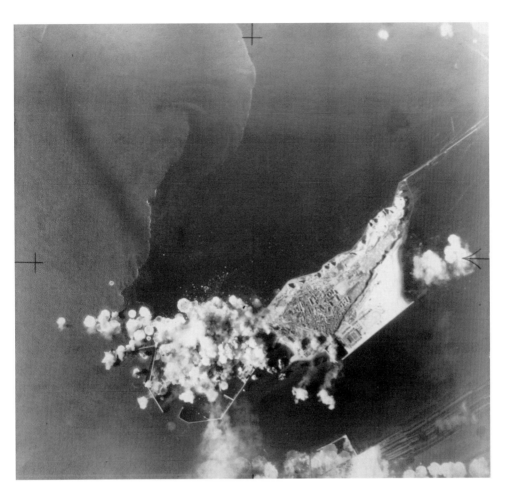

The bombing of the small island of Heligoland on 18 April 1945 when a daylight attack was made on the U-boat base, the airfield and the town by 969 aircraft – 617 Lancasters, 332 Halifaxes and 20 Mosquitoes. Bombing was accurate and the target areas were turned almost into crater-pitted moonscapes. Ninety-five per cent of all the houses on Heligoland were destroyed leaving 2,000 civilians homeless. Fifty German soldiers were killed and 150 injured. Three Halifaxes were lost. (via Derek Patfield)

Banff Mosquitoes attacking Leirvik harbour on 15 January 1945 when a formation of thirteen strike Mosquitoes, one Tsetse and two 333 Squadron outriders, led by Wing Commander Maurice Guedj commanding 143 Squadron were despatched. The Mosquitoes destroyed two merchantmen and an armed trawler and left them burning and sinking before they were jumped by about thirty Fw 190s of III./JG 5. Five enemy fighters were shot down but five Mosquitoes, including the one piloted by 'Maury' Guedj, were also lost. (via Andy Bird)

On 17 March two ships lying in the inner harbour at Ålesund and four more just outside were repeatedly strafed by thirty-one FB.VIs of 235 Squadron after they had been led in overland south of the harbour by two Norwegian crews in 333 Squadron. Twelve Mustangs flew escort, flak was heavy and two aircraft were lost but the Mosquitoes fired their cannon and RPs to deadly effect, leaving three of the ships sinking and three others crippled. One ship was holed thirty-two times with 14 below the waterline and another thirty-seven times, 31 of them below the waterline. (via Andy Bird)

Ground crew loading rockets on to FB.VI PZ438 of 143 Squadron. (Charles E. Brown)

Group Captain Max Aitken DSO DFC points out a spot on a map of Norway. Far right is Wing Commander G.D. Sise DSO DFC, a New Zealander commanding 248 Squadron. Wing Commander R.A. Atkinson DSO DFC*, Australian CO 235 Squadron (KIA 13 December 1944) is to Aitken's right. (via G. A. B. Lord)

night, had our usual fry-up and went to the ops room for a full briefing. We were told we were taking off in total darkness on navigation lights and when we had formatted on the leader satisfactorily the leader would switch off his navigation lights, switch on his formation lights and the rest of us would follow suit. We would then proceed to Lorient Harbour to look for the returning submarine and, if not found there, continue to sweep outwards into the Bay of Biscay on our search. A squadron leader was leading us with Flight Lieutenant Dobson as second in command.

All went well with the take-off on navigation lights on a pitch-black morning and we were all beginning to formate when the leader's navigation lights went out but his formation lights did not come on. Dobson immediately started calling over the R/T asking the leader to at least flash his navigation lights, so we could see where he was. Imagine a number of Mossies weaving about in pitch-black conditions. It had, in my opinion, all the ingredients for a collision, so I pulled well away and awaited developments. All this time Dobson was calling the leader to flash his navigation lights but to no avail. Then I switched all my lights off pulled further away and then the R/T went dead with no further communication from the rest of the group. So I asked Ron to give me a course for Lorient and said we would meet them there. By now the sky was becoming a little bit lighter and following Ron's directions, we went down to our usual 10-12ft over the waves whose foam was faintly visible. All the time Ron was directing me and pointing to a piece of land jutting out, faintly visible as dawn was breaking. He told me that when we rounded that piece of land Lorient would be on our port side with Ile-de-Groix on our starboard. He was quite right and to our amazement we passed directly over a U-boat [U-155 commanded by Johannes Rudolf] about 200-300 yards from the harbour entrance. I climbed up to about 1,200ft frantically calling the rest of the force but with no reply, opened the bomb doors, primed the two depth charges, went into a dive firing my cannons and machine guns and at approximately 50 yards from the sub. At approximately 50ft I released the depth charges. We then faced intense flak both from Lorient and Ile-de-Groix, so I took very violent corkscrew evasive action at a height of between 10 and 75ft. Thanks to the Mossie's speed we were soon out of range, so Ron routed me back to base where the lads found the fuselage OK but three stub exhausts on one of the engines had been half flattened by some shell having bounced off them. We found that, for some reason only known by him, the leader had decided to proceed to the Bay first and sweep in to Lorient. He had also changed the R/T channel, which was why I could neither contact nor receive them.[192]

Also during June 248 Squadron was joined at Portreath by 235 Squadron equipped with the Mosquito FB.VI. (Their last Beaufighter sortie was flown on

27 June). The Mosquitoes now flew escort for the Beaufighters and they were also used to intercept Dornier Do 217s, which carried Henschel 293 glider bombs for attacks on Allied shipping. On 30 June the Mosquito flown by Pilot Officer Wally Tonge and his observer Flight Sergeant Ron Rigby, was hit while on a anti-shipping strike off Concarneau in Brittany. They managed to ditch the aircraft and take to their dinghy but they did not survive. On 4 July Wing Commander Tony Phillips with Pilot Officer R.W. 'Tommy' Thomson DFC and Squadron Leader Jean Maurice (pseudonym for Max Guedj DSO DFC CdeG) with Squadron Leader H.C. 'Tubby' Randall, flew a costly 248 Squadron operation to the Brest Peninsula. They found a group of minesweepers anchored in Penfoul Cove and the Kercrdven docks. For greater accuracy the two Mosquitoes closed right in on their targets, skimmed over the masts of the enemy ships and dropped their bombs. AA guns were firing from Creach-Conarch heights and the ships. It is unclear if the Mosquito crewed by Phillips and Thomson was hit by flak. A witness claims that they hit the top of the mast of one of the ships. The Mosquito crashed near the Keranguyon Farm and the crew were ejected in the explosion. Phillips was found near the aircraft, Thompson falling a hundred yards away, in front of the doorstep of Madame Berrou's farm, which caught fire after being hit by flying debris. Two farm workers, Yves Glemarec and Yvonne Laurent, a young girl, had their clothes set alight. Glemarec badly burned, survived, but Yvonne died 12 hours later. For two days the airmen were left where they lay before a German officer gave the order to bury them.

On 11 July two Tsetses escorted by sixteen PB.VIs, made an evening raid on the approach to Brest harbour where a surfaced U-boat was proceeding slowly with no wake along the Goulet de Brest, escorted by three minesweepers and a *Sperrbrecher*. The shore batteries combined with the ships to put up an intense flak barrage. Undeterred, Flying Officer Bill Cosman and Flying Officer Freedman made a diving attack on the U-boat, breaking off at 50 yards and claiming two possible hits out of four shots fired. The Tsetse flown by Doug Turner and Des Curtis scored five hits on the *Sperrbrecher*. Cosman's parting shot was a salvo of two 57mm shells at the leading minesweeper, as the Mosquitoes weaved their way through the flak to the mouth of the harbour.

On 14 August 1944 Jim Hoyle was involved with another 'little adventure':

> I was not due to fly on that particular day and I had just partaken of my evening meal in the Sergeants' Mess when I received a message that Doug Turner was waiting to see me in the Reception. He asked me if I would be willing to accompany him on an operational trip. It seems that Doug had just been an onlooker to a briefing given by Wing Commander Gage D. Sise, a New Zealander always known as 'Bill' Sise who had just been appointed CO of 248 Squadron. Bill was due to fly a formation of Mosquitoes from 248 and 235 Squadrons right into the Gironde Estuary, where it had already been ascertained that there would be no shortage of

targets. [Bill Sise was later to receive bars to both his DSO and DFC whilst serving with our squadron]. Like me, Doug was also on a 'rest day' and his navigator Des Curtis had actually gone away for the day. Doug was obviously bubbling with excitement at the prospect of going on this mission. Though I thought that I might be 'pushing my luck' not to be flying with Hilly, my regular pilot, I felt quite flattered that Doug, who enjoyed a tremendous reputation, should have asked me to accompany him on what was likely to be a demanding trip. As I had not been at the briefing and time was pressing, it was just a case of grabbing my flying gear and getting airborne.

We took off at 19.00 hours D.B.S.T [Double British Summer Time] on a pleasant summer evening. At the tail end of a straggly formation of twenty-six Mosquitoes we followed the route down the French coast, passing the opening to the Gironde, where after a few miles we turned at right angles to cross the coast. When we arrived in the estuary some miles north of Bordeaux all hell was let loose with the heaviest barrage of anti-aircraft fire that I had ever encountered. Within a matter of seconds I saw one Mosquito spin out of control and watched it explode on impact as it crashed into a little hillock. I realised later the pilot of the plane was Taffy Stoddart, a well-known character in the Sergeants' Mess. There was no shortage of ships as we watched the other Mosquitoes make their attacks. Coolly taking his time, Doug was the last to attack and he selected what we took to be a *Sperbrecher* moored alongside a jetty. I was able to take some photographs, which were later to confirm that Doug's attack had been accurate and effective. As we broke away, we saw another Mosquito with both engines blazing furiously, skim low over the water before making a perfect ditching. Doug then went off on another circuit and as we flew low over the ditched plane we saw an inflated dinghy and both crewmembers standing on the wing and waving furiously to us. I was able to recognise Warrant Officer Bob Gennoe and his navigator 'Benny' Goodman.

After we had set off back on our homeward journey we heard Warrant Officer Harold Corbin say over the VHF that his plane had been very badly damaged and he asked for someone to escort him. Unfortunately, we could not see any sign of his plane, or for that matter, any of the other Mosquitoes. It really was quite surprising how such a large formation could disappear in such a short space of time. Nightfall was now setting in and as Doug was concerned about his fuel reserves, we hugged the French coast to reduce the length of the journey as far as possible and landed back at Portreath at 23.00 hours. We then heard the grim news that four aircraft were missing: Squadron Leader Cook, Bob Gennoe, Taffy Stoddart and Harold Corbin.[193] We were able to report our conversation with Harold and also that we had seen Bob make a successful ditching.

Harold Corbin and Flight Sergeant Maurice Webb, his observer, were flying in the van as part of the anti-flak effort. They attacked and damaged a Seetier-Class destroyer but return fire damaged three of the Mosquito's fuel tanks. They set course for Vannes airfield in Brittany, now in Allied hands, trailing fuel from their punctured tanks, the port engine knocked out and the other damaged. Harold Corbin continues:

We could see the tracers of the light flak hosing past us from behind. We could also hear it thwacking into our Mosquito as we flew at 50ft heading for the coast with hopes of a stretch of sand if we had to crash land. Using alternating rudder to yaw the Mosquito out of the line of fire and keeping right 'on the deck', not to be silhouetted against the sky for the German gunners' benefit, we made the coast. Being still airworthy we kept going out to sea away from the hail of light flak. Turning north in the fading light it had been a dusk attack we quickly checked for damage. Plenty of holes in the wings, petrol streaming out from several tanks, Gee set smashed and port engine fading with coolant all gone. On feathering the port engine we were spotted by one of our squadron who slowed down to escort us. The rest of the strike force headed back to Portreath. When black puffs of heavy flak suddenly bracketed us our escort veered in towards the coast to draw the fire away from us. A little later, with night coming on, he waved us 'Goodbye and good luck' and prudently put on speed to get back home.

Night fell. We decided to climb as much as we could after being unable to see Vannes aerodrome. Fuel was getting very low and the starboard engine was beginning to falter. It was obvious that we stood little chance of reaching England and with a night landing on one ropey engine if we did. The probability was that we'd be making a night ditching in the Channel. I recalled the 'Pilot's notes': 'This aircraft has been successfully ditched by day, but whenever possible bale out rather than ditch. I decided that baling out was the only option.

We had managed to achieve 4,000ft and we were over Brittany. We'd face the situation on the ground when we got there. My observer went out first kneeling down by the little, now released and discarded, entrance hatch and tumbling forward to fall out just behind the airscrew. It felt strange to be alone. I unplugged my earphones, undid my safety strap and went to leave my seat. I couldn't! The seat parachute wouldn't come free of the deep bucket seat as I could not lift my bottom high enough in the cramped cockpit. Struggling to keep the Mossie on an even keel I slowly edged the chute up and out until I was sitting on the side of the seat well.

Taking took a couple of deep breaths and leaving go of the control column, I made to kneel down and so out. But as soon as I took my hand away from the control column the remaining power of the starboard engine caused the starboard wing to lift sharply and a roll to begin. I got back quickly to the seat edge and grabbed the stick and levelled the Mossie. Whilst still retaining some control with my left hand I stretched as far as I could towards the escape hatch. As fast as I was able I let go, knelt down and did a forward roll out into the night. I counted up to three and pulled the ripcord. Nothing! It had come off in my hand! Suddenly there was a loud snap and my descent was seemingly arrested with a great jerk. I looked up and there was my lovely, glorious parachute canopy holding me suspended under the black sky. I could see the ground below but it didn't seem to be getting any nearer and hanging there, I began to wonder if it ever would. A great mushroom of light suddenly erupted from the earth and my immediate response was to think that the Germans were using flares to see me, but in the next moment I realised that it was my abandoned Mossie ploughing into the ground and blowing up. I prayed that it had not hurt any French people.

Jim Hoyle continues:

On 22 August Harold Corbin and Maurice Webb arrived back at Portreath where they had a remarkable story to tell. After Maurice and Harold had baled out in turn, separately, they were taken into safe custody by the French Resistance movement and within 24 hours they had a joyful reunion. They were soon passed over to members of the American Army, who by this time were advancing rapidly through Western France after breaking through the Falaise Gap. So, 8 days after being shot down, they were able to rejoin their squadron where they were quickly sent off on a well-deserved leave. Later Harold Corbin was awarded the Conspicuous Gallantry Medal, a very rare honour, whilst Maurice Webb was decorated with the Distinguished Flying Medal.[194]

It took Bob Gennoe and 'Benny' Goodman a few weeks longer to get back and by this time 248 Squadron had moved up to Banff. Bob told me that after Doug and I had departed from the scene, he and Benny were able to paddle their dinghy out to a deserted lighthouse at the mouth of the Gironde. Once they had managed to get inside, they found beds and blankets and as they were soaked to the skin they stripped off and went to bed for the night. The following morning some German soldiers arrived and took them back to a camp near Bordeaux as prisoners of war. After about a fortnight they, along with other prisoners, set off under escort and were told that they were to be taken to a prisoner of war camp in Germany. They had only marched a short distance however when they realised that their German guards had disappeared and that they had been left to their own devices. Within a few days they were picked up by the advancing American troops. I told Bob that I had been able to identify him when he stood on the wing waving to us. "Waving be buggered," he responded, "We were telling you to get the hell out of it before you also got shot down. Your plane was surrounded by flak bursts.

As the Americans continued their advance in western France our days in Cornwall were numbered and on 17 September 1944 all the crews were transferred up to Banff on the Moray Firth coast in Northern Scotland. Portreath had been our home for seven eventful months and it was with a feeling of sadness that we set off on the long flight north. For the residents if Portreath it must have seemed that peace had finally arrived, once our planes had departed but I am sure that the landlord at 'The Tap' at least would have been sorry to witness our departure. We were now to be in at the start of another adventure, this time as members of the Banff Strike Wing.

In September, enemy activity in the Bay of Biscay had decreased to such an extent that Coastal Command felt secure enough to post its two Mosquito squadrons north to Scotland. Four Mosquitoes of 248 Squadron flew the final sorties on 7 September in poor visibility near Gironde, while searching for U-boats. Then 235 and 248 Squadrons landed at Banff to form the Dallachy Wing together with 333 (Norwegian) Squadron. The Wing's Mosquitoes and Beaufighters were used in attacks throughout the remainder of the war on targets in Norwegian waters.[195] The first Banff Wing anti-shipping operation to Norway took place on 14 September when twenty-nine Mosquitoes and nineteen Beaufighters attacked shipping between Egero and Stors Toreungen Light. A flak ship and a merchantman were sunk. On the 17th they hunted U-boats. On 18 September Harold Corbin CGM and Maurice Webb DFM of 248 Squadron went on U-boat hunt and sighted U-867 on the surface near Bergen. Corbin strafed it with 20mm cannon and straddled it with his two depth charges to claim it as sunk. This was one of the few times that the crew returned from an op without sustaining any damage to their Mosquito but Corbin noted in his diary, 'I hope this is kept out of the newspapers'. (This was because his wife and parents had had so much worry with him being reported missing a month earlier).

On 21 September six Mosquitoes and twenty-one Beaufighters sought shipping in Kristiansund. The Dallachy Wing brought the month to a closing peak on 30 September with a Rover involving seventeen Mosquitoes and a dozen Beaufighters. On 28 September, the Banff Wing Mosquitoes were at last modified to carry eight rocket-projectiles (RP) on Mk.IIIA projector rails beneath their wings just like the Beaufighters.

On 19 October the flak alarm was raised by lookouts on three vessels at anchor at Askvoy at 13.30 hours as nineteen Mosquitoes streaked towards them. Flashes erupted from the nose of each Mosquito and spouts of water erupted in a line towards V-5116. Rounds struck the bridge and more triggered a fire, which the Tsetses fanned with their 57mm shells. Seven crew were injured. One said later that an aircraft carrying a big gun, emitting a long flame had attacked them. One 235 Squadron Mosquito was lost. With the departure of the two Beaufighter squadrons on 22 October to Dallachy to form a wing with 455 and 489 Squadrons from Langham, 143 Beaufighter Squadron at North Coates moved north to join the Banff Strike Wing and convert to the Mosquito Mk.VI. On 24 October two Mosquitoes of 235 Squadron attacked three enemy aircraft, the first seen by the strike wing. Warrant Officer Cogswell destroyed one Bf 110 while Flight Lieutenant Jacques finished off the second Bf 110 hit by Cogswell who had set an engine on fire. Jacques then destroyed the third aircraft, a Ju 88G. By the end of the month, five strikes had been made.

On 26 October, the Mosquitoes used rocket projectiles for the first time. During October 143 Squadron, Coastal Command, which was equipped with Beaufighters at North Coates, shed its virtual OTU status and moved to Banff to convert to the Mosquito as part of the Banff Strike Wing. The station commander was Group Captain Max Aitken DSO DFC, the son of Lord Beaverbrook. Aitken liked flying the Mosquito too. Legend has it that when informed by Group that 'station commanders do NOT fly on operations' he sent a two-worded message back, the second being '.... you!' Only a few isolated vessels were found and sunk in early October because the enemy operated at night in the knowledge that the strike wing could not fly in tight formation in the dark. On 9 October the Banff Wing tried out a system that had been tried at North Coates during early August 1944. A Warwick laden with flame floats and markers took off at 04.15 and 2 hours later, dropped them to form a circle 119ft in diameter 100 yards from Stavanger. Half an hour later, eight Mosquitoes of 235 Squadron followed by eighteen Beaufighters of 144 Squadron, traced the same course. At 06.20 the first aircraft arrived and began to circle. As dawn appeared, the formation set off heading for Egrsund. Led by Wing Commander Tony Gadd of 144 Squadron, at 07.10 they sank a German merchantman and a submarine chaser, while a Norwegian vessel was badly damaged. When they had recovered from the surprise the enemy gunners put up a fierce flak barrage but this was smothered by cannon fire. Three aircraft were damaged but all returned. On 28 September, while on anti-U-Boat patrol off Sondersund, Flying Officer Wallace Woodcock attacked a torpedo-boat and, despite accurate return fire from Christiansand, scored nine hits with the Tsetse and saw it sink.

George Lord, a Mosquito pilot who had been credited with sinking a U-boat, one probably sunk and one seriously damaged during a first tour of operations on Hudsons in North Africa in 1942, has vivid recollections of Mosquito shipping strikes:

We took off usually in the dark to arrive over our targets soon after first light when possible. We flew in a loose formation, usually without navigation lights, at a nominal 50ft above the North Sea. We had a primitive low-level altimeter with a tolerance of about +/- 17ft when set at

50ft. Not much of a margin, flying in the dark on instruments, no autopilot and occasionally hitting the slipstream of someone ahead, unseen. The altimeter had three lights: red, green and amber. Green was a datum, red if you went below; amber if you went above. With the long rollers of the North Sea the three lights usually flashed continually in sequence all the way across, so that our actual height above the sea must have varied down to something like 30-35 ft, all at some 220 knots cruising speed! Not much room for error!

We remained at low-level until either in sight of the Norwegian coast or if we knew enemy radar or aircraft had detected us. It was worse when we had to fly with a gaggle of Beaufighters (including some Beaufighters with torpedoes; these aircraft were called Torbeaus), whose cruising speed was 180 knots. The Mossie with a full war load was staggering a bit then and rather unpleasant in turbulence or someone's slipstream when you couldn't see the chap in front.

We flew the FB.VI with two Merlin 25s. It had four 20mm cannon and four .303-inch Brownings in the nose, with four rocket rails and drop tanks under each wing. Initially, the rocket heads were 60lb semi-armour-piercing explosive heads, used in the desert for tank busting. It was found these exploded on contact with ships and did only superficial damage. Moreover, if there was a 'hang-up', the rule was not to attempt a landing back at base but to bale out, because the slightest jolt once the rocket was armed would cause the head to explode, with disastrous consequences for the aircraft and crew. We went over to the 23-pounder armour-piercing rocket, which we delivered at 260 knots in a shallow dive. The rails had to be set so that they were parallel with the airflow at correct diving speed, otherwise the RPs would weathercock and either under- or overshoot the target. They would also miss if the pilot dived at the wrong airspeed. When making an attack on shipping, the Mosquitoes normally commenced their dive of approximately 45° at about 2,000ft and then opened up with machine gun fire at 1,500-1,000ft before using the cannons and lastly, at about 500ft, the RPs. The RPs were arranged to form a pattern spread on impact, so that if fired at the correct range and airspeed and angle of dive, four would hit the ship above the waterline and the other four would undershoot slightly to hit below the waterline. In the Norwegian fjords pilots usually had one chance, so they fired all eight rockets at once. After entering the ship's hull each would punch an 18-inch hole in the far side of the hull for the sea to flood in, while the remains of the cordite motor burned inside the hull to ignite fuel and ammunition in the ship.

These attacks were all at low-level, ending almost at ship-level. It was easy almost to overdo it by concentrating on aiming at the target and firing at the right moment. On one occasion, my navigator yelled "Pull up" and we just missed hitting the ship's masts! When there was a formation attack one sometimes suddenly saw another aircraft shoot across our line of fire, attacking from a different angle. When a number of our aircraft were involved the usual practice was to split into three sections of say three aircraft each. One would be top cover to watch out for any fighters; one would be anti-flak (the most dangerous, going in first to silence the anti-aircraft guns hopefully!); the third was the section making the actual attack; also pretty dicey. The idea was to rotate the order to give everyone a fair chance of survival (we had a rate of about one in five) and obviously the favourite was to be top cover and the worst to be anti-flak. An unusual hazard flying low-level along the Norwegian coast and into the fjords was shore-based artillery firing at us and the first one knew of it was when a huge plume of water rose up in front of us! If we had flown into it, it would have meant almost certain death. For our attacks, we would fly out in the dark and aim to arrive at first light. We had one of the earliest radio altimeters, which could be set for a given height to be flown say, say 50ft. It had three lights: amber in that case meant above 50ft, green was 50ft, red was below 50ft. With the long North Sea swells, you could see them recorded by the lights. When we heard the enemy jamming our radios, we knew we had been detected. Then we climbed up and went into the fjord in close battle formation. One scheme proposed was for a Warwick aircraft (a modified Wellington) to be out there in the dark, waiting for us to arrive and laying a circle of flares on the sea, perhaps a mile in diameter. We had to keep radio silence, we were dispersed and it was dark; but we were supposed to identify each other by the light of the flares. That was telling the enemy! Must have been thought up by a chap deep underground.

On 15 October, what was planned was an operation involving both Mosquitoes with rockets and Torbeaus. Just south of Christiansand, going west from Germany, was a ship of some importance, for it was escorted by flak-ships, balloon-ships and ships with parachute-and-cable devices. We reckoned we hit her on the stern with a 500lb bomb, but I think a torpedo caused the destruction. One minute the ship was there, then there was just an expanding cloud of smoke, a ring of fire over the sea, and in there were human beings with not a hope of surviving. Normally, one felt detached. This was one of the few occasions when I felt differently. It was probably a munitions ship or tanker. We had two Norwegian naval aircrews with us, familiar with the coastline, who had escaped and who carried out reconnaissance with us. Some of our information came from transmitters in Norway. The operators would put them on a bike, openly, knowing what would happen if they were caught, and push the bikes up into the mountains, often deep in snow; we heard that people would save their rations to give to the men who pushed the bikes. The German ships used to creep down the Norwegian coast in the dark and in daylight moor under sheer rock faces in a fjord. Our recce Mosquitoes would radio back a coded signal reporting the targets they had spotted and we would go out to attack. We would split into two or three sections as mentioned above for anti-flak, target attacking and top cover. As the ships were moored under the sheer rock faces, we had to make a very steep turn away after firing. Then we would scoot up the fjord hell-for-leather and then up the mountainside. Often there were little farms at the top and I have seen people come out, waving flags. The Focke Wulf 190s waited until the attack was over and the Mossies were coming out. Damaged Mosquitoes were slower and more liable to be caught. One trick the Germans used against us was to sling cables across the fjord. You couldn't see them.

George Lord flew an armed recce on 3 November and another on the 4th. Low cloud prevented bombing and he attacked a motor vessel alongside the quay at Floro with cannon and machine guns. Flak was intense and his mainplane and tailplane were holed. On 7 November 143 Squadron entered the fray for the first time since relinquishing its Beaufighters when two Mosquitoes carried out a search for enemy aircraft between Obrestad and Lindesnes. Frequent snow and hail were a feature of operations on 8 and 9 November when the Mosquitoes looked for shipping off Ytterîene, Marstein and Askvoll. The Banff Wing now began to operate in increasingly larger formations, including for the first time, on 13 November, a combined operation with the Dallachy Wing. The largest strike so far occurred on 21 November. New Zealand Wing Commander Bill Sise DSO DFC, who had taken over 248 Squadron on the death of Wing Commander Phillips, led a formation of thirty-three Mosquitoes, accompanied by forty-two Beaufighters and twelve Mustang III fighter escorts, in a shipping strike at Ålesund. Off Lista on 29 November a 248 Squadron Tsetse flown by Flying Officer Wallace G. Woodcock scored two hits on a U-boat, which he attacked with 20mm cannon and eight 57mm shells, while other XVIIIs attacked with depth charges and cannon. Woodcock recalls, 'This, at the time, was supposedly the nearest a Mossie had got to sinking one. I did hear a rumour that Halifaxes got it later when it had to surface, but this was never confirmed.'

Tsetses were again in action on 5 December when Bill Sise led thirty-four Mosquitoes in an attack on merchantmen in Nord Gullen. On the 7th, twenty-one Mosquitoes and forty Beaufighters, escorted by three 'Finger Fours' of Mustang IIIs of 315 (Polish) Squadron flying to the rear, set out to attack a convoy in Ålesund harbour. Landfall was made as briefed but Squadron Leader Barnes DFC led them further up the coast, towards Gossen airfield, whereupon they were jumped by approximately twenty-five Fw 190s and Bf 109Gs. They dived through the middle of the Mosquitoes and attacked singly and in pairs. The Mustangs shot down four fighters and two more collided. A Mustang and a Beaufighter were lost. Flying Officer Wallace G. Woodcock adds:

I was fairly lucky in most of my strikes. However, there was a problem sometimes for us, because we had to leave the formation when near the target to climb to 5,000ft while the others stayed low. For instance, on 7 December, a formation of about ninety aircraft (the entire Banff Mossie Wing, plus the Beaufighter Wing from Dallachy) was sent to prang a large convoy holed up in Ålesund harbour. We had a very ambitious leader, but even I, a mere pilot, could see our landfall was spot on target. Nevertheless he turned north and led us up the coast for about 60 miles until we were near a *Luftwaffe* airfield, when we were jumped. The four Mark XVIIIs, flying at 5,000ft above the rest, were jumped first. Bill Cosman and K.C. Wing (both Canadians) and Brian Beathe (a South African) went down. I was able to chase an Me 109 off Brian's tail, then I went down and strafed the airfield, but was jumped later. However, I made it back to Sumburgh in the Shetlands (I think I was still taking evasive action, even then!). Bill and K.C. didn't make it. In the Ops Room at Sumburgh the leader was claiming we were jumped at Ålesund. We soon disillusioned him on that point!

On 12 December the Mosquitoes were escorted to Gossen again, but no fighters were seen. The following day 30 year old, Australian Wing Commander Richard Atkinson DSO DFC, CO of 235 Squadron, who a few days earlier been awarded a bar to his DFC, led an attack by eighteen Mosquitoes of 235, 248 and 143 Squadrons, against German shipping in Eidsfjord on the Norwegian coast. Six Mustangs of 315 Squadron escorted them and an Air-Sea Rescue Warwick also accompanied the operation. At 12.21 the Mosquitoes began taking off. Making landfall near Utvaer Light, a tall red tower protruding from the rocks just after 14.00 hours. While outriders searched along the inner Leads the remaining aircraft flew outside the Leads. At 15.07 hours Norwegian Lieutenant Stensrud sent a radio message, 'Target in Eidsfjord'. The Mosquitoes swept in towards the daunting mountain terrain gaining height turning towards Eidsfjord. D/S *Falkenfels* was the only merchantman in convoy Al-1097 together with two escorts Vp. 5503 and Vp. 5110 on watch. The eighteen Mosquitoes went down in sections led by Atkinson. Projectiles of all calibre streamed towards them from the flak ships and shore batteries and shells enveloped the formation. As Atkinson and his 20 year-old navigator Flying Officer Valentine 'Val' Upton RAFVR thundered towards the target German gun crews at the fortress at Furuneset got his Mosquito in their sights and began firing. Suddenly Flying Officer Harold Corbin CGM of 248 Squadron saw an explosion in front of him and knew that Atkinson's aircraft had received a hit. Corbin tells how, 'I followed "Dickie" down, directly behind him slightly to starboard. Tracer passed us and kept coming. Suddenly there was a burst and it ripped off his starboard wing. Fragments embedded themselves into our aircraft as I continued looking through the sights. Our Mosquito juddered from the blast. Atkinson's aircraft just spiralled in.'

Lieutenant Dymek (USAAF) and Flight Sergeant Harvey in their respective

Mosquitoes hit the anti-aircraft positions with rockets, machine gun and cannon fire, causing many casualties. Lieutenant Stensrud circled to take photographs but owing to increased intensity of flak he was unable to. It was not only anti-aircraft fire that caused damage to the Mosquitoes. As he pressed home his attack Flying Officer Angus McIntosh of 248 Squadron encountered a Mallard duck which damaged his port mainplane. As the Mosquitoes set course back to Banff, led by Wing Commander Maurice, in Eidsfjord the *Falkenfels* was left burning. The bodies of Atkinson and his navigator, Flying Officer Val Upton were never recovered. The remaining Mosquitoes landed at Banff at 16.46 hours. Dick Atkinson's wife Joan, who was lodging at 'Distillery Cottage' near the Mosquito base, heard the aircraft return that evening and did not hear the usual low flying over the house. She had an overwhelming feeling that her husband was not there, so she was waiting in dread for the knock on the door, which came about an hour later.[196]

On the 16th the Mosquitoes winkled out a merchantman and its escort, lurking in Kraakhellesund and made two attacks, the first in line astern! Two of the Mosquitoes were shot down. On 19 December Mustangs escorted them to Sulen, Norway, but again no fighters appeared. On Boxing Day twelve FB.VIs of 235 Squadron led by Squadron Leader Norman 'Jacko' Jackson-Smith, with two outriders from 333 (Norwegian) Squadron attacked two motor boats at Leirvik harbour, about 70 miles up the Sogne Fjord, with machine guns and cannon. One was left on fire, the other smoking heavily. Light flak was experienced from ships and heavy flak from the harbour area. One of the Mosquitoes was crewed by Flying Officer Bill Clayton-Graham DFC and Flying Officer 'Ginger' Webster, which was hit as Clayton-Graham recalls:

> After attacking the nearest ship I went on to attack the second ship, when I was hit in the port engine. One ship was left sinking, the other on fire. Our strike force totalled twelve aircraft. As I broke off the second attack, smoke was pouring from my port engine, which I feathered and I flew round the headland to go down the fjord and out to sea, having climbed to 1,000ft. Heavy flak burst around me in the fjord and then I saw fighters in line astern flying with me about 1,000ft above and slightly astern to my right; about twenty-four of them. As they peeled off to attack I turned into them and attacked with machine-guns (my cannon were spent), which forced about twelve of them (Me 109s and Fw 190s) to dive past my nose and through my line of fire. I saw one hit well and truly and I must have tickled quite a few others. I was not hit but was a sitting duck with only one engine. I turned back on course out to sea, dived onto the wave-tops with the good engine at full throttle and awaited the second attack, which never came. They had all gone on to attack another aircraft flown by my good friend, Flying Officer Jim Fletcher, whom they shot down. One enemy fighter was reported by the Norwegian underground to have been shot down.

Our strike leader, Squadron Leader 'Jacko' Jackson-Smith, who had seen my predicament but had lost sight of me, called me up and told me to fire a Very light so that he could come and escort me. I replied, "Not bloody likely, they'll see me, too", and pressed on! About 20 miles out to sea, I called up the patrolling Air-Sea Rescue Warwick, which carried a lifeboat. He homed in on me (I was doing about 170 mph) and escorted me back the 300-odd miles over the North Sea to Banff. The Mossie handled beautifully and I made a safe wheels-down landing. A piece of shrapnel was found, which had cut a coolant pipe in my port engine. A change of underpants and several pints of beer were the only repairs needed by me.

Harold Corbin and Maurice Webb in Mosquito 'N' had been hit by flak, which had damaged one engine, causing a loss of glycol coolant. Corbin recounts:

Seeing the German fighters waiting for us as we came out of the fjord I risked full throttle, got down on the deck and hoped the damaged engine would last until we were out of danger and that no German would pick on us. We were lucky and finally out of danger, but the damaged motor, having done what was necessary was finished, so I feathered the prop and once again headed for home on one motor. Having got safely back to Banff I then misjudged the approach and realised that I was going to touch down in a field 100 yards short of the aerodrome boundary and runway. I was not unduly worried until just after touch down. I saw a stone wall at the aerodrome edge. Just as we hit this I switched off to avoid possible fire and selected 'wheels up' on the undercarriage to allow the wall to knock the wheels back up. I felt we might somersault otherwise and end upside-down. Well, dear old 'N' hit the wall, flat on our belly, both props and wheels torn off but otherwise on an even keel. Maurice and I were trapped in the wreckage but within seconds Max Aitken had raced around the perimeter track in his station wagon and dragged us out. He then took us to the station hospital. We were only slightly injured and soon recovered, but when 248's CO, Bill Sise DSO DFC, came to see us he said, "I'm giving you a rest. No more ops, but I want you to stay with the Squadron to help newcomers." We then went off to an aircrew officer's course at Hereford. After a month or so we returned to find the Squadron had suffered many losses during our absence. Bill Sise had been posted to 143 Squadron, many friends were gone and the biggest blow of all was that our dear, our beloved, Wing Commander Maurice Geudj had been lost.

On 9 January 1945 eighteen FB.VIs of 235 Squadron returned to Leirvik and attacked eight merchant ships in the harbour with cannons and machine-guns, as Flying Officer Bill Clayton-Graham DFC recalls:

We left three ships on fire. The Norwegian underground later reported one ship sunk at its moorings and four others severely damaged: One of the ships on fire had unloaded ammunition, which was stacked alongside the quay. Happily this did not go up during our attack. We had a fighter escort of twelve Mustangs, but they were not needed on this occasion.

Two days later there was more success when Flight Lieutenant N. Russell DFC shot down two Bf 109s and another Mosquito pilot claimed a Bf 109 during an anti-shipping strike in Flekke Fjord by fourteen Mosquitoes and eighteen Beaufighters. The Mosquitoes returned to Leirvik harbour on 15 January 1945 when a formation of thirteen strike Mosquitoes, one Tsetse and two 333 Squadron outriders, led by Wing Commander Maurice Guedj, now CO of 143 Squadron, were despatched. 'Maury' had survived a tour on long-range day Beaufighters with 248 Squadron and he got back on ops by threatening to resign his commission and join the Free French commandos. The Mosquitoes destroyed two merchantmen and an armed trawler and left them burning and sinking before they were jumped by about thirty Fw 190s of III./JG5. Tsetse 'Z' fired four shells at an Fw 190. Five enemy fighters were shot down but five Mosquitoes, including the one piloted by 'Maury' Guedj, were also lost. (Guedj was the most decorated Free French pilot and a Paris street was named after him). The rest fought their way back across the North Sea pursued for a time by nine fighters. This sudden rise in Banff Wing losses caused concern at Northwood. After this attack 248 Squadron's short-range Tsetses were transferred south to North Coates in Lincolnshire to operate with a Torbeau squadron.

In February the Mosquitoes began to widen their horizons and, operating independently of the Beaufighters now, ranged far and wide over the Norwegian coast seeking specific targets. On 11 February delayed action bombs were dropped in a narrow fjord off Midgulen to roll 'Dam Buster' style down a 3,000ft cliff to explode among the ships in the harbour below. On 21 February 235 Squadron carried RPs for the first time when a 5,000-ton ship in Askevold Fjord was attacked. Taking part for the first time were spare aircrew from 603 Squadron, who had flown Beaufighters in the Middle East, led by Wing Commander Christopher N. Foxley-Norris DSO, who had flown Hurricanes on 3 Squadron in the Battle of Britain. During the first few days of March the installation of new Mk.IB tiered RP projector rails enabled long range drop-tanks to he carried in addition to the rocket projectiles. Nos. 235 and 248 Squadrons were now able to operate at an increased range but with a 50 or 100-gallon drop-tank and four RPs under each wing, the Mosquitoes tended to stagger on take-off!

On 7 March forty Mosquitoes led by Wing Commander R.K. Orrock DFC, CO, 248 Squadron attacked eight self-propelled barges and a large merchantman with an escorting flak ship in the Kattegat with machine guns, cannon and rocket fire. A dozen P-51 Mustangs provided top cover and two Warwicks of 279 Squadron were in attendance to drop lifeboats to ditched crews if called upon. Orrock decided that the eight well-laden barges were the more important and he called for them to be attacked. Two Mosquitoes from 235 Squadron shot up the flak ship with machine guns and cannon fire and twenty-four more Mosquitoes of 235 and 248 Squadrons and fourteen aircraft from 143 Squadron attacked firing rocket projectiles. Four outriders came from 333 Squadron. All eight barges were destroyed. No enemy fighters showed but two of the Mosquitoes collided shortly after the attack.

On an armed reconnaissance in the Skagerrak and Kattegat five days later, eight Bf 109s intercepted the force of forty-four Mosquitoes and twelve Mustangs. The Mosquitoes shot down one of the enemy machines and another was claimed as a 'probable' for no loss to their number. On 17 March two ships lying in the inner harbour at Ålesund and four more just outside were repeatedly strafed by thirty-one FB.VIs of 235 Squadron after they had been led in overland south of the harbour by two Norwegian crews in 333 Squadron. Twelve Mustangs flew escort. Flak was heavy and two aircraft were lost but the Mosquitoes fired their cannon and RPs to deadly effect, leaving three of the ships sinking and three others crippled. One ship was holed thirty-two times with fourteen below the waterline and another thirty-seven times, thirty-one of them below the waterline.

On 21 March 235 and 143 Squadrons made short work of another ship at Sandshavn. Two days later nine Mosquitoes attacked a troopship, the 7,800-ton Rothenfels, at anchor at the end of Dalsfjord. The strike leader, Squadron Leader Robbie Read and one other were shot down. In the afternoon Wing Commander Foxley-Norris led another strike, attacking a motor vessel at Tetgenaes. On 24 March some crews in 404 'Buffalo' Squadron RCAF arrived to convert to Mosquitoes while the remainder attacked merchantmen at Egersund using Beaufighters. Three days later a freight train near Naerbo was attacked. On 30 March a warehouse on Menstad quay full of chemicals and vessels at Porsgrunn-Skein harbour which the Germans used to evacuate troops from Norway came under attack by thirty-two rocket-firing FB.VIs led by Wing Commander A.H. Simmonds, CO of 235 Squadron. Eight more Mosquitoes who remained on station on the lookout for enemy fighters covered them. None appeared and the eight FB.VIs detailed as escorts provided accurate suppression fire against gun positions in the sides of the fjord. The attackers flew so low that they crested the wave tops. When Flight Lieutenant Clause and Flight Lieutenant Royce Turner went after a merchantman tied to the quay they could even see the Plimsol marks on one of the vessels. Clause scored hits with all the rockets aimed as one of the vessels and as he came off the target 'three separate plumes of smoke were building up to a great height'. He then swooped down and sprayed a 4-gun battery on the side of the fjord with cannon. Two Mosquitoes, one crewed by Flight Lieutenant Bill Knowles and Flight Sergeant L. Thomas, which struck an overhead electric cable and crashed, failed to return. The attack had proved devastating with over 120 rocket projectiles holing three merchantmen. One merchantman was hit by twenty-eight rockets, another by thirty-nine and a third vessel by more than sixty RPs. All of them sank and a fourth merchantman was badly damaged.

New crews replaced those lost. Among them was Flight Sergeant John R. Smith, a navigator in 248 Squadron and his pilot, Flight Lieutenant Peter McIntyre, whom he had teamed up with at the OTU at East Fortune in the autumn of 1944 on one of only two Mosquitoes (the rest were Beaufighters).[197] Smith recalls:

> The first day on the squadron we were not flying and so I went on the roof of Flying Control to see the 'famous' formation of three Mosquitoes take off on the runway at the same time. Group Captain Max Aitken was watching too. He turned round and said to me, "They are a beautiful sight, aren't they?" He added, "You're new at the Banff Wing?" I said I was. He then said he believed all pilots and navigators should be commissioned officers, as in the American air force and would recommend me if I went and saw him after I'd done a few operations.

April dawned and on 2 April the Mosquitoes flew an operation to Sanderfjord. Navigator Frank Hawthorne relates the details:

> Flight Lieutenant Bob Golightly and I were briefed and set course from Banff on a reconnaissance flight to South West Norway. Our flight plan was to cross the coast where the anti-aircraft site, as we knew, was equipped with lesser armament than our Mosquito. In the event we crossed the Norwegian coast heading directly towards the anti-aircraft site, menacing them with our cannon and machine guns. This elicited no response until we were practically overhead when they opened fire and caught us with their first burst; very commendable deflection shooting considering we had increased speed for the transit. We hurriedly vacated the area heading westward over the coast to the North Sea where we tried to evaluate the damage. It appeared we had been hit in the fuselage, fortunately aft of the cockpit, but Bob discovered he had to hold the stick back to maintain level flight. I gave him a course for Banff but in these circumstances he felt his arms would not cope satisfactorily in landing the aircraft and we should change seats (as we had done frequently on previous occasions) and I would fly the aircraft back to base. On our arrival at Banff, we changed seats and Bob set about landing the aircraft. However on selecting undercarriage down, only one leg came down, the other remaining stubbornly retracted in spite of Bob doing manoeuvres to shake it down. Use of the emergency hand pump proved fruitless in bringing one leg down or pumping the other leg up. So we were committed to this asymmetric attitude for landing. Tightening our straps. As we approached Bob selected 'undercarriage up', bounced the one leg at the beginning of the runway, sending it to the retracted position and we settled down to an

orthodox belly landing. Hitting the runway with a thud it seemed to me that something fell to the floor of the cockpit. We skidded along the runway to a halt and fortunately there was no fire. Bob and I exited through the top escape hatch and jumped down onto the runway. Checking later I found that the starboard propeller had ripped through the side of the fuselage, flicked my trouser leg and exited again. Just another day?

On 5 April thirty-seven Mosquitoes escorted by Mustangs flew across Denmark to attack a widely spread out and heavily-armed convoy in the Kattegat. Every ship in the convoy was left on fire and sinking and an estimated 900 German soldiers were lost. One *Sperrbrecher* sank with all hands, 200 bodies being recovered by Swedish vessels. An escorting Mustang was shot down over Denmark and a Mosquito crash-landed with the crew picked up by the Danish Underground.

With the war almost over the Mosquito crews had yet to obtain a confirmed U-boat 'kill' all to themselves. All that was about to change on 9 April when thirty-one rocket-projectile FB.VIs of 248, 143 and 235 Squadrons led by Squadron Leader Bert Gunnis DFC with five others as fighter cover and DZ592, a 2nd TAF photo-Mosquito were despatched to Norway on the look out for enemy shipping. Flight Sergeant John R. Smith recalls:

> This was my most memorable day. It began with the morning briefing for a wing sweep through the Skagerrak and Kattegat, looking for enemy shipping to attack. We were told that our Mosquito, Q-Queen was unserviceable, but as our new Wing Commander, Jackson-Smith, wasn't flying that day, we were told we could have his K-King, a brand new aircraft. When we prepared for take-off it refused to start for some minutes. When we were finally ready, all of the others were airborne and heading for Peterhead to get in formation. We had some difficulty getting off the runway, nearly removing the top deck of a passing bus! We flew flat-out to catch up and take our position in the formation. We went through the Skagerrak without seeing anything and were heading back to Banff when we saw three U-boats[198] line astern on the surface of the Kattegat, coming from Denmark and heading for Norway. We did not hear any order to attack[199] but when the leading aircraft in our formation attacked the leading U-boat, Peter decided to attack the middle one with our rockets and cannon. He scored direct hits and the U-boat blew up. We normally flew at about 50ft to beat the German radar but we were well below this; probably only about 20-25ft. As we passed over the U-Boat, straight into the explosion, some debris hit us and it knocked out our starboard engine.[200] We had been told that in the event of serious trouble, not to try to get back to base but to make for neutral Sweden. So we announced over the wireless we were making for *Brighton*, code-name for the day for Sweden. We did

not hear any reply. It would seem we were transmitting all right, but our receiver was out of order.

We set off for Sweden on a course I had given and managed to gain several hundred feet. We passed over what I believed to be the Swedish coastline when some anti-aircraft guns opened up. It brought immediate panic from Peter and even though I had been pretty sure I knew where we were, I began to worry a little. He shouted, "This isn't Sweden; it's Norway! And you know what the Germans are doing to PoWs." (It was rumoured that they were castrating Allied aircrew.) It was Sweden. The Swedish AA gunners must have been practicing, as the shells did not burst near us. We limped on and some minutes later I recognized a viaduct that was marked on my map. It gladdened my heart, for I knew we were spot-on course for an airfield I had headed for. Peter immediately brightened up and told me to get rid of the ARO, which was secret.

We came upon the airfield and he made a perfect one-engined landing far superior to the practice ones he had made at home. I pressed the two small buttons on my right, which destroyed the IFF and Gee box. When we got out of the aircraft, Peter got down on his knees and kissed the ground. He got up, put his arm around me and said, "Good old Smitty. You knew where you were all the time, didn't you?" I didn't say anything. A Swedish Air Force officer with a revolver in his right hand wasn't taking any chances, but he shook hands with us with his left. "Welcome to Sweden," he said, in perfect English.[201]

On 11 April thirty-five Mosquitoes made another attack on Porsgrunn. Bf 109G-14s shot down two, although the remainder left four merchantmen sinking. Next day an FB.XVIII of 248 Squadron, one of five Tsetses sent on detachment to 254 Beaufighter Squadron at North Coates, attacked a U-boat in the North Sea. The Tsetse detachment was used primarily for operations against midget submarines and U-boats, with Spitfire XXIs for cover. Two Tsetses found five U-boats on the surface on 18 April. The XVIIIs got off just one round each before the submarines crash-dived. On 19 April the FB.VIs at Banff sank U-251 in the Kattegat. On 21 April forty-two FB.VIs of 235, 248, 143 and 333 Squadrons led by Wing Commander Christopher Foxley-Norris, CO, 143 Squadron, engaged eighteen Junkers Ju 88s of KG26 inbound from Gardermoen, Denmark to attack convoy JW66, which had left the Clyde three days before. Twenty-four Mustang escorts missed the mêlée, having sought and gained permission to return early for a party at Peterhead! The Mosquitoes shot down five Ju 88A-17 and four Ju 188A-3 torpedo carrying aircraft. Two of the Ju 88s were shot down by two 333 Squadron crews, Lieutenant Thorlief Eriksen and 2nd Lieutenant Johan Hansen-Just and Flight Lieutenant 'Bob' Golightly and Flying Officer Frank Hawthorne. Hawthorne remembers:

We approached from the port quarter. Bright flashes emitted from the Junkers machine gun positions and Bob returned fire with a three-second-burst and these ceased. On our firing again the Ju 88 exploded at 15ft above sea level. Debris embedded itself in the plywood as we took avoiding action.

The next day 404 'Buffalo' Squadron RCAF flew its first operation from Banff since replacing its Beaufighter Xs with Mosquito VIs in March. They sank a Bv 138 flying boat at her moorings but the squadron had little time left to make an impression as the war in Europe was now drawing to a close. However, on 2 May, a strike by twenty-seven Mosquitoes in the Kattegat resulted in the sinking of U-2359. On 4 May Wing Commander Christopher Foxley-Norris[202] led forty-eight Mosquitoes of 143, 235, 248, 333 Norwegian and 404 'Buffalo' Squadrons, escorted by eighteen Mustangs on the last large-scale shipping strike of the war to the Kattegat. Three ASR Warwicks with airborne lifeboats were available should they be needed. The Mosquitoes sighted a very heavily armed convoy, which they immediately attacked at low level. Flight Lieutenant Gerald Yeates DFC* with his navigator Flight Lieutenant Tommy Scott of 248 Squadron attacking a German destroyer flew so low that they carried away, in the nose of their Mosquito, the top of the mast of the destroyer complete with pennant. The wing had its last loss when Flight Lieutenant Thorburn DFC failed to return. This final, massive, battle was the end of the shooting war for the strike wing but patrols for U-boat crews who might be inclined to continue the fight, went on until 21 May, when four Mosquitoes of 143 and 248 Squadrons found only passive E-boats.

The Banff Wing provided escorts for the King of Norway as he sailed back to his country under heavy naval escort. Days later a schnorkel was seen and attacked by a single Mosquito from 404 'Buffalo' Squadron RCAF. By 25 May the rapid run down of the anti-shipping wing had begun. No.489 Squadron RNZAF converted from the Beaufighter Mosquito FB.VI in June when the war was over and disbanded at Banff on 1 August 1945.

CHAPTER SEVEN

Star and Bar

In the summer of 1942, Colonel Elliott Roosevelt brought two squadrons of Lockheed F-4 Lightnings and a squadron of B-17F 'mapping Fortresses' to Britain. The President's son was preparing his group for the invasion of North Africa and was to work with the RAF until ready. Given a Mosquito B.IV for combat evaluation, Roosevelt discovered that the aircraft outperformed his F-4s and had five times the range. The first of the Canadian-built Mosquitoes had already given demonstrations at Wright Field. It was so good, General Arnold ordered that no US aircraft were to be raced against the Mosquito, to avoid embarrassing American pilots! Arnold asked that Mosquitoes be obtained to equip all American photo-reconnaissance squadrons in Europe, almost 200 aircraft for 1943 alone! In 1943 thirty Mosquitoes were diverted from British production after the Canadian allocation of 120 for the Americans had been reduced to just sixty B.XXs because of RAF demands. These, plus eleven Canadian-built F-8 models, were delivered to the 802nd (later, 25th) Bomb Group at Watton in Norfolk. However, these were not as popular with the pilots and navigators as the British-built Mosquitoes and they were soon reassigned to a bomb group in Italy.

The 802nd, with the 7th Photographic Group, became part of the 325th Photographic Wing, which was commanded by Colonel Elliott Roosevelt. Many personnel who were transferred into the 802nd Bomb Group had to be retrained. Mechanics, who had never seen a Mosquito night bomber, attended a two-week course at the Rolls-Royce engine school in Derby. Others attended the airframe school at the de Havilland factory in Hatfield. Most of the aircrew, many of whom were P-38 Lightning pilots from the 50th Fighter Squadron in Iceland and who were used to the P-38's contra-rotating propellers, had never experienced the take-off and landing characteristics of the Mosquito bomber; especially its high landing-speed and tendency to swing on take-off. They had also to remember to open the radiator shutters just prior to take-off to prevent the engines overheating.

The 652nd Bomb Squadron was equipped with the B-17 and B-24 while the 653rd Bomb Squadron used Mosquito T.III and PR.XVI aircraft on meteorological flights, known as 'Bluestockings', gathering weather information from over the continent. PR.XVIs used a two-stage, two-speed supercharger that would cut in automatically at altitude. The superchargers were independent on each engine and a small difference in adjustment caused one to change gears hundreds of feet before the other. The resulting bang and surge of power to one engine could wrest control from the unwary pilot and give the impression that the aircraft had been hit by flak. Several Airspeed Oxfords and three dual-control Mosquito T.IIIs were assigned for training. The 654th, or the 'Special Squadron', flew day and night 'Joker' photo missions and scouting sorties just ahead of the main bombing force, transmitting up-to-the-minute weather reports back to the task force commander to prevent him leading his bombers into heavy weather fronts. On Joker missions the Mosquitoes dropped 1,000,000-candlepower-type M-46 photo flash bombs (PFBs) to illuminate and obtain evidence of enemy troop movements and bridge construction conducted under the cover of darkness.[203] American Mosquitoes were also used on Skywave long-range navigation missions using LORAN. Daylight missions code-named PRU, using still and motion picture photography and H_2X 'Mickey' flights. Mosquitoes brought back bomb-approach-strips, or target run-ups, which were used to brief the key radar navigator-bombardier of the bomber mission and to sight the bomb target through the overcast during the actual bombing. Three Mickey sorties flown at night failed to return and later, four P-38 Lightnings were assigned to escort the H_2X missions going in at high altitudes.

The date for the D-Day invasion was determined by intelligence gathered on 'Dillies' (night photography missions of coastal defences). A local storm front, forming suddenly east of Iceland on 5 June and monitored by the Bluestockings, postponed the invasion for one day until 6 June. On D-Day a Mosquito flown by Lieutenant Colonel George O. Doherty, the 25th Bomb Group CO and Major John C. Walch flew a morning photography mission over the Normandy beachhead. Later that day the 25th Bomb Group suffered its first Mosquito loss when Captain Walter D. Gernand and Sergeant Ebbet C. Lynch, an 8th CCU cameraman, were killed returning from a photo reconnaissance mission to the beachhead and beyond when they hit a hill in darkness near High Wycombe. A month later, on 6 July, 1st Lieutenant John J. Mann and 2nd Lieutenant William L. Davis were lost over the Channel on a weather scouting mission for the 1st Bomb Division. In August another weather scout Mosquito was lost when a PR.XVI failed to return from the last leg of the 8th Air Force Russian Shuttle mission from Italy to England. (Light Weather Squadron PR.XVIs fitted with LORAN accompanied the two 8th AF Frantic shuttle bombing missions to the Ukraine).[204] Lieutenant Ralph Fisher, who had flown a 653rd Squadron Mosquito on the first shuttle mission, briefed 1st Lieutenant Ronald M. Nichols and 2nd Lieutenant Elbert F. Harris, who would fly scout on the second. Nichols had flown a tour of missions on Fortresses and the shuttle mission would be his 57th mission. For Harris it was his 20th. Seventy-six Fortresses escorted by sixty-four P-51s were to bomb the Focke Wulf plant at Rahmel in Poland *en route* to the Ukraine and later fly home via Italy and France. A US Navy team arrived at Watton prior to departure and installed the LORAN receiver in their PR.XVI and checked Harris out on the equipment. He recounts his experiences:

> We took off on schedule, flew parallel to the bomber stream going to Berlin, caught up with our task force and proceeded to the target area. The weather was clear over Germany and Poland; no problems. We spotted four fighters slightly above and some distance to the right, but they didn't come after us. We waited in the area for the bomb drop and were pleased to report an excellent pattern on the target. Shortly after, we left and passed the bombers and fighters on our course, which took us 75-100 miles to the west of Warsaw. The Germans were suppressing the Polish underground uprising and the city was being destroyed while the Soviets sat idly by on the outskirts of the city. Most of the city seemed to be in flames. There was a huge plume of smoke rising to about 30,000ft, which could be seen from 200 miles away on our course. Our orders were to drop to 6,000ft at Kiev and to remain at this altitude to Poltava. Lieutenant Fisher told us about the tendency of the Soviets to fire AA and the Soviet fighters to attack American planes and since we believed we were the lead plane contingent, we were most apprehensive during our descent. As it turned out, the other Mosquito arrived slightly ahead of us and there were no incidents. We received good reception on the LORAN from Britain till we let down to 6,000ft at Kiev. The Italian chain signal was good at first. Then it became intermittent until we lost it over Poland. Since the weather was good, I could cheek against both Gee and pilotage, finding good agreement between the fixes. We landed at Poltava and were guided to a parking spot. Our fuel was low but not critical when we arrived.

The B-17s arrived and flew a bombing mission later against a Polish synthetic-oil refinery. Nichols and Harris flew scout for the mission, which was uneventful and the bombing pattern excellent. Then, on 8 August, the shuttle force took off for San Severo, one of many B-17 bases in the Foggia area of Italy, bombing two Rumanian airfields *en route*. On 12 August the force flew back to Britain on the last stage of their shuttle, bombing the French aircraft complex, Avion Sud and the adjacent Francazal airfield at Toulouse *en route*. Nichols and Harris flew ahead scouting the weather, reporting back to the bomber leader. At about 11.45 hours, north of the target area, their PR.XVI was attacked by P-51s of the 357th Fighter Group who mistook the Mosquito for a Ju 88. Harris recalls:

> Tracers passed above us. Nick began evasive action but too late. The next burst was in and around the right engine and we were on fire. The tracers kept coming around and into the Mosquito. I was wearing a chest chute harness. As I leaned down to pick up my chute pack, the Mosquito tilted and I was thrown violently against the floor. I strained to push myself up but couldn't move. The Mosquito had gone into a high-speed stall and followed with a tight spin. Nick was fighting the controls but the Mosquito

wasn't responding. A sheet of flames extended from and along the trailing edge of the right wing, caused by gasoline pouring from the right wing-tank. As I shoved my escape kit into my shirt front I was considering my alternatives: bale out the top hatch and be killed by the tail stabilizer, or go out the bottom, catch fire and be burned to death. Judging that there was little time left before the aircraft exploded, I decided to take my chances on the tail. I pulled the release for the top hatch and it flew off. I climbed out and pushed out and down. Before closing my eyes I glimpsed fierce flames under the fuselage. There was a roaring sheet of flame from under the right wing with streamers of fire. I was hit by the horizontal stabilizer, bounced off it and fell away spinning...

The Mosquito went out of control into a spin and crashed at Pujaudran, a small village 15 miles west of Toulouse. Elbert Harris, who had burns and a bullet wound in the shoulder, survived but Nichols was killed. Harris was picked up by Yves Busquère and Denise Gaby, who rendered first aid, gave shelter and then passed him to the local French Underground. Harris was picked up by a 161 Squadron Hudson on 5 September and flown back to England where he called 'Nick' Nichols' fiancée, a dietician in an army hospital near Plymouth.

American Mosquitoes accompanied Project Aphrodite and Anvil pilotless drone operations using war-weary B-17s and PB4Y-1 Liberators respectively. Each aircraft was packed with 18,000lb of Torpex, a nitroglycerine compound and was flown to a point over the English coast or North Sea where the pilot and co-pilot baled out. The drone would fly on and be directed onto its target (normally a V-1 or V-2 site) by remote control via a Ventura 'mother ship'. Strike analysis depended upon the films brought back by the accompanying Mosquitoes to determine the success, or failure, of the mission. Each Aphrodite and Anvil mission was preceded by a Bluestocking weather reconnaissance flight over the target by a 653rd Bomb Squadron Mosquito. After the drone was airborne, a Mosquito in the 654th Bomb Squadron joined the mission carrying an 8th Combat Camera Unit (CCU) crewman. The mission was to fly close to the drone and photograph its flight and its effects. These photographs were used to analyze all angles of the flight and to improve methods and equipment used on such missions. Some of the 8th CCU cameramen came from the Hal Roach Studios in Hollywood, where they trained alongside movie stars making training films, such as Ronald Reagan (the Administrative Officer), Alan Ladd, Van Heflin, John Carroll and others.

On 4 August 1944 of four Aphrodite B-17s, or 'Babies', despatched to No-ball sites in the Pas de Calais, one crashed in England, killing its pilot: the second refused to dive over the target and was destroyed by flak; the third overshot and the fourth undershot. On 6 August two Aphrodite drones crashed and exploded. The missions were photographed by Staff Sergeant August 'Augie' Kurjack and 1st Lieutenant David J. McCarthy in 25th Bomb Group Mosquitoes. Kurjack ran about 50ft of movie film of the crash in England. McCarthy's Mosquito, flown by 1st Lieutenant Robert A. Tunnell, an American from Eureka, California, who had enlisted in the RCAF in 1941 and then joined the USAAF in 1943, picked up some flak and flew home on one engine. The US Navy's first Project Anvil mission went ahead on 12 August. Some 21,170lb of Torpex was distributed throughout the PB4Y-1 Liberator, together with six demolition charges each containing 113lb of TNT. The pilot for the Anvil mission was Lieutenant Joseph P. Kennedy Jr, at 29, the eldest son of Joseph Kennedy, the former US Ambassador to Britain and who had flown a tour of missions from Dunkeswell with VB-110. 'Bud' Willy was co-pilot. Their target was a secret weapon site at Mimoycques, which concealed a three-barrelled 150-mm artillery piece, designed to fire 600 tons of explosives a day on London.

A Mosquito flown by Tunnell, with McCarthy in the right-hand seat, followed behind the formation of two Ventura 'mother ships', Kennedy's Liberator, a navigational B-17, a P-51 Mustang and a P-38 Lightning. The mission proceeded satisfactorily to Blythburgh when, at 1,500ft, two explosions ripped the Liberator asunder. McCarthy reported:

> We had just decided to close in on the 'Baby'. I was flying in the nose of the plane so that I could get some good shots of the 'Baby' in flight ahead of us. The 'Baby' just exploded in mid-air. As we heard it I was knocked halfway back to the cockpit. A few pieces of the 'Baby' came through the Plexiglas nose and I got hit in the head and caught a lot of fragments in my right arm.

McCarthy crawled back to the cockpit and lowered the wheels. Tunnell concludes:

> I didn't get a scratch but I was damn near scared to death. The Mosquito went up a few hundred feet and I didn't get any response from my controls. I was setting to reach for my parachute but decided to check the controls again. This time they responded and I decided to try and make a landing. One engine was out and the other was smoking. We were near a field so I headed straight for it. We made a good landing and then the second motor cut out. I had just enough speed left to get the Mosquito off the runway, but I couldn't taxi onto a hardstand. I'm sure glad that the pictures of our previous mission were good because I don't think we're going to get that close to the 'Baby' again.

A dozen drone missions were flown before the British advance overran the Pas de Calais area. Several attempts were made to convert Mosquitoes into 'mother ships' but they were not used operationally.

On 13 August 1st Lieutenant Dean H. Sanner and Staff Sergeant Augie Kurjack filmed the flight paths of Disney glide bombs released from under the wings of B-17s at U-boat pens at Le Havre, France and photographed any damage to the submarine pens. Captain Edward Terrell RN had invented the 18ft long, 2,000lb bombs, powered by a rocket motor in the tail and they were designed to pierce 20ft of concrete before exploding. The first was not going to hit anything, so Sanner broke off the pursuit and climbed back to follow the second glide bomb. At the Initial Point the second bomb was released and he zigzagged back and forth considerably to hold the faster Mosquito behind the slower glide bomb. As Sanner flew over the bomb it exploded. The blast blew him out of the aircraft. His cameraman was killed. Sanner suffered a broken leg and injuries to his right arm and was captured within the hour. He finished the war in *Stalag Luft* I.

On 7 August a 654th Squadron Mosquito flown by 1st Lieutenant Walter W. Thompson and 2nd Lieutenant Carl C. Edgar failed to return from an H_2X (Mickey) photography mission to Salzbergen, Germany. Two weeks later, on 19 August a 654th Squadron Mosquito with pilot, 1st Lieutenant Ray L. Musgrave and navigator, 1st Lieutenant Harold F. Fordham took off shortly after 23.00 hours. Their mission was an H_2X (Mickey) to photograph a radar approach to Bremen from an initial point about 20 miles north-north-east of Bremen. The aircraft failed to return, as Fordham explains:

> After becoming airborne we climbed for altitude over the North Sea. We entered Germany near the mouth of the Elbe River and then cut back south and west toward Bremen. From the initial point we began a series of H_2X photos toward a military industrial target. Shortly before I completed the series of photographs, however, sudden and erratic movements seized the aircraft. Erratic movements spoil approach photos and I immediately called the pilot and asked what was happening. He replied, "I don't know. We're caught in the lights." Though confused, I had to accept his explanation for the moment. Being in a closed, dimly lit cubicle in the rear fuselage, I was oblivious to external conditions. Still, when the aircraft fell off on a wing and went into a slow downward spiral, I became concerned. The action was not a normal evasive tactic. I glanced at the altimeter and the needle reflected our fast descent. I attempted to contact the pilot on the intercom but received no response or reply. As the centrifugal force from the spiral grew more intense and the altimeter needle continued to drop I concluded we were going to crash.
>
> I was buckled in my backpack parachute and sitting on my flak suit. We had a dim light inside the fuselage and the escape hatch was on my right hand side. I released the escape hatch and eased the lower half of my body through the cramped opening. I tried to squeeze further through the hatch but the parachute snagged on its rim. I was stuck halfway out of the hull with my legs in the slipstream, banging against the outside fuselage. After rocking and squirming over the opening I fell clear and immediately pulled the D-ring of my parachute. It opened with a jolt. We had lost a considerable amount of altitude. Though we had been flying at around

25,000ft for photography I baled out below 10,000ft. As I fell away I could neither see fire or flames nor other indication that the Mosquito had been damaged in flight. Neither was there a later explosion or fire to indicate the crash of the aircraft. Musgrove had said, "We're caught in the lights." Now, suspended in the descending parachute, I could not see any searchlights nor anything to indicate a source of blinding lights. Except for the stars above I could see nothing. I was in complete blackness and swinging like a pendulum. This oscillation became a major concern. Oscillating about 1° to each side could make landing difficult. Below was black featureless void that gave no hint as to distance to the ground. Until I struck the ground I had no indication of its proximity. I landed in a field, fell over backwards and lay there dazed for a minute or two. In the distance I heard soldiers singing and for a moment considered a possible connection between the singing and my stunned condition. I tested each body part for damage as I gathered myself from the ground. I snagged the pan chute to shreds on the barbed wire of a fence, dug a hole and buried it. Taking stock of my situation I had parachuted a short distance west of Bremen from a clear starlit sky. Using Polaris, the North Star, as a guide I sought to travel in a westerly direction: I hoped, thereby, to reach the border with the Netherlands and perhaps find a friendly resident. My boots were conspicuous and I tore the tops off them to make them look like black Oxfords similar to those worn by German males. This proved to be a serious mistake. Without the tops, the shoes were loose and shapeless. My feet blistered and became badly swollen. I travelled at night and, during the day, concealed myself in haystacks or in whatever screening shelter I could find. I avoided villages and their inhabitants where possible but could not avoid the numerous canals and channels. At each waterway I gathered the branches from trees and made a raft. I undressed, placed my clothing on the raft and swam across. I redressed on the other side. Though the routine was time consuming it was much too cold to wear wet clothing. For ten days I roamed free but without a bite to eat. My escape kit had been kept in a pocket of my B-3 jacket. The pocket was not snapped shut. All the contents, including food, were lost when I pulled the ripcord of my parachute.

Exhausted, Fordham was finally apprehended by a *Luftwaffe* officer in a Dutch church on the edge of a village where he had sought a short, comfortable rest. Fordham was driven to a *Luftwaffe* airfield. After two days a train took him to *Dulag Luft* interrogation centre in Oberursel, a suburb of Frankfurt. Each day for the ten days he was there Fordham was interrogated. After the tenth day he was transferred to *Stalag Luft* III. Musgrave, who had been killed, was buried at Cambridge American Cemetery.

In September 1944 the Allies attempted to capture bridges on the Rhine in

Holland at Veghel, Grave, Nijmegen and Arnhem, using Britain's 1st and America's 82nd and 101st Airborne Divisions. Operation Market Garden was planned to cut off the Germany Army in the Belgian sector and save the bridges and the port of Antwerp for the American army units and British XXX Corps advancing north from the Dutch border. First Lieutenant Claude C. Moore, a Mosquito navigator, recalls:

> On the night of 16 September three Mossie crews were called in and told that we would go out early next day at staggered intervals. No details. One plane was to take off at 2 am, one at 4 am and one at 6 am. Next morning, just before take-off, we were given the details: the Nijmegen-Arnhem area. Find the base of the clouds in the area. How thick and how low. Go down to the deck if necessary. Radio back that information. We were the last flight, at 6 am. Jimmy Spear was the pilot. The sky was already light when we left. It was only a matter of minutes from Watton to Holland. We skimmed across at 2,000–3,000ft. Soon we were at the target area, which, I learned later, was where the parachute drops were made and the glider-borne assault troops were landed. There were large clouds, intermittently broken, so we descended. At around 500ft we were finding the base of the clouds. Apparently High Command was not waiting for our information; there were planes everywhere. I had never seen so many fighters up close. Below us, above us, around us, on every side they were climbing, diving, milling like a swarm of angry bees. They were really beating the place up. We reported thick, low, occasionally broken, white clouds and smaller, grey puffs of clouds and gave the cloud base as approximately 400-500ft. The smaller, grey puffs of clouds were spaced all around. Only, I finally realized, they weren't small clouds. They were shell bursts. We were being shot at!
>
> I was startled to see a plane coming off the deck, climbing straight at us and closing; a snub-nosed, radial-engined plane. From the markings and the silhouette I took it to be from Hermann Goering's own elite group: the cowling painted in a distinctive yellow-and-black checkerboard pattern. 'Focke-Wulf 190' flashed through my mind. 'Damn', I thought. 'This is it!' I'm sure that, mentally, I was frozen in space. But the next thing I knew, the snub-nose had zoomed past us. I did a double take. It was a P-47 Thunderbolt. We stayed in the area a little longer, made a few more weather reports, then headed back to Watton. At the base we were debriefed. We went over to the Combat Mess for breakfast and settled into the day's routine.

On 18 September the Germans counter-attacked and forestalled an American attempt to capture the bridge at Nijmegen. Just over 100 B-24 Liberators dropped supplies and ammunition to the American Airborne forces at Grosbeek, in the

Nijmegen-Eindhoven area. Five Mosquito weather scouts were despatched to Holland. 1st Lieutenant Robert Tunnell and his navigator-cameraman, 19-year old Staff Sergeant John G. Cunney, failed to return. They appeared over the German airfield at Plantlünne far from their objective and were caught in a searchlight, which blinded the pilot. Tunnell took evasive action, hit an oak tree and crashed on a hillside near Lignin on the Dutch-German border. The Mosquito exploded killing both crewmembers. They are now interred in the American War Cemetery at Neuville en Condroz, Belgium.

Bad weather during Operation Market-Garden made regular air reconnaissance over the Arnhem bridge impossible, so on 22 September three 25th Bomb Group Mosquitoes were despatched. Lieutenant 'Paddy' Walker's navigator, Roy C. Conyers, remembers:

> We were to dip as low as possible to try to establish by visual observation who controlled the bridge, the Germans or the British. I thought that this regularity was crazy and mentioned it to Edwin R. Cerrutti, 654th navigator. His only comment was that the German Command wouldn't believe that we were that stupid.

As 'Paddy' Walker flew over the north end of the bridge just below the fog, at under 500ft, he and Roy Conyers could see Germans running for their anti-aircraft guns. Walker states:

> Ground fire began almost immediately. This continued as we flew over and past the other end, on towards the coast. Tracer fire could be seen coming up around us and the plane was hit. I saw the left wing drop-tank disintegrate and jettisoned both. The right engine was shut down and the propeller feathered. The fire went out, but the engine was inoperative. I was flying as low and as fast as possible to get out of range. As we crossed the coast additional fire was received, spurts of water coming up near the plane from the barrage; however, we were not hit. After we got out of range, I climbed up into the weather to gain enough altitude to make an emergency Mayday radio call, to get a 'steer' to the nearest base where the weather was suitable to land. We steered to Bournemouth. My Mayday call was answered by the sweetest girl's British accent: 'Tommy' Settle, a beautiful blonde WAAF at Tangmere. During the days that it took to repair the plane she and I became better acquainted and after the engine change and other repairs I took her on the test flight. It was her first airplane ride and in a Mosquito. Unfortunately, I was at Tangmere for only a week.

On 25 September another Bluestocking mission was launched as evacuation of the surviving paratroops from Arnhem began. 1st Lieutenant Clayborne O. Vinyard and his navigator, 1st Lieutenant John J. O'Mara, took off at 01.26 hours in poor visibility. Vinyard recounts the mission:

The fog was thick. We climbed to 30,000ft but were unable to rise above the overcast. We were depending on our LORAN equipment for navigation and flew beyond our Netherlands objective. We reached the outskirts of Frankfurt before turning back. Returning toward our objective, we descended to 18,000ft where a *Luftwaffe* night-fighter picked up our presence with his radar. Near 04.30 hours our aircraft was struck by cannon fire. Tracers set the right engine ablaze and rounds penetrated the fuselage. I immediately banked the aircraft to the left and dived in a spiral dive to 12,000ft, hoping, thereby, to lose the night fighter and coincidentally extinguish the blaze. The German fighter did not follow me in the dive but the engine fire would not extinguish. I levelled the flight of the aircraft in preparation for parachuting. John O'Mara pulled away the inner door of the hatch but the outer door would not open. Getting out of my seat and leaving my controls, I stamped my foot on the outer door. It released and I moved back to the controls. O'Mara pulled himself through the open hatch and without hesitation I followed. The air stream blew off my English flying boots as I stuck my feet out the exit. I fell into the darkness and slowly counted to fifteen. There was no sound in the dense, moist air until I pulled the ripcord of the parachute. Drifting down in the clouds, however, I could hear the wind in the risers.

The cloud layer opened up above a farming community and I landed in the tallest of pine trees. Fragile and brittle limbs covered its upper section. I grasped the trunk of the pine, released the parachute and slipped down a very long, limb-less trunk. I had landed on a hill, in woods, somewhere in western Germany. In these tall pines there is no underbrush. I enjoyed my freedom for perhaps four hours but after daylight I was located by a group of civilians, one of whom carried a gun. They had been alerted by the crash of the aircraft and had located John O'Mara. I was taken to Erlangen, a small town of perhaps twenty houses and held for the arrival of a military guard. The military guard took me to a neighbouring town where I joined O'Mara, the navigator. Together we were taken by bus and by train to an air base and placed in a cell. The next morning we boarded a train for Frankfurt. The railway station on our rail line at Frankfurt had been bombed out and we had to walk several miles through the ruined city to another railway station. O'Mara was wearing his wool-lined flying boots over his GI shoes. This was burdensome and he gave the flying boots to me to wear. They were much too large for stockinged feet and I had to drag them to keep them from sliding off. Angry civilians followed us during our march through Frankfurt. Our young guards spoke some English and cautioned us. We could talk with the civilians but should they attack there was nothing the guards could do to protect us. We walked fast, looked straight ahead and disregarded the insults and missiles that came our way.

From Frankfurt we went by train to an interrogation centre, where we were placed in separate quarters for perhaps a week. Each day we were taken into the office of a military officer for interrogation. Once the interrogation was over, O'Mara and I were lodged in a compound together. Shortly, we were entrained for imprisonment near Barth. Approaching Berlin we found ourselves near the target area of a massive air attack. The train stopped while the guards sought the protection of the woods. We, of course, remained locked in the railroad cars. There were seven or eight of these coaches, filled with prisoners of war. Though they carried no PoW identification, they were not attacked. After the attack the train continued its journey, taking us to *Stalag Luft* I and we remained there for the duration.[205]

The 653rd Bluestocking Squadron suffered a run of fatal crashes. On 1 November 1st Lieutenant Robert C. Grimes and 1st Lieutenant Clarence W. Jodar were returning from a Bluestocking mission in a furiously stormy night when a wing-tip clipped a tree and they crashed inverted. Three weeks later, on 22 November 1st Lieutenant Malcolm S. 'Mac' MacLeod, who had flown in the RAF and 2nd Lieutenant Edward G. Fitzgerald and 1st Lieutenant Russell E. Harry and 2nd Lieutenant Milford B. Hopkins were killed returning from another Bluestocking mission in much the same circumstances. MacLeod's Mosquito crashed at Saham Toney and Harry's aircraft crashed at Thompson near Watton. Just a few weeks' earlier Hopkins and Clarence Jodar had celebrated with friends the arrival of their first-born sons.

The 654th Squadron had its losses too. On 25 October the Mosquito flown by 1st Lieutenant George M. Brooks and 2nd Lieutenant Richard C. Taylor failed to return from a Night Photography (Joker) mission to Duisburg. Brooks was killed but Taylor survived and he returned. Then on 1 November the 654th Squadron lost a second Mosquito. Second Lieutenant Vance J. 'Chip' Chipman and 1st Lieutenant William G. Cannon took off on a Mickey mission at 19.30 hours from Watton. Chipman was a former racetrack driver from Chicago who had joined the Royal Canadian Air Force when war started in Europe. To some he was '...a strange chap in USAAF uniform with both RAF and USAAF wings. His chest was splattered with combat decorations and he sported a long handlebar moustache. In a crisp British accent he introduced himself, mentioning that he would be assisting in Mosquito pilot training.' Chipman and Cannon's objective was H_2X photos for a bombing run to Schweinfurt. They never returned from their mission. This was the third successive H_2X photo mission to fail to return and it strengthened suspicions that German Ju 88s were homing in on H_2X radar equipment. It proved, however, to be an exception. At the IP, 50 miles from Schweinfurt, cameras were started. The run was completed at a target near the centre of the city and the Mosquito banked and headed for home. On leaving the city the Mosquito received a direct hit of anti-aircraft fire. The right engine caught fire and Cannon was hit by shrapnel in his right leg and on the back of his head. Chipman gave the order to bale out but received no reply from Cannon, who had the usual difficulties in exiting the Mosquito but his descent was smooth. The impact with the ground in the black of night was unexpected and rough and broke his injured leg in three places. He had landed near an anti-aircraft battery whose crewmen found him within minutes.[206]

Chipman meanwhile, performed the cockpit controls bale-out routine, exited the bottom hatch, opened his parachute and from his descending parachute watched his aircraft explode. After landing and burying his parachute and Mae West, he took stock. He had lost one tooth, split his lip, cut his tongue and torn a ligament in his left leg. He had retained his escape supplies during his jump, however. Chipman made his way toward France during the night and sought available hiding places during the day. From some farmer's storage hill he filled his trouser leg pockets with raw beets and potatoes. From a small shop he stole a bicycle. With the use of the bicycle he was covering distance until an aged tyre blew out. Thereafter he walked pushing the bicycle. One night Chipman passed two German soldiers who became suspicious and shone their torch on him. Seeing the blood and torn military clothing they took him to a *Luftwaffe* aerodrome and locked him in a cell. Later he was given the freedom of a hallway.

A day or two later at breakfast he found a door unlocked. Walking out the door he made his way to one of several Bf 109s parked in a blast bay. He planned to start the aircraft and head for England and everything seemed to be working smoothly but he found that a lone person inside the aircraft could not start a Bf 109. Chipman was still trying when he was discovered and hustled back into the guardhouse. A guard, using one-inch rubber tubing, beat Chipman over the head until he was unconscious. When he recovered he was taken to the *Dulag Luft* in Frankfurt where he was interrogated. Chipman answered all questions with the usual name, rank and serial number but perhaps in a frivolous manner. Thus, in an effort to make him talk, his captors gave him a doped cigarette. It made him very dizzy and very sick but he did not lose his control. Rather, he answered their questions with imaginative and ridiculous accounts of activities as if it were the effect of the drug. This included a revelation about a flying submarine. From Frankfurt, Chipman was taken to *Stalag Luft* III at Sagan.[207]

On 6 November 1944 1st Lieutenant Otto E. Kaellner's Mosquito crashed in England following a Mickey night radar-mapping mission to Cologne using the H2S radar system. Kaellner was killed and his navigator, Lieutenant Edwin R. Cerrutti, was seriously injured. Flight Officer James D. Spear and Lieutenant Carroll Bryan were killed on a local training flight on 23 December when their Mosquito crashed at Debden. Meanwhile, the loss of the three aircraft and crews on three consecutive night photography missions led Major (later Colonel) Roy Ellis-Brown, Group Operations Officer, to cancel operations pending further evaluation. Ellis-Brown, who had flown with the RAF and had been awarded the

DFC, paid a visit to 100 (Special Duties) Group at Bylaugh Hall in Norfolk and got the low down from the RAF on why the Americans were losing Mosquitoes at night. He was told that 'stooging along alone', especially at low level for a hundred miles was 'asking for it'. Despite opposition from the 654th Squadron commander, Colonel John Larkin, Ellis-Brown, supported by Colonel Leon Gray the 25th Bomb Group CO, all Mickey flights at night ceased forthwith and new ways of flying the missions in daylight were tried. Beginning on 19 February 1945, the 654th Bomb Squadron switched to light-weather missions.

Pete Dustman, an American pilot from the western Rocky Mountains in Idaho, who, while serving as an instructor at RAF Leconfield early in the war, had met and married Lorna, his English wife, wanted night fighters when he finished training. His roommate wanted training command. "You guessed it," says Dustman. "I was posted to Upavon to become an instructor on Oxfords and my roommate went to night fighters. After various assignments 2nd Lieutenant Dustman wound up ferrying B-17s, B-24s, Dakotas, the P-47 and one Boulton Paul Defiant that the US borrowed to tow targets and then didn't use. On one trip he heard about the formation of a Mosquito base at RAF Watton, so he made a stop on his next delivery to talk to the commander. Since he had flown RAF aircraft Dustman was immediately accepted and he joined the 25th Bombardment Group and was assigned to the 654th Bomb Squadron, as he recalls:

> As I joined the squadron they were working to modify the Mossie to fit Chaff dispensers, night photo equipment with 24-inch cameras for high altitude (24,000ft) and to install radar on the Mickey ships. In the interim we had one B-25 and three B-26s to take night photos at 12,000ft, short range, slow and low. I flew five in the B-25 and three in the B-26 over France to cover railways at night and the building of the new V-1 sites. I flew my first mission in a day photo Mosquito along the French coast. I imagine it was a just a feint to keep the Germans guessing, which is about all it did as the groundcrew forgot to turn on the cameras before we left. As others on their first mission, I flew my first trip with my heart going at top speed, but I saw nothing except a few clouds along the route. Other missions of the 654 were a bit more exciting. Two missions that I flew verified the old saying that 'flying is 90 per cent luck and 10 per cent skill', although that might be overstating the skill part. On my 28th birthday on 21 February 1945 I started out on a routine night photo mission with a target at Memel, west of Hamm in the Ruhr Valley with Lieutenant Len A. Erickson as navigator. The scheduling team had fouled it up as I was approaching Essen at the same time as the RAF was having a major strike in the same area. It was interesting to watch, as we were getting ready to start our run-in at 22,000ft. Naturally everything was lit up with flares going down and flak coming up. As I started my photo run and dropped my first of a string of thirty flares, flying straight and level to keep the camera

in focus, I heard a loud English voice say, "Mossie rock your wings". We assumed that a British night-fighter was on our tail but couldn't make contact. I didn't want to miss the pictures, so I kept going hoping to complete the mission. Then again I heard the same voice saying "Blue Leader, this is Blue 4, this Mossie won't rock his wings" and the faint reply, "Shoot the bastard down then!" My wings were rocked vertical and sideways with flash bombs going in every direction, with no pictures taken that night. I did have words at debriefing on return that night about their scheduling.

On a night flight over Germany to take photos, a new navigator was with me. His training had been primarily on radar, with very little on navigation. On this flight we had a strong wind shift (now known as jet stream shift), which was unexpected. The navigator thought it was just the Gee navigation system that had messed up and didn't consider the wind shear accurate, although the Gee was good for the target run. On return he did not allow for the wind shift and we drifted so far south that we missed not only our base in East Anglia but England! Since our radios had also packed up, we let down hoping to find land and get our position in the moonlight, but the top of one cloud was just like all others. I kept trying the radio and finally received a steer of due north, landing at Bournemouth with 10 minutes of fuel left. Since the navigator had also forgotten the camera switches, the mission was a complete loss.[208]

On 24 March 1945, a daylight mission using a Mosquito fitted with British radar equipment was tried. After having the radar fitted at Malvern the Mosquito, piloted by 1st Lieutenant Carroll B. Stubblefield and his navigator-radar operator, 1st Lieutenant James B. Richmond, took off from RAF Defford and headed for East Anglia. The Mosquito was joined by eight P-51 Mustangs of the 479th Fighter Group from Wattisham. The purpose of the mission was electronic and radar surveillance over German fighter bases in the Siegen-Kassel area in Germany. The group flew to the Antwerp, Aachen and the Remagen bridgehead, thence to Limburg and Siegen and turned north-easterly toward the Kassel area. The Mosquito flew a criss-cross pattern at 18,500ft. The escorting P-51s were thus able to maintain the pace and flew at 19,000ft altitude and 1,000 yards behind. At 17.00 hours the Mustang leader reported unidentified aircraft at the 2 and 1 o'clock positions. They were identified as P-47s, heading west at 17,000ft. The P-51 pilots attempted to call them on Channel 'C' but they received no response. As the P-47s came up the Mosquito had turned into them, making a tight, descending 360° circle, to present its clear US and Red Tail identifications. It then returned to its north-easterly direction, informing the group leader that it was again on course. Once again the Mosquito began to weave and criss-cross its course. As the Mosquito turned left the two Thunderbolts, flying on the right of the Mustangs, turned inside and closed on the Mosquito. A Mustang pilot warned the Mosquito that the P-47s were apparently attacking and the Group Leader yelled, "Break" but the Mosquito remained level, turning more to the left. Richmond had his head in the shroud over the CRT display screen. His first indication of danger was Stubblefield's exclamation, "Damn! We're being chased." Richmond jerked his head out from under the shroud to find streaks of tracer bullets flashing through the cockpit. The port engine caught fire and the starboard engine died. Stubblefield feathered the starboard engine prop and shouted: "Get out of here, Rich. Go." Richmond kicked out the trap door and struggled through the opening. He was still struggling when the aircraft exploded. Stubblefield was killed but Richmond was blown free and his parachute opened safely at 10,000ft. Richmond landed near a village about 50 miles west of Kassel on one foot, injuring the leg. Within moments, a cluster of civilians carried him into the village and placed him in a holding cell. After 48 hours he was transferred to an interrogation centre at Pinneburg about 10 miles from Hamburg. Two days later he was transported to *Stalag Luft I* at Barth on the Baltic. The two P-47s that had fired at the Mosquito were from the 23rd Squadron, 36th Fighter Group, of the 9th Air Force.

Next day 1st Lieutenant Bernard J. Boucher and his navigator, 1st Lieutenant Louis Pessirilo were killed during a Bluestocking mission over Germany. Five other Mosquitoes on weather reconnaissance returned safely.

Some 352 'Chaff' (Window)-dispensing sorties, code-named Gray-Pea (after Colonel Leon Gray[209] and Colonel (later General) Budd Peaslee), were carried out by Mosquitoes of the 653rd and 654th Bomb Squadrons using an electric dispensing mechanism in their bomb bays. On 3 April 1945 six Gray-Pea Mosquitoes were detailed for Chaff-screening for the 8th Air Force, five more scouted for the B-17s and seven flew weather reconnaissance over the continent and seas around Britain. On 3 April 1945, six Mosquitoes of the 654th Squadron took part in a Gray-Pea mission in support of a First Air Division bombing of Kiel on the Baltic coast just south of Denmark. Lieutenant Colonel Alvin Podwojski, pilot and Captain Lionel A. Proulx, navigator, were the first to take off at 15.00 hours. Once all six aircraft were airborne they climbed for altitude, flying toward Cromer on the coast. They left Cromer at 9,500ft and climbed *en route* to 25,000ft. They met no enemy opposition *en route* to the IP. The weather was good. Podwojski remembers:

> Our aircraft was unable to reach a proper airspeed of 220 mph with the engines turning at their normal rpm. To attain this normal speed I had to rev our engines to 300 rpm above normal. This was too fast and it was necessary to keep the cowl flaps open to cool the engines. I considered turning back, but with the mission time estimated at only 3 hours and 15 minutes, we continued on. I could throttle back, I thought, after clearing the target. The flight plan called for us to pull ahead of the bombers 30 to 35 miles south-west of the target. I contacted the lead aircraft of the bomber force to coordinate our flight and was informed that they would be

at the IP in only 7 minutes. This was disturbing. At my limited speed we could not overtake the bombers at the IP in 7 minutes. After I had instructed Captain James M. McNulty to take the lead and attempt the rendezvous, the bombers called back and reported that a mistake had been made. They were 12 minutes from the IP, rather than 7 minutes. The bombers would be at the IP at 16.30 hours. To add to our difficulties our VHF was not cutting in and out. Still, I resumed the lead with engines rotating at 2,750 rpm plus 8, much too fast. Though our starboard engine was overheating badly, a perfect rendezvous was made. Our six Mosquitoes flew line abreast ahead and above the bomber formation. We were spread wider than the B-17 formations to drop Chaff over an extended track. The Chaff had its intended effect and no flak was observed bursting near the bombers. Twelve to twenty bursts of flak were directed at our Mosquito, however, accurate for altitude but trailing our flight by 100 yards.

Lionel Proulx takes up the story:

After we had discharged the aluminium foil at the prescribed level approaching and over the target area we turned, leaving the bombers behind us. We planned to separate and start for home. There was no need to stay in formation unless German jet fighters were in evidence and with our poor aircraft performance we planned to throttle back. As we were making the turn and still heading north-east, I loosened my seat belt and stood up to see if there were any enemy aircraft in our proximity. I did see three aircraft to our rear, identifying them as Me 109s. I yelled at Pod but he was already aware of their presence. At that moment something, possibly flak, hit the starboard engine. The performance of the starboard engine was of immediate concern, particularly during the left bank. Pod was a powerful figure of a man and he managed to keep the aircraft at a favourable level and complete the turn. I leaned over to help him but at that time we entered the clouds. The decision to divert to Sweden was reviewed by Alvin Podwojski:

The oil temperature gauge on the starboard engine was reflecting the heat; the radiator temperature was high; the oil pressure was down to 15 lb and the port engine started running rough. There was a direct head-wind of 100 mph above 25,000ft over the North Sea. I asked Proulx for the time to England and received the answer of 2 hours and 10 minutes. He estimated it would take 1 hour and 50 minutes to reach friendly lines at low altitude and with two engines. In answer to my further enquiry, Proulx reckoned that, with the wind in our favour, it would take 40 minutes to reach Sweden. He added, "You fly the damn plane. I'll do the praying." So saying, he pulled out his rosary beads. The decision was thus left to me. I called

McNulty and instructed our flight to proceed without us. We were due west of Flensburg when we turned east toward Sweden. Meanwhile, Proulx sorted his maps and gave me compass directions.

Lionel Proulx recalls:

With the starboard engine smoking and steaming and the oil pressure down to 10lb from the normal 70lb, Pod cut the starboard engine and feathered the propeller. Though the port engine was turning 2,650 rpm, our air speed was only 160 mph. Pod tried to jettison the drop tanks on the wings but only one dropped. The port tank would not jettison. It broke loose later when we were in a banking curve while checking for enemy aircraft. Keeping close watch to the rear, I observed over Svendborg, Denmark, German fighters either pursuing or shadowing us. We were yet a full 30 minutes from Sweden. With our slow descent through broken clouds, the German fighters lost interest. Flying by instruments, we came down out of cloud cover over the Swedish coast at approximately 9,000ft. The Royal Swedish Air Force flying Seversky P-35 fighters immediately intercepted us. Their SAF insignia, three gold crowns on a blue background, was distinct. They escorted us to an airfield outside Malmo called Bulltofta.

As the Mosquito approached the airfield and before the crew had lowered their landing gear the port engine died. With the loss of their air compressor Proulx had to wind down the landing gear manually. It was slow and exhausting work but he prevailed. With the landing gear extended Podwojski made a 'dead stick' landing on the south-west runway. Immediately upon touchdown, Swedish fire trucks raced parallel to the runway with their nozzles trained on the Mosquito in case it burst into flames but the aircraft rolled to a stop at the end of the runway after almost three hours in the air. The fire trucks encircled the Mosquito and Swedish Air Force personnel brandishing weapons immediately surrounded the Americans. Podwojski was allowed to inspect the starboard engine and he found what appeared to be flak holes in the bottom of the cowling. Internment in Sweden was not without its compensations but one night a black limousine arrived at the American's hotel and took them to Bromma Airport where they waited in the darkness for a black B-24 that stopped nearby with engines running. They boarded the bomber and took off on their return flight to England.

Seventy-four Mosquito Red-Tail sorties (named after their red tails, so coloured to distinguish them from enemy aircraft) were flown from bases in East Anglia, each carrying the Command Pilot of 8th Air Force bombing missions. On 4 April 1945 1st Lieutenant Theodore B. Smith, pilot, 653rd Squadron and Colonel Troy W. Crawford, Commanding Officer, 446th Bomb Group, lifted off in a Mosquito on a Red Tail mission. Crawford had been selected to coordinate operations of the front third of the formation of B-24 Liberator bombers of the 2nd Air Division targeted for Parchim Airfield, west of Berlin. Parchim airfield was closed-in and the mission was diverted to Wesendorf airfield. At about 09.30 hours Crawford called the leader of the bomber force by radio to inform him that he was joining the formation. The mission was Smith's thirteenth mission in a Mosquito. He had completed one tour with a bomber group. His first twelve missions with the 25th Bomb Group were weather missions, however. This was his first Red Tail mission. He had not been briefed on procedure to adapt his routine with either his fighter escort or with bomber formations. The Mosquito must weave to allow escorting P-51s to keep pace. Bomber gunners were instructed to fire on all planes that approached within a specified range. The briefing was the responsibility of the 2nd Bomb Division.

Crawford was impressed with the formation flown by his pilots. At 10.30 hours he instructed Smith to fly around to the left of the formation to a position where he could get some good photographs. It was at this time that an Fw 190 and between eight and fifteen Me 262s attacked the formation. Smith drew too close to the bomber formation. Gunners in the lead squadron, seeing an aircraft resembling the attacking Me 262s, opened fire. The right engine of the Mosquito was hit in its cooler and died. It was followed in moments by the left engine. There was no fire and the aircraft peeled off under control. Crawford was not familiar with the escape mechanism on Mosquitoes. Smith explained how to work the lock on the escape hatch and the colonel jumped. He was followed shortly by Smith. Both landed safely and Smith and Crawford were captured but some Germans who, realising that Germany had lost the war, later freed Crawford. He returned to the USA.

John W. 'Jack' Green, a pilot in the 653rd Squadron recalls:

My navigator Johnny Mink and I were diverted on one occasion to Exeter in the south-western region of England. Two other weather mission aircraft were also diverted there. The three weather missions in one night had to be staggered to obtain insight into the movement of foul weather in the area. Our descent began at approximately 20,000ft into the cloud layer that covered all England. Our vectors or headings for us to fly were established by three receiving stations and were set to circle us down and into the somewhat narrow valley in which the airfield was located. To circle us down required a triangulation plotting from the three, registering our direction from each. Directional lines of the three must cross to determine our point of location. The ceiling was at 500ft, well below the level of the tops of the mountains surrounding. As the descent progressed the radius of the circle we were in became shorter and shorter. Finally vectors were coming one after another. We received them all and then acknowledged as we circled all the way from 20,000ft to 500ft, the ceiling level. Then came touchdown. After we parked, a staff car drove us to the front of operations command and there we were greeted by a Wing Commander with, "Wot? A Yank flying a Mosquito?" After pleasantries and curiosities were satisfied and after being introduced to his staff we were escorted to the main vector unit where we could meet the officer in charge, the one who had made the quick triangulations. With a degree of pride, I believe, and interest in us, he explained how all had been done on the board in front of him. It was quite remarkable that he could receive directional lines from two other stations register his own and plot our next bearing so rapidly. He had been very busy!

In January 1945 flying with Lieutenant Ralph E. Fisher, I returned from a mission with one engine out, dead tired, at four in the morning. There was no airfield open in all of the UK, a not uncommon occurrence for the 653rd. We were directed to head for Manston on the south-east tip of England on the surmise that the weather there might break and open for us. As we approached the coast the ceiling lifted to 200ft with visibility a quarter of a mile. But then, as we descended, we were informed that Manston had closed-in again. It was suggested that we fly west on the chance that there would be an opening somewhere. We were 200ft off the deck of the sea, south of the cliffs of Dover, in black conditions, nothing visible and still on one engine. Imagine again relying in the dark, on altimeter settings at 200ft, hoping that you are indeed, clearing the deck. And the coastline and cliffs of Dover off the starboard wing! And, what about the feelings of my navigator? This was Fisher's first flight with me. We flew for about 15 minutes when 'Blue Frock', the code name for Manston, called us back. They reported visibility had improved to a quarter of a mile again so back we went. My approach was 'hot'. I planned it that way. With only one engine it would be necessary for Lieutenant Fisher to hand pump the landing gear down and commit to some flaps for the round-out before arriving at approach speed. It worked. After all that and being dead tired, we learned that there was a small US contingent stationed at Manston to handle those Yanks landing in emergencies.

We were directed to a Nissen hut where a USAAF supply sergeant furnished OD [Olive Drab] blankets. And then told us to find a cot somewhere? The treatment received from the USAAF supply sergeant and his telling us to look for a cot somewhere, after his supplying us with the thinnest of OD blankets, could only be something of a shock to us. We had not been treated so before. But we ate the standard scrambled eggs that were furnished before turning in. We had been spoiled by the far different treatment we had always received when diverted. Usually, and hopefully, it was always an English airfield, where the Mossie could be handled and serviced by those familiar with it. Perhaps our reception at English aerodromes would be considered unusual by our standards. This was wartime. But that in itself underscores how considerate and hospitable the English everywhere were and especially when encountering the Yank flier.

Even civilians in the countryside extended themselves within the limits of their capabilities, one might think. Frequently, the extension seemed to go way beyond that.

But it was nearly morning and a moment of glory came at 8 o'clock. Not being able to sleep, I needed my diversion kit, which had been left in the aircraft. I went off to ops for help. Where had we parked the Mosquito? The duty officer, a WAAF, asked for the number of our aircraft, then left the room. She came back shortly with wide, wide eyes. "You're a 'Paint Jar!' " "Yes-?" I replied. "I've always wanted to meet a 'Paint Jar'". On a number of occasions 'Blue Frock' people had been startled late at night or in early morning when, with no radio activity, weather being so bad that no one was flying, yet a 'Paint Jar' would be heard calling for a vector. 'Paint Jar' was a mystery. Just who were they, those 'Paint Jars', the only ones aloft in such miserable weather? And on their secret missions? 'Paint Jar' was the call sign of the 653rd Squadron. My call sign was 'Paint Jar 57'. And of course my chest puffed up a bit! But I was too tired to follow up.[210]

By early 1945 several anti-Nazi agents were ready to be parachuted into Germany from American aircraft, but there were problems. In France agents had successfully used the long-established, but weighty, S-Phone device; but making air-to-ground contact with the agents once they had landed in Germany was more difficult. A large and heavy suitcase was highly suspicious and safe houses were few and far between. And anyway, the S-Phone had an effective range only up to 10,000ft, well within reach of the German flak batteries. Stephen H. Simpson, a Texan scientist with the honorary rank of Lieutenant Commander and Dewitt R. Goddard came up with a transmitter-receiver system so small that the agent in the field could easily carry it. Yet it could transmit a radio beam so narrow that it was practically immune to detection by the German 'Gonio' (Radio-goniometry) vans. The new system was named Joan-Eleanor, after Major Joan Marshall, a WAC and Goddard's wife. Goddard and Simpson's invention was modified and installed in a Mosquito after all unnecessary equipment was removed. An oxygen system was installed in the bomb bay and adapted to accommodate the Joan-Eleanor device and an operative. Eventually, five Mosquitoes were made available for Joan-Eleanor and agent-dropping missions, the latter being known as Redstockings in the hope that the German Abwehr would think they were connected with Bluestocking weather missions. Lieutenant Marvin R. Edwards, a navigator who served on B-24 and Mosquito flights, recounts:

The Joan-Eleanor radio equipment was battery operated. The transmission and receiving package carried in the Mosquito weighed about 40lb. It could pick up a voice on the ground in the 60-mile radius of the cone at 40,000ft. Beyond that, the Joan-Eleanor radio transmission and receiver equipment would not work. The transmitter and receiver were called Eleanor. The OSS agent on the ground carried the Joan section, which beamed UHF transmissions. It only weighed about two pounds and it measured only 6.5 inches x 2.25 inches x 1.5 inches. While the transmitter used by the agent on the ground spread to about a 60-mile circle at 40,000ft. The cone narrowed to just a couple of feet at ground level. Therefore the chance of the conversation being picked up by German direction finders was almost nil. The special operator in the Mosquito recorded the conversation that took place on a wire spool, which was rushed to OSS HQ for analysis. It was then immediately given to the Allied High Command, who used the information in planning future operations and strategy against Germany.

On 22 October the first test flight was made with Steve Simpson and his equipment in the rear fuselage. On 10 November 1944 the first agent, code-named Bobbie was dropped during the night at Ulrum on the German border with Holland. Bobbie was Anton Schrader, a 27-year-old Dutch engineer and the son of a Netherlands governor-general in the Dutch East Indies. An agent was given a line of 100-150 miles, anywhere along which he could use his radio. He was never to use it in the same place twice. He should broadcast from a 50-yards clearing in a forest because trees and shrubbery would quickly absorb the spreading frequency waves. The BBC would broadcast an innocuous sentence : 'Mary needs to talk to you Thursday the 10th,' at a pre-arranged time. This meant a mission would fly the line on that date after midnight and call continuously. When the agent responded he was acknowledged and the aircraft continued for 20 miles. The point was then orbited at a radius of 20 miles as the Mosquito flew in a 40-mile circle above 30,000ft. By using direction finders in the Mosquito, the contact man located the point from which the agent was transmitting. By using synchronized instruments the contact man in the plane could direct the pilot.

Simpson's first two attempts to contact Bobbie failed. Both missions were flown in Mosquito NS676, the second of two Mosquitoes supplied by the RAF, crewed by Captain Victor S. Doroski, pilot and Lieutenant Bill Miskho, navigator. On the first try the Mosquito's elevator controls jammed and control of the aircraft was wrenched from Doroski's hands. On the second effort Bobbie could not be contacted. On 22 November Simpson made a third attempt to make contact with Bobbie. Mosquito NS707 was used as NS676 had been badly damaged on landing after the abortive second trip. As they crossed the Dutch coast, Doroski lost height and the Redstocking Mosquito started circling at 30,000ft at a pre-set time and at an established rendezvous point to enable Simpson, crouched in the bomb bay, to record the conversation on the wire recorder There was no response from Bobbie. Simpson ordered Doroski down to 20,000ft in an effort to pick up the agent's signal, but still there was no response. Below the Mosquito there unfolded a barrage of fireworks. The aircraft shuddered with each burst. Simpson shouted on the intercom, "We're in a storm, Captain. You'd better get us out of here!" The reply came, "Commander, that's no storm. We're being shot at!"

Doroski climbed back up to 30,000ft and cruised around the area again. At midnight Simpson finally made contact with Bobbie. Through heavy static the agent informed Simpson that he was 'quite all right'. He said that a *Panzer* regiment was headed towards Arnhem and pinpointed a railway bridge over the Ems Canal at Leeuwarden. If Allied bombers destroyed the bridge, he said, they would paralyze traffic from this key junction into Germany. Bobbie finished abruptly. "I am standing here near German posts. It is very dangerous." Simpson said goodbye and told Doroski to head for home. (Doroski was subsequently lost on a night-photography Joker mission on 8 February 1945.)

On 12 December the seventh mission in contact with Bobbie was flown. Simpson's pilot was 'Paddy' Walker; Captain Bill Miskho flew as navigator. Bobbie told Simpson that the IX SS *Panzer* Division was in a rest camp in the area but had been ordered to move in 48 hours. He added ominously that, "...it is almost impossible to travel as all railroads, cars, trucks and buses have been taken over and are moving troops and supplies. Something big is about to happen." The message was clear and in English. After receiving and recording the full communication from Bobbie the Mosquito headed for Watton. On arrival, the recording wire was transported to London and reported to Secret Intelligence, but the significance was not realized. On 16 December Field Marshal Karl von Rundstedt's Panzer divisions attacked the Allied front-line in an area of the Ardennes where American units were in rest and rehabilitation. The German offensive achieved complete surprise and caused widespread confusion and a salient, or 'bulge', was opened. The Ardennes Offensive had proved that the German Army was not finished and agents were needed in Germany. Bobbie was later apprehended by the Abwehr, who used him to transmit deceptive intelligence, but by a pre-arranged code OSS knew that he had been 'turned' and contact missions continued to be flown regularly by the 25th Bomb Group. However, the stripped-down Mosquito flew above 45,000ft to avoid German night-fighters and interceptors. Two months later Bobbie returned to England equipped with a German radio, having persuaded the Abwehr that he would make a good double agent!

Lieutenant Marvin R. Edwards adds:

These Mosquito missions involved a crew of three, the pilot, the navigator and a special operator who spoke to the agent on the ground. A compartment was designed to hold this operator in the belly of the aircraft. After I had been shown how the Mosquito navigation equipment operated I had few problems. The navigator on the B-24 had not only to wear an oxygen mask but a heated suit and heavy gloves as well. The outside temperature at 20,000ft in December was well below zero Fahrenheit. The navigator's desk on the B-24 was located over the nose wheel and there was no air seal! Thus the temperature where the navigator stood was the same as outside the plane. Some of the navigational work required removing the gloves and thereby risking frostbite. Thus the Mossie heating system was a refreshing change. Mosquitoes used were Mk.VIII and the IX. They had Merlin 72 engines. Heat in the pilot-navigator cockpit area stayed at room temperature. These models were not pressurised so oxygen masks had to be used. We later learned that the Mossie was not designed to carry a passenger in the modified compartment. Happily, except for the great discomfort of the special operator, the plane handled well on most occasions. We all noted that the engines in American aircraft seemed to roar, while the Merlins seemed to purr. We were also impressed with the automatic supercharger that was activated at about 20,000ft, as we climbed to an altitude of 28-40,000ft. The thrust was so strong that it seemed as though we were taking off again. Once we reached 40,000ft we felt secure. The German flak could not reach us. The only German planes that presented any threat were the jet fighters that the Germans developed near the war's end. Their numbers were very limited. Since our plywood plane was at such a high altitude, we felt that the German radar would have difficulty in spotting us. This was important. To maintain both our speed and altitude, our Mossie was stripped of what was considered all excess weight. We had no armament of any kind. Even our IFF (Identification Friend or Foe) was removed. Eliminating the IFF did present a problem on occasion when we returned to England.

On 21 January 1945 a team code-named Troy was dropped into Stuttgart. They were followed on 28 February by a second team code-named Anzio, who were also dropped into Stuttgart. On the night of 1/2 March 1945 a lone A-26 Invader dropped two agents code-named Hammer near Berlin (the Mosquito could carry only one agent). The mission required two weeks of preparation, which included collecting all information from British sources regarding territory covered in flight. The crewmembers were familiarised with enemy gun batteries, enemy flying fields and enemy radar installations, enemy fighter control points and enemy navigational aids. Drop-points near large watercourses, which could be seen in the dark of the moon, were selected. Specialised navigational equipment was installed. The selected course was plotted on a special LORAN and Gee trainer attached to a link trainer. Major John W. Walch and William G. Miskho, the two navigators and Robert Walker the pilot, spent days in training for a fully co-ordinated exercise. The mission was flown on a moonlit night at fence-top level all the way. The flight took a zigzag course, following rivers and other features discernible at night. It skirted mountains and defensive areas. Major John W. Walch sat in the nose reading maps and observing the terrain. Bill Miskho operated specialised equipment. The weather was good of course. A weather observation flight to Berlin in a Mosquito had preceeded the mission and reported conditions as clear and favourable. The mission was successful.[211] On 12 March a Redstocking Mosquito flying 30,000ft over Berlin successfully established contact with one of the Hammer agents by using Joan-Eleanor. The total exercise resulted in one of the most valuable intelligence commitments of the war.

On 20 March when over 400 B-17s and B-24s raided the shipyard and dock area at Hamburg a very eventful Chaff-dispensing mission was flown by four Mosquito XVIs of the 654th Bomb Squadron, as Lieutenant Roger W. Gilbert, one of the pilots, relates:[212]

The four aircraft began take-off shortly after 14.00 hours and contacted the bombers at the initial point one hour later. We took position ahead of and below the bombers at 26,000ft, flying four abreast. Over Stade, Germany 30 miles west of the target we began discharging chaff. This continued to and over Hamburg. We had received at least three radio transmissions warning us of Me 262 jets in the area. On the last call Lieutenant Norman R. Magee, pilot in the lead aircraft, called for us to break left because the jets were coming through our flight. Lieutenant Raymond G. Spoerl, my navigator, checking from the observation bubble, reported that one jet appeared to be coming toward us from six o'clock high. A moment later Spoerl reported that the jet was firing at us and I broke as hard as I could to the left. We had turned about 45° when we began taking 30mm hits in the cockpit, the instrument panel, the observation canopy and the left wing. The battle damage to the left wing helped us turn even tighter to the left, taking us out of the line of fire. The 30mm shells had worked the wing over, however. We were going down out of control in a tight spiral. The jet flashed by us on our right. Spoerl, who had been monitoring the jets' activities from the observation bubble and without his safety belt, was thrown to the floor by gravity forces. This occurred as the cannon fire punched the hole in the observation bubble. As I looked down at Ray on the floor I thought that he had been shot. I was concerned that I could not get out of the tight spiral because of the damage to the left wing, but with a high power setting on the left engine the Mosquito straightened up. By keeping a much higher power setting on the left engine than the right, the Mosquito flew fairly well and, with the lifting of gravity forces, Raymond lifted himself up and proved to be OK: his lucky day.

Taking inventory of the damage, we found that the left wing-tip was lost. The flap and aileron extended perhaps two feet beyond the shredded main structure of the wing. The ailerons that had been jammed temporarily in the left turn position now worked only part way and the radio was inoperative. We had dropped 8,000ft below the flight, could not communicate and were no longer part of the team. We were on our own as we turned toward Watton. I did not experience further control problems unless my speed slowed to 170 mph. Then the aircraft would fall off to the left. Without the radio we could not communicate with the Watton control tower. To alert their personnel to our problems I raced across the field and by the control tower with the damaged wing on a level with and near its windows. Fortunately the control personnel saw it. I circled the field and set the wheels down at the edge of the runway at just above 170 mph. We stopped comfortably and taxied to our dispersal area. The crash and fire equipment were already on their way. They were followed shortly by the maintenance officer and the operations staff of the Squadron. The damaged wing was attracting concern combined with wonder and we were suddenly VIPs.

The other three craft on the Chaff dispensing mission escaped damage from the attack of German jets. Though the Mosquito of 1st Lieutenant Joseph A. Polovick and 1st Lieutenant Bernard M. Blaum had been attacked directly by one jet, they evaded its line of fire with the accepted tactic of breaking and diving for several thousand feet. The three Mosquitoes regrouped and completed their mission beyond the target. The jets, which had apparently reached their fuel limits, did not follow them.

Once the three Mosquitoes turned toward home German defences lost interest in them. Two of the Mosquitoes developed mechanical problems while Findley's Mosquito purred back to Watton without a misfire. Lieutenant Norman R. Magee and Lieutenant Len A. Erickson were forced to feather their starboard engine propeller and drop out of the flight but they returned to Watton alone and without further concerns. The Mosquito flown by Polovick and Blaum was the one Mosquito that did not return. They and the Mosquito flown by Lieutenant Charles Findley and Lieutenant Robert Balser were still flying in formation and in good form until they were exiting Germany over the North Friesian Islands. Over the island of Fohr one engine of Polovick's Mosquito ceased to function, followed shortly by the other, caused, apparently by a vapour lock in the fuel lines. As their Mosquito glided toward the central part of the island Findley and Balser circled over them. Two parachutes opened. Both Polovick and Balser became prisoners of war and were held in *Stalag Luft* I at Barth. (They were liberated in early May by Russian forces and were flown by Allied aircraft to a staging area near Reims, France. Polovick returned to Watton but Balser was transferred directly back to the United States from France).

On 13 March operations had moved to Harrington, where 492nd Bomb Group 'Carpetbagger' Liberators, commanded by Colonel Hudson H. Upham were used on covert missions. B-24 and B-17 night leaflet crews arrived from Cheddington at the same time and chaos ensued. Mosquito maintenance suffered drastically and, eventually, RAF ground personnel were brought in to maintain the aircraft. OSS regained control over all Mosquito operations and 25th Bomb Group pilots and navigators flew the aircraft until enough 492nd Bomb Group personnel were available. A 492nd Bomb Group pilot and navigator carried Commander Simpson on their first communications mission on 31 March 1945.

One of Lieutenant Marvin R. Edwards' 'most meaningful' rendezvous Mosquito flights was in mid-April 1945:

> Our assignment was to fly in orbit at a point in the Munich area. There had been reports that the German military were planning a last ditch stand in the mountains near Munich known as the 'Redoubt'. That concept was first talked about after the failure of the last massive German counter attack in December 1944 in the Battle of the Bulge. Certain members of the German High Command had believed that underground fortifications and factories connected by tunnels could be constructed in the Alps. They believed that such a complex would be impregnable, even from air attacks. Many of those defending the facility would be German SS Storm Troops. Shortly after the war's end, in May 1945, I went to OSS HQ in Grosvenor Square in London. I was informed that the OSS agent contacted in Bavaria had reported that there would be no organised German resistance in that area. The plan never got off the ground. The Germans offered no resistance to the American army assigned to that sector of operations.

Taking off from Watton on 6 April 1945 the right engine of 1st Lieutenant John A. Pruis and 1st Lieutenant Claude Moore's Mosquito suddenly burst into flames. Pruis immediately chopped the throttle and feathered the right propeller. He gave more power to the right-hand engine, corrected flight altitude and worked to gain altitude. They levelled off at 1,000ft and got on the downwind leg but the right engine fanned into flame again and the prop began windmilling out of control. Pruis held extra power to compensate for the loss of the engine and as a result they were half way down the runway when they touched down. Moore jettisoned the escape hatch overhead and at the same moment pulled up the landing gear. Within seconds they were skidding, spinning around and coming to a very abrupt halt. Both men got out before the Mosquito was engulfed in flames, which were extinguished by fire fighters. Pruis and Moore were debriefed, reports were written up and they were given another Mosquito and sent up again, all within the hour. Moore was philosophical: 'Just another day.' He was also resourceful: he had rescued his parachute and, after giving it to a buddy nearby, it somehow made its way back to the States where silk cloth was unavailable, even with a ration card, and it furnished material for parts of a young bride's trousseau!

Three days after the crash John Pruis and Claude Moore took off again, this time on a Gray-Pea mission with three other Mosquitoes to escort a long, maximum-effort mission by B-17s of the 1st Air Division to Oberpfaffenhofen, a suburb 20 miles north of Munich in south-eastern Germany. The reconnaissance flight rendezvoused with the bomber formation prior to the IP, 28 miles from the target. At the IP they climbed 2,000ft above the bombers and began to dispense chaff. Cameras were activated as the Mosquitoes massed over the target area to obtain photo coverage before the bombing began. After passing over the target, the

Mosquitoes orbited and followed behind the bombers to obtain pictures of damage to the target area. After the damage assessment circuit over the target Pruis still had unused film. They obeyed a duty-conscious impulse and flew over the target once again, taking more pictures of the damage. Their concern for good pictures distanced them far behind the other three Mosquitoes. They set their course on a 314° heading to catch and to make eventual contact with the Mosquitoes and return to base.

This was Pruis' third Mosquito mission with the 25th Bomb Group. He had completed a tour in B-24 bombers. As pilot he was concerned with fuel consumption and, considering the distance of the mission, he had good reason. Though fuel consumption would be close, all concerns for engine and aircraft performance were minor. Flying at 20,000ft they could see three aircraft in the distance on a course toward England and presumed these to be their companion Mosquitoes. As they approached closer, however, they decided that the aircraft were P-51s but they were without American markings. The P-51s banked to the left and Pruis and Moore dismissed them from their thoughts. Some minutes later Moore was noting observations on his navigational chart or log when there was an explosion. With two engines running, an indication of an explosion was not so much a noise as a jolt. Not until Pruis slumped over the wheel did Moore become fully aware of the circumstances. He attempted to help Pruis but was unable to move him. The Mosquito began a right-hand spin with the right engine in flames. With the right-hand spin the flames from the right or starboard engine blazed across both the canopy and the bottom escape hatches. Black smoke poured from the right side of the nose between the cockpit and the nacelle. Still, Moore did not know what had happened. He had not seen any enemy aircraft from the back of their Mosquito.

Moore never wore a parachute on his missions. A seat pack placed him too high in relation with the canopy and the work table. A chest pack pushed him too far from the plotting table and was burdensome to work with. He stored his parachute pack on a small shelf behind the pilot. The centrifugal force from the spinning aircraft was formidable. Moore experienced a difficult time reaching for his chute behind the pilot. It took the strength of both arms to grasp the pack and pull it toward him. He then attempted to connect it to his harness but, due to the centrifugal forces, he managed to connect only one side. He had more trouble than he thought he should and later, in the hospital, he learned the reason for his awkwardness. He had shrapnel wounds in his left arm from aircraft cannon shells.

An exit from the bottom hatch would be normal but Moore was afraid the flames would rise into the cockpit. He wasn't able to help Pruis but, if Pruis should regain consciousness and was able to do something for himself Moore did not want the flames coming into the cockpit. Thus, he released the canopy escape hatch and it flew off. Leaving the craft from the canopy escape-hatch was, of course, a high-risk endeavour. The probabilities of being struck by the vertical stabilizer were disturbing. Moore struggled through the hatch but he became entangled with the oxygen and communication cables inside the aircraft. He became stuck half in and half out of the top opening. He had been working without his helmet and wore no gloves. Flames lashed his upper body, seared his face and scalp and burned flesh from his hands and wrists. Fortunately he still wore his Rayban sunglasses as tongues of flame from the right engine lapped at him. Blood covered his left arm and the earth below swirled closer. He pulled himself back into the cockpit to remove the tangled cable obstructions that prevented his escape. Now, back in the cockpit the obstacles restraining his efforts alarmed Moore. It was enough to unnerve the less contrary.

Moore was weaker from the burns and wounds than in his first attempt to exit. The pain was driving through the tension to his senses. The centrifugal forces of the spinning aircraft became more intense by the second. There was no sensation of up or down, just the vision of an earth spinning closer on a collision course. He felt his first and only taste of discouragement. Perhaps Pruis was fortunate in finding peace in the sky. Pacific submission was out of character for Moore, however and his hesitancy was replaced with defiance. Pruis was dead or unconscious but Moore's limbs still responded to his will. A reaction of rage against the obstacles thrust all thought of his frailties from his mind. With a profane utterance he made his utmost and final effort to climb through the hatch. As he pulled out he glanced at the altimeter. It read 1,000ft. He later interpolated that he left the aircraft at 800ft. He was not fully conscious when he pulled the ripcord. Moore was jolted heavily to consciousness by the opening of the parachute. He was swinging violently in circles as he descended, probably due to the right chest hook being unfastened. He attempted to pull the risers to get the chute buckle fastened but with the burns and injuries to his arms and hands he failed. It was then that he noticed the bleeding from his left upper arm and forearm.

As Moore descended fighter planes circled him. They were P-51s with the roundel markings of the Free French Air Force. These Mustangs circled only minutes then left the vicinity. Moore had not seen the aircraft that had fired at their Mosquito but he knew that the shells entered the fuselage diagonally from the left rear side. He knew that Pruis and the starboard engine had received the brunt of their effects. He also remembered that three P-51s, flying ahead of them, had banked to their left and had flown past them to their rear. Moore turned his attention to the ground where he could see the impacted Mosquito. The fire was confined to the right engine and had not spread to the rest of the aircraft. Its nose and the forward part of the fuselage were intact. At that moment a gust of wind swept his Rayban glasses from his eyes. He was fortunate that they had shielded his eyes from the flames as he exited the escape hatch. Below him Moore saw evergreen trees with tall spindling trunks and an abundance of weak, flimsy limbs. He attempted to guide the parachute to smaller fruit trees nearby but failed in the short drop. The parachute caught in the top of a tall green tree, leaving him hanging by the risers 50 to 75ft above the ground.

There were several armed German soldiers near the base of the tree where he was hanging. They seemed to be contemplating his plight but did not seem concerned. He passed out soon after hitting the trees and when consciousness returned the German soldiers were gone. Moore unfastened the harness of his chute but with difficulty. His hands were burned raw; his arm was bleeding and his face felt like it was on fire. His first-aid pack, attached to the parachute harness, had been torn off as he ploughed through the branches. He attempted to climb down the pine tree but the limbs would not support his weight. Suddenly the branches were snapping and he was falling. He fell straight down in an upright position. Moore attempted to stand but the pain was intense. His back, left ankle, knee and foot were injured. He thought of using a limb for a cane to get to help. Physically, it was hopeless. Moore looked at his wristwatch and, except for the rim around the dial, the face was burned. It said 17.45 hours. The forest was beginning to darken. He needed medical attention. He could hardly see. He decided that he had to take his chances. Moore always carried a whistle attached to the zipper-pull of his pocket. This was an RAF custom that he had appropriated. He blew the whistle and heard the rustle of twigs and brush. He blew again and a soldier appeared holding his rifle at the ready across his body. Luckily they were soldiers of the 103rd Infantry Division. They took off their shirts and jackets, gathered two large tree branches and made a stretcher to carry Moore down a hill to two jeeps. They placed him diagonally on the flat platform of one of the jeeps and held him closely to prevent jostling on the bumpy ride. He was carried to a first-aid station located in a commandeered German home.

Moore remained in hospitals for the better part of two years. For several months after his arrival at the hospital in Reims the doctors concentrated on his broken back, a ruptured cartilage in his knee, an injured ankle and the shrapnel wounds in his arm. He was then transferred to two burn centres in England where his hand, face and scalp received skin grafts and other attention. Later, he was transferred to the States where he received attention at two more hospitals. When married, years after the mission, he was still wearing a body cast. Pruis is buried in Lorraine American Cemetery, France.

On 12 April President Roosevelt passed away in Warm Springs, Georgia. His son was relieved of his command and a recommendation for a Presidential Citation for the 25th Bomb Group was discarded. Requests for awards for the 325th Photographic Wing, signed by Elliott Roosevelt, were returned, stamped 'Denied'. After 3 May 1945 Redstocking missions became an all-492nd Bomb Group operation. Animosity between Upham's bomb group and OSS reached a peak and negotiations at the highest level were held in London to resolve the matter. The outcome was that the 492nd Bomb Group extended its B-24 operations to include central Germany and beyond. And, as Lyon had proved unsuitable for Carpetbagger operations, new bases were established at Bron Field, Dijon in France and at Namur, Belgium. The OSS was anxious to despatch their growing number of anti-Nazi agents to Germany. Carpetbaggers flew eleven Redstocking missions (and twelve communications missions from England, only, two of which were successful). Between 19 March and 28/29 April 1945, thirty-one successful Joan-Eleanor missions and forty-seven unsuccessful Redstocking sorties were flown.

The 25th Bomb Group expected to be sent to the Pacific, but soon orders arrived to return their Mosquitoes to the RAF Lieutenant Warren Borges wrote: 'We came home…after flying our beloved Mosquitoes into a field ('Boondocks'…the grass was two feet high!) in Scotland; what a sad day!'

Quietly, without ceremony or flag-waving, the Americans' involvement with the Mosquito was over.

CHAPTER EIGHT

The Reich Intruders

From 1943 to 1945 Mosquito FB.VI (and later NF.XII and NF.XIII squadrons) in 2nd Tactical Air Force intruded over the Reich, bombing and strafing German lines of communication and *Luftwaffe* airfields. In 2nd TAF the FB.VI is probably best remembered for daylight precision operations, particularly pinpoint raids on Gestapo buildings in occupied Europe. No.2 Group had been transferred to 2nd TAF on 1 June 1943. Air Vice Marshal Basil Embry replaced Air Vice Marshal d'Albiac at HQ, Bylaugh Hall with the task of preparing 2 Group for invasion support in the run-up to Operation Overlord: the invasion of France. Embry was an excellent choice for the newfound role. He successfully fought off an attempt to re-equip 2 Group with Vultee Vengeance dive-bombers and saw to it that his Lockheed Ventura-equipped squadrons were re-equipped with the Mosquito FB.VI, which was armed with four cannon for night Intruder operations. Re-equipment began in August 1943 with 140 Wing at Sculthorpe, when 464 (RAAF) and 487 (RNZAF) Squadrons exchanged their obsolete Lockheed machines. No.21 Squadron closely followed them in September, all three squadrons moving to Hunsdon in December 1943. On 15 October 138 Wing at Lasham began operating FB.VIs when 613 (City of Manchester) Squadron joined 2 Group. In December they were joined by 305 (Polish) Squadron converted from the Mitchell and in February 1944 107 Squadron converted from the Douglas Boston. It was planned to transfer 138 Wing to airfields in France when the outbreak from the Normandy beachhead came. As part of the newfound offensive, the main work for the FB.VIs of 138 and 140 Wings was Day and Night Ranger operations and Intruder sorties from England.[213]

In 2nd TAF the FB.VI carried out precision attacks, often on individual buildings, by day and night. Probably the most famous of these was Operation Jericho, which went ahead on 18 February 1944 after snowstorms and thick cloud had led to several postponements. In January information had been received in London that over 100 loyal Frenchmen, among them Monsieur Vivant, a key Resistance leader in Abbeville, were being held in captivity in Amiens prison. Several attempts by the Resistance had been made to rescue them but had failed. Dominique Ponchardier the leader of the local Resistance requested an urgent air strike to break open the prison walls. There would be casualties, but better to die from RAF bombs than be shot by a German firing squad. A dozen prisoners were due to be executed on 19 February. The prison was built in the shape of a cross and surrounded by a wall 20ft high and 3ft thick. To help identify the target area a model of the prison was prepared, as Embry recalled:

> When called upon to destroy that kind of target, we constructed a model of it and also of the town. We then placed the town model on a table and examined it at eye level, obtaining exactly the same oblique view, in miniature, as if we were flying over the town at a height of 50 feet. We then selected a combination of easily recognisable landmarks, such as church spires and factory chimneys, which we adopted as navigational markers to define our approach route to the target. At the start of the approach the landmarks might be as far as two miles apart, but the distance between markers would be gradually narrowed down until eventually it was as if we were flying down a visual beam of approach. On the town models we marked the known positions of all light flak guns and took these into account when selecting the approach route. We used the target model to help the crews to recognise their objective and to decide aiming points, especially if the attack was being made by more than one sub-formation of six aircraft. Sometimes the models were photographed and copies issued to crews at their briefing which they took with them in the air to help in their final approach and identification of the target.

The plan was to breach this wall by using 11-second delayed action bombs dropped by five FB.VIs of 464 Squadron RAAF led by Wing Commander R.W. 'Bob' Iredale and six of 487 Squadron RNZAF led by Wing Commander Irving S. 'Black' Smith. The concussion from the bomb explosions should open the cell doors to give most of the prisoners a chance to escape. Wing Commander 'Black' Smith was pleased to be going on this mission:

> After four years of war just doing everything possible to destroy life, here we were going to use our skill to save it. It was a grand feeling and everybody left the briefing room prepared to fly into the walls rather than fail to breach them.

If the first two waves of Mosquitoes failed, six FB.VIs of 21 Squadron led by Wing Commander I.G. 'Daddy' Dale had orders to flatten the prison complex. Embry was forbidden to go on the raid because of his previous exploits in France and Group Captain Percy C. Pickard DSO DFC, CO 140 Wing was in overall command of the raid. He and his navigator Flight Lieutenant John Alan 'Peter' Broadley DSO DFC DFM flew in F-Freddie (HX922), a 487 Squadron Mosquito and flew with the 464 Squadron formation. (Pickard, a brave and revered leader, as a Flight Lieutenant he and Wellington F-Freddie had appeared in the British wartime film, *Target for Tonight*.) Flight Lieutenant Tony Wickham, in DZ414/O, a specially equipped Film Photographic Unit Mosquito IV with a cameraman,

Pilot Officer Leigh Howard, would film the bombing operation. Typhoon IBs of 174 (Mauritius) Squadron and 245 (Northern Rhodesia) Squadron at Westhampnett were detailed to provide the Mosquitoes with escort cover.

The formation of nineteen Mosquitoes took off from Hunsdon at 10.55 hours with snow falling and headed for their rendezvous with the Typhoons over Littlehampton. Over the Channel the weather improved but by then Flight Lieutenant E.E. Hogan and Flight Sergeant D.A.S. Crowfoot and Flight Sergeant A. Steadman and Pilot Officer E.J. Reynolds, in 21 Squadron were forced to return. Two Typhoons in 245 Squadron aborted with fuel problems and 174 Squadron failed to make the rendezvous at all. About 10 miles from the target Flight Lieutenant B.D. 'Titch' Hanafin and Pilot Officer C. Frank Redgrave of 487 Squadron RNZAF were forced to abort 10 miles short of the target because of an engine fire. They extinguished the fire and flew home on one engine. Hanafin was again hit by flak, which paralyzed one side of his body. He was met and escorted home by 'Black' Smith and he made a perfect landing at a forward airfield in England. The remaining Mosquitoes descended to 100ft and they pressed on at no higher than tree-top level, avoiding power lines and known flak batteries. The formation swept around to the south of Albert and the crews picked up the long, straight tree-lined road to Amiens. Descending to 10ft their propellers swirled wispy snow clouds in their wake. The poplars on the road ended abruptly and a mile in the distance the prison stood out in fresh snow. The Mosquitoes split up and attacked in four waves from two directions at 12.01 hours precisely as the guards were eating their lunch.

The first bombs were dropped on the outer walls on the east and north sides of the prison by the four 487 Squadron FB.VIs led by Wing Commander 'Black' Smith. The five FB.VIs of 464 Squadron and Pickard's Mosquito closely followed them. Their target was the main building and the guards' quarters at the east and west ends of the prison. Eight Typhoons of 174 Squadron provided escort over the target while six Typhoons of 245 Squadron covered Wing Commander I.G. 'Daddy' Dale's four remaining 21 Squadron Mosquitoes, which orbited 10 miles to the north, ready if needed. The first bombs blew in almost all the doors and the wall was breached. Wing Commander R.W. 'Bob' Iredale said later:

> I pinpointed the guards' quarters, let go my bombs so that they would skid right into the annex, with the sloping roof of the prison inches from the belly of my plane as I climbed over it.

Flight Lieutenant Tony Wickham made three passes over the ruined jail, which was now disgorging smoke and flame and fleeing men and Pilot Officer Leigh Howard filmed the flight of the prisoners.

Pickard was the last over the prison and after dropping his bombs he circled the area at 500ft to assess the results. Satisfied that the Mosquitoes had done their work, the success signal 'RED-RED-RED' was radioed to 'Daddy' Dale so that they could return home. Almost immediately Fw 190s of II/JG26 attacked the

Mosquitoes and took on the Typhoons. *Feldwebel* Wilhelm Mayer[214] singled out F-Freddie and sent it crashing in flames and Pickard and Broadley were killed. *Leutnant* Waldemar 'Waldi' Radener of 7./JG26 shot down a 174 Squadron Typhoon flown by Flying Officer J.E. Renaud north of Amiens and the pilot was taken prisoner. Squadron Leader Alexander Ian McRitchie and Flight Lieutenant R.W. 'Sammy' Sampson's Mosquito in 464 Squadron RAAF was downed by flak. The Australian second flight leader was wounded in twenty-six places and he crash-landed at over 200 mph near Poix. McRitchie survived and was taken prisoner but Sampson was dead.[215] Pilot Officer Maxwell Sparkes and Pilot Officer Arthur Dunlop of 487 Squadron suffered a flak hit in an engine and they were escorted home by 'Black' Smith. Sparkes put down safely at a south coast airfield in England. Foul weather over the Channel claimed another 174 Squadron Typhoon, flown by Flight Sergeant H.S. Brown. (Group Captain Peter Wykeham-Barnes DSO DFC* became the new 140 Wing commander). In March 1944 Dominique Ponchardier sent the following message to London.

> I thank you in the name of our comrades for the bombardment of the prison, we were not able to save all. Thanks to the admirable precision of the attack the first bomb blew in nearly all the doors and 150 prisoners escaped with the help of the civilian population. Of these, twelve were to have been shot on 19 February. In addition, thirty-seven prisoners were killed; some of them by German machine guns and fifty Germans were also killed.

On 15 February George Murray and Harry Batt and Gordon Bell-Irving,[216] Bert Hott, Flight Lieutenant J.L. 'Les' Bulmer, navigator and his pilot Flight Lieutenant Ed McQuarrie RCAF had joined 21 Squadron at Hunsdon. This was a surprise to them for having completed the Night Intruder course at 60 OTU High Ercall they expected to join one of the three Intruder squadrons: 418, 605 (both in the UK) or 23 in Malta. Les Bulmer remembers the move:

> When we joined, 21 Squadron's principal occupation was attacking V-1 (Noball) sites at low level. We had no experience of low-level navigation so we spent all February practising low-level cross-country and formation flying. On 18 February we watched all three squadrons of the wing take off in a snowstorm for what we later discovered was the Amiens prison raid. The only time I saw the 140 Wing CO, Group Captain Charles Pickard, was in the Mess the night before the raid. The whole squadron was sworn to secrecy when we heard he was missing in case he had got away but it was not long before we received news that he was dead.

Flight Lieutenants Les Bulmer and Ed McQuarrie RCAF flew their first 21 Squadron operation, a Night Intruder, to the airfield at Montdidier on 2 March.

> Although we were new boys, because we'd been trained as Night Intruders

we had more night-flying experience on Mosquitoes than the old hands. We took off at 19.55 and returned at 21.55. It was uneventful. I was not sure what to expect as we crossed the French coast but I rather imagined it would be flak and searchlight all the way in and all the way out. Instead there was just total darkness, with the odd glimmer of a light and nobody seemed to be interested in us at all; or was a night-fighter creeping up on us? I kept constant lookout rearwards. The night was very dark and Gee was jammed once we crossed the coast, so navigation had to be by dead reckoning. We were somewhere in the area but could not locate the airfield and the Germans would not co-operate and put on the lights for us, so we returned home somewhat disappointed.

No.2 Group Mosquitoes tried various techniques in attacking Noball sites. The normal method was to go low-level all the way but this had resulted in aircraft sustaining damage by 20mm flak when crossing the coast. On 4 March we were one of four aircraft to attack two sites. Our target was near Esclavelles and we took off at 08.10. Noball targets were far too small to get four aircraft over them within 11 seconds, which was the delay we had on the 500lb bombs. The squadron CO, Wing Commander I.G. 'Daddy' Dale, led with 'A' Flight Commander Squadron Leader Joe Bodien as his No.2. As a 'sprog' crew we were to stick with Flight Lieutenant Mike Benn, who was one of the squadron's most experienced pilots.[217]

We crossed the Channel at low level and climbed as we reached the coast to about 3,000ft to avoid the flak. There we split into pairs for our respective targets and got down on the deck. Not long afterwards I noticed a red glow on the edge of a wood on the starboard side. This became several red balls that travelled rapidly towards us. It was then that I realised what flak looked like from the wrong end. The stream of 20mm appeared to be heading along the wing and into the cockpit, so Mac and I instinctively ducked. Luckily it passed overhead and we went thankfully on our way.

At briefing we had arranged to fly beyond the target, turn and attack on the way out. We arrived at the turning point but nothing happened. There was strict radio silence so we couldn't ask Mike and his navigator, Flying Officer W.A. Roe what they were doing. We just had to stick with them and hope that they knew where they were. Eventually they did start to turn and all hell broke loose. In fact, Roe had missed the turning point and when he did eventually start to turn he led us into a real hornet's nest. Everything happened so fast but we suddenly found ourselves in a valley with a railway in the bottom and rows of huts up the valley sides. I don't know what the area was but they obviously objected to our presence and the sky erupted in 20mm flak from all directions. Mike Benn started to climb out of harm's way and we followed behind but were surrounded by streams of tracer and we had an uncomfortable few seconds when flak intended for

Mike was crossing in front of our nose, while that for us was crossing just behind the tail. Mac said, "Sod this, I'm going down" and shoved the stick forward. As he did so there was a loud bang. I checked to see if we were on fire or losing fuel but everything was normal.

By this time we had lost sight of Mike Benn and were somewhere south-east of the target. If we tried to make the target on our own we might arrive just as his bombs were due to explode, so we headed for a secondary target in a wood. We duly dropped our four 500-pounders on a hut in the wood and fled at high speed towards the coast. We flew low over a large chateau outside which German troops were milling around, then I told Ed to climb before we hit the coast. Unfortunately I left it too late and we were on top of the coast as we started to climb. Up came the flak, hosing around us and down went the nose as we sped out to sea, weaving like mad and followed by the now all too familiar tracer. Soon we were clear and heading for home, somewhat relieved to find ourselves still in one piece.

When we got back to Hunsdon we found that a 20-mm shell had come up underneath us from the port and entered the starboard nacelle. It blew a large hole in the inboard side of the nacelle and a smaller one in the outboard side. Shell splinters had knocked chunks out of the starboard flap and out of the fuselage side just about where I was sitting. I was thankful that a Mosquito had a thick skin; if it had been metal I would probably have had a sore bum. The shell struck in the only part of the nacelle where it couldn't do any damage: in the rear fairing. Any farther forward and it would have smashed the undercarriage.

For another Noball, on 7 March, to near Les Essarts, our leader was Flight Lieutenant Duncan A. 'Buck' Taylor, with Squadron Leader Philippe Livry-Level as his navigator.[218] We decided to stay high after crossing the coast, identify the target, dive on it, then climb back up to 3,000-4,000ft until clear of the coast on the way back. There was a flak position on the right of our approach to the target, so we arranged that we would both fire our cannons as we dived, hoping that this would make them keep their heads down until we were clear. Everything went according to plan and we arrived over the target and went into a steep dive, both of us firing cannons on the way down. There was no problem from the flak position but as we pulled out of the dive and released the bombs a burst of 20mm shot up vertically in front of us. Buck was clear but we had no choice but to fly through it. As we climbed away I looked back to see the whole site erupt as 4,000lb of high explosive went off. I must say that I've always had a grudging admiration for the guy who shot at us. To be blasted with eight cannons and yet have the nerve to jump up and let fly at us, presumably aware that he was about to get eight 500lb bombs around his ear holes took some courage.

Ed said, "Check around. I think we've been hit." There was so much racket from the cannons as we dived that I hadn't heard any bang but I checked for fire and loss of fuel. The fuel gauges were reading normal, so we joined up with Buck for the return trip. We climbed to 4,000ft and stayed there until clear of the coast, then dropped down to sea level over the Channel. Soon after we were clear of the French coast Buck's aircraft fired off a Very cartridge and he was obviously in trouble. I checked the list of the colours of the day but the one he'd used wasn't on it. We were puzzled and expected him to ditch at any moment but nothing happened. I tackled Philippe at debriefing and he explained that he had to have a smoke, he used a long cigarette holder, and since the designers of the Mosquito had forgotten to include an ashtray in the specification, he was forced to improvise. An empty Very cartridge case would fill his requirements, so he emptied one! Smoking in or near an aircraft was strictly forbidden but Philippe was a law unto himself.

Ed had been right in thinking that we'd been hit; a 20mm shell had exploded in the port spinner. It appeared that bits of it had gone rearwards through the engine, because the bottom cowling had a number of carbuncles that weren't there when we started. And yet the engine and propeller pitch mechanism had functioned perfectly, which gave me a great deal of confidence in the Merlin. I was beginning to think that if these sort of trips were the norm then sooner of later a shell would find a vital spot and our chances of completing a tour of ops looked none too promising. In the event these were the only times that we sustained damage although they weren't the only times the enemy took a dislike to us and let fly.

Our next two ops were also against V-1 sites but employed a very different technique. Six aircraft, in two vics of three, joined up with two Pathfinder Mosquitoes fitted with Oboe, at the coast. We followed the lead Oboe aircraft up to 20,000ft while the second Oboe aircraft tagged along behind in case of equipment failure in the lead aircraft. We had an escort of six Spits, which was some comfort. The idea was that we would maintain close formation on the Oboe aircraft. His four bombs were set to drop in a stick and the boffins had calculated that, by the time the third bomb appeared out of the bomb bay, we would have woken up and released our bombs also. So the leader's third bomb was supposed to be on target, with the first two undershooting and the last one overshooting. The only snag with this system was that Oboe required that we fly in tight formation, straight and level for 10 minutes until bomb release. This was not exactly amusing, since the Germans were somewhat hostile and slung a lot of heavy flak at us as we approached the target east of Abbeville. It was a long 10 minutes, sitting there at 20,000ft, having to take everything that was thrown at us and not being able to take avoiding action. You just prayed that your name was not on any of the bits of metal that were being flung into the sky. The Spits, wisely, kept well clear of the formation at this time, as did the stand-in Oboe aircraft, who only closed in tight at the last minute.

With bombs gone we turned for home. From that height Dungeness looked so close. The rest of the formation had adopted a 'last man home's a sissy' attitude and were hell bent for the English coast. With wartime camouflage it was difficult to see an aircraft from above; it merged very effectively with the ground below. So suddenly Ed and I found ourselves all alone in the sky and, reckoning that we'd outstayed our welcome, stuck the nose down and went, hell for leather for Dungeness and safety. We were travelling so fast that even with the throttles right back and the undercarriage warning horn blowing continuously the ASI was indicating well over 300 mph. And I was wondering at what speed the wings came off. Part way across the Channel we caught up with another Mosquito and tried to maintain some form of decorum by flying in formation with him. One of the Spit escort managed to catch us up in mid-Channel and stayed with us until we crossed the Kent coast when he did a victory roll and headed for his base, wherever that was. At debriefing the flight leader, Squadron Leader Ritchie issued a rocket. He said we'd behaved like naughty schoolboys who'd been breaking windows and then run away. I don't think we cared that much, as long as we'd broken the right windows. Sadly, we hadn't. The much-vaunted Oboe had caused us to drop our bombs several miles, I believe, from the target. So, as a penance for our sins, we had to go out next day and do it all over again and this time we did all come back together. For the rest of March and the first half of April our ops were all Night Intruders on airfields in Holland and France. We never spotted any aircraft but we did bomb and strafe the runways and dispersals. At Evreux the Germans were most co-operative and switched the lights on for us. We made what we thought was a bombing attack, that is, until we got back to base and I found a dark object hanging under each wing, which shouldn't have been there. Ed had forgotten to select the bombs.

The last raid on Hengelo by twelve Mosquitoes of 140 Wing, 2nd TAF took place on 18 March 1944. Although the Stork Works was no longer on the target list there was still the important target of Hazemeyer. The low-level raid was led by Wing Commander R.W. 'Bob' Iredale DFC and involved four aircraft from each of 487 Squadron RNZAF, 464 Squadron RAAF and 21 Squadron RAF at Hunsdon. A Mosquito of 487 Squadron aborted its sortie 5 miles south-west of Lowestoft after an engine failure while another hit a tree when it took evasive action to avoid hitting another Mosquito. Three remaining aircrews bombed the target at 16.36 hours and very good results were claimed. The whole area was seen to have numerous fires. No.464 Squadron bombed a minute ahead of 21 Squadron and crews succeeded in hitting the central part of the main building and setting it on fire. Fifteen-year old Henk F. van Baaren was among those who took shelter in the cellar at the family shop in Hengelo. He recalled:[219]

> Some bombs fell in the town centre, one killing a German officer in the street. A couple of houses were damaged and two civilians were reported as having been killed. After the raid I saw two girls running away from the bombed centre area of the town. There was blood all over their faces and dresses but later I heard that they had been in a grocer's shop when the blast of the exploding bombs had blown debris from tomato juice and jam containers over them! Later when my father and I were talking together on the pavement in front of his shop window, there was a loud bang followed by the sound of broken glass. At that moment an ammunition train near the railway station exploded and the force of the huge blast blew out our shop window scattering glass all over us. Buildings in a large area around the station, including much of the main shopping centre, the main offices of the Stork Works and other factories nearby had all their windows shattered. Two German guards were killed and a number of soldiers were injured. The German AA gunners, having been in action on the roof couldn't leave their positions after the bombing as numerous fires surrounded them. The German fire brigade arrived to rescue them but when they connected the hoses to the fire hydrant they couldn't get any water. They were rather irate and angry and accused the local firemen, who were called in from other factories nearby, of sabotaging the supply! Peace was eventually restored between the two parties and the AA crews were rescued. The fire brigade report reads: 'forty-eight 250kg HE TD eleven bombs dropped of which forty were on target; twelve bombs hit the factory interior at 16.36 hours after which the factory clocks stopped! It took until 3 am to extinguish the last of the fires in the factory.'

No.464 Squadron had also bombed the primary target but the Mosquito flown by Squadron Leader W.R.G. 'Dick' Sugden and Flying Officer A.H. 'Bunny' Bridger was hit by flak in the starboard engine, which caught fire. The Australian crew crash-landed in Albergen not far from the target area and they were slightly injured. Luckily Dutch farmers living nearby helped them out of the aircraft but they were disturbed to discover that there were still bombs on board. Some Germans, who quickly arrived on the scene, took Sugden and Bridger prisoner. They were taken to hospital for a check up and three weeks later Sugden was sent by train to Amsterdam and from there with a group of American aircrew to Frankfurt. He ended up in *Stalag Luft* I Barth where he was reunited later with 'Bunny' and with his former flight commander, Squadron Leader Ian McRitchie who had been shot down on the Amiens prison raid in February, which Sugden and Bridger had also flown. The Russians liberated all three airmen on 1 May 1945.

More low-level pinpoint daylight raids, for which 140 and 138 Wings would become legendary, took place in 1944. In April Mosquitoes of 2nd TAF were once again called upon to fly a very important low-level strike mission, this time to Holland, when 613 Squadron, commanded by Wing Commander R.N. 'Bob' Bateson DFC, was directed to bomb the *Huize Kleykamp* in The Hague. Before the war the five-storey, 95ft high white building on Carnegie Square had been used for art exhibitions. Now occupied by the *Gestapo*, it housed the Dutch Central Population Registry and duplicates of all legally issued Dutch personal identity papers so that identity cards falsified by the Dutch Underground could be checked and recognized as false. Jaap van der Kamp and a few other Underground members had managed to infiltrate the Bureau staff in the building and sketches of the interior layout and its immediate surroundings were prepared. The *Huize Kleykamp* was strongly defended day and night and the ID card duplicates were stored in heavy metal cupboards so a raid by the Underground was just not possible. In mid-December 1943 London received word from Holland requesting that the building be destroyed from the air. It would be the most difficult job that a bomber squadron had ever had to face.

Light anti-aircraft weapons defended the *Huize Kleykamp* and it was tightly wedged among other houses in the Scheveningsweg, which made accuracy very difficult and heavy civilian causalities could be expected. By March 1944 there was no alternative; the building had to be destroyed. Planning for the raid therefore had to be meticulous. The attack would have to be carried out when the building was occupied on a working day so that the files would be open and the card indexes spread out on desks, otherwise they could not be destroyed by fire. The Dutch underground was not overly concerned with the deaths of the *Kleykamp* personnel as they were regarded as collaborators anyway. Finally, the time of the attack was scheduled for midday so that most civilians would be off the streets and having lunch. A scale model of the building, perfect in every detail right down to the thickness and the composition of the walls was built. Meanwhile, scientists developed a new bomb, a mixture of incendiary and high explosive, which was designed to have the maximum effect on the masses of *Gestapo* files and records. Bateson picked his crews carefully and put them through weeks of intensive training. Embry insisted that the mission could not go ahead until visibility of at least 6 miles was available. At last, on Tuesday 11 April all was ready.

In the early morning Bateson led six Mosquitoes off from Lasham and set course very low over the North Sea to Holland with Spitfires for escort. The Mosquitoes climbed to 1,400ft and flew a feint from the head of Goeree via Lehornhoven to the Reeuwijk Lakes near Gouda. No.2 in the second pair led by Squadron Leader Charles Newman and Flight Lieutenant F.G. Trevers was Flight Lieutenant Ron Smith:

I was completely occupied in flying the aircraft at very low level in formation and listening to Flying Officer John Hepworth, my navigator, on what landmark to expect next. The way in was deliberately made very roundabout in order to confuse the enemy of our objective and to achieve maximum surprise.

As they approached the Dutch coast Bateson and his navigator Flying Officer B.J. Standish noticed something strange. There were no recognizable landmarks; they found themselves flying over a vast expanse of water, dotted with islands where no islands should have been. Unknown to the aircrew, the Germans had opened the sluice gates on the River Scheldt inundating a large area of the flat Dutch countryside. There was relief all round, when, after flying on for a few more minutes, they finally got their bearings and leaned that they were on track for the objective. As they approached The Hague the Mosquitoes split up into pairs, following in line astern, sweeping across the rooftops the narrow streets shuddering to the din of their engines. Bateson's and Flight Lieutenant Peter Cobley's, the first two FB.VIs, lined up to attack while the other four circled Lake Gouda allowing the 30-second 500lb delayed action bombs carried by the first two aircraft, to explode. The third and fourth aircraft carried incendiary and the fifth and sixth aircraft, two HEs and two incendiary. Rob Cohen, an ex-student at the Delft Technical University who had escaped to England by canoe, flew one of these Mosquitoes. Bateson's Mosquito streaked towards the target, bomb doors open, its port wing-tip missing the tall spire on top of the Peace Palace diagonally opposite the *Huize Kleykamp* by inches. Cobley, following Bateson, saw the leader's bombs drop away. He had a hazy impression of a German sentry throwing away his rifle and running for his life, then he saw Bateson's three bombs quite literally skip through the front door and the large windows of the first floor of the building. A. Korthals Alter wrote later:

> Immediately after there were two large explosions. A streetcar about to turn into the Javastraat, stopped and the conductor, driver and passengers ran for cover. At the corner of Scheveningsweg and Laan Copes van Cattenburgh people lay flat on the ground. The only sound that followed after the explosions was that of broken glass and a dull rumbling noise resembling a distant thunderstorm. During the first few moments, people were so bewildered that no one uttered a sound. Only when the second Mosquito came rushing in and heavy explosions were again heard did people realize what was happening. "They are bombing" they called out. A frightful noise then announced the second attack.

> Cobley dropped his bombs in turn, pulling up sharply over the roof of the building. Two minutes later, with dense clouds of smoke already pouring from the shattered building, the second pair of Newman and Smith made their own attack. One of the Mosquito crews could barely see the target. After a further interval, the third pair, led by Flight Lieutenant Vic Hester and Flying Officer Ray Birkett, finished off the mission by

dropping HE and incendiary bombs. By now little of the *Kleycamp* building remained and Hester's bombs flew through the air and hit the Alexander barracks. Cohen, whose bomb drop failed, but who took photographs, was killed later that summer on a sortie over France. Flight Lieutenant Ron Smith's final recollection was of coming out over playing fields filled with footballers before crossing the coast north of the city to be escorted home by waiting Spitfires. The *Gestapo* building had been completely destroyed and the majority of the identity papers destroyed. The card files lay buried under the burning wreckage or fluttered over the Scheveningsweg carried by the heat of the fire. The state police who rushed to the scene forced passers-by to pick up the file cards from the street and even made them search the wreckage, threatening them with their cudgels. Most realised why the raid had occurred and they slyly dropped file cards into the flames or destroyed the photos. Fire brigade personnel kept people away from the devastated building instead of trying to save people in the Kleycamp. Among the dead lay Van der Kamp and some of fellow Dutch Underground workers. Buildings that surrounded the Kleycamp had suffered only slight damage but sixty-one civilians were killed, twenty-four seriously injured and forty-three slightly injured. All six Mosquitoes got back safely, without a shot being fired at them. Five weeks later a report reached the RAF that the operation had been highly satisfactory. For his leadership of this operation Bateson was awarded the DSC and received the Dutch Flying Cross from Prince Bernhard of the Netherlands. An Air Ministry bulletin later described the raid as 'probably the most brilliant feat of low-level precision bombing of the war.

The main work for 138 and 140 Wings also was Day and Night Ranger operations and Intruder sorties from England. On 12 April Flight Lieutenant J.L. 'Les' Bulmer and Flight Lieutenant Ed McQuarrie of 21 Squadron were intruding over the airfield at St. Dizier when a searchlight was turned on them. Les Bulmer remembers:

We took exception to that, so we flew right down the beam, firing our cannons as we went. That soon put it out. Didn't do our night vision a lot of good, though, we were almost blinded for a while. On our return journey we ran into searchlights near Abbeville and there were so many that we were in and out of them for about 10 minutes. There was no sign of flak so I kept a sharp eye out for night-fighters but didn't see any. I was beginning to wonder where I'd taken us, because a concentration of searchlights such as this was normally reserved for large cities and I was convinced that we were nowhere near a town, let alone a city.

All was revealed when we got back to debriefing. While we'd been away the flak map had been changed and where before there had been no flak position, there was now a large green area with '800' marked against it. This meant that we had just flown through a large defended area with 800 light AA guns in it. It seems that the Germans, in a bid to stop the destruction of their individual V-1 sites, had concentrated a number of them into one large area heavily defended against low-level attack. I think someone might have told us before we took off.

For the second half of April Ed and I were on a Gee-H course at Swanton Morley. This was to be our precision blind-bombing aid. Although I got good results in practice raids on Boston Stump and the central tower of Ely Cathedral, on operations it, and sometimes I, were something of a failure, so this piece of equipment was not much used. In fact I only carried out three Gee-H sorties. On the first the equipment packed up. On the second we dropped our bombs from 20,000ft on the Seine crossing at Duclair, at least that was where they were supposed to go. I have a feeling that they were nowhere near. The third and last I put down in my log-book as Gee-H trouble but some unkind person came along afterwards, crossed out Gee-H and inserted 'finger' and drew a small picture of Percy Prune's award of the highly Derogatory Order of the Irremovable Digit.

FB.VIs of 2nd TAF continued their night-fighting role and bombing of German targets in France and the Low Countries. Meanwhile, the first PR.XVI production examples had been urgently despatched to 140 Squadron, 2nd TAF where they supplemented PR.IXs on reconnaissance and mapping duties as part of the build up to D-Day. As photo-reconnaissance Mosquito crews of 'B' Flight left their crew room at Northolt on the evening of 4 June on their way to tea they were astonished to see that their blue PR.XVIs had been painted with broad black and white stripes. Geoff Curson, one of the radar-navigators, states:

No explanation was given buy our flight commander, my pilot, Squadron Leader Robert 'Bobby' W. Pearson DFC. We wondered…. The weather was foul and we had been stood down for the night. After dinner most of us headed for the 'George' in Ruislip to drink and dance the night away. Next day we reported as usual to the Flight buildings at about 14.00 hours and carried out the normal night-flying tests on our aircraft, ready for operations, if needed, that night. At 17.00 hours, three crews were detailed for briefing; 'Bobby' Pearson and myself, Harry Cartmell and Mark Hubert, Ray Batenburg and Walter Le May. When we entered the briefing room (a tent) we were amazed to see Group Captain Lousada, OC 34 Wing waiting to brief us. This was most unusual and had never happened before; we knew that the invasion of France was to take place the next morning and that the troops were already at sea, on their way to the Normandy beaches. Our task was to be over there before them to photograph the road junctions behind the beaches in the early hours of the morning to see if the German forces had been alerted and were moving troops into the area. He ordered total secrecy, no one else was to know what was on and he asked for our maximum effort.

The usual briefing by the Met man and Army liaison officer followed and we were given individual targets. The cloud base was about 4,500ft and the fuses on our flash-bombs were set accordingly. My targets were Granville, St. Lô and Vire; the most westerly of those allotted. This meant that we had to approach them by a roundabout route from the direction of the Channel Islands to avoid the prohibited area of the sea crossing. Back in the crew-room we carried out detailed planning for the flight. Bobby said, "We will go out and back over Start Point, that should keep us clear as far as the Navy is concerned!" He left the rest of the planning to me, while he checked the serviceability of the aircraft and the other crews' navigation plans.

I decided to climb all the way to Start Point and cross the Channel at 25,000ft. Bobby liked to be high crossing the enemy coast where the main defences were; out of range of flak. Our height over the target would be 4,500ft and we would drop a string of four flashes over each target (we carried twelve). Gee would be used as the aiming points for all targets, so I worked out the co-ordinates for each and our best line of approach. At 23.00 hours we went out to the aircraft; the ground crew saw us safely on board and gave me the twelve safety pins from the flashes, showing me they were armed. We taxied out to the runway and took-off. I entered the time 23.25 in my log as 'airborne' and we set course for Exeter, to stay over land all the way and started our climb. After a while I could see a red light to port flashing 'TG' and recognised Tangmere's beacon and knew their night-fighters were probably active. A little while later the aircraft rocked; Bobby said, "We hit someone's slipstream, its probably one of their fighters having a look at us!" By the time we reached Exeter we were at our desired height of 25,000ft and turned for Start Point. At 00.16 we crossed out over it and set course for Granville across the sea. It would take 20 minutes to reach our first target. After 5 minutes on course we could see Guernsey in front. The enemy coast was in sight. Crossing Guernsey we had to lose 20,000ft in 6 minutes. We were at 5,000ft over Jersey and moving very fast.

I had set up the Gee for the target but the signals we were receiving were not good as they became weaker as we descended. 'B' signal for our approach was strong but 'C' was weak and I needed it for the flash release. It was only a tiny blip that kept rising and falling. When we were in line I released the first four flashes and by their light I could see the harbour at Granville beneath us. I set Gee for St. Lô. It was now 00.35 on 6 June.

The Gee signals picked up as we turned. Suddenly our cockpit was filled with brilliant light. A searchlight had flashed straight onto us. I looked downwards, it was on the end of the jetty and coming up the beam was a stream of tracer shells from the flak gun beside it. "They are shooting up the beam", shouted Bobby and as the shells streaked past our starboard wingtip he pushed the nose down, stood the Mosquito on its port wingtip in a violent turn away. We swung round and lost height into the safety of the dark. We levelled out at 2,000ft and had to climb swiftly back on to East for the approach line to St. Lô. St. Lô and Vire were photographed without incident. Instead of turning for home, Bobby decided to do a low-level reconnaissance towards the Seine along the Le Mans–Paris road. We were 500ft above the ground but the night was dark and no lights were visible. Little did we know at the time, but we passed over three Panzer Divisions in the area. All I saw were fields and hedges. Navigation was no problem; I could fix our position using Gee whenever it was needed. About 5 minutes short of Paris we turned West and headed back for home, crossing out from France at St. Malo and keeping well clear of the Channel Islands on our way back to Start Point. We were back over England at 02.20 hours and followed the route taken out, back to base.

Near Salisbury we saw the most amazing sight. In the sky above us, coming down from the North, were row after row of lights. It looked as if there was a runway in the sky flying towards us. I was astonished. I could see then that they were the navigation lights of aircraft. It was the Airborne Brigade on its way over, planes and gliders from all over Britain in a steady stream that seemed never-ending. We finally landed at Northolt at 03.00 hours. All three crews operating that night returned safely. On this occasion we waited up for the photographs to be processed. We viewed them wet; they were excellent both from the point of view that our objectives were covered and the information obtained. The Army was delighted, it looked as if the invasion was going to take them completely by surprise. That was the news they were longing to hear. We went off to our tents to sleep, well satisfied with our night's work.

On the night of 5/6 June on the eve of D-Day, all six of 2nd TAF's Mosquito fighter squadrons carried out defensive operations over the invasion coast. In night operations on 7/8 June 1944 seventy Mosquitoes of 107, 305 and 613 Squadrons operating to the west on rail targets at Argentan, Domfort and Lisieux, sealed approaches to the bridgehead in Normandy. The opportunity for breakout and the eventual invasion of Germany was now within reach and 2nd TAF would go all the way with the ground forces. On 11 June six Mosquitoes of 464 and 487 Squadrons led by Wing Commander Bob Iredale and Flight Lieutenant McCaul attacked petrol tankers in a railway marshalling yard at Châtellerault at the request of the Army. Wing Commander Mike Pollard of 107 Squadron and his six Mosquitoes arrived at 22.44 hours to find fires burning in an area 300 x 200 yards with smoke rising to 4,000ft. The night attacks continued on railway targets and fifty aircraft from 88, 98, 107, 180, 226 and 320 Squadrons bombed the railway

Flying Officer Sid Seid DFC of 418 (City of Edmonton) Squadron RCAF leaning out of the cockpit of FB.VI TH-J with his dog 'Mostitch' and Flight Lieutenant Tommy Mathew alongside him on the wing. Seid, an American-Jew from California who enlisted in the RCAF was hell bent on destroying the Nazis, and would apparently stop at nothing to get at them. Sid's usual navigator was Flying Officer Dave Mcintosh DFC who postwar wrote a book entitled *Terror in the Starboard Seat* about his experiences flying with Sid Seid. The emblem seen painted on the cockpit access door was an unofficial 418 Squadron crest (Stephen M. Fochuk)

Pilot Officer Harry Randall-Cutler (right) and Pilot Officer Hubert Cohen of 305 (Polish) Squadron beside FB.VI LR303 A-Apple at Hartford Bridge in October 1944. 305 Squadron carried out night intruding over the continent from Hartford Bridge and Lasham that October before moving to Epinoy near Cambrai in November 1944. (Harry Randall-Cutler)

FB.VIs MM417/EG-T, EG-V and EG-D of 487 Squadron RNZAF on 29 February 1944 each carrying two 500lb bombs beneath their wings. (Jerry Scutts)

B.IX LR503I/F-Bar for Freddie of 105 Squadron, which completed a Bomber Command record of 213 operational sorties, pictured on 23 April 1945. Flight Lieutenant J. Maurice W. Briggs DSO DFC DFM (right) and navigator Flying Officer John C. Baker DFC*, themselves veterans of 107 sorties, flew the Mosquito on a goodwill tour of Canada in May 1945 taking with them as a passenger, de Havilland engineer Edward Jack. They landed at Calgary airport on 9 May after performing quite an aerial display to signal their arrival. Just after 1600 hours on 10 May the crew took off on a flight to Red Deer and Lethbridge from where they were to return to Calgary. They decided to 'beat up' the control tower to thrill a crowd that had turned up to see them off. Briggs made two passes at very low level and on the third pass Freddie failed to pull up in time and struck the top of the tower and a metal pole used for the release of weather balloons. The port wing and a piece of the tail-plane sheared off before the Mosquito plunged into the ground and was consumed by flames. Despite having been thrown clear of the aircraft, Briggs and Baker were killed. They were buried next day at Burnsland cemetery, Calgary in its Field of Honor. (via Jerry Scutts)

FB.VI with port propeller feathered. (DH)

NF.XXX MV529 is prepared for test flying at Leavesden in September 1944. Following its delivery to the RAF, the Mosquito saw service with 25 Squadron at Castle Camps until it was destroyed in a mid-air collision with fellow squadron aircraft MT494 on 23/24 January 1945. MV259 was crewed by Squadron Leader J. Arnsley DFC and Flight Lieutenant O.M Reid DFC at the time of the collision, which occurred over Camps Hall, Cambridgeshire during an AI practice interception. The second crew involved were Flight Lieutenants O.L. Ward DFC and E.D. Eyles. (BAe via Philip Birtles)

On Tuesday, 11 April 1944 six Mosquito FB VIs of 613 Squadron led by the CO, Wing Commander R.N. 'Bob' Bateson DFC attacked the Dutch Central Population Registry in The Hague. The Gestapo building was completely destroyed in what an Air Ministry bulletin later described as 'probably the most brilliant feat of low-level precision bombing of the war'. (BAe Hatfield)

On 19 August 1944 613 Squadron Mosquito crews, led by Squadron Leader Charles Newman carried out a daring low-level attack on a school building at Egletons, fifty miles SE of Limoges, believed to be in use as an SS troops' barracks. Fourteen of the Mosquitoes located and bombed the target, scoring at least twenty direct hits and the target was almost completely destroyed.

One Mosquito, crewed by Flight Lieutenant House and Flying Officer Savill, was hit in the starboard engine over the target area and failed to return but the crew survived and returned to the squadron just five days later. (Vic Hester)

Flight Lieutenants Landrey and 'Steve' Stephens of 157 Squadron at Hunsdon in 1943. (Brian Whitlock Blundell Coll)

Lieutenant James Luma DFC and his regular navigator Flying Officer Colin Finlayson of 418 (City of Edmonton) Squadron RCAF examining the hole in their Mosquito following a successful sortie over the continent in 1944. (Stephen M. Fochuk)

Ground staff working on the starboard Merlin engine of a 684 Squadron Mosquito. (Denis Moore Coll)

Flying Officer 'Collie' Knox and Flying Officer 'Tommy' Thompson of 81 Squadron at Seletar making the final operational flight of a Mosquito in the RAF, on 15 December 1955. This sortie by PR.34A RG314 was a Firedog sortie over Malaya. (via Jerry Scutts)

A dramatic low-level beat up of Seletar in PR.34A RG177 by Flight Sergeant Anderson of 81 Squadron in May 1953. (Aeroplane Monthly)

Silver FB.VIs of 47 Squadron in Burma in the spring of 1945. (via Andy Thomas)

junction at Le Haye, west of Carentan. Two nights later forty-two Mosquitoes of 107, 305, 464 and 613 Squadrons strafed and bombed troop movements between Tours and Angers-Vire, Dreux and Falaise and Evreux and Lisieux.

Les Bulmer reported:

> The scene over France, had changed completely. Whereas before D-Day there had been almost total darkness, now there were lights everywhere and most of the Normandy towns burned for several nights. Navigation was much easier; you just flew from one fire to the next.

On 14/15 June Mosquitoes wreaked havoc on the continent and 2nd TAF Mosquito crews shot down eight enemy aircraft. On the night of 22/23 June Flight Lieutenant Mike Benn DFC was killed. He took off on his 31st Mosquito operation with his navigator, Flying Officer W.A. Roe, on a Night Ranger from Thorney Island in FB.VI G-George. On becoming airborne he found that his ASI (airspeed indicator) was not working and so he radioed Control that he had problems and was returning to base. Another Mosquito crew was able to formate with G-George and led them into the approach to ensure that they were at the right speed but Benn's approach was such that he touched down too far down the runway. He overran the end of the runway and the Mosquito went over the low sea wall at the airfield boundary and bounced on the shingle strip. The undercarriage and wheels were torn off as they hit the barbed-wire fence entanglement beyond the shingle and the tail dropped when it hit the mud flat. The fuselage snapped completely off near the tail fin and the aircraft's nose dropped and dug into the mud bringing the aircraft to a halt about 30 yards from the sea wall. Bill Roe survived but the sudden stop caused the armour plate behind the pilot's seat to hurl itself forward and this broke Mike Benn's back. They were in shallow water and Roe managed to keep Benn's head above water and carried him some way back to the airfield before the ambulance finally found them. Benn died the following day in St Richard's hospital, Chichester. The Squadron records stated, 'Michael was a favourite of the Squadron and his death is a great shock to us all'.[220]

The 2nd TAF and Air Defence Great Britain (ADGB) destroyed at least 230 aircraft at night over the Channel, France, the Low Countries and Germany, June 1944–April 1945. Until suitable airstrips could be made ready, the Mosquito wings flew operations from Thorney Island and Lasham. Some spectacular pinpoint daylight operations against specific buildings were flown. On 14 July, Bastille Day, the Mosquitoes of 2nd TAF carried out a daylight low-level attack on a special target at Bonneuil Matours, near Poitiers. Crews were told that the raid was on a Gestapo barracks and was to punish those responsible for the murder of some British prisoners of war who had been clubbed to death with rifle butts in a nearby village square.[221] The Mosquitoes' target was a collection of six buildings inside a rectangle just 170 x 100ft, close to the village, which had to be avoided. The Mosquitoes took off in the late afternoon to hit the target at dusk, when the occupants of the barracks would be having dinner. There were eighteen aircraft with crews from 21, 464 and 487 Squadrons led by Group Captain Peter Wykeham-Barnes DSO DFC* and Flying Officer Chaplin. Wing Commander 'Reggie' W. Reynolds DSO* DFC led the four FB.VIs of 487 Squadron in shallow dives and dropped 9 tons of bombs on the barracks while the Germans were eating dinner. On 30 July the SAS learned that 2,000-3,000 Germans were massing for an anti-Maquis/SAS sweep and the majority were billeted in the Caserne des Dunes barracks at Poitiers. This resulted in a raid by twenty-four FB.VIs of 487 and 21 Squadrons escorted by Mustangs on 1 August. Meanwhile, the SAS learned that the survivors of the 158th Regiment were now in the Chateau de Fou, an SS police HQ south of Châtellerault. This and Chateau Maulny, a saboteur school was attacked by twenty-three FB.VIs of 107 and 305 Squadrons on Sunday 2 August. It is estimated that 80 per cent of the regiment were killed, so that unit paid dearly for its actions. That same day, 613 Squadron attacked a chateau in Normandy, which was used as a rest home for German submariners. It appeared that Sunday was chosen because on Saturday nights the Germans had a dance, which went on rather late. The FB.VIs attacked early in the morning, with rather devastating results. AVM Embry under the alias 'Wing Commander Smith' and the Station Commander, Group Captain Bower, took part.

In July Squadron Leader David F. Dennis DSO DFC became the CO of 21 Squadron. He had rejoined the squadron when the build-up to D-Day was in progress and on 29 July he flew his first operational night-sortie of his third tour. Having carried out an interdiction sortie in Southern Germany with his navigator Flying Officer Grantham his Mosquito was hit by flak, which put one engine out of action. The propeller refused to feather and only by maintaining full power on the other engine could he maintain flight, albeit in a slight descent. Arriving in darkness at the recently recaptured area around Caen in northern France he found an emergency landing strip and put the aircraft down without injury to himself or the navigator but the Mosquito was a write off. The next night he was back at Thorney Island carrying out night-flying training and at that time it was not unusual to carry out two 2 hour 30 minute operational sorties in one night.

No. 140 Squadron provided photo coverage throughout the winter of 1944-45, moving to France in September to keep in touch with the action.[222] Flying Officer Arthur T. Kirk, a pilot in 140 Squadron, recalls:

At the end of July 1944, Sergeant Mike Pedder my navigator and I set off on our first trip over France. Our target was a stretch of country between Grand Courronne and Hautor. The excitement got to Mike a bit and he kept looking round behind. I said, "Look Mike, I've been on night-fighters and it's no good you looking round behind. If there's anything up our rear end, we'll know about it soon enough!" It did the trick and we settled into the task. On our second op we photographed the road between Thury-Harcourt and Caen, as our troops were bogged down and needed information about opposing forces. The third trip was to the Falaise area, which was soon to be a scene of bloody carnage as German armour was caught and savaged by rocket-firing Typhoons and other fighter-bombers. We returned to find our cameras had obtained only three photographs instead of the dozen expected from each camera. It appeared that this had occurred on all of our sorties so far as, somehow, we had got the camera programming sequence wrong. After a sort-out, we did a lot better.

In August, sixty-seven of 140 Squadron's long-range mapping sorties were at night. We carried out three night operations, two of them along the River Orne and another from Barentin to Pavilly, when we saw Rouen under the shellfire. Mike navigated using Gee, sometimes Rebecca, or even Oboe. We carried twelve flashes in the belly of the Mossie and as they were released, they exploded at the set height, operating the camera shutters by photo-electric cells. On a good op we got twenty-four pictures of troops, trucks, trains and armoured columns. Sometimes we'd be sent to photograph river crossings supposedly in use by the Wehrmacht and anything the Army wanted to know about movement in the area, or was considered important to the overall strategy, we photographed. We plotted our track to enter France unnoticed if possible, with Fecamp, on the coast, being a favourite landfall. The 'natives' didn't seem to be too unfriendly there! Occasionally, jamming or on-board malfunctions would frustrate us and we had to rely on more basic techniques: dead reckoning, or map-reading, if conditions allowed. We were not the only aircraft inhabiting the night sky. Sometimes we would see Bomber Command unloading their deadly cargoes, from the target indicators, splashes of vivid reds, greens or yellows saturating the aiming points, followed by exploding bombs, flak and searchlights probing until they lit one or more of the bombers like a moth in a candle-glow. Once or twice we saw them pounced on all and sundry and, amid the flashing streams of tracer and billowing smoke, catching fire. We always looked for parachutes and hoped they all got out. On night reconnaissance we didn't lose a crew, or have one injured, while I was with the unit, although aircraft did suffer damage through flak. The Mosquito was an elusive bird, even more so at night![223]

In August seventy-seven enemy aircraft were destroyed in the air by the seven night-fighter and fighter-bomber squadrons of 2nd TAF. On 18 August Fifteen FB.VI crews of 613 Squadron at Lasham led by Squadron Leader Charles Newman, carried out a daring low level attack on a school building at Egletons, 50 miles south-east of Limoges, believed to be in use as an SS troops barracks. Fourteen of the Mosquitoes located and bombed the target, scoring at least twenty direct hits and the target was almost completely destroyed. One Mosquito crewed by Flight Lieutenant House and Flying Officer Savill was hit in the starboard engine over the target area and failed to return but the crew survived and returned to the squadron just five days later.

On 25/26 August 138 Wing took part in all-out attacks on troop concentrations and vehicles in the Rouen area which were attempting to retreat across the Seine. Attacks continued on the night of 30 August against railways in the Saarbourg and Strassburg areas. Les Bulmer wrote:

> August was a very busy month for 21 Squadron, we were out nearly every night and there was no time for Night Flying Tests. It was just a case of flying and sleeping when we could. This was the period of the breakout from the beachhead and encircling the Germans at Falaise. At night it was awe-inspiring to see the huge circle of gun flashes pouring fire into the Falaise Gap. Those that got out were caught by the Typhoons by day and us by night. We had a field day attacking transports. We harried the Germans in retreat. Sometimes it was sheer slaughter as we found roads jammed with enemy transport just waiting to be set on fire. Ed and I flew eighteen sorties that month, sometimes two in one night. On the 18th we took off at 00.10 for our thirty-ninth op and patrolled the Seine crossing and bridges over the River Risle. We bombed on the western approach of the bridge at Brionne and made two attacks with cannon. We were back at Thorney Island by 01.45. We refuelled and rearmed and were off again at 03.50 to patrol roads in the Lisi-Evreux area. We dropped a flare on the road northeast of Bernay but nothing was seen. We dropped another flare on the road south of Orbec and we could see transports burning but we did not attack. We bombed and strafed transport in the southern outskirts of Obec underneath someone else's flare and landed again at 05.30. After debriefing and a meal, we snatched a few hours sleep before attending briefing for the next night's raids. We were off at 23.10 that night and back at 01.10 on the 19th. Once again we refuelled and rearmed and were off at 04.15, returning at 05.50. So in less than thirty hours we had carried out four operations. Coming back over the Channel on the last one I must have dozed off because I awoke with a start when the aircraft gave a violent lurch. Ed had also fallen asleep and woke just in time to stop us spiralling into the sea.

On 26 August, the day after Paris was liberated; Les Bulmer and Ed McQuarrie had a change from beating up transport, as Bulmer explains:

> By late August the main effort was concentrated in trying to stop the Germans retreating across the Seine. A lot of the crossing points had been knocked out but there still remained the railway bridge in Rouen the 'heavies' could have blanketed it with bombs but this would have caused many French casualties so 2 Group were called in to try a pinpoint attack. It had to be at night because the enemy was desperate to keep it open and it was well defended. Four aircraft, working in pairs, were allotted to the task. One of the pair would fly in at around 3,000ft and drop three flares

using Gee for the other one, which would be waiting underneath. Meanwhile the other aircraft would stooge around at low level waiting for the bridge to be illuminated and then nip in and bomb it. Then the two would reverse roles. Mac and Flight Lieutenant Winder tossed for who should be the first to drop the flares and we won (or lost, depending on your point of view). Since we were carrying flares in the bomb bay, we could only carry two bombs each under the wings. Flight Lieutenant Swaine and another crew took off first. We, together with our partner Flight Lieutenant Winder, left at 22.35, thirty minutes or so later. On the way over to France Swaine called up on the R/T to say that it was pretty hot in the target area and that he'd been hit. He recommended that we abort. Ed and Winder had a brief conversation and decided to give it a whirl. I was more than happy to call it a day but I wasn't consulted.

We went in at about 3,000ft. The enemy took a dislike to us at Cap d'Antifer as we crossed the coast, then we settled down for a straight run in to Rouen. I had my head stuck in the Gee set following a Gee line that should take us over the bridge from the north-west. Ed was concentrating on following my instructions to stay on the line and waiting for me to give him the order to drop the flares. Thus neither of us was aware of what was going on around us. This was just as well, because afterwards Winder said that he could see exactly where we were above him because of the flak that was following us in. Ignorance is a wonderful thing at times. You can't weave when you are following a Gee line. The usual glow appeared beneath us as we let the flares go. But by the time we'd turned to check that we'd dropped them in the right place, two of them had been shot out and the third had its parachute damaged and was burning on the east bank of the river. We saw Winder go in to attack and since the flare was still illuminating the scene, we saw his bombs burst on the south-west end of the bridge. Mac stuck the nose down and we dived on the bridge before the flare burned itself out. We let go the bombs just as the flare went out so I couldn't see the results. We then called up Winder to tell him that he needn't bother to drop his flares. I think he was as relieved as we were to get the hell out of it as soon as possible. We never heard if we'd had any success. I rather doubt it. Dive bombing at night is a bit of a hit and miss affair. Still, I expect that the powers-that-be thought it worth a try and we were more or less expendable.

On 31 August, a huge petrol dump at Nomency near Nancy was destroyed by Mosquito fighter-bombers and twelve FB.VIs of 464 Squadron attacked a dozen petrol trains near Chagney from between 20 and 200ft and caused widespread destruction.

At Hunsdon in summer 1944 Pilot Officer Dudley Hemmings' pilot in 464 Squadron completed his tour with him and was rested. The young navigator met

Squadron Leader Don Wellings DFC 'a tall, unassuming man', who had completed a tour on Blenheims at a night-vision course.[224] He explains:

> During the period June to October 1944 Don and I did thirty-five ops, thirty at night and five low-level trips by day. We commenced our first ops on the V-1 flying bomb sites in Northern France. The targets were difficult to locate in the woods, the ramps not much longer than a cricket pitch. I must say I was scared on my first trip when 50ft over the sea we saw the heavily defended French coast ahead. Low-level tight formation in Vics or Boxes was a must for the squadrons. This was difficult for some pilots to do continually. Wellings was a fearless man and could fly a perfect course from his navigator. During night attacks in Normandy he would press hard to destroy the target going as low as possible for accuracy; hence I would yell out to him altimeter readings fearing he was getting too low for my liking!
>
> A typical night op: Take-off Lasham 23.00 hours then 16 minutes to Littlehampton on the coast and across the Channel at 50ft. When the French coast was coming up we climbed to 3,000ft, crossed the coast in a weaving dive to escape any flak then down to about 1,500-2,000ft and patrolled a given area in the battle zone. Eventually to find a moving train or transport column, climb a bit and drop a flare over the targets. It would burn on a parachute for about 7 to 10 minutes turning night into day. Bomb the train, the engine if possible; the train would stop; rake the train with machine guns and cannon and set it on fire. Sometimes we received flak and the cockpit filled with cordite smoke, which nearly made me sick as I called out altimeter readings to Wellings in our dives. I would identify the location with a Gee fix if possible and when all armaments expended set course for the French coast and back to base. Then a debriefing, bacon and eggs, and on to our camp stretchers for sleep around 3am.

In September the Allies launched Operation Market Garden, the aim of which was to cut the German-occupied Netherlands almost in half and to prepare the way for the invasion of Germany that would bypass the northern flank of Germany's Westwall fortifications (The Siegfried line). The Allied plan was to capture bridges on the Rhine in Holland at Veghel, Grave, Nijmegen and Arnhem, using Britain's 1st and America's 82nd and 101st Airborne Divisions. They were to cut off the Germany Army in the Belgian sector and save the bridges and the port of Antwerp for the American army units and British XXX Corps advancing north from the Dutch border. On 17 September the operation took place. Thirty-two FB.VIs of 107 and 613 Squadrons in 138 Wing were detailed to attack a German barracks at Arnhem, while 21 Squadron at Thorney Island bombed three school buildings in the centre of Nijmegen, which were being used by the German garrison. Both raids were to eliminate the opposition before the airborne forces went in later that day. Dudley Hemmings and Don Wellings, who in August had moved to 613 Squadron, recalls:

The attacks were scheduled to begin 5 minutes before midday Dutch time to soften the German defences ahead of the invading paratroopers. As was usual with all Mosquito daylight raids, low-level flying and careful routeing into the targets to gain surprise was essential for success. Whilst by late 1944 the *Luftwaffe* had diminished in the air, enemy anti-aircraft guns were still heavy around German held positions. The task given the Section led by Squadron Leader Don Wellings DFC and I as his navigator, was to attack the barracks in the centre of Arnhem.

The thirty-two FB.VI Mosquitoes of 107 and 613 Squadrons in 138 Wing were to attack, in shallow high-speed dives at between 800 and 1,500ft, two German barracks complexes in Arnhem, the *Willemskazerne* in the centre of the town and the *Saksen-Weimarkazerne* in the northern outskirts. Fifteen Mosquitoes of 21 Squadron in 140 Wing were to bomb three school buildings in the centre of Nijmegen, believed to being used as billets for the German garrison. One of the crews who took part was Canadian Flight Lieutenant Ed McQuarrie RCAF and his navigator Flight Lieutenant 'Les' Bulmer, who were flying their last operation as a crew. Bulmer recounts:

> It was intended to be another of 2 Group's pinpoint raids but it turned out to be a total cock-up. Both raids were to eliminate the opposition before the airborne forces of Market Garden went in later that day. We were still based at Thorney Island, so we would have quite a way to go to reach the target. As a result we had to carry wing tanks, which meant that our bomb load was confined to two 500-pounders in the bomb bay. At briefing we had the usual 2 Group model of the town that Basil Embry's model shop always produced for these sort of pinpoint raids, so that we could familiarize ourselves with the target and the run-in over the town. There would be fifteen aircraft in five sets of three in echelon starboard. Wing Commander David F. Dennis DSO DFC DFM led with Squadron Leader 'Jock' Murray as his No.2. We led the third echelon with Flight Lieutenant Bert Willers as our No.2. To ensure that all fifteen aircraft would be clear of the target before the bombs exploded the leading aircraft (the first ten) had 25-second fuses, whereas the rear echelons had the normal eleven-second delay. To stay clear of trouble we planned to fly across the Channel and up to the front line at high level. Once over enemy territory we would drop down to the deck and head for a road that ran north-west from Cleve into Nijmegen. The road would give us an accurate run-up to the target, which consisted of three large buildings forming a semi-circle facing the direction from which we planned to attack, so it would be easy to identify.

On 17 September 1,113 medium and heavy bombers escorted by 330 fighter aircraft carried out bombing attacks to eliminate the opposition before the airborne forces of Market Garden went in later that day. The first airlift alone involved 360 British and 1,174 American transport aircraft and 491 gliders, accompanied by 910 fighter escorts. During the course of the operation 20,190 parachutists, 13,781 glider-borne troops, 5,230 tons of equipment and stores, 1,927 vehicles and 568 pieces of artillery were landed behind the German lines. The bombing strikes included seventeen Mosquitoes of 107 Squadron and sixteen Mosquitoes of 613 Squadron at Lasham and sixteen Mosquitoes of 21 Squadron at Thorney Island. No.107 Squadron finally began taking off at half-minute intervals at 10.51 hours after a few last minute hiccups, as Dudley Hemmings continues:

> We formed up in tight formation and set course for Southwold on the English coast for the 750 miles round trip. Across East Anglia we had a marvellous view of the sky filled with the great armada of some of the 2,000 transports and gliders *en route* to their drop zones several miles west of Arnhem. Crossing the English coast at Southwold we soon left the brave Red Berets behind and skimmed over the North Sea at 50ft and 250 mph; IFF off and bombs switched to 'Fire'. As lead navigator I was map reading each pinpoint every 2 minutes to keep on track knowing there were seven crews behind relying on our lead. Our routeing into Arnhem was circuitous and required good timing, pinpoint map reading and the use of Gee over the 130 miles of sea to the Dutch coast. Midway over the North Sea we turned slightly to port at a DR position in order to cross the Dutch coast one-mile south of Egmont, a position presumed undefended. Landfall without incident was made as planned and we swept across the lowlands of Holland, lifting up over some high-tension lines east of Alkmaar. At a headland on the Zuider Zee near Hoorn we turned south-east to cross 32 miles of the Zuider Zee, making for a checkpoint at Nijkerk where a railway ran 90° to our track. We crossed the town of Nijkerk at house top level and looking behind us it was good to see the flight still in close formation.
>
> We were now 8 minutes to our time on target. About 10 miles west of Arnhem we turned on an easterly course and climbed rapidly to 3,000ft, the others breaking the box formation to line astern. I had an oblique photo of a model made from aerial photographs and knew that a white gravel road led straight to the barracks. We flew in a shallow dive down this road. I pointed out the target to Don Wellings and we dropped our bombs from 1,000ft. The Mossies behind us did likewise. We carried instantaneous bombs on this trip and could not bomb at low level for fear of blowing up either the following aircraft or ourselves. When really low level bombing was done, eleven-second delay bombs were carried. Pilot aimed bombing became quite accurate after much practice by pilots on the bombing ranges back in England. Up came some flak and with the bomb doors open Wellings opened up with the firepower in the nose as our bombs were

released. The Section followed us in. Until now the crews had maintained radio silence but soon after flattening out past the target I heard one of our crews over the radio call out "We've got it!"

On 21 Squadron meanwhile Ed McQuarrie and 'Les' Bulmer had taken off at 10.45 for Nijmegen and the Mosquitoes formed-up into tight formation. Les Bulmer continues:

Somewhere short of the front line we shed our drop tanks: empty tanks could be lethal if hit by flak. Just after crossing the front line we came under heavy ack-ack fire near Weert. There was nothing we could do to avoid it, as this would have destroyed the formation. But this didn't stop No.2 in the second echelon from trying to weave. He was a bigger menace than the flak. As far as I know nobody was hit, although a message came over the R/T calling someone by name, which we didn't catch, telling them that they were on fire. I think it probably came from some other formation because there were no signs of fire in ours. But I reckon it caused a mild panic among all our crews. On the deck it was hard work for the pilots trying to keep one eye on the ground and the other on the rest of the formation. Somewhere along the way there was a cry of "Wires, wires!" and we had to climb to get over an electricity pylon. I was amazed to see that Willers on our right seemed to fly underneath! In fact, I found out afterwards that he'd taken advantage of the droop in the cables to stay low.

Our turning point on the Cleve-Nijmegen road came up, which we planned to follow into Nijmegen but we carried straight on, then circled starboard to come up on Cleve from the east. I had no idea what was going on. Every navigator in the formation, except the leader, must have been wondering what the hell was happening. I could hardly believe my eyes when the leading aircraft opened their bomb doors. Ed followed suit and I yelled at him that this wasn't the target and not to release our bombs. Poor Ed was totally confused and probably thought I had gone off my head since the leaders were obviously intent on bombing whatever was coming up. After what seemed ages but was probably only seconds the leader's bomb doors closed and I breathed a sigh of relief as we shot over Cleve. On the straight road, with houses on either side and a larger building, which could have been a church or chapel, people were standing watching us go over. I looked back to check that the rear echelons had noticed that bomb doors had been closed. To my surprise I saw a huge cloud of black smoke and dust from bombs which some of the rear six aircraft had let go. (According to later official reports three aircraft bombed a barrack square in Cleve and machine-gunned troops). South-west of Cleve is the *Reichwald,* a large forest and we proceeded to career around this. By now there was not much formation left, just a gaggle of aircraft milling around waiting for someone to make a decision. Suddenly I saw two aircraft haring off in the right direction. One of them, I later discovered, was Jock Murray. I told Ed to follow and we chased after them, with everyone else tagging along behind or beside us. We were now fifteen aircraft all flying individually towards Nijmegen. And we had no means of knowing whether any of the leading planes were the ones with the short fuses.

We sped up the road to Nijmegen and I could see the bridge over on the right. Then we were over the town looking anxiously for the target. It seemed to be chaos, with Mosquitoes going in all directions, flak coming up and Mustangs milling around above us. I noticed one Mosquito climbing away to the north and wondered where the hell he was going. Then another Mosquito shot underneath us almost at right angles. I shall never know how he found room between the rooftops and us and I wondered why he was going in that particular direction. Then I realised that he'd seen the target and was heading straight for it. I yelled to Ed to pull round and pointed to the target, by now almost on our port wing-tip. He put us into a tight turn but we couldn't make it in time. We shot over the town and I saw a green train in the railway station with a crowd of people on the platform looking up and, presumably, wondering what was happening. In a flash we were clear and out over farmland where we dumped our bombs and got out fast. The element of surprise was long gone so it as suicidal to go round again. Many others did the same. We were fortunate in not having a rearward-facing camera connected to the bomb release so no one was aware that, in our haste to get away, we'd omitted to drop them safe. I just hoped that no one would be passing that way within the next 25 seconds. (Those who had such a camera got a rocket at the subsequent debriefing). On the way in and on the way out the farmers and their families were standing in their doorways waving like mad. Probably they were cheering on 'the brave RAF' while we were thinking, 'what the hell are we doing here, let's get the hell out of it.' We found another Mosquito, which seemed to be going in the same direction as us, so we joined him for the journey home. This was uneventful; we didn't even get shot at over Weert this time. Maybe the Germans didn't consider two aircraft to be worth wasting ammunition on. And besides, we were heading for home.

We returned to Thorney Island (one crew was missing) where the full story of the confusion over the target route unfolded. Wing Commander Dennis had a bird hit his windscreen just before reaching the turning point. In retrospect it might have been wiser for him to pull out and hand over to Jock Murray immediately but he chose to carry on, not being able to see properly and hence the mess we finished up in. Only five aircraft claimed to have located and bombed the target. Most of the rest did as we did and dumped them in fields, apart from those who had already got rid of theirs over Cleve. I've always felt that it was a mistake to have fifteen planes in one formation. The usual formation on previous raids of this sort was groups of six in two vics of three. Because each of the following echelons had to be stepped down on the one in front to avoid slipstream problems, it meant that the leader had to keep a reasonable height above the deck. Otherwise the rear echelons would be ploughing a furrow across the countryside. In the event, it was impossible to avoid hitting slipstreams and we were being thrown all over the place and at tree top height this is not the healthiest of situations. To cap it all we learned afterwards that the German troops were not in their barracks at the time, so all we succeeded in doing was probably to kill a few innocent Dutchmen and some German civilians. Such is war. In wartime I suppose you can't very well admit to the world that you made a cock-up.

Dudley Hemmings concludes:

Safely back at Lasham after 3 hours in the air; a debriefing, some discussion of the other Sections' experiences (two aircraft failed to return); a beer at 'The Swan' in Alton nearby clouding the knowledge that tomorrow was another day, another 'op'. As to whose bombs hit the barracks or went astray I do not know. It is best not to know as a number of Dutch civilians were killed during the raid. For navigator and pilot on such missions it was purely a test of one's navigational and flying skills, a hope .of survival under fire, a task completed as ordered and a mental isolation from the outcome on the ground. When my CO told me my operational tour was completed and to take Rest Leave Wellings said to me that the CO had told him the same. While he insisted I go, Wellings stated that he would ask to stay on because he wanted to 'see out the war'. Sadly, when I was on leave he took a new navigator and went missing on 9 October 1944.

On 18 September the Germans counter-attacked and forestalled an American attempt to capture the bridge at Nijmegen. Market Garden has been described in an official report as 'by far the biggest and most ambitious airborne operation ever carried out by any nation or nations.'[225]

Altogether, nine Mosquito bomber squadrons now equipped 2nd TAF. In September 1944, following the outbreak from the Normandy beachhead, plans were in progress to move them to airfields in France. As part of the newfound offensive, Mosquito squadrons outside 2nd TAF also made daylight Rangers from France and intruder sorties over the Continent. Late in October another daring low-level raid, this time on Aarhus University, the HQ for the *Gestapo* in the whole of Jutland, Denmark, was ordered. The University consisted of four or five buildings just next to an autobahn, which ran 10 miles in a straight line up to the buildings. In College No.4 was also the HQ of the *Sickerkeitsdienst des Reicksführers Schutzstaffeln* or SD, the police service of the Nazi party. The precision attack was scheduled for 31 October by twenty-five FB.VIs of 21, 464 and 487 Squadrons each carrying 11-second delayed action bombs. Included in the Mosquito formation, which was led by Wing Commander 'Reggie' W. Reynolds DSO* DFC and Squadron Leader Ted Sismore DSO DFC, was AVM Basil Embry and his navigator, Peter Clapham. On 30 October the crews at Thorney Island had no idea what their target was, as Les Webb, Ern 'Dunks' Dunkley's navigator in 464 Squadron, explains:

> The Flight Commanders were called in by the CO, Group Captain Peter Wykeham-Barnes,[226] who would lead the third wave. 'Dunks', an Australian, was one of the Flight Commanders. They were told that we were going on a special raid and he wanted each flight commander to pick six crews, see that their planes were all right, tell them to carry an overnight bag and they'd get instructions to go off tomorrow. Nobody knew where. The crews were to fly to Swanton Morley in Norfolk. The advantages of doing it from Swanton Morley were two-fold. One was that it was nearer to the coast but the other one was the that it was a Mosquito training area so if anybody was looking they were used to seeing Mossies in that area.

Humphrey-Baker in 487 Squadron who was navigator for pilot Wing Commander 'Peter' Thomas adds:

> On 31 October we took off from Thorney Island at 7 am, landing at Swanton Morley to refuel and to link up with aircraft from 21 Squadron.

Les Webb continues:

> We all flew up singly and landed at Swanton Morley. After we landed we were told that we were now under guard. We couldn't go out, we couldn't make telephone calls and there would be an early dinner. The food at Swanton Morley was out of this world; it was absolutely superb. Immediately after dinner a little Dane who had been parachuted into Denmark and who then got all the information before coming out by submarine, briefed us. His information enabled a large model to be constructed showing all the surrounding area and even the colours of the roofs. It was an incredible model.

Escort was provided by eight Mustang IIIs of 315 (Polish) Squadron, 12 Group, which flew to Swanton Morley from their base at Andrews Field in Essex, led by the CO, Squadron Leader Tadeusz Andersz and rendezvoused with the Mosquitoes over the North Sea. Humphrey-Baker in 487 Squadron takes up the story:

> We were carrying wing tanks, which would be abandoned, over the North Sea. It was rather alarming to see these grey torpedo-like shapes whipping

by in close proximity. As we approached the target already shrouded in smoke, I could see that the right-hand building, which we had to attack, had the centre section completely destroyed while the two end sections were still standing. As we crossed the target I felt the aircraft being hit on the starboard side. Soon afterwards Peter Wykeham Barnes called Peter to feather the starboard prop, as the engine was on fire. Once we were on one engine we headed for 'Sally', our code name for Sweden. I read later that we had been hit by debris from an exploding bomb; despite the fact that they all had delayed-action fuses to allow each box of six aircraft to pass without risk. We crossed the Kattegat and reached the coast without further incident and upon finding a suitable field, Peter brought the aircraft down for a very efficient wheels-up landing. Once the shaking had ceased it was very quiet. Peter placed the firebomb in the navigator's bag and the plane was soon in flames and we took off up a hill towards some trees.

With surprising speed a squad of grey-clad soldiers arrived with an antiquated fire engine in tow. They waved guns at us and we thought it advisable to stop. We were rather amused at their efforts to quell the flames, as the weak jet from their machine would not reach the aircraft. They soon made it clear that their concern was to know if there was anybody else in the aircraft or if there were still bombs aboard. We were taken to a neighbouring farmer whose wife prepared an excellent meal at short notice. We were then taken to Gothenburg and placed in a large room at the top of a tall hotel. The room was equipped with a telephone directory and from this we were surprised to learn that there was in fact a British Consulate in the town and we resolved that we would try to reach it if the opportunity presented itself.

Les Webb, 'Dunks' Dunkley's navigator continues:

'Daisy' Sismore was leading. As we crossed the coast there was a small village a few miles inland and as we flew across, he flew straight over the village and went on. The other three formations did a circuit and then the next one peeled off. We were the last ones in. We orbited until it was our turn. In a field below were a couple of farm horses with a plough that seemed to be on their own. By the time we had done three circuits, everybody realised that we were RAF aircraft and they were waving and cheering in the streets. The interesting thing was that a farmer dressed in blue dungarees and blue hat who must have ducked down between the two horse stood up and held the horse's heads at the salute as we went past. I thought that was superb.

We went in, in formation, echelon starboard. We turned and saw the building. The problem now was we had broken up into pairs, whether intentionally or not and we were flying Number 2 at that point because

Bedford, Bill Langton's [the CO, Wing Commander A.W. Langton DFC] navigator had called that he had handed over to somebody else. Clayton had gone up to No.1 and Dunk and I were flying No.2. By the time we got to the target we were flying with Clayton, coming in together. We were slightly starboard. The smoke from the site, unluckily, was blowing towards us and as we entered the smoke it was pretty obvious that the left-hand building was more damaged than the right-hand building. Clayton saw it before we did because he was slightly ahead of us. In all his glory he made a smart turn onto the target, which left 'Dunks' with absolutely nowhere to go. 'Dunks' did a brilliant bit of flying. He just went oomph, oomph and we went under Clayton, across and then swung round. We were at nought feet and two people on the main road to Aarhus dived into the gutter! We still had time to drop our bombs on the target, then off and away. We formed into formation again before we got to the coast and went out over the North Sea again. The Mustangs were still with us and later they went off and left us. We came straight home to Thorney. On the way home 'Dunks' lost track of the CO and called over the radio, "Has anyone seen the old man?" He came back saying, "We are not home yet, shut up!" The whole flight took 4 hours 45 minutes.

Inside one of the college buildings, 40 year-old Pastor Harald Sandbäk, arrested on 11 September on suspicion of complicity in acts of sabotage, was about to have his final interrogation. Sandbäk had helped distribute illegal publications in Jutland and in 1942 had become involved in the reception of arms dropped by the RAF before he assumed the leadership of a small group of saboteurs. The longest interrogation he endured was 39 hours without any rest, after days of whipping and tightening of string around his handcuffs. Sandbäk recalled:

I was taken to an office where Schwitzgiebel the *Gestapo* Chief in Jutland and his deputy Werner were and they told me that this would be my last chance to tell the truth. I declared that I had no more to say, after which those devils handed me over to the torturers. They half dragged and half carted me up to the attic of the college, took off all my clothes and put on new handcuffs. To these a string was attached which would be tightened and caused insufferable pain. I was thrown on a bed and whipped with a leather dog whip. I was then taken down to the office again for further interrogation by Werner and his two assistants. Suddenly we heard a whine of the first bombs, while the planes thundered across the university. Werner's face was as pale as death from fright and he and his assistants ran out of the room. I saw them disappear down a passage to the right and instinctively I went to the left. This saved my life because shortly afterwards the whole building collapsed and Werner and his assistants were killed. I was later rescued by Danish patriots.[227]

The operation was carried out at such a low altitude that Squadron Leader F.H. Denton of 487 Squadron hit the roof of the building, losing his tail wheel and the port half of the tail plane. The New Zealander nursed the Mosquito across the North Sea and managed to land safely. The university and its incriminating records were destroyed. Among the 110-175 Germans killed in the raid was *Kriminalrat Schwitzgiebel,* head of the *Gestapo* in Jutland and SS *Oberstumführer* Lonechun, Head of the Security Services.

Later that evening in Gothenburg, a young officer, who informed them that he was a schoolmaster doing his period of compulsory service, collected Wing Commander 'Peter' Thomas and Humphrey-Baker. Humphrey-Baker recalls:

He was to escort us to Falun where we would be detained for an indefinite period. He was very pleasant and we all got on very well. He escorted us to the railway station and while he was busy getting our tickets, we took off at speed into the night. After the brilliant lights of the station the square outside looked very black. It was raining and the macadam glistened in the light of the high-street lamps. We raced across the empty space, Peter was to my left and we had not gone far when he took a flying leap over a low parapet and disappeared; a second later I heard a loud splash. I thought that this was in keeping with Peter's somewhat flamboyant style. Peter was blond and handsome and played the role of an RAF Wing Commander excellently. His wife was equally glamorous.

Within a few seconds of our escape I was on my own. I ran on for a few yards to a bridge. I ran across and doubled back on the other side of the canal. I called out to the soggy Peter to see if he was OK or if he needed help. He told me to carry on, which I had every intention of doing, as I could dimly see people appearing on the other side of the canal. I ran on and followed the road round to the right. I continued until I came to a junction and turned right and soon came upon a woman about to enter her home. I asked her in what I fondly thought was a mixture of German and Swedish where the British Consulate was. She replied in English, "Why should I help you?" which was not surprising, as I must have been somewhat bedraggled and hatless. I mumbled that I was in a hurry and wet. She replied that it was only a few doors further on. So to my intense surprise and relief I had located it in what seemed to be a very short time. I really do not think I could have run more than 1 km. The Consul's son opened the door and I was taken in. It was a remarkable stroke of luck to get there so quickly and at night. Soon afterwards with Schnapps in hand we saw a guard being posted at the gate. The Consul had no option but to return me and a few Schnapps later I arrived at the Police station in the company of the Consul and his son to find a somewhat disconsolate Peter Thomas sitting wrapped in a blanket.

We had wrongly thought that if we could reach the Consulate we could be repatriated. This of course would only have happened if we had escaped from occupied Europe, but did not apply to anyone stupid enough to escape from the hospitable hands of the Swedes. We were handed back to our chagrined guard who could not understand why we should have wanted to run away from him. We were escorted back to the station by the Consul, placed on a train and locked into a very comfortable sleeping compartment. On arrival at Falun we had to go before a local doctor for an FFI [French Force of the Interior] inspection. I was somewhat alarmed at his vigorous approach and was relieved to depart still entire, although I was also amused at the wooden trumpet with which he tuned in to my heart. Every possible thing in Sweden seemed to be made of wood. I watched local businessmen stoking up the boilers mounted on the back of their Volvos to generate the producer gas, which powered their vehicles. In thick overcoats and wearing gloves they would shove wood into the little furnace and then slowly drive away. We were lodged in a pension at Korsnas run by Miss Sundberg, a very nice old lady. There were about sixteen of us, mostly Australians I think, including the crew of a Lancaster that had been damaged on the final successful attack on the *Tirpitz*.[228] The numbers dwindled rapidly as the rate of repatriation had increased following an influx of German soldiers from Finland. There was also a large camp of about 600 Americans nearby. Peter Thomas who had to go to Malmo to move a Mosquito said that there were over 100 serviceable American aircraft at the Lingschoping airfield where they would arrive in droves.

Among the attributes of our pension was a still made by earlier residents and a stock of Munchen Lowenbrau beer. It was my first introduction to this beer and I have enjoyed it ever since, when I can find it. We were given a lot of freedom and I very much enjoyed my time in Falun. Meeting some members of the Danish Resistance movement, which, of course we had set out to help, heightened my enjoyment. They took me around and we had a great time until we had to return to Stockholm prior to flying home. Peter Thomas, as a result of his senior rank, stayed at the British Consulate while I was sent to a dirty and evil smelling hotel. I protested immediately, but was told we would be leaving that night. Fortunately my Danish friends had given me the address of the local Danish Resistance office in Stockholm, which I quickly visited. They were eager to help and took me to a nicer hotel where I spent several nights until flown out. I also met a charming young Danish girl Henny Sindunq, a resistance worker from Copenhagen. She took me around Stockholm and we had supper together every evening until like Cinderella, I had to leave to head out to the airport in preparation for flying home. Fortunately the weather was bad and we were returned to our respective lodgings in the small hours of the morning. Henny would dutifully turn out the next day and we would dine at a different restaurant of her choice. This went on for four or five nights until I finally crept off in a very cold DC 3 finally landing at Wick in Scotland after an absence of 24 days.[229]

By November 1944 107, 305 (Polish) and 613 Squadrons of 138 Wing finally arrived in France, to be based at Epinoy near Cambrai, France. On 21 November, 136 Wing was created within 2nd TAF by the arrival, from Fighter Command, of 418 and 605 Squadrons, which transferred to Hartford Bridge. That month 2nd TAF Mosquito night fighters shot down fourteen enemy aircraft. In December 464 RAAF and 487 RNZAF Squadrons sent advance detachments to Rosieres-en-Santerre, France. In February 1945 the two squadrons, along with 21 Squadron, all of 140 Wing, left southern England and landed at Amiens-Rosieres-en-Santerre. Their arrival coincided with the first anniversary of the Amiens raid by 140 Wing Mosquitoes in February 1944, when the 'walls of Jericho' had come tumbling down.

The *Luftwaffe* was powerless to stop the Allies' inexorable advance westwards but there was one last attempt to try to halt the Allies. Since 20 December 1944 many *Jagdgeschwader* had been transferred to airfields in the west for Operation Bodenplatte, when approximately 850 *Luftwaffe* fighters took off at 07.45 hours on Sunday morning 1 January 1945 to attack twenty-seven airfields in northern France, Belgium and southern Holland. The 4-hour operation succeeded in destroying about 100 Allied aircraft, but it cost the *Luftwaffe* 300 aircraft, most of which were shot down by Allied anti-aircraft guns deployed primarily against the V-1s. During January 2nd TAF's Mosquito night fighters exacted a measure of revenge, shooting down seventeen enemy aircraft.

On 22 February 9,000 Allied aircraft were pressed into action for Operation Clarion to deliver the coup de grace to what remained of the German transport system. Their targets were railway stations, trains and engines, crossroads, bridges and ships and barges on canals and rivers, stores and other targets. No.2 Group put up every available crew and every serviceable aircraft, flying 215 sorties, 176 from the Continent and the remainder by 136 Wing in England. It was to be the last time that the Mosquitoes operated in daylight in such numbers. One of the Mosquito crews in 21 Squadron that took part was Bert Willers and Les Bulmer, who had teamed up with his new pilot after Ed McQuarrie had finished his tour.[230] Les Bulmer remembers:

Clarion was a change from night operations. Each Mosquito squadron was given a particular area to patrol and 21 Squadron was given the area north of Hanover. By this time we were based in France at Rossieres-en-Santerre and we flew north to the Zuider Zee and then turned east. At Dimmer See 'A' Flight broke away to the NE and 'B' Flight continued east until we approached Nienburg. Here we split into two groups of four, one of which led towards the Hanover area. We found some engines and trucks in Schwarmstedt station and deposited our two bombs upon them plus a burst of cannon. Our No.2, Pilot Officer Bolton did the same but there was not enough left for the other two aircraft so they went off to do their own thing. On the way back west we saw a column of smoke from a train at Lemforde and we turned towards it. But we'd been seen and a lot of 20mm flak came our way even though we were some distance off. We decided that discretion was the better part of valour and we left well alone. As we headed west a single-engined aircraft, which we couldn't identify, passed above us going in the opposite direction. Things were uneventful until we neared the Zuider Zee when we spotted two trucks travelling south. We were almost on top of them before we saw them so we tried to emulate a Stuka and dived almost vertically and gave them a burst of cannon. Bolton probably wondered where we had gone. All the way from Hanover he'd kept about a mile behind us and we couldn't think why. He later told us that he didn't want to get caught up in the flak, which we were attracting. Bert and I were blissfully unaware of this and thought what an uneventful trip it had been.[251] On 10 March Bert Willers was called into the CO's office after we returned from our 23rd trip together and he was told that it was our last one. I'd been on the Squadron since 15 February 1944 and done seventy-five ops. It was rather like getting a reprieve from a death sentence.

During the remaining months of the war, 2nd TAF squadrons and those of Fighter Command and 100 Group flew Bomber Support, Lure and Intruder operations to preselected airfields on the other side of the 'bomb line'. E.S. Gates, George Topliss' navigator on 613 Squadron, who had flown their first operation on 23 July 1944, recalls:

I vividly recall the atmosphere in the cockpit of our elegant and powerful Mk.VI Mosquito bomber as we thundered down the main runway at RAF Lasham at the start of another trip. I would settle into my seat with a complete sense of security and accepted perhaps naively, that our aircraft would see us through another operation. A gentle easing back of the stick and up we would climb into the night sky. Somehow it felt reassuring to place one's faith in a complicated mass of machinery. The persistent, powerful drone of the Rolls Royce engines, a steady vibration through the warm, snug cockpit, the pale opalescent glow of the instrument panel and the green flickering haze from the Gee set, all created a unique tiny world, completely remote from the reality of the earth below and the unpleasant war in which we were engaged.

Each navigational log has its own story to tell. Our first operation on 613 Squadron was to patrol a small area of northern France for an hour, searching out enemy road and rail transport. After my meticulous navigational planning and exceedingly thorough preflight checks by George, we were on our way. Crossing the coast near Littlehampton we flew south-east to enter enemy occupied France at Quiberville. Acting as he had been instructed, George commenced evasive action to confuse any enemy aircraft and flak. Unfortunately, his actions confused us more than the enemy. George later admitted that he scared himself to death as he nearly lost control by making over-violent manoeuvres. On all future operations we took no evasive action, relying on the speed of the Mosquito to take us quickly beyond any enemy coastal defences.

On one pitch-black night we dived steeply to attack a light in Germany and saw the dark silhouettes of trees rush past on the starboard side as we abruptly climbed away, a split second from oblivion. Then there was that occasion when, working as an Intruder pair, Frankie Reede dropped a flare as we took up a favourable position to attack the target. Naked under the yellow light and bear blinded by its brilliance, we were engulfed by a tangled trellis of coloured tracer shells. Identifying nothing and with the instinct of self-preservation uppermost, we dived away into the blackness beyond the flare.

The terse comment, 'weather bad' in my log for our operational trip on 4 November 1944 sets the scene but in no way does it portray the fearful experiences we encountered in heavy thundercloud over the North Sea. The aircraft writhed and creaked in the terrifyingly violent air currents; rain and hail spun off the propellers, the inherent charges of static electricity making them glow like huge Catherine Wheels; then there was the clatter of ice against the fuselage as chunks spun off the blades. Finally, after what seemed an interminable period of terror, we broke out of the clouds to find ourselves flying serenely down a huge valley between mountains of cumulonimbus. A half moon illuminated the massive towers and turret tops in a cold, pale glow and black fearful shadows were cast in the depths from which we had just emerged. Such images are forever indelibly etched in the memory. I can recall even more distinctly, those visages of squadron friends who flew off into the night never to return. The reality of life was often brought home to us at the termination of an operation. Frequently, fellows with which one had shared the previous evening's entertainment in the mess were posted missing. Every crewmember on the squadron was known to the others and each time an aircraft failed to return we all felt the loss. Nevertheless one carried on, inevitably thinking 'Its never going to happen to me'. And the Fatal Sisters, as they accompanied us on sixty-six operations against the enemy, decided not to sever one's life thread. We completed our last Intruder trip with 613 Squadron on the night of 19 April 1945. As our Mosquito trundled towards the end of the runway on our return from northern Germany I made my final entry in my last operational log of the war. '04.35 hours – landed safely.'

CHAPTER NINE

The Shell House Raid

Dr. Karl-Heinz Hoffmann, the *Gestapo* chief in Denmark, was a troubled man. He knew that Germany had lost the war but that was not his main concern. The 31-year old SS *Sturmbannführer* concluded that the successful pinpoint raid by Mosquitoes of 2nd Tactical Air Force on the headquarters at Aarhus on 31 October could be but a prelude to an even bigger raid on his own headquarters in the centre of Copenhagen. Hoffmann had expert knowledge of the resistance movements and had arrived in Copenhagen in September 1943 to direct *Gestapo* operations. In May 1944 his expanding organisation had moved from the Dagmarhus, a large building in the city hall square and had taken over the Shell House overlooking St. Jørgen's Lake in the centre of the city.[232] The *Shellhaus* had been built in 1934 as the new headquarters of the famous international oil company, A/S Dansk Shell. Each of the five floors of the building, which also had a cellar and an attic, was made of steel-framed reinforced concrete and on the outside the *Gestapo* installed screen walls with firing slits and barbed-wire barricades. As a deterrent against air attack, the Shell House had been camouflaged with green and brown stripes. (In fact, as it turned out, the stripes proved to be an added recognition aid as the building was the only one in the city to be camouflaged!) Following the D-Day landings in Normandy in June resistance activity in Denmark increased and the *Gestapo* began a new reign of terror against Danish saboteurs and resistance groups and the population at large. On 7 October in an effort to eradicate railway sabotage, Hoffmann decreed that captured resistance members and saboteurs would be carried on all trains transporting German troops. It had no effect and the *Gestapo* headquarters in Aarhus, Copenhagen and Odense stepped up interrogation and intelligence gathering. At the same time the *Gestapo* records within *Shellhaus* became the key to wholesale discrimination of the resistance movement.[233] Telephone taps on the lines between German High Command in Copenhagen and Berlin, had revealed plans to wind up the resistance movement in Copenhagen conclusively; the consequences of which would have allowed the release of 100,000 German troops to bolster the Battle of the Rhine. Such an event could have caused a major Allied defeat.

By the end of October 1944 the *Gestapo* had managed to capture several members of the Freedom Council, an underground movement, *Frit Danmark* (Free Denmark) and other groups. Not only was the capture of several key members of the Freedom Council a blow to the efficiency of this organisation, it was also a serious threat to Danish Resistance and the SOE organisation in Denmark. Signals to England requesting the bombing of *Gestapo* HQ were being received on an almost daily basis by the middle of January 1945. As the attack on Aarhus had showed, air attack was the only effective way of destroying these heavily defended headquarters. (The Danish police had made attempts to destroy the headquarters but they were unable to penetrate the heavily guarded buildings). In Copenhagen Hoffmann moved quickly and ordered the immediate conversion of the Shell House attic space into a prison complex. In all, twenty-two cells for hostages and six holding cells together with cooking, storage and washing facilities were to be built. Most held two prisoners, although sometimes the 'prisoners' were Danish informers put there to try and pick up information from the hostages. The cells themselves measured 3 metres by 2 metres, with one small window measuring 20 by 10 centimetres. Each cell had a two-tiered bunk bed, a table with drawers and two wooden chairs. A single 15-watt bulb was provided.[234] Hoffmann thought that with this human shield, the Gestapo would be immune to air attack.

Normal procedure required that a special pinpoint attack, which was to take place in friendly occupied territory, had to be sanctioned by the Air Board. Studies revealed the great risks involved in hitting a single target in a city centre. Civilian casualties were estimated at 300 and the percentage of aircraft losses could be considerably high. The Air Board passed responsibility for the final decision to Air Vice Marshal Basil Embry DSO** DFC* AFC, CIC 2 Group, whose 140 Wing 2nd Tactical Air Force, sometimes known as the 'Gestapo Hunters' would be the ones to carry out such a daring pinpoint raid. Embry in turn insisted that the final decision should come from someone in the field. This person would have full possession of the facts from both sides and up-to-date knowledge on the requirements of the Resistance. Furthermore, realistic estimates of casualties and possible damage had to be determined.

Ole Lippmann, Chief of Operations in the field and Allied representative of the Freedom Council (Danish Resistance), was the only man qualified to assess the risks. Around 10 February 1945 he was sent back to Denmark to make an appraisal and consequently the final decision for the attack on *Shellhaus*. Lippmann discovered that the situation was critical. On 4 March Lippmann wrote that it had been a very black week in Denmark. The *Gestapo*'s efficiency had improved markedly over the last few months and great damage had been done to the network in Copenhagen. He also said that he had still not been able to get a clear picture of the current situation. A week later Lippmann signalled: 'All military leaders have been captured. Also all the Resistance action plans have fallen into German hands and without doubt the *Gestapo* knows of the whole Resistance organisation'.[235] He urgently requested that 'Carthage' be destroyed. Carthage was the code he was briefed to use. On 15 March he repeated the request and sent the following message: 'Military leaders arrested and plans in German hands. Situation never before so desperate. Remaining leaders known by Hun. We are regrouping but need help. Bombing of SD Copenhagen will give us breathing space. If any importance at all to Danish resistance you must help us irrespective cost. We will never forget RAF and you if you come.'

Despite the risk of civilian casualties and heavy defences, the raid was finally sanctioned, although Embry admitted that he was horrified by the thought. He wrote later:

> The idea of killing our own friends weighed heavily on my mind; it was indeed a hateful responsibility I had to carry alone both then and on several further occasions before the war ended. Those who have not borne such responsibility can never fully appreciate the mental torment of the commander who says, 'Yes, we will do it and this is how it will be done.'

Nevertheless, as the request had come from 'The Field', the raid would take place and the actual date and time were closely guarded secrets. In the months leading up to the raid, the SOE worked closely with the Danish Resistance and British Intelligence to gather an enormous amount of material. Most of this came from the staff under the command of Major Svend Truelsen the dynamic Chief of Danish Military Intelligence. From this they were able to construct a highly detailed relief scale model, depicting a square mile of Copenhagen City centre. Meanwhile, time was fast running out for the Danes imprisoned in *Shellhaus*.

Ove Kampmann was a young Danish engineer who had worked on the construction of the Shell House. Now he shared cell 13 in the attic with a Danish Nazi informer. Kampmann's crime was hiding refugees and passing them through the escape routes to freedom in Sweden. Later he began to act as a liaison contact between the Copenhagen military groups and the communications systems. The SD[236] had come for him early in the morning of 24 February. He was dragged from bed and taken to *Shellhaus*. For 48 hours, almost without a break, he was whipped and beaten. The SD knew that he was due to attend an important meeting at 9 o'clock on the following Monday morning to exchange information with a number of resistance leaders. Again and again the same question was repeated: 'Where is the meeting to be held?' He had never considered himself a brave man but if he could hold out until after 9 o'clock, he could then tell them what they wanted to know. If he did not arrive within 5 minutes of the appointed time the other resistance members would realise that something was wrong and they would not wait. By 9.15 they would have scattered and the meeting place would not be used again. Kampmann's iron will conquered. He painfully watched as the hands of the clock moved passed the time of the meeting. At last with triumphant relief he told them what they wanted. The beating stopped, he was untied and dragged to his cell. His interrogators had done a better job than he knew. During the night, while he was unconscious, they had altered the clock. Unwittingly he had given the *Gestapo* the location of the meeting with time enough for them to arrange an ambush. More arrests were made. Kampmann tried to warn his two comrades in the next cell by pushing a note through a crack in the partition. However, they had already guessed the worst and immediately pushed the message back to him.

The *Gestapo* also arrested Ove Gessø Pedersen in February, as a suspected member of the resistance group *Frit Danmark*. He was immediately imprisoned on the sixth floor of *Shellhaus* along with twenty-three other prominent members of the underground. At first he shared cell No.14 with Professor Brandt Rehberg, a Freedom Council member and scientist who had been arrested with Colonel E.V.C. Tiemroth on 26 February. (The capture of Tiemroth had alarmed intelligence services in London because he had detailed knowledge of the Resistance throughout Denmark). Pedersen was later moved into Cell No.9, one of the so-called 'arrest' cells, together with Lars Hansen Christiansen, who was arrested early in February 1945 for his part in a sabotage group.

Ebbe Wolfhagen, a Commander in the Royal Danish Navy, had scuttled his ship in Copenhagen harbour and he had joined the resistance organisation, *Holger Dansker,* a sabotage group. On the afternoon of 21 February 1945 Wolfhagen and another resistance member were apprehended whilst walking down a street in Copenhagen. Imprisoned in *Shellhaus* Wolfhagen's interrogations started with a broken nose and a black eye, then a beating and questioning for 16 hours without a break. He had a feeling that the situation was not very favourable and he waited each day in his cell to be told of the hour of his execution. On 19 March 1945 he had been taken down to the interrogation rooms again. The *Gestapo* placed some papers in front of him, covered except for one small space at the foot of the final page. They ordered him to sign. He refused, saying that he could not put his signature to any document that he had not read. After some argument he was allowed to read his 'confession'. Throughout his interrogations he had refused an interpreter and had answered all questions himself in German. He had decided upon this as a precaution against being forced or tricked into revealing secret information, as he could always plead that he had not understood the question and had therefore answered it incorrectly not untruthfully. With this as his excuse, he insisted upon the deletion of all the most incriminating evidence. He was then sent back to his cell and on the following day a new typescript was presented for him to sign. Although not all the incriminating material had been removed, he signed. The *Gestapo* officers were friendly and congratulated him on his good sense. His interrogator then asked him one final question. 'How many murders have you committed?' Wolfhagen truthfully answered, 'None'.

'Not even one little one just before you were arrested?' He was asked.

His reply, firmly and in all honesty was, 'I am unable to distinguish between little murders and big murders. I have not committed murder of any kind.' At 3 o'clock in the morning of 12 March Ebbe Wolfhagen was moved from *Shellhaus* to Vestre Prison, a move that may have saved his life.

A day earlier eighteen FB.VIs from 140 Wing (21 RAF, 464 RAAF and 487 RNZAF Squadrons) plus two FPU (Film Production Unit) specially modified Mosquito B.IVs, were detached from Rosiéres en Senterre in France to RAF Fersfield in Norfolk. The move was made so that the route over the North Sea to Denmark would avoid flying over enemy-held territory with all the attendant risk of flak and radar detection. However, this stretched the Mosquitoes' range to the limit of endurance, a total flight time of over 8 hours. Group Captain R.N. 'Bob' Bateson DSO DFC** AFC and Squadron Leader Ted Sismore DSO DFC, the leading tactical navigator, would lead the operation. Air Vice Marshal Embry, alias 'Wing Commander Smith', would fly in a Mosquito loaned by 107 Squadron, in the first wave, with Squadron Leader Peter Clapham as his navigator. The crews were briefed intensely on 20 March and before take-off the next day and kept in a confined and closely guarded area away from the other personnel on the base. The twenty Mosquitoes would attack at minimum altitude, in three waves of 7, 6 and 6 aircraft respectively. Included in this total was one FPU Mosquito IV (DZ414/O) flown by Flight Lieutenant Ken Greenwood and Flying Officer E. Moore of 487 Squadron, which carried two 500lb HE and two 500lb M76 incendiaries and was to fly with and bomb with the first wave. The second FPU Mosquito IV, Q-Query, flown by Flying Officer R.E. 'Bob' Kirkpatrick of 21 Squadron and Sergeant R. Hearne of 4 FPU. Kirkpatrick was born in 1922 in Souris, Manitoba, Canada of American parents who moved back to Cleveland, Ohio, when he was one year old. On 8 December 1941 he tried to enlist in the US Marines but a medical revealed a heart murmur and he was turned down. Kirkpatrick travelled to Windsor, Ontario where, upon questioning his physical condition, he was told, "If you can see lightning and hear thunder you can be a pilot!" The RCAF accepted him for pilot training and after flying Beaufighters in a Coastal Command OTU in September 1944 he joined 21 Squadron at Thorney Island. He and Hearne had the unenviable task of flying behind the third and last wave to film the results. In total the twenty Mosquitoes carried a lethal load of forty-four 500lb bombs. Because of the very low levels flown and to prevent damage to following aircraft, the leading aircraft of each wave had 30-second delayed action bombs and the remainder, 11-second delayed action bombs. A proportion of the first and third waves carried M76 incendiaries.

At Fersfield the Mosquito crews were joined by 31 Mustang pilots of 64, 126 and 234 Squadrons (11 Group Fighter Command), which flew in from RAF Bentwaters. The fighters, who were to escort the Mosquitoes and eliminate flak positions in the target area, were led by their Belgian Wing Commander (later Lieutenant General Avi.e.r.) Mike Donnet CVO DFC CG, born of Belgian parents in Richmond, England in 1917, had escaped to England on 5 August 1941 after Belgium had capitulated, in a two-seater Stampe biplane with a fellow officer. Twelve Mustangs of 126 Squadron would escort the first wave and six from 64 Squadron; two from 126 Squadron would escort the second wave and eight

Mustangs of 64 Squadron, the third wave. Three Mustangs from 234 Squadron would sweep from 10 miles north (Værløse air base) towards Copenhagen.

At 08.55 on 12 March the formation was airborne, forming up over Fersfield; 5 minutes later it crossed the English coastline north-east of Norwich, with a direct course for the first checkpoint 375 miles away at Hvide Sand in Jutland. The weather was stormy, with surface winds gusting at 50 knots, making it difficult to control the aircraft. After crossing the North Sea at 50ft to avoid radar detection, the windshields had become coated with salt spray, which reduced visibility; some pilots tried slowing down so that they could clear patches of their screens with gloves or cloths. The checkpoint was dead-on with the force making landfall at Hvide Sand at 10.20. Three Mustangs were forced to turn back due to bird-strike damage. Over Jutland, the aircraft, still flying at minimum height, begun to attract attention of Danes and Germans alike. The *Jagdfliegerfuhrer* (German Fighter Control) received continuous reports as they flew across Denmark but failed to advise Copenhagen until after the bombing began. The formation flew on by way of Give and along the northern side of Vejle Fjord to Juelsminde and then across the Great Belt. On the island of Zealand the checkpoint was Tissø, an almost circular lake chosen as an easy landmark. Here the formation spilt into the three wave formations ready to be escorted by the Mustangs. The first wave, lead by Group Captain Bateson, set course for Copenhagen at minimum altitude with an escort of eleven Mustangs, one having been forced to return due to bird-strike damage. Flying on Bateson's port side was Air Vice Marshal Embry and Peter Clapham. The remaining aircraft carried out 'rate-one turns' (orbits) of the lake, once for the second wave, twice for third and three times for the remaining FPU Mossie. This gave a distance of approximately 9 miles between each wave, an interval of approximately two minutes flying time.

On the outskirts of Copenhagen the first wave began to pick out the details of the target area. Despite the bumpy conditions Ted Sismore identified the target by the green and brown stripes and Bateson led his force over the rooftops. The aircraft began to move into attack formation, bomb doors were opened, bombs fused and speed was increased to 300 mph. The escorting Mustangs increased speed and began to seek out their targets, the flak positions, most being unmanned at the time. The first wave continued their run-in towards the final checkpoint when 800 yards from the target tragedy struck. The leading aircraft of the second flight, the fourth Mosquito in the first wave, collided with a 130ft high floodlight pylon in the marshalling yards at Enghave and went into a vertical dive. The pilot, Wing Commander Peter Kleboe DSO DFC AFC, aged 28, was the newly appointed CO of 21 Squadron.[237] His navigator was Canadian Flying Officer Reg Hall aged 30. Flight Lieutenant T.M. 'Mac' Hetherington RCAF and Flight Lieutenant J.K. Bell were flying No.6 on the starboard side of, and slightly behind, Kleboe's aircraft. Hetherington observed:

We watched each other and attempted to follow the leader by 'biting hard into his tail' and at the same time, staying clear of his slipstream. We followed each other like shadows. We were altogether; 12ft lower than the first three aircraft. We knew that we had to turn, but apparently Wing Commander Kleboe had not seen the pylon or had reacted too slowly. Suddenly, through the side window I observed his aircraft climb at a very steep angle and fall off to port. Squadron Leader A.C. Henderson and I instinctively threw our aircraft to starboard and continued on towards the target.

Flight Lieutenant Ken Greenwood, flying on the port side of Kleboe's aircraft, was just 25ft away on Kleboe's port side. He adds:

About 10 to 15 seconds before the accident, bomb doors had been opened, copying the leader. Kleboe's aircraft lost height, some 15ft, and I suppose by peripheral vision, I saw the pylon and realised that he was going to fly into it. As the aircraft struck the pylon, part of the port engine was damaged. The Mosquito rose almost vertically and then rapidly to port. I had to take violent evasive action to prevent a mid-air collision and swung to hard to port. Kleboe's two bombs struck a building in Sønder Boulevard (one, a dud, failed to explode) and eight civilians were killed. The Mosquito was observed waggling its wings and trailing smoke before it crashed on the Alleenberg garages at 74 Frederiksberg Allé adjacent to the *Jeanne d'Arc* School, a catholic institution run by St. Joseph sisters and known as the French School. The force of the explosion from the fuel created a huge pall of black smoke. Kleboe died instantly. His Canadian navigator, Reg Hall, was flung out of the aircraft in the impact and his body fell through the roof of the Frederiksberg Theatre, landing at the feet of the female director who had just poured herself a cup of coffee.[238] At the time of the Mosquito crash the pupils at the French School were all in their classrooms and the Sisters quickly ordered the children to the cellars. [In the confusion it appears that at least one Mosquito bombed the school by mistake, one bomb hitting the west wing and another striking the staircase by the east wing and chapel]. Before all could take refuge the first of the Mosquito's bombs had begun exploding. The north-west and eastern corners of the school building collapsed killing many of the children and Sisters and trapping others on the upper floors. In the cellar shelter, after the first wave of bombing, some of the children escaped through the windows only to fall victim to the second wave.[239] Then the cellar began to flood from a broken water pipe. A fire broke out on the upper floors but the emergency command centre received the alarm very late due to the breakdown on the emergency communication system. Meanwhile, the main fire department force was sent to the *Shellhaus*. Passers-by and the Sisters, together with fifteen firemen, struggled to rescue those trapped in the school, fight the fire and drive the ambulances. The water supply failed due to the ruptured mains and, aided by the strong wind, the school burned to the ground in less than two hours. Two firemen were killed when walls fell on them. When the fire was at last extinguished and the rescuers reached the cellar they found forty-two children huddled together, having died from drowning or other injuries. Altogether, eighty-six children lost their lives and sixty-seven were injured but 396 were saved. Ten St. Joseph Sisters died and thirty-five were injured.[240]

The remaining aircraft of the first wave continued over the target area. Group Captain Bateson being the first to attack with his bombs going in between the second and third floors of the west wing at 11.15: right on schedule. Air Vice Marshal Embry and Squadron Leader Peter Clapham and Squadron Leader Tony Carlisle and Flight Lieutenant N.J. 'Rex' Ingram got their bombs away. Carlisle followed with Embry directly behind and observed the Air Vice Marshal's bombs strike the building at street level. Henderson and 'Mac' Hetherington each put their two bombs through the roof of the Shellhaus. Embry moved into Henderson's flight path, which forced him to go over Embry. Henderson's navigator, Bill Moore, said, "Look, the old man's going sightseeing!" After getting their bombs away, the first wave scattered and exited Copenhagen at roof-top height in a north-westerly direction over the city and made for home. Until now, the Germans had not sounded the air-raid warning. The Danish Civil Air Defence had also followed the path of the aircraft, realizing the danger to the city it tried to persuade the Germans to sound the alarm. By the time the Germans took action, bombs were already smashing into the *Shellhaus*. Official records have revealed that the German officers responsible for this negligence were court-martialled. As the Mustangs crossed the target area, the second loss of the day occurred. Flak tracer shells bracketed Flight Lieutenant David Drew DFC's Mustang. The aircraft had sustained a hit and a thin black line of smoke appeared from the underside of the aircraft. Drew banked his Mustang and turned north. It disappeared over the rooftops and crashed in Fælled Park. Drew was killed. He was later buried at Bispebjerg Churchyard together with Peter Kleboe and Reginald Hall.

As the attack started and the first bombs exploded, tiles began to fall down leaving a hole in the roof of the *Shellhaus*. In a panic reaction, Ove Kampmann, one of the twenty-six Danish prisoners imprisoned on the sixth floor, laid himself down on the bed with a blanket over his head. The sound of banging on doors was heard. Together with the other surviving prisoners, Kampmann made his way across the empty attic area on the east side of the building. The stairs were slippery with blood from the dead and dying and it was almost impossible for the prisoners to find space for their feet. When they reached the first floor level they saw that the carnage was even more appalling: every stair was piled high with bodies. Stumbling and slipping over the dead Germans, they made their way to the ground floor and the main entrance. There was not a guard in sight. The men split into pairs or went off alone.

One of the hostages, Poul Borking, an SOE operative who had been parachuted into Denmark, was being interrogated on the fifth floor and was seated so that he could see out of a window. A *Gestapo* agent was telling Borking that as an SOE officer he could expect to be shot when at that precise moment he spotted the Mosquitoes streaking towards the building. He leapt to his feet and turned over the table in front of him onto his interrogator and ran from the room past another stunned *Gestapo* man who was standing by the door. The first bombs exploded as Borking reached the third floor and when he reached the main door he found all the guards dead. Borking continued on to the main railway station where he boarded a train escaping from Copenhagen. Another prisoner, Christian Lyst Hansen, in cell 6, was reading in his bed when he heard the roar of engines followed by two violent explosions. With a solid wooden stool he was able to batter his cell door open and take the cell door keys from the panic-stricken SS guard. Hansen began opening the other cell doors, freeing all the prisoners from cells 7 to 22 although it was not possible to reach cells 1 to 5 because a bomb had blown a large hole at the corner of the corridor on Nyropsgade.

Aage Schoch, a member of the Freedom Council who had been captured on 2 September and held in one of the attic cells and Dr. Mogens Fog, another Freedom Council member who was arrested on 14 October, made their way down a rear stairway. When they reached the second floor they thought that they would have a better chance to escape if they used a main stairway. They moved to the front of the building only to find the stairway littered with dead and dying Germans as a bomb had exploded on a guard post just outside, killing everyone on the street. The blast caught those who were fleeing down the stairway inside. To reach the street the escaping prisoners were forced to step over and walk on the dead.[241] Ove Gessø Pedersen in cell No.9, one of the so-called 'arrest' cells, with Lars Hansen Christiansen, remembers, 'After the first bombs had struck the building I was possessed with only one thought, to get out.' Upon hearing the sound of aircraft engines, Christiansen's first thought was that they were German.

> Then we [Christansen and Gessø Pedersen] heard the first bombs exploded and the building seemed to lift itself up. Dust and debris fell from the ceiling covering us from head to toe. After discovering that three rather weak hinges supported the numerous locks the *Gestapo* had put in the door, we tried to break the door down.

Pedersen continues:

> First I tried to smash the door with a folding chair but this fell to pieces. Then I tried with a stool, which proved to be stronger, with this, I was successful in smashing the door.

Christiansen got out onto the corridor and turned right towards the empty attic area.

I ran across the to the east stairway where I had to climb over the dead and wounded lying on the stairs. Nobody tried to stop me. I ran out onto the street still covered in white dust and over to Vestersøhus [an apartment building next to *Shellhaus*]. I rang a number of door bells, the people opened up their doors and asked where I came from, when I replied from *Shellhaus*, nobody would take the chance of hiding a fugitive from the *Gestapo,* so the doors shut in my face. Eventually I got into an apartment at number 42 where, over a glass of brandy, I sat back and watched *Shellhaus* burn.

Meanwhile, in the corridor outside cell No.9 Pedersen noticed a single SS guard, rooted to the spot, covered in dust and shaking with fear.

Close by was huge gaping hole cut by the first bombs and a marvellous view over the rooftops of Copenhagen. As I stood outside the cell, I realised that I had forgotten a coat that my brother had lent to me. Feeling rather embarrassed, I ran back to collect the coat. I returned to the corridor and swung myself down through the hole by means of a thick length of insulated electrical wiring. I then made my way to the second floor. I had to push my way through a crowd of panic-struck people on the stairs and came out into the street where I jumped over the barbed wire. I made my way towards Svineryggen (Street) by the lakes. From this point I managed to see aircraft from the second wave of Mosquitoes attack the *Shellhaus*, I then ran off down the street.

The five cells on the west Nyropsgade wing took direct bomb hits. Bombs passed through cells 2 and 3 killing Admiral Carl Hammerich, Chief of the Danish naval staff, Ole Stang, a resistance leader, and a Danish collaborator who shared Stang's cell and penetrated to the lower floors of the south-west corner before exploding. (Stang's body was found later but no trace of Admiral Hammerich or the informer was ever found). Three prisoners on kitchen duties were killed when the room opposite Cell 1 used for washing-up received a direct hit. Captain Peter Ahnfeldt-Mollerup was killed while he was being interrogated in an office next to Pøul Borking's cell. Professor Brandt Rehberg in Cell 14 survived and out in the street he and Ove Kampmann made their way to a safe house before escaping to Sweden. Pøul Bruun, Pøul Sørensen, Karl Wedell-Wedellsborg and Mogens Prior, the four prisoners in the remaining three cells, found themselves lying in the rubble on the floor below their cells. They were not seriously injured but were trapped by fire on one side and a huge hole in the floor on the other. They made up a makeshift escape rope from belts and lowered themselves down to the fourth floor. Desperate to get away from the clutches of the *Gestapo* and not having any other way to escape, they jumped one at a time to the pavement four floors below. All received serious injuries and were recaptured by the Germans. Mogens Prior received no proper medical attention and he died on 26 March. Karl Wedell-

Wedellsborg also died having received no medical treatment except that from fellow prisoners. Against all the odds Bruun and Sørensen survived their terrible injuries and were gradually nursed back to health. Colonel Tiemroth and another prisoner left behind in the attic corridor with their guard did not try to escape once they reached the safety of the street, mainly because they feared reprisals against their families. After they had helped two fellow prisoners to flee to safety they awaited recapture.[242]

The second wave of six Mosquitoes of 464 Squadron RAAF led by Wing Commander Bob Iredale DSO DFC RAAF and Flying Officer B.J. Standish arrived over Copenhagen some 2 minutes behind the first. By this time the sky over Copenhagen was being criss-crossed by flak. The smoke coming from Kleboe's wrecked aircraft was greater than that coming from the *Shellhaus* and it distracted the leading three crews. Confusion reigned and the force was split into two. (The Mosquitoes, together with the Mustang escort, began to circle the area to clarify their position. In the first manoeuvre some Mosquitoes were too far left of the target and only those aircraft closest to *Shellhaus* were able to bomb). A split-second decision had to be made. Iredale broke off his attack and circled to come in again. At the same time the three remaining Mosquitoes of Blue Section led by Flight Lieutenant Archie Smith DFC and Flight Sergeant E.L. Green had realised the mistake and located the target slightly to the right of their track. Smith made two orbits of the target area before bombing. His bombs struck the outside of the east wing, destroying a pillbox situated on the corner. Both Iredale, who got his bombs away on the east end of the *Shellhaus* and Smith, who also attacked a flak position at Hundested, managed to bomb *Shellhaus*. During his orbit, Flight Lieutenant W. Knowle Shrimpton DFC and Flying Officer Peter R. Lake RAAF in the No.2 position behind Iredale in the second wave came into conflict with the incoming third wave. Shrimpton explains:

> We came up to the lake where we would drop our wing tanks. I had to keep the Mosquito level and straight during this part of the operation, no skidding, so that the tanks would fall away cleanly without rolling into the tailplane. This was no easy task due to the extremely high turbulence. Peter was then concentrating more on map reading whilst I concentrated on accurate flying. I prayed that he had memorized the track. Then on the outskirts of the city I recognized the first landmark shown on the briefing model. Flying became precise; height 50ft, engine revs and boost. We wanted 320 mph but settled for 305 to 310, which was about all we could get. I set the bomb fuses and opened the bomb bay doors. We were getting close. Flak was looping over the target from the right with not much room over *Shellhaus*. The next event was a shock. Peter yelled, "Don't bomb, smoke to port!" He signalled to me that something was wrong. Were we on target? This all took place 10-15 seconds from what we believed to be the target, time enough to see that the building in question was not damaged

but not enough to evaluate all the facts. Therefore, I aborted the attack, cleared the building and closed the bomb doors. Throttling back and keeping low, I commenced a left-hand orbit. After a moment we had left the flak area and I reduced the rate of turn. We then had the opportunity to assess the situation and make a plan. The building which we were confident was the target was not damaged, no fire or smoke. We decided that the preceding aircraft had probably bombed the wrong target. Was the fire a decoy? We decided to get ourselves into position for another run up to the target. Then, realizing that we were alone without orientation of our position, we commenced another orbit. After about 325° we both became re-orientated, first by Peter's recognition of the run-up track and as a result of that, my identification of the target. Here we determined that *Shellhaus* had been hit. We could see dust and smoke. I continued to turn on the run-up and as we came in we both agreed that the job had been done. We observed heavy damage to the base of the building and lots of dust and smoke. More bombs might have unnecessarily endangered the Danes in the building so we aborted the attack. Later, on the long flight home, there was a distinct sense of failure or at least disappointment that we still had our bombs.

Two of the Mosquitoes from Blue Section in the second wave were hit by flak over the north of Zealand on the return flight. Flying Officer Ronald G. 'Shorty' Dawson RAAF and Flying Officer Fergus T. Murray, ditched near Lisleje Strand. Flying Officer John H. Spike Palmer RAAF and Sub Lieutenant Hans H. Becker, a Norwegian, ditched in Samsø Belt. There were no survivors from either aircraft.[243] The third wave consisting of the six 487 Squadron FB.VIs, led by Wing Commander F.H. Denton DFC* and his Australian navigator Flying Officer A.J. Coe had navigation problems. They approached Copenhagen from the north-east; a completely different direction to the planned flight path. This wave had been observed in front of the returning aircraft from the first wave as they left the target area. Delayed by some minutes they were caught up by Q-Query, flown by Flying Officer R.E. 'Bob' Kirkpatrick with Sergeant R. Hearne that had departed the Lake Tissø area 2 minutes behind the other six Mosquitoes. By mistake, four crews in the third wave bombed the area around the school. Denton and Coe, who located Shellhaus, saw so much damage already that the pilot aborted his attack and jettisoned their bombs in the sea. Flak tore away the starboard flap and knocked out the hydraulic system but Denton managed to nurse his flak-damaged FB.VI back and belly-landed in England.[244] Q-Query also limped home after taking a flak hit over the target. Kirkpatrick recounts:

As we approached the city I could see a huge pall of black smoke dead ahead and at the same time, some Mossies in a tight left turn. Our courses were converging. As they straightened out towards the smoke I had only a second to decide to join them close enough to avoid the 11-second delay bombs, rather than risk a right turn with the cruddy windshield [which had become coated with salt spray low over the North Sea]. The Mossies levelled off on track and I tucked in close, just as their bomb doors opened. I opened mine and saw their bombs drop just before we entered the smoke. I dropped my bomb load, then we got a pretty good wallop in the smoke and after breaking out I lost contact with the other Mosquitoes.

On the outskirts of the city, I saw two Mossies at about 3 o'clock on a northerly heading. I joined up with them only to see that one was smoking badly from the starboard engine. [Flight Lieutenant David V. Pattison and Flight Sergeant Frank Pygram's Mosquito had been hit by flak from the cruiser *Nürnburg* moored in the harbour]. The escorting Mosquito waved me off, as without guns, I would be just a burden and their course was not towards England. I turned back west just in time to see a sandbagged gun pit with two guns firing at the three of us. We had inadvertently got close to a large barracks, a fenced area with several low buildings. The best and quickest evasion was to go straight towards the gun pit and dive. I opened the bomb doors to get their attention and spoil their aim. As the doors opened the gunners abandoned their guns and ducked down. We were gone in a flash, right over them.[245]

On the return trip we sweated fuel for over an hour. When we spotted the English coast and, not too far inland, an air base, I went straight in. I got the wheels down, but nothing for flaps or brakes, so I coasted to a stop on the grass by the runway. We had found a B-24 base [Rackheath] near Norwich. Hearne and I were escorted by MPs to the control tower to explain our presence.

Pilot Officer R.C. Hamilton RAAF's Mustang in 64 Squadron sustained damage over the target area and he lost oil pressure before being forced to ditch in Ringkøbing Fjord near Tarm, Jutland. Hamilton survived to be taken prisoner and he was later sent to *Stalag Luft* I at Barth in Germany. In all, four Mosquitoes and two Mustangs failed to return, for the loss of nine aircrew.

Ebbe Wolfhagen imprisoned in Vestre prison heard the explosions in the distance:

My first reaction that day was of shock. Later I asked a guard for a pencil and paper so that I could write a note to *Shellhaus* to ask for permission to smoke and read. The guard replied, "You can forget that: *Shellhaus* is in flames." I was at that time very concerned about my colleagues' fate, were they dead or had they survived?

If all the Mosquitoes' bombs had been dropped on *Shellhaus* it is doubtful that anyone would have survived. Had the air-raid warning been sounded on time, civilian casualties may have been much less. Casualties among the *Gestapo* were less than expected as Karl Heinz Hoffmann and all the leading *Gestapo* staff were attending the funeral of an officer who had shot himself two days previously. (After the war Hoffmann defended himself at his trial and served four years imprisonment). The total number of dead was seventy-two, with twenty-six members of the *Gestapo* and thirty Danish collaborators. The remainder were innocent Danes. The escape of so many Danish patriots provided the Resistance with the much-needed breathing space. The tragedy at the *Jeanne d'Arc* School marred this success, as one can never balance the lives of innocent children against those of resistance fighters, nevertheless there has never been any retribution shown towards the RAF for this costly operation. After the war, a fitting memorial was raised to the children and adults killed at the *Jeanne d'Arc* School. Likewise, at the new Shellhaus building there is a memorial to the Resistance members that lost their lives. Today at *Shellhaus*, there is a memorial to the nine aircrew members that laid down their lives in the fight for Denmark's freedom.

No.140 Wing had one more low-level pin-point raid to fly. On 17 April six FB.VIs of 140 Wing, led by Group Captain Bob Bateson DSO DFC** AFC and Squadron Leader Ted Sismore DSO DFC* taxied out for a daylight strike on a school building on the outskirts of Odense, which was being used by the *Gestapo* as an HQ. Air Vice Marshal Basil Embry went along, as usual. Bateson led the Mosquitoes over the building three times before he could positively identify the target, even breaking radio silence to ask the other crews if they could see it. No enemy fighters showed and once found, the six Mosquitoes destroyed the Gestapo HQ. The delay in bombing gave the Danish civilians time to flee and no Danish casualties were reported. Eighteen days later Denmark was free.[246]

CHAPTER TEN

'The Forgotten Front'

One of the myriad problems facing South East Asia Command (SEAC) in India in 1943 was how to perform aerial reconnaissance over Burma and Malaya from its bases in Ceylon and India. Only four camera-equipped B-25C Mitchells of 681 (PR) Squadron at Dum Dum in Calcutta possessed the range and speed for such flights over the Bay of Bengal and the Rangoon area. No.681 Squadron's aircraft situation was causing great concern, for the two of the serviceable Mitchells had been in use for over 12 months and there were no aircraft in the command, other than Mosquitoes, with equivalent operational range and high speed. At the beginning of April 1943 three Mosquito FB.IIs and three FB.VIs were allotted to 27 Squadron at Agartala. Three were for performance tests and familiarization, three to be used for weathering trials during the coming rainy season under the supervision of Mr. F.G. Myers, de Havilland's technical representative in India. Late in the month, however, it was decided that the Mosquitoes should supplement the squadron's Beaufighters for Intruder operations. The first Mosquito operation over Burma was a reconnaissance on 14 May 1943. It is reported that Major Hereward de Havilland, visiting 27 Squadron, was horrified to find that the FB.IIs were being put to operational use. He attempted to have them grounded because he considered that the casein glue with which they were bonded was unlikely to withstand insect attack and the tropical weather. The FB.VIs, yet to arrive, were supposedly bonded with 'waterproof' formaldehyde adhesive. No.27 Squadron used the FB.IIs again on only one occasion. One crashed and another was damaged by ground fire on 5 June.

After experiencing a delay while Air Ministry approval was sought to allow the conversion of the several Mosquitoes into PR aircraft at 1 CMU, Kanchrapara two B.IIs and their flight crews were transferred in August to the twin-engined flight of 681 Squadron. These were followed by three newly arrived B.VIs. All five were fitted with vertical camera mountings but they did not have the four cameras of the 'PRU type' or the additional fuel tanks nor, in the case of the 'B' Flight, provision for fitting underwing fuel tanks. On 23 August Flying Officer Dupee DFM reconnoitred the Mandalay-Shewbo-yeu-Monywa-Wuntho area. The following day a second Mosquito sortie was flown when Flight Lieutenant Picknett made a reconnaissance of Akyab Island. During September 681 Squadron flew eight PR sorties over vast areas of Burma and on occasion an

FB.VI was employed. One of the Mosquitoes became a victim of enemy action, but after a forced landing, it was repaired and returned to Calcutta after three weeks. The feared deterioration of fuselage bonding adhesives did not happen, despite the aircraft being continually exposed to high temperatures and humidity, so approval was given for the delivery of more Mosquitoes to India.

On 29 September 684 Squadron was formed at Dum Dum from the twin-engined flights of 681 Squadron and it was planned that they have an establishment of twenty PR Mosquitoes. However, the unit was initially equipped with four B-25 Mitchell IIIs, two Mosquito Is and three VIs. Photographic coverage of targets such as Bangkok and Sumatra could only be reached by the Mosquito PR.IX, which had a safe range in excess of 1,250 miles. One was delivered to 681 Squadron on 18 October. A second crashed the same day on landing at Ranchi, killing the crew. Three days later 684 performed the first of thirty-three PR sorties over Burma when Flight Lieutenant F.B. McCulloch and Sergeant T.S. Vigors flew over Rangoon and Magwe. Another PR.IX arrived on 23 October. Next day McCulloch and Flight Lieutenant Henry Reeves reconnoitred the Andaman Islands to bring back photos of Japanese shipping and flying boat activity. Three Nakajima Ki-43 'Oscar' fighters tried to intercept the high flying Mosquito but none got near the British aircraft. Later that day Flight Sergeant Johnson and Sergeant Willis returned safely with photos of Rangoon despite another attempted interception by two fighters and AA fire at 27,000ft.

No.684 Squadron's first Mosquito loss while on operations from India occurred on 2 November when Flying Officers Fielding and Turton failed to return from a photo recce of the Rangoon area. Two days later the supply route from Moulmein to the Sittang bridge was covered. All Mosquito operations came to an abrupt end on 12 November, however, when a series of accidents resulted in a signal being sent to all units grounding the aircraft, pending inspection. On 9 December the six remaining Mosquitoes and four B-25Cs of 684 Squadron moved to Comilla in East Bengal, where it formed part of 171 PR Wing, Air Command SE Asia, which had come into being on 16 November. Their stay was a short one, for after just month it returned to Dum Dum on 30 January 1944. On 10 December Sergeant Boot and Sergeant Wilkins flying a Mosquito II were shot down over Rangoon and a second Mosquito crashed near Feni on 23 December following structural failure, killing Flying Officer Orr and Sergeant Johnson. Operations now involved distances of over 1,000 miles from base and 8-hour operational duration was not uncommon. On 15 December Squadron Leader Basil S. Jones the CO and his observer, Flying Officer R.C. Hawson reconnoitred Bangkok for the first time. The sortie revealed new information on Japanese reserve positions and the use of 'lay-back' airfields and earned both men the DFC. No.681 Squadron meanwhile, moved east also to Chandina.

On Christmas Day 1943 27 Squadron, equipped with a mixed inventory of Beaufighters and Mosquito FB.VIs, despatched its first Mosquito sorties proper.[247] In January 1944, the Air Ministry decided to equip twenty-two bomber and strike squadrons with FB.VI aircraft to replace the Vultee Vengeance and some Beaufighters. De Havilland was to produce replacement airframe components at Karachi. Mosquito reconnaissance operations now covered distances of up to 1,000 miles from base and an eight-hour duration was not uncommon.

In February the PR Force (PRF) was formed under Group Captain S.C. Wise to bring together 681 and 684 Squadrons and the US 9th PRS. No.684, now back at Dum Dum and commanded by Wing Commander W.B. Murray, received nine pressurised PR.XVIs, which enabled higher altitudes to be flown. The remaining Mk.VIs were retired and they became a valuable source of spares, as parts were always in short supply. At the beginning of the month 684 Squadron had begun a photographic survey of Burma, while reconnaissance flights to islands in the Indian Ocean also continued. On 7 February Squadron Leader Basil Jones DFC and Flying Officer R.C. Hawson DFC tussled with a 'Hamp' (a modified 'Zero' with clipped wings) fighter over Port Blair in the Andaman Islands. On 23 February PR.IX 'L' returned from a 'Special Areas' sortie with engine trouble and had to be written off. Two days later Flight Lieutenant F.B. McCulloch and Flight Sergeant T.S. Vigors flew to Mergui, then south down the coastal road to Tavoy where five Zeros intercepted them at 22,000ft. McCulloch climbed away and they were not attacked.

Flying Officers Jack Winship RCAF and Peter Haines had been involved at Cawnpore with experiments to attach a 90-gallon jettison tank under the belly of a PR.IX. Using this tank, the crew took off from Dum Dum on 29 February and flew across the Bay of Bengal on a recce of the Andaman Islands, with a stop at Ramu. Duration of the flight was 8 hours 25 minutes and the return flight was flown in the most violent weather Winship had encountered. He and Haines covered Port Blair, Stewart Sound and Port Bonington before meeting a Zero, which was unable to catch them. Another PR.IX developed engine trouble on the outward flight and later had to be struck off charge. By the end the month few Mosquitoes were available due to a shortage of spares.

In March 1944 684 Squadron made regular flights to the Andaman Islands and reconnoitred the Japanese railway system in Burma. One of the pilots on the squadron at this time was Flight Lieutenant Robin M. Sinclair (later the Right Honourable Viscount Thurso of Ulster). Robin Sinclair made many social contacts in Calcutta. Indeed, he often brought interesting people into the mess, including the Maharajahdirajah of Butdwan (whose palace was used as the squadron airmen's' mess) and the monocled Colonel Bernard Fergusson, one of the Chindit leaders. The young pilot would also fly to the forward landing ground with 'Popsie', his little dachshund bitch who had her own parachute! On the 22nd Sinclair and Flying Officer Reggie W. Stocks were briefed to reconnoitre southwards along the Siam-Singapore railway as far as petrol and prudence allowed. This trip reached into northern Malaya and established a record for that time of 2,490 miles, lasting 8 hours 45 minutes. Sinclair and Stocks landed back at advance base with 30 gallons of petrol remaining. This was the first sortie by an RAF aircraft over Malaya since the fall of Singapore.

Five days after this epic flight, on 27 March, Flight Lieutenant Kossuth 'Kos' J. Newman DFC* RNZAF and Flight Sergeant Ron Smith DFM in 684 Squadron flew a 1,860-mile trip to photograph a stretch of the Burma railway and airfields at Bangkok and Hua Hin. On the same day Warrant Officer J.A. Johnson and Flight Sergeant F. Wells flew a sortie to the Nicobars to cover Port Blair airfield and the radar site at Mount Augusta. The final sortie of March (flown on the 31st) saw Flying Officers Dupee DFM and McDonnell obtain the first photos of Car Nicobar Island.

In April 684 Squadron experimented with long-range flights as far afield as Khun Khaen, in central Siam and Vientiane in Laos, to see if they could fly over the monsoon weather so as to cover Japanese rear areas when the weather had passed. Until 13 April these sorties were flown from Dum Dum but then Ramu in the south was used. The Mosquitoes flew in the evening before their sorties so that they could take-off at first light and reach their objectives early in the day before cloud built up. On 4 April Sergeant T. Cocks and Flight Sergeant C. Smith set out to cover Metgui but found the Tenassetim coast covered in cloud. On the return journey, however, they photographed the Mokpaiin area and the Sittang bridge on the Burma railway, which had been damaged during a recent bombing raid. Their photos revealed that repairs had been carried out and the rail line was free between Mattaban and Rangoon. Four days later the bridge was heavily bombed by B-24s. A photo-reconnaissance carried out on 10 April by Warrant Officer J.A. Johnson and Flight Sergeant F. Wells showed that the two western spans of the bridge had been destroyed.

Meanwhile, on 5 April Flying Officers Jack Winship and Peter Haines, now on their second op, had a close call during a sortie to cover Kaun Cean and some new enemy airfields in north-east Siam. Winship explains:

> Peter and I flew from Dum Dum to Ramu in MM294 to refuel for our PR flight. When the fuel tanks were all topped-off we set out for Kaungean located near the eastern border of Siam, close to the Indo-China area. After take-off we ascended to the desired altitude. The procedure was first to consume fuel from the main tank located in the bomb bay to make room for transfer of petrol from the outer-wing drop tanks. We had 50 gallons in either drop tank, so all we needed was to use 100 gallons from the main tank before we could transfer fuel from the outer drop tanks. Eventually, I had reduced the main tank by some 120 gallons or so and tried to transfer fuel. I immediately received a red light indicating there was a vapour-lock and fuel would not transfer. So I switched back to my regular tank again. According to the manual, if you have trouble like this and you can't transfer

fuel, return to base. You don't fly around with 50 gallons of fuel in either drop tank. Now, I had done this before, had vapour-locks and continued my flights. After a while as things cooled, the lock usually disappeared and you could pump fuel from the drop to the main tank. I had never returned from a trip and I had no intention of this being the first flight I would have to scrub. We had good altitude of 35,000ft and a terrific tail wind. Peter was surprised when he computed us having over a 100 mph or so tail wind; we couldn't believe it. We must have climbed up into a jet stream and were doing just beautifully with a terrific ground speed.

We continued flying along and everything by then was getting cooled down. I was ready to transfer fuel from the drop tanks when I noticed my port engine temperature climbing as I glanced at the gauge. I looked out and there was this horrendous plume of vapour trailing from the engine: just a colossal cloud! Startled, I realised it was my coolant and immediately shut the engine down, feathering the prop before the Merlin heated up to seize. Then it dawned on me that this was the engine I needed to transfer the fuel. The Pesco pumps were located on this engine and we needed them to pump fuel from the drop tanks. We were approximately two and a-half-hours from Ramu by this time and had covered nearly 800 miles. Peter right away gave me a reciprocal heading. This I did making the turn with the single engine. The drop tanks were of no use to me now. It was 100 gallons of fuel we needed badly. Without the tanks, you don't have the extra weight or the drag, but there was no way I was going to utilise this fuel. So I had to get rid of it and pressed the jettison button. The tanks dropped off and I maintained airspeed by sustaining a slow rate of descent. You cannot hold 35,000ft on one engine. In the meantime, Peter was plotting out a course for me and managed to send off an SOS on the key. We were too far to reach Ramu by VHF. Another thing, the generator was on the feathered engine. We wanted to be careful to keep the batteries strong and operating as long as possible, considering the circumstances. Using the VHF radio would have drained them. Peter dropped the trailing aerial in an attempt the pick up any messages, but nobody seemed to have received our emergency distress signals, for we received no replies, but that was not our main worry.

Our main concern was whether we had enough fuel available to return to Ramu. According to the manual, the fuel consumption on one engine meant we were not going to make it. Peter suggested that maybe we should fly on to China, which was closer than Ramu. I had doubts about this, as we would have to fly through mountainous areas with very few airstrips and I don't know if the natives in the area would be friendly to us. My thoughts were to fly as far back towards Ramu as possible, then crash-land in a riverbed, get our escape kit out and try to work our way back to the coast somehow. Even if it was going to take me months, I was determined to reach our lines. When you are young and foolhardy, you don't realise how grave the situation is or could be.

At this time, we were gradually losing altitude when all of a sudden the aircraft gave a shudder and the other engine began running rough. Peter was getting ready to bale out, thinking we had lost both engines. I told him to hold on, sit tight for a moment. Suddenly it dawned on me that the superchargers had cut-out. They cut-out after you descend to a certain altitude with the increased density of the air. When they cut-out it was like losing another engine, so I immediately opened the throttle again to retain my boost. Finally, with my boost regained I was able to hold the aircraft on an even keel at around 14,000ft with no difficulty. I kept the engine running hot and it behaved properly. The radiator inlet was controllable and when opened, caused drag. I made adjustments opening the inlet enough to maintain speed and engine temperature barely below the danger point. The over-burdened engine seemed to run smoother when it was hot. A Rolls-Royce representative later told me that a certain safety factor was built into the engine and as long as vapour (overheating) doesn't come off my engine, I was not running it too hot. The prop I had feathered was windmilling slightly. It had not feathered completely and was causing the aircraft to wallow, resulting in a loss of airspeed. I had a difficult time controlling the aircraft as it was! I unfeathered the prop, held the starter button, the engine turned over. I then punched the button again to get the prop feathered. It went into fine pitch immediately. I was able to trim the aircraft and found it would fly with hands off the wheel; it flew beautifully! Again our concern was whether enough petrol was left. According to the manual, we would be approximately 100 gallons short, running empty a few hundred miles from base. There were mountains ahead to go over yet. We took a direct route passing over known enemy airfields, still maintaining 14,000ft. You could see Japanese aircraft parked on the airfields below, located around the Irrawaddy Valley plain. We were not putting out any con-trail and I'm sure they must have heard the droning sound of our engine on the ground, but no one bothered to come up and investigate. If an enemy aircraft did come up, all we could do was dive for the ground and attempt to fly as far as possible. We flew over the Japanese aerodromes, escaping detection and then sighted the bluish hue of the far distant Andaman mountain range. We were doing 200 mph at this time and were surprised the aircraft would maintain this speed on one engine. We had close to 800 miles to reach Ramu and it would take us slightly over four hours to return.

At this time, we did not realise our SOS was not picked up at Ramu but had skipped and gone all the way to Calcutta. Our wireless officer there was working on a receiver when he suddenly heard the SOS coming through. He immediately wired Ramu and asked what their contingency plans were. They replied, having no knowledge of the situation we were in, they would dispatch Spitfires to escort us in. By this time we were flying over the inhospitable Andaman mountain range at 14,000ft and this was why I wanted to maintain altitude. If we ever had to dive down, it would be difficult to regain this altitude or to navigate our aircraft through the remote valleys and high ridges. Everything was going well and fuel consumption was better than anticipated. We were obtaining 90 gallons to the hour, where the manual said it would be around 125 gallons per hour. We encountered no head winds compared to the terrific tail wind at the high altitude we enjoyed on the outward journey. We still had some petrol in our tanks as we neared Ramu.

As our aircraft approached the strip, another Mosquito pilot entering the circuit heard our RT conversation with the field. He orbited then followed me to make sure I maintained my airspeed coming in on one engine to a fairly short strip. There were two runways at Ramu called 'Reindeer 2' located next to each other. The fighter aircraft used one and the other was for Mosquito aircraft to land on. All of a sudden this other pilot begins yelling that I'm landing on the wrong strip. I said the hell, wrong strip or not, there is one ahead of me. But he had mistaken the strips and we landed on the correct runway. On a previous occasion, I had made a single-engine landing at Ramu during an op. On another flight they brought me in downwind and I overshot, having to have the aircraft towed out of the mud by truck. But the landing I was presently making was the best I had ever made. When you have a single engine encounter like this, you're working on it. You are so careful in bringing it in that you ease the aircraft onto the runway. Whenever I made single-engine landings, I always made perfect ones. It was when I had good conditions, two engines and was lax, that I had my ropey landings. We had been in the air over six and a-half-hours. Peter figured we had flown a distance close to 790 miles on one engine.[248]

In May 1944 a 684 Squadron detachment began operations from Alipore, a suburb of Calcutta. On the 6th Flight Lieutenant 'Kos' Newman DFC* RNAZF and Flight Sergeant Ray Smith DFM took off to fly a reconnaissance sweep of Nancowry Harbour in Great Nicobar to ascertain whether there was any Japanese shipping in port. Ray Smith explains:

The trip (2,256 miles) was thought to be at the extreme range of the PR.IX and at the time it was felt that we might not be able to get back to our advanced landing ground at Ramu from where we had taken off. To cover this contingency the Royal Navy had placed caches of food and survival kits on some islands off the Arakan coast. If we thought that we would not be able to make it back to Ramu, we were to make a forced landing on the sea adjacent to one of these islands and, hopefully, we would be picked up by the Royal Navy. Fortunately, we were able to make it back, although we flew for about 10 minutes with our fuel gauges reading zero.[249]

No.684 Squadron received some additional PR.XVIs in May and June. By this time the monsoon weather was affecting the number of successful operations being flown and eighty-one of the 110 sorties in June were abortive. On 22 July Flying Officers Tebb and Fletcher in a PR.XVI fitted with a 90-gallon jettison tank reconnoitred three airfields on the Andaman and Nicobar Islands. At the beginning of August a 684 Squadron detachment was based at Yelahanka, near Bangalore, in southern India for aerial survey work. The weather over the Indian Ocean was clearer than over the Bay of Bengal, so, on 11 August, the squadron sent a detachment from Alipore to China Bay, Ceylon, for operations with 222 Group. The detachment's task was to make the first air survey of northern Sumatra and nearby islands. To ease maintenance and processing problems, the Yelahanka detachment also moved to China Bay a few days later. The Ceylon detachment began operations on 15 August when a PR.IX crew flew a recce of Nancowry and Sabang Islands. On 23 August a flight was made to Sabang and Car Nicobar and two days later a PR.XVI crew flew to Sabang and along the west coast of Sumatra to Sibolga harbour. A further lengthy sortie to Sumatra the following day discovered a previously unknown Japanese airfield at Padang Tidji, near Sigh. By the end of August, however, the Mosquitoes had almost ceased operations due to the monsoon. In spite of the weather on the 28th Squadron Leader Kos Newman DFC* and Flight Sergeant Ray Smith DFM covered a section of the Burma-Siam railway adjacent to the side of a mountain just south of Moulmeio. They came under heavy AA fire and were lucky to escape, as Ray Smith recalls:

We were greeted with intense anti-aircraft fire whilst flying at about 500ft and just as we had completed the job the aircraft was hit in the air intake of the port engine and also in the nose, smashing Kos' oxygen economizer. Not knowing the extent of the damage, which had been caused to the port engine, we climbed to 25,000ft, since we did not want to get caught at low altitude with only one engine functioning properly. We then decided to try and make out way to Chittagong above the Irrawaddy valley, where we felt that the weather would not be quite so severe. We were right in this assumption and upon successfully reaching the Chittagong area we decided to carry on to our base at Alipore, as the port engine appeared to be functioning normally. Whilst we were flying at high level we both had to use my oxygen supply alternately as became necessary.

As a result of this remarkable operation the area was heavily bombed a few days later, which caused a massive landslide that completely blocked the track. Newman was awarded a bar to his DFC.

No.684 Squadron's activities at China Bay were halted until mid-September 1944, when a PR of parts of Sumatra was flown and were then halted again until October. That month, 684 Squadron Mosquitoes at Alipore used Cox's Bazaar, at the mouths of the Ganges, to make long-range flights into Burma. All Mosquito operations came to an abrupt halt on 12 November 1944, when following a spate of crashes, a signal to all units required Mosquito aircraft to be grounded pending inspection.[250] The cause of the accidents was, supposedly, destruction by 'termites' and deterioration of glue. It was supposed that, as the aircraft were left standing in the open, extreme heat has caused the glue to crack and the upper surfaces to lift from the spar; but it soon became clear that the adhesive was not the cause of the trouble. In March 1944 production of the first batch of Mosquitoes in Australia had been disrupted when it was discovered that components in the wing failed to 'mate'. Consequently, gaps occurred in the glued joints between the main spar and the plywood stressed-skin of the wings (under load the plywood upper wing surface could become detached and the box-section spar assembly could collapse). The wings for the first twenty Australian-built aircraft were scrapped.[251] The effects of the accidents in India were far-reaching. The intended manufacture of components at Karachi was abandoned and the re-equipping of squadrons delayed. Structural failures and added troubles with the engines meant the wooden aircraft was never a favourite with the crews of 27 Squadron, who preferred the Beaufighter for their low-level strafing sorties. All fourteen FB.VIs in 110 (Hyderabad) Squadron, which a few days earlier had retired its Vultee Vengeance aircraft, were grounded by 6 November. De Havilland still maintained that the failures in India resulted from climatic conditions and ordered the destruction of all parts made with casein glue.[252] A meeting at the Air Ministry on 1 January 1945 heard an explanation of the Mosquito defects from Major de Havilland on his return from India. He again attributed the faults to the entry of water, differential shrinkage and unsatisfactory glueing; admitting that there was scope for improving manufacturing techniques, particularly the method of assembling glued joints. Records show that accidents classified as caused by 'loss of control' were three times more frequent on Mosquitoes than on any other type of aircraft. However, the Air Ministry forestalled possible loss of confidence in its Mosquito squadrons at home and abroad by holding to Major de Havilland's assertion that the accidents in India were caused by 'faults largely due to climate'.[253]

On 4 July 1944 meanwhile, 82 (United Provinces) Squadron at Kolar and 84 Squadron at Quetta, India were to begin conversion to the FB.VI from the Vultee Vengeance III dive-bomber.[254] No.82 Squadron began conversion at Kolar, 35 miles to the east, in July but 84 Squadron never did convert to the American aircraft owing to the lack of available Vengeances. In October the Squadron disposed of all its Vengeances and on 31 October moved to Yelahanka near Bangalore to re-equip with the Mosquito FB.VI. In November advice was received that, owing to technical problems with the Mosquito, the squadron would re-equip with Vengeance IIIs and return to the forward area. Two weeks later they were instructed to continue the conversion to the Mosquito owing to lack of suitable Vengeances and the Squadron was instructed to continue the conversion to the Mosquito! (The Squadron's first Mosquito arrived in mid-February 1945). Meanwhile, heavy monsoons prevented any operations at all until mid-September but 45 and 82 Squadrons moved, in turn, to Ranchi, just over 200 miles west of Calcutta, for attacks on Japanese targets in Burma.

On 1 October 45 Squadron flew their first Mosquito sortie. On 9 November Flight Lieutenant Cliff Emeny led six of the Squadron's Mosquitoes on a dawn raid on Meiktila aerodrome. Emeny, who as an NCO gunner/observer on Defiants on 225 Squadron destroyed a German bomber attacking Hull on 9 May 1941, destroyed a Japanese bomber taking off. However, his Mosquito was then hit by flak, which set the port engine on fire and caused the starboard engine to lose coolant. He was attacked by two Oscars, who were driven off his tail by another Mosquito and this enabled him to make a controlled crash-landing in the Burmese jungle. The Mosquito exploded on impact and cut a swathe through the trees before coming to a halt. Emeny and his navigator were subsequently reported 'missing believed killed' but though they were burned and injured they had both survived. On every operation Emeny carried a special axe with a very short handle and by using it he was able to cut himself free of the wreckage before he was badly burned. The Japanese captured him and his navigator, denied them medical treatment and after very brutal interrogation sentenced the pilot to death by beheading. Probably the advance of the 14th Army saved his life and he was imprisoned in Rangoon. In prison he saved the lives of many of the prisoners after persuading the Japanese to let him set up a rudimentary hospital. On liberation he weighed just 6 stone 10lb.[255]

In late November all Mosquito VIs were grounded because of faults with the main wing-spars. The pilots were transferred to Cox's Bazaar to bring out wounded from the Kaladan in Tiger Moths and Vultee-Stinson Sentinels and the navigators were sent on leave. Meanwhile, 47 Squadron had moved to Yelahanka on 7 October followed by 110 'Hyderabad' Squadron three weeks later. When 110 Squadron was first formed during the First World War the Nizam of Hyderabad had met the cost of the aircraft as a contribution to the war effort. It was said that if any member of the Squadron was in the vicinity of the Nizam's palace, there was a welcome awaiting him with lavish hospitality! Starting in December 1944, 47, 82 and 110 Squadrons commenced day and night Intruder sorties on the Japanese road, rail and river network system. On 18 December the Australian CO of 82 Squadron, Wing Commander Lionel V. Hudson and his navigator Pilot Officer Shortus failed to return from the squadron's first operational sortie when they crashed in the Irrawaddy. They both managed to reach an island in the middle of the river and the Japanese took them prisoner. Hudson's replacement was newly promoted Wing Commander F.W. 'Freddy' Snell DFC. On 19 December 45 Squadron resumed Mosquito operations after their aircraft had been passed airworthy with an attack on the Saye-Kinu railway. Next day the Squadron destroyed the Alon railway bridge. On 23 December a glide bombing attack with 500lb bombs was carried out at night on Meiktila aerodrome. Daylight attacks on locomotives and rolling stock and a night raid on the marshalling yards at Ywataung on the 27th followed. On 29 December six Mosquitoes of 45 Squadron made a dawn dive bombing attack on Meiktila aerodrome. Six Japanese Oscars intercepted them. Ben Walsh, pilot of one of the Mosquitoes managed to get a prolonged cannon and machine gun blast at one of them and he believed that he damaged it but he could not get confirmation since his was the last of the six Mosquitoes in the attack. All the Mosquitoes returned safely. Walsh tells his story:

These low level attacks were made over inhospitable terrain and were often pressed home in the face of heavy ground flak and small arms fire. The dive bombing technique involved approaching from around 4,000ft and then diving to 1,000ft whilst aiming the bombs at the target. The bomb load varied between 2 x 500lb and 4 x 500lb loads, often fitted with instantaneous fused bombs, which gave little margin for error. From 3 January 1945 onwards it was a time of intense operational activity even though the weather at times was totally unhelpful because of the small monsoons. Jap airfields, especially Meiktila, were the primary targets for low-level bombing, strafing and night patrols. Road communication, railways and bridges got their fair share of attention too. On 8 January we made a dive bomb attack on Jap troop concentrations at Sagaing. On the 12th a Rhubarb[256] was flown to Chindwin and the Irrawaddy to Sagaing and Jap installations at Konywa waterfront were bombed. A further ten ops were flown during the month and MT transport, railway installations, bullock carts and sampans were bombed and strafed. On the 16th there was a dawn strike on Meiktila and a Rhubarb on the Irrawaddy-Chank road. Jap ground fire hit the starboard spinner and main spar of the aircraft close to the starboard radiator. The outer fuel tanks were hit but the crew completed the op safely. Later inspection of the Mosquito revealed that the damage was superficial. On the 18th the Jap HQ at Koko was hit with four 500lb bombs and the following night ricer traffic was shot up between Sagaing and Yenang Yaung. We were despatched on a night attack on the 23rd to bomb either Heho airfield or Meiktila but the weather was duff and instead we dive bombed Myingyan with five 500 pounders fitted with instantaneous fuses. The round trip took 4 hours 20 minutes to complete. On the 26th a daylight attack was made on petrol dumps in Port Duffern and three MTs were shot up on the Mandalay road. On take-off next day our Mosquito developed a hydraulics fault and the operation had to be aborted. On the 29th a night attack was made on the Myitnge bridge. A considerable amount of flak was put up and this burst uncomfortably close to the aircraft. Jap stores at Ywabo were bombed on the 31st and transport was attacked along the Irrawaddy-Myingyan-Magwe road and railway. Some Jap ground fire hit the Mossie in the fuselage during this part of the operation.

On 10 February my navigator, Warrant Officer Orsborn and I were sent out as a single aircraft operation over the 8-10,000ft mountain range. It was an Army support operation to drop 'Parafex' containers (simulating hand grenade, mortar shells, machine-gun and rifle fire) in a predetermined spot on the Irrawaddy River to assist in an army crossing. Near the target we experienced a total electrics failure and believing we had dropped our 'Parafex' on target we endeavoured to make our way back to base without radio. Needless to say with no moon, flooding and swollen rivers and increasing high cumulus especially over the mountains we got hopelessly lost and were very low on fuel. We were almost at the point of baling out when, by a sheer stroke of luck, we spotted lights of a very small landing strip and made an emergency landing (downwind as it happened) on a short, forward landing strip at Onbauk near Mandalay. The plane overshot the lights and ploughed through a burnt out DC-3 and was badly damaged and because of the electrics failure we found the 'Parafex' still on board. Jap ground forces were all around and often attacked at night with mortar and machine gun fire. The next morning we got a transport to Imphal and then back to base.

Between 5–31 March 45 Squadron kept up a relentless and intense bombing and strafing campaign against the Japs. Road and rail transport was shot up at every opportunity and bridges were bombed. My bridge bombing efforts included Thamakan (missed), Thwatty (badly damaged), Sinthe (damaged) and Toungoo. By the end of the month we had notched up 64 hours day and 14.30 hours night operational flying. One of the best results was obtained on the 26th/27th when Salin was bombed at first light. Four 500lb bombs were dropped accurately on a Jap camp. The following day a Rhubarb was carried out on the railway and road between Kyaukpadauna and Pyinmana. Two locos were shot up and a 3-ton MT was set alight before the ammunition ran out!

Sergeant (later Warrant Officer) A.H. 'Alf' Pridmore of 45 Squadron, whose pilot Flight Lieutenant Dick Campbell RCAF had been killed in the crash of a Mosquito on 10 October,[257] adds:

March was a very active month indeed for 45 Squadron, which completed a record 287 day sorties and sixty-five night sorties. This shows the high operational activity of the Squadron. My pilot, Flying Officer Don

Blenkhorne a Canadian from Nova Scotia and I completed a total of twenty sorties during the month, with only one abort. As the Japs retreated the Squadron used the forward airfield at Thazi. On 4 March we took off from Khumbirgram in north-east Assam on a 45 minute flight to Thazi at 16.20 in Mosquito HR332. After refuelling and taking a rest we took off again at 00.25 on the 5th to carry out an Intruder op. We bombed Pyinmana aerodrome and then did a patrol followed by a Rhubarb between Magew-Allenmyo-Myolalin. A sampan and a motor transport were attacked. The four-hour trip home was made with a short stop over at Kalemyo. A similar operation was carried out in a dawn operation on the 7th when Tennant aerodrome was hit and a locomotive was shot up.

On 15 March we took off for Yenanyang oilfield. Flying out of Khumbirgram we always had to cross the Naga Hills at about 10,000ft before heading for a distinctive bend in the Irrawaddy we called point 'A' and then setting course for our target area at lower levels. Final attacks were usually shallow glide-bombing where the pilot waited until the target passed under the nearside engine nacelle and immediately he would wing over and dive on the target. The Squadron approached the target line abreast flying flat out, over the treetops. Each aircraft carried short delay bombs and we released ours in the target area and then headed for home. The Japs put up a moderate amount of flak but did no damage. The operation lasted 3 hours, 20 minutes. Two days later the Squadron returned to the target area, bombing this time from high level. The bomb load carried was usually two bombs in the bomb bay and two more under the wings if drop tanks were not needed. Attacks on airfields could be dangerous but they were necessary, as it was important to try and keep the Jap aircraft on the ground. In March these operations were often carried out at night or timed for dawn, but in May we carried out 'cab rank' operations to keep a constant patrol over an airfield to prevent aircraft from taking off. Unfortunately this did not prevent the Japs from calling up aircraft from other fields and we did suffer some losses. However we must have been lucky for we never met a Jap aircraft and any damage was usually the result of ground fire. The general terrain we flew over was also a major threat as the Naga tribes were still headhunters at that time and our escape kit included 'blood money' in addition to revolvers and machetes. One of our major roles was to destroy supply lines ahead of our advancing troops. The XIV Army carried out a brilliant and speedy advance through Burma and the speed of their advance left many isolated pockets of Japanese still fighting. After the fall of Mandalay we overflew a column of British tanks out on the open road sweeping towards Rangoon, the crews waved to us from their tanks.[258]

Ben Walsh and Warrant Officer Orsborn's last operation on Mosquitoes, their 40th in total, nearly ended in disaster. On the afternoon of the 4 April they took off for the advanced landing ground at Thazi, *en route* to Zinga. After an hour they landed to refuel, taking off again on the final 1 hour 40-minute flight to the target. On board were two 500lb bombs and two 500lb incendiaries. As the evening light began to fade they ran in to bomb Zinga village and as they left the target it appeared that it had been accurately hit. The return trip took three hours in the dark and after a time it became apparent that the fuel situation was not good. Estimates indicated there would be insufficient fuel to enable the aircraft to reach base. Ben Walsh called for an emergency homing to Monywa. Insufficient numbers of flares were laid, the Mosquito overshot having made a final approach from 5,000ft with very little fuel left and crashed through a gun position. The Mosquito was a 'write-off'. The crew sustained no injuries. After an overnight stay at Monywa they hitched a lift to Tulihall in a 221 Communications Squadron Warwick and waited for the Dakota mail plane to take them back to base the following day. This completed their operational tour with 45 Squadron and a short time later they were posted away from the squadron to take up non-operational communications, ferrying and plane-testing duties.

Meanwhile, in November 1944 Wing Commander W.E.M. Lowry DFC had assumed command of 684 Squadron. All Mosquito operations came to an abrupt halt on 12 November, however, when yet another signal to all units requited Mosquito aircraft to be grounded, pending inspection. The cause of the accidents was supposedly destruction by 'termites' and deterioration of glue. But the actual cause resulted from faulty construction of the wing spar. The number of aircraft available to 684 Squadron for instance, dropped from twenty-one in October to just four airworthy PR.IXs by 20 November. With the arrival of refurbished and replacement aircraft, the squadron soon had twelve Mosquitoes available for operations again and in January 1945 684 Squadron flew over seventy sorties, including 2,100-mile round trips to survey Phuket Island, which had been first covered on 30 December. Squadron Leader Newman and Flight Sergeant Williams obtained complete coverage of Phuket on 5 January during a round trip of 2,286 miles. No.1 Detachment at China Bay, near Tricomalee in Ceylon, made similar long-range sorties to the Andaman and Nicobar Islands and the tip of Sumatra, flying almost 1,000 statute miles across the Bay of Bengal. Each sortie lasted mote than eight hours.

The Japanese forces in Burma were always a difficult target because so much movement took place in heavily wooded or jungle territory. The weather was always a threat, particularly over the mountains rising to 10,000ft or so, which had to be crossed in all flights to and from base at that time. Charles Carruthers, a navigator on 82 Squadron flying out of Khumbirgram in the early months of 1945 in support of the 14th Army, recalls a Rhubarb flown on 24 February 1945. Their mission was to attack the road and railway NE from Mandalay to Lashio and then south along the road for more than 100 miles:

This was the most exciting trip yet. Warrant Officer Ron Murkin and I set course from base with Flight Lieutenant Dick 'Mac' Mackenzie DFC and his navigator Flight Lieutenant Ray Pears DFC leading. Arriving at Sadang we proceeded to detour around Mandalay, as there are very strong ack-ack positions there. Turning south we finally located the road and railway and proceeded to follow it. Everything was going quite well and I was keeping a wary eye on our tail for Oscars: those nasty little Jap fighters. After a quarter of an hour or so we spotted a loco in a bamboo hut (the Japs' poor attempt at camouflage). This we strafed and saw dust and possible steam rising from it. Proceeding happily up the railway line, weaving from side to side, suddenly the sky was filled with little black puffs of smoke. They looked quite harmless, but having known what Bofors can do it caused us no little anxiety. Our nose went down immediately, throttles open, and we left with great speed. Having thought we were out of range I glanced behind and was shaken to see those little black puffs following closely on our tail. Luckily, however we got away with it. Mac thought he got hit as he told us over the R/T, so we turned for home. But apparently his aircraft was functioning OK so we carried on after a couple of minutes. There is no doubt that they had been waiting for us, as their fire was so accurate. I think it was because of the fact that we unconsciously flew right over their position without seeing them that it might have surprised them a little. Anyway, that was that and eventually we located the road leading south and started to patrol it. Then like a bolt from the blue, we heard Mac yell, "Bandits, for God's sake open her out". So once again down went the nose and throttles through the gate this time and we hurtled along at a steady 350mph right on the deck. It didn't take us long to outrun them. Possibly they didn't see us but there is nothing like 'safety first'. They were probably sent up to intercept us as they were heading north along the road and we were coming south. However, once more we managed to avoid danger.

Seeing as there were enemy fighters in the vicinity we turned west for our lives. Thinking the danger was past we were more or less peaceful in mind. Then a further Oscar was sighted, which caused us great alarm, as he appeared to be turning in to attack us. This time it was not so easy because as we were flying at about 50ft, right in front of us was a range of mountains. Somehow we managed to top the rise and screamed down the other side approaching the 400-mph mark. The old Merlins were dragging at their anchorings and the whole kite was shuddering. This was the least of our worries and finally we reached our lines and set course for base. We landed OK after four hours of very exciting and nerve-racking experiences. While taxiing back to dispersal the groundcrew seemed to be taking undue interest in us. Imagine our surprise when we got out and saw part of the starboard wheel cover torn and bent by shrapnel. Peculiarly enough Mac thought he had been hit and hadn't. We didn't notice a thing at the time we were shot at and yet a stray bit of shrapnel had damaged us. Ignorance is bliss! The Intelligence Reports of 200 Jap fighters having been moved up into the battle area from Rangoon was causing some consternation. So far, bandits had amounted to practically nothing in the way of opposition.

Since December 82 Squadron was based at Kumbhirgram in India, to the west of the Manipur/Chin Hills, which rise to around 9,000ft. Gordon Thewlis, an Observer, remembers a flight he did with his pilot, Flight Lieutenant B. V. 'Vic' Hewes, an American from Atlanta, Georgia:

It was one of my most unforgettable operations. We were usually sent out to attack predetermined targets in support of the advancing XIV Army. Quite a lot of our intelligence for targets was obtained via Force 136. These were small groups of men, usually four in number, with a wireless operator in the team, working in the jungle behind Japanese lines, sending information back on targets to attack. On this occasion, the Japanese were trying to hoodwink us, as they were always vulnerable to air attack if keeping to jungle roads during daylight hours. Medical supplies were urgently required for the Japanese troops of 33rd Division. They utilised local bullock carts, disguised with a hay top covering. Force 136 discovered this ruse as they monitored a convoy of 8-10 carts making their way north towards the front line. The Japanese 33rd Division was retreating down the Chindwin valley to the south and west of Mandalay. Taking off from Thazi, a forward landing-strip to the east of the Chin Hills, as dawn was breaking, we set course in a south-easterly direction.

The target given to us was Ywadon, but the bullock cart convoy had moved on a little by the time we arrived there. After a few moments searching in the general direction they were heading we spotted them in line astern, about eight of them in total, edging along a narrow track banking, alongside rice paddy fields. Making a broadside approach we hit the first two, made a steep turn to port and made a similar attack on the rear three, finishing off the trapped middle three with a third strafing.

Our ammunition belts on both the .303 Browning machine guns and the 20mm Hispano cannon had been loaded with extra incendiary bullets and shells to cause the most effective damage. Flame and smoke damaged medical supplies would be of little use. The horrifying part was seeing the bullocks in the shafts falling to the ground, having been hit with either stray bullets or shells. It was also unfortunate for the Burmese Teamsters who were caught up in the attacks. They had probably been drafted into this job under duress by their Japanese conquerors.

My conscience didn't play any part at this point. We were a highly trained crew. We had to do a job, which we did to the best of our ability. But we did come to realise that this was the horror of war at close hand! With our complete domination of the air, Japanese motor transport was usually kept well hidden in the jungle during daylight hours. Carts drawn by bullocks would generally be less vulnerable to attack. Hence our reliance on Force 136. On this occasion we were to continue our sortie [Rhubarb] to Ywathit where we strafed a lone truck heading north and then more 'business' as we spotted four more covered trucks also heading north, which we duly strafed and certainly caused considerable damage. We were by this time south and west of Mandalay near Monywa on the Chindwin. It was time for home.

On all these low level sorties the cockpit became extremely hot with sweat stinging the eyes and the body saturated in perspiration. The sickly acrid smell of burnt cordite fumes, all added up to make a sortie a very unpleasant and unforgettable experience.

On the return flight we were obliged to land at Thazi, a jungle refuelling strip in the Kabaw valley (Death Valley), north-west of Mandalay and one hour short of our home base at Kumbhirgram, due to a very dangerous build up of cumulus over the Manipur Mountain range. Our operational flight time for this operation was a gruelling 3 hours and 40 minutes, arriving knackered at Thazi to the point of collapse. Had the weather been clear I doubt if we could have made it to our home base. Perhaps God was on our side in clamping down the weather. As it was we were again diverted from Thazi to Imphal because of bad weather, taking off later for base at Kumbhirgram. All in all this one operation had taken nearly two days to complete. It was then debriefing and bed to recover. In many ways it was a sortie which left little sense of satisfaction, as it was difficult to see if the end, with native Burmese and bullocks killed, justified the means.

Max Howland an Australian Mosquito pilot on 684 Squadron at Alipore, Calcutta in 1945 states:

On my course at OTU at Dyce most English were posted to Benson. Us 'colonials' got India. "Tough luck old chap, glad we're not going with you" they said and then they got a rugged time over Germany. I think the squadron was efficient. It was certainly informal. Briefing was individual, no crews together. The CO gave each new crew on arrival a 2-3 hour run-down on the strategic situation and on operating conditions. We were warned that we would fly through the monsoon and that unless we set aside our preconceived ideas of weather and developed new standards we wouldn't be long for the squadron. The monsoon rain was heavy. We were told that we would not be able to tell the difference between blue sky and black cloud. I think most of us doubted it, until it happened to us. Later, I was at 33,000ft beside a Cu Nimb and I wasn't even half way up. A black storm looks bad but we were warned of the daddy of them all: a brown storm. Of course we couldn't photograph through cloud. On one trip I flew from right on the deck over Jap territory and up to 35,000ft to avoid the cloud and was supposed to photograph from high-level above 22,000ft from 8,000ft. Once to maintain 300° from my navigator's plot I actually steered 270, 180, 330, 265, 360°. You'd have fabric coming off from the rain you couldn't dodge. You'd try unsuccessfully to avoid flying in cloud because you could still see Cu-Nimb sticking up after clearing stratus at 25,000ft. Our liquid-cooled engines on the high altitude models didn't like ground running in the midday tropics. After starting-up we taxied like hell to take-off doing the rest of our cockpit check on the run. If we got held up we had to shut down. Our job was to give notice of any Jap reinforcing. We did this by photographing every town, every tin-pot port, every 'drome, roads, and every inch of the railway system within a thousand miles (equivalent of London to right across Poland). We could keep track of every railway wagon they had. If the Japs had mislaid one we could have told them where it was. We had a line shoot: 'Jap stationmasters can't even go to the toilet without our knowing' (or words to that effect). When covering a railway line we flew over the whole length taking sixty overlapping photos, any adjoining pair of which made a stereo or 3D pair. The camera took shots automatically about every 6 seconds: set to suit height, airspeed, wind. A red light gave warning of the next exposure. For gentle curves we skidded the aircraft round between shots. For a 90-degree bend, say, we would turn off the camera and turn through 270°. We could virtually guarantee to fly vertically over a target. In Burma wind at height was seldom a problem. However, we did have our problems: we flew alone, unarmed, in daylight, one thousand miles at heights from the deck up. The Japs were more thinly spread than the Germans and the targets were fewer but we visited them more often.

A typical good weather op to Akyab, Ramree Island and finally north of Rangoon consisted of a briefing for two days, completed about lunch time. Then we'd fly to the most forward strip at Cox's Bazaar. At daybreak, fill the 100-gallon drops. Take off as soon as possible hoping to start photographing about 09.00 and be out over the Bay on the way back by early afternoon when the storm lines built up along the Malay coast. And we'd be hoping to arrive back in time for a swim in the coffee they called the Bay of Bengal. At height we ran the bomb-bay tank dry and calculated how long we could stay in the air. We would give ourselves 15 minutes safety though we would sometimes pinch five minutes to finish a job. While still 15 minutes out all tanks would read empty and you'd pray the navigator had learned his arithmetic right and that another Thunderbolt wouldn't prang and drop a bomb on the only runway. My longest trip was 8 hours and I had 40 gallons left. I know others that have been much closer and completed an otherwise successful op but an op was a failure unless we got back. Land and refuel and then fly back to Alipore. First interpretation ready after dinner and a selection of photos back to the flight within 48 hours.

Word got round some time after the German surrender and before the atomic bombs, that all Australians were being sent home. Official word came from Delhi, it was true when we could be spared. I had an interesting war and a lucky one. I like the philosophy of what an American wrote: 'War is the ultimate adventure; the ordinary man's means of escaping from the ordinary.'

During February 1945 89 Squadron at Baigachi began converting from the Beaufighter to the Mosquito FB.VI but they were never used. In March 82 Squadron flew 269 sorties, while 47 and 84 Squadrons were used on bomber support operations for the Army. Two crews of 82 Squadron had a lucky escape on 8 March returning from a raid by six Mosquitoes of 82 Squadron on a bridge over the Sittand River at Pyinmana and a nearby airstrip. The Mosquitoes dropped their 11-second delayed action bombs close to the target without hitting the bridge. The lead aircraft flown by Squadron Leader F.W. 'Freddy' Snell DFC, who had flown Fairey Battles at the beginning of the war and had then gone to Canada as an instructor, and Flying Officer Arthur Maude was badly damaged by an explosion beneath the aircraft. Despite the aircraft being riddled with holes, Snell managed to get the Mosquito back to Kumbhirgram. It was thought that the explosion had been caused by the detonation of a land mine.

After attacking the bridge Flying Officer Ron 'Babe' Wambeek DFC and Warrant Officer Brian Mooney swept low over Lewe II airstrip in the hope of catching Japanese fighters on the ground but their Mosquito was hit by accurate bursts of machine-gun fire. The port engine streamed glycol and the hydraulic system was damaged. Wambeek feathered the port propeller and set course for Sadaung about 200 miles to the north, the most advanced airfield at which the aircraft could be repaired before crossing to their base in Assam. Without hydraulics they were committed to a crash landing but that would put the strip out of action for several hours so they carried on a to a small satellite strip about 5 miles to the south-east, although it was unlikely that it was in Allied hands at the time. Uneven ground, trees and large boulders precluded a crash landing elsewhere so the crew reasoned that it was better to take their chances evading the Japanese than risk almost certain death over the jungle terrain. Wambeek landed without flaps and with his undercarriage down at an alarming speed before the Mosquito ground to a halt. At the last moment the Mosquito slewed round to the right and the fuselage broke in half just behind the wing roots before ending up about 30 yards from the trees at the end of the strip. Both men scrambled out of the top hatch and disappeared into the scrub and undergrowth. A sticky stench of rotting flesh pervaded the whole area. An estimated 4,000 Japanese had been killed in the fighting. Two hours later an army patrol in two jeeps picked up the two downed fliers and ran the gauntlet of enemy snipers. As they passed along the shores of Meiktila Lake they could see numerous bodies floating high on the water in the shimmering haze and heat of the afternoon, all with huge, grotesque, gas-inflated bellies. While waiting their turn to be evacuated Wambeek and Mooney were given cups of hot, sweet tea. Wambeek wondered if the water had come from Meiktila Lake![259]

Meanwhile, on 10 February at China Bay the No.1 Detachment commander, Flight Lieutenant Henry C. Lowcock and his navigator Flight Sergeant D.W.R. Lewin photographed five Sumatran airfields. Four days later Wing Commander W.E.M. Lowry DFC and Flight Lieutenant Gerald Stevens flew the first of a series of low-level reconnaissance flights over the notorious Burma-Siam railway. By the end of February 684 Squadron was back to full strength with twenty-two Mosquitoes, including three which were detached to China Bay. By March 1945 the Squadron was making record-breaking flights of around 9 hours to Phuket Island to reconnoitre possible landing beaches. The approaching monsoon and build up of tropical storms in the Bay of Bengal caused operational problems. On 10 March Flight Lieutenant Jack Irvine and Flight Sergeant Bob Bannister flew through one such storm to photograph possible landing beaches on Phuket Island during a flight that lasted almost 9 hours. Twelve days later, Irvine and Bannister carried out a sortie, which lasted 8 hours 45 minutes and covered 2,493 miles, to photograph the Bangkok-Singapore railway to a point just south of the Malayan border. (This was to be the longest sortie flown by a Mosquito PR.XVI in any theatre of the war.)

On 5 April Flight Lieutenant R. Stoneham and Flying Officer R. Burns had a lucky escape. At the beginning of their run along the Burma-Siam railway, their starboard engine speed began to increase from 2,000 to 3,000 rpm. Stoneham throttled back but this had no effect. Propeller pitch was altered with the same result and the Mosquito began vibrating as the engine speed reached 5,000 revs. Burns, who was in the nose, saw that the engine was on fire and the extinguisher was operated. The aircraft lost height rapidly and by the time it cleared the coast near Moolmein it was down to 1,000ft. A height of 600ft was maintained over the Gulf of Mattaban and when land was again sighted neat Basseit, Stoneham jettisoned the wing-tanks, enabling the aircraft to climb to 1,500ft and return to Cox's Bazaar. On 18 April Stoneham and Burns had another lucky escape when they were caught in severe storms *en route* to Victoria Point. They returned to Cox's Bazaar with only 10 minutes' fuel remaining. The Mosquito's leading wing edges and tailplane were damaged, requiring repairs before the crew could continue to Alipore. However, Flight Lieutenant Newman and Flight Sergeant Preston were killed on a sortie from Alipore to Cox's Bazaar when the Mosquito crashed in bad weather *en route*. Four days later Flight Lieutenant T. Bell and Flying Officer J. Plater were lost in similar circumstances on a sortie to Nancowry Island. It was assumed that they had crashed into the sea that same day

Operation Dracula, the seaborne invasion of lower Burma via the port of Rangoon, took place on 1/2 May with support from 82 and 110 Squadrons but the PR.IXs of 684 Squadron were grounded by bad weather. For this operation 82 Squadron was detached from their home base at Kumbhirgram to a satellite strip at Joari, north of Akyab Island on the Arakan coast. This permitted crews to fly due south over the coast and on a due east course to the Irrawaddy estuary, then north-east to Rangoon, which allowed them to miss the highly dangerous monsoon clouds building up further inland in Burma. The task of 82 Squadron was to neutralise the ground artillery and anti-aircraft positions protecting an oil refinery at Syriam about 5 miles to the south of Rangoon. It was essential to put these guns out of commission. Royal Marine commandos were coming up the estuary in landing craft, which would have left them like sitting ducks. Each Mosquito was armed with two 500lb 11-second delay, fused bombs, with four cannon and four Browning machine-guns for strafing purposes. The whole trip took 5 hours and 15 minutes. Gradually, conditions improved proved and by the end of the month the Mosquitoes, using Kyaukpyo on Ramree Island, as an advanced landing strip were flying regularly as far as Bangkok, Phuket Island and the Siam railway. Most of the sorties were carried out by the China Bay detachment, which continued its coverage of the Indian Ocean islands.

On 24 May Wing Commander W.E.M. Lowry DFC and his navigator, Flying Officer Gerald Stevens of 684 Squadron flew to Tenassetim and Kra via the advanced landing ground at Kyaukpyu to take high-level vertical photographs. Then they dropped to just 50ft for oblique photos of St. Luke, St. Matthew and the Domel Islands. On 28 May Flying Officer Cliff C. Andrews DFC RNZAF and Warrant Officer H.S. Painter, a former schoolmaster at Enderby House, Narborough reconnoitred targets in the Siam Valley and covered Don Moang airfield at Bangkok, the waterfront at Sattahib and bridges on the Bangkok-Phnom Penh railway line. A 'first-sighting' message was radioed back about shipping observed at Sattahib. As a result, Liberators made attacks on two merchant ships and the port installations on 30 May and 1 June.

In early June the PR Development Flight was formed at Ratmalana in Ceylon with two PR.XVIs and two Oxfords under the command of Flight Lieutenant Henry Lowcock. Before Operation Zipper, the invasion of Malaya, could go ahead in September 684 Squadron had to obtain full coverage of a 10-mile stretch of coastline in the region of Port Swettenham on the east coast of Malaya. A new Mosquito, the PR.34, a VLR version of the PR.XVI, was available and if based on the Cocos Islands, 1,050 miles south-west of Singapore, reconnaissance missions to Kuala Lumpur and Port Swettenham were possible. On 27 March Squadron Leader Kos Newman DFC* and Warrant Officer Ray Smith DFM returned to

England to test the aircraft's suitability. They flew back in a PR.IX (which they had brought out in December 1943) so it could be inspected by de Havillands to determine how Mosquitoes were coping with tropical conditions. Warrant Officer Ray Smith explains:

> We found the PR.34 to be entirely suitable to our requirements and at dusk on the evening of 29 May we took off from Benson for Karachi (in RG185/Z) in company with three other aircraft crewed by UK personnel, refuelling at Cairo West. This flight was to take the form of a race to establish a new England to India record. After we had been airborne for a short time, however our starboard engine started giving trouble and Kos decided that he would have to feather the propeller and return to Benson on one engine. The only problem with that was that we had about three tons of fuel on board, so it was decided to continue until we were over the Channel and jettison the drop tanks. We were over complete cloud cover at the time and my ETA for the Channel coast was slightly out, culminating in our dropping the drop tanks on a farm in Kent. From the farmer's point of view, it was a pity that the tanks did not remain intact. Kos had never landed a Mosquito at night on two good engines, let alone one. On the final approach to the runway, he asked me to call out the airspeed and altitude for every 50ft of descent, to enable him to give his undivided concentration to the actual flying. I had just uttered the words, "120 and 50ft" when we came into violent contact with the end of the runway but Kos rectified the situation in his own inimitable manner and we were once again safely back on terra firma and so to bed. The following day we received information that the fastest time put up by one of the other three aircraft was 12 hours 27 minutes. The fault on our starboard engine having been rectified, we took off again that evening and did the trip in 12 hours 25 minutes, thus establishing a new England to India record.

The four PR.34s were taken on charge by 684 Squadron, which, on 9 June became part of 347 (PR) Wing, RAF. During June 684 was able to fly only six sorties from Alipore. With their operations restricted by monsoon storms, on 16 June Flight Lieutenants G. Edwards and Jack Irvine flew north to the peak of Makalu in Nepal, then to Mount Everest, 10 miles further west. Edwards circled the mountain for 20 minutes, taking photographs with cameras mounted in wing-tanks. Nepal was a neutral country and the Everest flights[260] caused a minor diplomatic upset when details were released to the Press. It was explained that the aircraft were lost due to the extensive cloud cover and were only able to fix their positions by recognising the mountain. On 28 June 1945 the four PR.34s flew from Alipore, via China Bay, to the Cocos Islands, arriving the next day and forming (No.2) Detachment at the recently completed airstrip. No.3 Detachment was established at Chittagong in July but bad weather prevented all except one sortie being flown. On 1 July another flight was made to Mount Everest by two Mosquitoes from Alipore. One aircraft was fitted with cine cameras but heavy cloud and snowstorms prevented a clear view of the mountain.

On 14 June Wing Commander Michael H. Constable-Maxwell DSO DFC was appointed CO of 84 Squadron, which was now based at Chakulia. Constable-Maxwell, who had eight victories in Europe, was on his fourth tour. He brought with him to India his navigator Flight Lieutenant John Quinton DFC who participated in the destruction of at least three enemy aircraft and others damaged whilst serving on 604 Squadron in 1944 but the war with Japan ended before they saw any further action.[261] At the end of June the Squadron moved to St. Thomas Mount, Madras, with a detachment moving to Guindy. Constable-Maxwell insisted that the squadron carry out dive-bombing sorties with the Mosquito and practice dives commenced on the ranges in the Madras area. However, dive-bombing was cancelled after a fatal crash of one of the Squadron's Mosquito on 22 July when the crew made an error of judgement and hit the water after a practice dive.

Meanwhile, on 3 July a PR.34 flown by Wing Commander W.E.M. Lowry DFC and Flight Sergeant Stan Pateman made that model's first reconnaissance sortie from Cocos Island, to Point Pinto via Morib and Port Swettenham area via Gedong and, finally, Sumatra. Next day seven runs were made by Kos Newman and Ray Smith over airfields at Kuala Lumpur and Port Swettenham and on the return flight, Fort de Rock airfield, north of Padang in Sumatra. Ray Smith remembers:

> The trips from the Cocos Islands were usually in the region of nine hours' duration. We used to make for Suncling Island off the coast of Sumatra, 613 miles from Cocos and then set course to the particular area we were required to cover. The idea was that if an aircraft had to ditch the ASR Catalina in the Cocos and crewed by a Dutch crew would know along which track to search for survivors.

By the end of July seven PR.34s of No 2 Detachment from Cocos Island[262] had completed twenty-five sorties and a further thirteen more were flown by VJ-Day. No operations at all were flown during the first week of August, however because of bad weather *en route* to Malaya. Indeed, some of the proposed invasion beaches were never photographed because of high tides. The photos were only useful if taken at low tide. Operation Zipper never went ahead because Japan unconditionally surrendered on 14 August following the dropping of the two atomic bombs on the 6th and 9th on Hiroshima and Nagasaki. The surrender brought added responsibilities for the PR Mosquitoes, which were required to bring back further information on PoW camps and Japanese dispositions in Malaya. On 12 August 47 Squadron flew its last sortie of the war before its Mosquitoes were taken out of service to have rocket projectiles fitted. (These were used late in 1945 against Indonesian insurgents in the Dutch East Indies.) With the unconditional Japanese surrender on 14 August 1945, the Mosquitoes were sent to reconnoitre the oilfields at Palembang in Sumatra and Japanese dispositions and PoW camps in Malaya.[263] Some of the flights, which included reconnaissance of Penang and Taiping in northern Malaya, lasted over 9 hours. The oilfields at Palembang on Sumatra were also photographed.[264]

On 20 August eight FB.VIs of 110 Squadron were used to dislodge Japanese troops at Tikedo, east of the Sittang River, who had refused to surrender. It was the final RAF operation of the Second World War. Ironically, 110 Squadron had also flown the first operation of the war, when equipped with Blenheims in France. A more contrite band of Japanese soldiers welcomed the crew of a 684 Squadron PR.34, which put down at Kallang on Singapore Island with engine trouble on 31 August following a photographic reconnaissance of the Palembang oil refineries, rather than risk the long overwater flight back to Cocos Island. Amid great excitement Squadron Leader Cliff C. Andrews RNZAF and Warrant Officer H.S. Painter disembarked wearing their .45 revolvers. As they opened the inner hatch to disembark, the Japanese ground staff opened the outer. The two aircrew were helped to disembark but were not disarmed. In fact the Japanese, including officers with swords, courteously greeted them and there was much bowing and heel clicking. They were taken to the mess and were dined after the Japanese who arranged for some RAF PoWs in Changi jail to repair the faulty engine. The crew were the first Britons, apart from a British medical officer parachuted into the country to attend to PoWs the previous day, to arrive in Singapore since the surrender. On 12 September General Itazaki, Japanese Southern Area Commander, formally surrendered to Vice-Admiral Lord Louis Mountbatten in Singapore, thus ending the war with Japan. The official history had this to say. 'PR in SE Asia was of greater importance than in other theatres, owing to the comparatively meagre ground intelligence available and for the RAF's purposes alone it provided an indispensable factor in the maintenance of Allied air superiority, a vital factor in the defeat of the Japanese forces.'

After VJ-Day 684 Squadron's PR.34s flew a high-speed courier service throughout the Far East, while small detachments at Mingaladon in Burma, Batavia in Indonesia and Labuan in North Borneo carried out survey work in the region. Navigator Flight Lieutenant Bill McLintock who with his skipper Flight Lieutenant K. 'Sam' Rawcliffe, arrived in Alipore in a PR.34 from the UK on 5 October, recounts:

Of all the detachments, the most memorable was probably Labaun. We were accommodated in tents and shared the site with a small signals unit. Crews would fly out from Singapore carrying out a survey *en route* and landing at Labaun. Some surveys would be carried out from the island and on the return flight to Singapore a survey of Sarawak was included. On one memorable trip Warrant Officers McDonald and Radford left Seletar and ran into a typhoon over Borneo, leaving them with insufficient fuel to return to Singapore and they crash-landed in a rice field in Borneo. It took about ten days to get then back to the squadron.

By 16 October the China Bay detachment was withdrawn to Indo-China where a revolt against the French had broken out. On the 19th three of 684 Squadron's PR.34s and Spitfires of 273 Squadron flew a demonstration over Dalat, 130 miles to the north-east, where Annamite rebels had taken control. On the 21st six PR.34s left Alipore for Tan Son Nhut, near Saigon, to provide PR and survey support. Bill McLintock recalls:

The weather was bad and at the briefing we were told not to return to Alipore. We climbed through cloud before emerging into clear skies at about 23,000ft. After about two-and-a-half hours we got a glimpse of the ground and found that we were very far off course heading south-east and eventually picked up our position over Siam. I suggested a diversion to Bangkok, but Sam decided to press on, although I pointed out that if we encountered more bad weather our fuel position would be precarious. After about 5 hours we reached Saigon, with the gauges reading almost zero. We were met by Squadron Leader Newman and were very surprised to find that we were the first to land. After a period of waiting, a signal arrived stating that three Mossies had diverted to Bangkok. A later signal confirmed that Wing Commander W.E.M. Lowry DFC with Gerald Stevens as his navigator had crashed at Mingaladon on course but with a seized-up starboard engine and associated problems. Unfortunately, the Mosquito crewed by Flight Lieutenant Mike Workman and Warrant Officer Jimmy Fawkner was missing and was never located. It was later assumed that the plane had crashed into the Bay of Bengal. PR sorties were flown during the subsequent weeks to establish the location and disposition of Annamite rebel forces in the area.

Early in November 1945 the seven PR.34s on Cocos Island flew to Seletar, Singapore for survey work in Malaya and the East Indies. Wing Commander Lowry DFC and Flight Lieutenant George Jones in a PR.34 were lost during the long transit flight and the newly-promoted Wing Commander Kos Newman DFC* assumed command of 684 Squadron. At the end of January 1946 684 Squadron moved to Don Muang to take up more survey duties. The Seletar detachment stayed until early March when it too moved to Don Muang. In April Wing Commander John Merrifield DSO DFC* assumed command. In May a detachment was sent to Kemajoran in Java where a bloody civil war with Indonesian rebels was in progress. No.684 Squadron's main task was to make a four-month topographical survey of Java before the Netherlands East Indies Army finally took over from the British. In late August 684 Squadron moved to Seletar where on 1 September it disbanded by renumbering as 81 Squadron. On 1 August 1947 Spitfires were transferred to the unit, which became the sole PR asset in FEAF and took on the responsibility of PR and aerial survey work for the entire region.

The last RAF Mosquitoes to see RAF service anywhere were the PR.34As of 81 Squadron at Seletar. In 1946-47 the unit had carried out an aerial survey of the country. A state of emergency in Malaya was declared on 17 June 1948 when a full-scale communist uprising began and 81 Squadron's Mosquitoes reverted to their PR role as part of Operation Firedog, which began in July 1949. By the end of 1952 the unit had flown over 4,000 sorties and photographed 34,000 square miles. No.81 Squadron flew no less than 6,619 sorties during its eight years of operations in Malaya, with the honour of flying the RAF's very last Mosquito sortie, on 15 December 1955, going to RG314 and Flying Officers A.J. 'Collie' Knox and A.B. 'Tommy' Thompson. The crew successfully completed a Firedog reconnaissance sortie against two terrorist camps in Malaya.

NOTES

Chapter 1

1   Mosquito Aircrew Assoc (MAA) *The Mossie* No.36 September 2004.

2   W4064/C FTR on 31 May 1942 when it was hit by flak on the operation to Cologne and was ditched 10 km SW of Antwerp, at Bazel on the bank of the Schelde. Pilot Officer William Deryck Kennard and Pilot Officer Eric Raymond Johnson were killed.

3   Simmons was later killed flying a Turkish Air Force Mosquito.

4   A further 60 Mosquito bombers were on order, but they would not start to arrive until the following February. For now, 105 Squadron had to make do with W4066, the first Mosquito bomber to enter RAF service. This aircraft arrived at Swanton Morley on 17 November watched by the AOC 2 Group, Air Vice Marshal d'Albiac and his staff. Three other B.IVs – W4064, W4068 and W4071 – were delivered at intervals to Swanton Morley by Geoffrey de Havilland Jr. and Pat Fillingham.

5   Losigkeit had proved very effective during Operation *Donnerkeil* (The 'Channel Dash') during which the three German warships *Scharnhorst, Gneisenau* and *Prinz Eugen* had escaped from Brest to Norway February 1942. On his return to Germany he formed IV Gruppe, JG1.

6   Klemens Rausch, whose job it was to keep the plot. (See *The Mosquito Log* by Alexander McKee. Souvenir Press. 1988). DK295/P crashed at Tilburg and the crew, were killed and were laid to rest in the Reichwald Forest war cemetery. Bugaj who in March 1943 received the *Eisern Kreuz I* (Iron Cross First Class) was killed at Achmer flying Fw 190A-4 'Black 8' on a non-combat flight on 12 April 1943. See *Defending The Reich. The History of JG1*, Eric Mombeek (JAC Publications 1992).

7   On 15 June 1941 Edwards led a formation of three Blenheims in successful attack on a 4,000-ton merchantman and on 1 July he was awarded the DFC for this daring low-level exploit. On 4 July a raid on Bremen (Operation *Wreckage*, as it was code-named) was led by Edwards. Although four crews were lost, successful attacks were made on the docks, factories, a timber yard and railways and great damage was caused to the tankers and transports that were loaded with vital supplies. All the aircraft were damaged. After the target Edwards proceeded to circle Bremen and strafed a stationary train that had opened up on them, before leading the formation out of Germany at low level. Edwards, his aircraft minus part of the port wing, the port aileron badly damaged, a cannon shell in the radio rack and a length of telegraph wire wrapped round the tail wheel and trailing behind, reached Swanton Morley where Edwards put down safely. *Operation Wreckage* received considerable publicity and on 21 July it was announced that Wing Commander Hughie Edwards DFC had been awarded the Victoria Cross for courage and leadership displayed on the operation. He thus became only the second Australian to receive this award (the first having been awarded to Lieutenant F. H. McNamara of the RFC during the First World War). Edwards later embarked on a publicity tour of the USA. Then, during the last week of July 1941 ten tropicalised Blenheims of 105 Squadron, led by Edwards, arrived at Luqa on Malta to relieve 110 Squadron on shipping strikes from the Mediterranean island. The 105 Squadron detachment returned to East Anglia in September 1941. In the winter of 1941–42 Edwards became CFI at Wellesbourne Mountford.

8   *The Men Who Flew The Mosquito* by Martin W. Bowman (Leo Cooper 2003 and 2005) has the full story of Tommy Broom's escape to England. In London they were interrogated by MI9 at the transit camp at the Grand Central Hotel in Marylebone and eventually issued with a certificate to take to RAF Uxbridge. Then they were free to send a telegram home and were taken to Air Ministry. They were given a written note stating their identity, had a couple of interviews, and asked where they wanted to be posted. Tommy Broom was told 105 Squadron had now moved to RAF Marham and 1655 Mosquito Training Unit was being formed and he agreed to be posted there. Squadron Leader Costello-Bowen AFC was killed in August 1943 while CFI at 1655 MTU when he was a passenger in a 487 Squadron Ventura flown by Flying Officer Sydney C. B. Abbott DFC RAAF, pilot on the Oxford Flight of 1655 MTU. After a rest as Chief Ground Instructor 1655 MTU, Tommy Broom resumed operations with Flight Lieutenant Ivor Broom (no relation) on 571 Squadron, 128 Squadron, and then 163 Squadron; Ivor as Wing Commander and Tommy as Squadron Leader. 'The Flying Brooms', as they were known, flew 58 operations together (21 to Berlin) in 8 Group Pathfinder Force. Ivor later became Air Marshal Sir Ivor Broom KCB CBE DSO DFC** AFC. Tommy was awarded the DFC and two bars.

9   KIA 13.11.42. See Squadron Leader Tommy Broom DFC** published by Pen & Sword.

10   Piffer, an Austrian, was killed on 17 June 1944 when USAAF P-47 Thunderbolts shot his Fw

190A-8 'White 3' near Argentan. He was posthumously awarded the *Ritterkreuz* (Knight's Cross) on 20 October 1944 for his 26 victories in the West. *Defending The Reich: The History of JG1*, Eric Mombeek (JAC Publications 1992).

11 'In September 1942 the Mosquito had ceased to be a secret. After a display in Canada of the aeroplane's capabilities, the Station newspaper of 5 SFTS reported both the demonstration and the fact that the machine was being manufactured in Canada - much to the fury of the rest of the media, who had been cheated of a scoop by the littlest of little brothers. After much futile fuming and recrimination, an Official World Press Release was made on 26 September, 1942. On 27 October, the *Daily Express* ran a two-page spread under the headline SWIFTEST BOMBER-FROM WOODSHOP, telling how a firm, which had formerly made 'bookcases and bedroom suites' was now making the fastest warplane in the world. And the report listed three main roles: Long-range day bomber; Long-range fighter-bomber or escort bomber; Long-range picture-gathering reconnaissance machine. The dimensions were given but, naturally, not the performance figures. More technical articles appeared in *The Aeroplane* of 15 January 1943, *Flight* of 6 May 1943, and *Aircraft Production* for June 1943.' *The Mosquito Log* by Alexander McKee. Souvenir Press. 1988.

12 Rowland, a post war captain for BEA, learned this at a stopover in Hamburg in 1963. Klein had later lost a leg in a crash-landing after he was shot down by a P-51 Mustang. In July 1993 Parry met Fenten face-to-face also, when the German flew his light aircraft to Horsham St Faith (Norwich Airport) and they flew a memorable flight around the city!

13 Oberfeldwebel Timm was KIA on 28 May 1944 flying Bf 109G-6 'Yellow 3'.

14 Kirchner had been awarded the *Eisernes Kreuz II Klasse (EK II* or Iron Cross 2nd Class) after shooting down a 9 Squadron Wellington III (Z1577) on the raid on Duisburg on the night of 23/24 July. He was killed on 19 April 1945 when his Heinkel He 162A-2 *Volksjäger* jet fighter crashed after he had claimed a Spitfire shot down. II Gruppe JG1 earned something of a reputation shooting down Mosquitoes and before the end of the year nine pilots had been awarded the *Eisernes Kreuz II*. They included Feldwebel Erwin Roden of 12./JG1 who had shot down the Mosquito flown by Sergeant K. C. Pickett and Sergeant Herbert Evans over Belgium on 6 September. Pickett survived to be taken prisoner but Evans was killed. Two days later Oberleutnant S'trohall had been credited with a Mosquito also. A complete account of the loss of Lang and Thomas is contained in *Mosquito Thunder* by Stuart R. Scott (Sutton 1999). See also, *Defending The Reich: The History of JG1*, Eric Mombeek (JAC Publications 1992).

15 See *The Mosquito Log* by Alexander McKee. Souvenir Press. 1988.

16 See *Mosquito Thunder* by Stuart R. Scott (Sutton 1999).

17 Eindhoven was Mike Carreck's final op on 105 Squadron. His tour over he was posted to 17 OTU 'on rest' as an instructor.

18 107 houses and 96 shops were completely destroyed and 107 Dutch workers and civilians living around the factory were killed and 161 wounded.

19 See *The Mosquito Log* by Alexander McKee. Souvenir Press. 1988.

20 *The Mossie, Mosquito Aircrew Association*, Vol.18 January 1998.

21 Flight Lieutenant John Gordon DFC and Flying Officer Ralph G. Hayes DFM, who were lucky on 26 April when their petrol tank was hit by a Bofors shell over Eindhoven but the shell failed to explode, saw their luck finally run out on 5 November 1943. They were killed in a crash at Road Green Farm, Hempnall about ten miles south of Norwich returning from the operation to Leverkusen on one engine.

22 By the end of the year he had taken up an appointment in Air Command Far East Asia and held the rank of SASO (Senior Air Staff Officer) until the end of 1945. He remained in the post-war RAF and was awarded the OBE in 1947. In 1958 he was promoted to Air Commodore and finally retired from the service in 1963. He returned to Australia, was knighted and in 1974 became Governor of West Australia.

23 Thompson and Horne were KIA on 1 May 1943 shortly after take off from Marham, while forming up for the raid on the Philips Works at Eindhoven.

24 *Bommen Vielen op Hengelo* by Henk F. Van Baaren, translated in The Mossie - Mosquito Aircrew Association, Vol. 16 April 1997.

25 Brown, who had a similar experience 6 days later after taking part in an attack by 15 Mosquitoes on the Renault works at Le Mans, was killed shortly after on a raid on the engine sheds at Malines in

Belgium. His Mosquito was hit by coastal flak and finished off three minutes later by two Fw 190s.

26   The first was flown by Reggie Reynolds with Ted Sismore, then number two Flight Sergeant K. H. N. Ellis with Flight Sergeant Donald, then Pilot Officer L. T. Weston with Flight Sergeant G. 'Jake' Brown

27   9.8 tons of bombs were dropped on the John Cockerill works. Pace and Cook crashed into the Ooster Schelde off Woensdrecht. A full account of this raid is contained in *Mosquitoes to Liège* in *2 Group RAF* by Michael J. F. Bowyer and in *Mosquito Thunder* by Stuart R. Scott.

28   Wooldridge spent 3-months in command of 105 and on 25 June he was posted to 3 Group at RAF Stradishall. On I September 1943 he was posted back to the PWD. His replacement at Marham was 109 Squadron's Wing Commander Henry John 'Butch' Cundall AFC (later Group Captain Cundall CBE DSO DFC AFC. After the war Wooldridge wrote *Low Attack* and having studied with Sibelius, he composed music, worked as a conductor, with the Philharmonia Orchestra especially, and wrote many plays, orchestral suites, incidental film music and film scores. His most famous was *Appointment in London* (1952), for which he wrote the music and also the squadron song. Wooldridge died in a car accident on 27 October 1958.

29   *The Mossie,* Mosquito Aircrew Association, Vol. 19 April 1998.

30   *Bommen Vielen op Hengelo* by Henk F. Van Baaren, translated in *The Mossie* - MAA, Vol. 16 April 1997.

31   They were buried at Maubeuge Centre cemetery on 5 April. On 30 July 1943 Mackenstedt crash-landed his Fw 190A-5 after being hit by return fire from a 8th Air Force B-17 and he died of his injuries in hospital. (See *The JG26 War Diary*, Vol.2 1943-45, Donald Caldwell (Grub Street 1998).

32   *The Mossie* No.31 May 2002.

33   Mosquitoes of 140 Wing, 2nd TAF flew the 11th and final RAF raid on Hengelo on 18 March 1944 when they bombed the Hazemeyer works.

34   On 28/29 June 1942 Oberleutnant Reinhold Knacke, Staffelkapitän, 1./NJG1 had been the first *Nachtjagd* pilot to claim a Mosquito kill, when he shot down DD677 of 23 Squadron at Haps, Southern Holland). Guided by Leutnant Lübke, *Jägerleitoffizier* of *Himmelbett* box *Eisbär* ('Polar Bear') at Sondel, Northern Holland, Lent power-dived onto a Mosquito west of Stavoren from superior altitude and at 500 kph fired a burst of cannon shells at the Mosquito. NF.II DZ694 of 410 Squadron flown by Flight Sergeant W. J. Reddie RCAF and his navigator, Sergeant K. Evans, who were on a Night Fighting Patrol over Holland, were KIA. Lent was noted for experimenting with new methods of attack. He would practice and perfect a diving attack, which would give him sufficient speed to overtake a Mosquito and shoot it down. For being one of the first German pilots to overcome this versatile aircraft he received special praise from Göring. Lent eventually rose to the rank of Oberst with a position of high command in the night fighter arm. He achieved 102 night-victories and 8 day-victories before being killed in a flying accident on 5 October 1944.

35   Shand remains missing while the body of his navigator was washed ashore at Makkum. Linke, with 24 night and 3 day victories was killed on the night of 13/14 May 1943. After shooting down two Lancasters (W4981 of 83 Squadron and ED589 of 9 Squadron) and Halifax DT732 of 10 Squadron over Friesland, he suffered an engine fire. He baled out near the village of Lemmer in Friesland but he struck the tail unit of his Bf 110 and was killed. Linke's *Bordfunker* Oberfeldwebel Walter Czybulka baled out safely.

36   Flight Lieutenant Harold Sutton DFC and Flying Officer John Morris and Flying Officer Fred Openshaw and Sergeant Alfred Stonestreet, of 139 Squadron.

37   Unable to find the target by DR Patterson identified and attacked Weimar railway station from 300ft. Patterson completed two tours of daylight operations on Mosquitoes and he was awarded the DSO early in 1944. Squadron Leader Blessing DSO DFC RAAF was KIA on 7 July 1944 on a PFF marking sortie over Caen.

38   *The Mossie*, Mosquito Aircrew Association, Vol.21, January 1999.

39   Flying Officer F. M. 'Bud' Fisher DFC and his navigator Flight Sergeant Les Hogan DFM were prevented from attacking the target by the balloon barrage bombed the town from 200ft. (Fisher and Hogan were KIA on the night of 29/30 September 1943 when their Mosquito crashed near West Raynham returning from the raid on Bochum). Flying Officer Don C. Dixon, an Australian from Brisbane and his navigator Flying Officer W. A. Christensen, a fellow Australian from New South Wales, attempted three runs on the target. They were also prevented from bombing by the balloons and

intense flak and they dropped their bombs on a goods train at Lastrup. Pilot Officer Ronald Massie and Sergeant George Lister who were last seen as the formation entered cloud prior to reaching the target crashed near Diepholz and were killed.

40 By March 1945 Roy Ralston was CO of 139 Squadron and still managed to fly on operations. He had been awarded the DSO for 'outstanding leadership and determination' and he was awarded a bar to his DSO after his 83rd op, promoted to wing commander and given command of 1655 Mosquito Training Unit at Marham. At the end of the war Ralston was listed for a permanent commission but a medical examination revealed that he had TB and he was invalided out of the RAF in 1946. Wing Commander Ralston DSO* DFC DFM AFC died on 8 October 1996.

41 Flight Lieutenant William S. D. 'Jock' Sutherland and Flying Officer George Dean in a 139 Squadron Mosquito were seen to bomb their target but both crew were killed when they crashed at Wroxham railway station. They had flown into high voltage overhead electric cables when attempting to land at RAF Coltishall on their return. Flying Officers Alan Rae DFM and Kenneth Bush died when their Mosquito crashed while they tried to land at Marham on one engine.

42 Wing Commander Reynolds was awarded a bar to his DSO, Flight Lieutenant Ted Sismore and Squadron Leader Bill Blessing received the DSO, Bud Fisher the DFC and his navigator, Flight Sergeant Hogan the DFM.

43 At 1655 MTU all pilots had to complete a laid down syllabus of 30 hours flying - ten in the Dual Flight and 20 in the Bomber Flight, the latter complete with navigator. No pilot was allowed to touch the controls of a Mosquito until he had 1,000 hours as first pilot under his belt and had been selected to fly Mosquitoes.

Chapter 2

44 Work began on the Mosquito prototypes, the first (E-0234, later W4050) flying on 25 November 1940. By January 1941 W4050 was proving faster than a Spitfire in tests at 6,000ft, and by February it was recording speeds of around 390 mph at 22,000ft. PR prototype W4051 was the second Mosquito completed at Salisbury Hall. While it retained the short engine nacelles and tailplane of the prototype, it differed in having longer wings (by 20 inches), and carried three vertical cameras and one oblique. At first the camera mounts were made of steel, but these were later changed to wood, as these helped reduce camera vibration and improve image quality. The nightfighter prototype became the second Mosquito to fly when the fuselage originally intended for W4051 was used to replace W4050's fuselage, which had fractured at Boscombe Down in a tail wheel incident. W4051 received a production fuselage instead, which later enabled the prototype to fly on operations - it completed its maiden flight on 10 June 1941.

45 W4064-72.

46 W4054 and W4055 followed on 22 July and 8 August respectively. Beginning in September, No.1 PRU received seven more production PR.Is - W4056 and W4058-63 (W4056 FTR in April 1942. W4057 became the B.V bomber prototype. W4058 failed to return from a sortie to Oslo on 17 October 1942). Four of these (W4060-63) were later modified with increased fuel tankage for long range operations and two, (W4062 and W4063) were tropicalised. W4060 was seriously damaged in a flying accident in July 1942. W4067 FTR on 27 July 1942. W4089 FTR in July 1942. The standard Mosquito camera installation at the time consisted of four vertical cameras. These were the F24 Universal oblique camera for day and night photography. The F52 20- or 36-inch high altitude day reconnaissance camera (which entered service in May 1942) and the American K-17 survey and mapping camera with 6-inch lens, plus a single F24 camera mounted in the lower fuselage. The fit depended on the type of sortie flown, with one of the most widely used being a single K-17 (or K8AB with 12-inch lens) forward and a split vertical F52 installation behind the wing, and an F24 oblique camera facing to port. This was sometimes changed to a split vertical F52 camera installation forward, two standard vertical F52 cameras and one F24 aft of the wing. The split vertical camera installation was basically two cameras (F24s or F52s) mounted at slightly differing angles to double the field of view, while retaining the 60% overlap needed for stereoscopic coverage of the target area. The split vertical F52 36-inch camera installation gave the PR.I lateral coverage of three miles from 35,000ft and 255 mph. Besides these installations, some late model PR Mosquitoes were fitted with two forward-facing F24 14-inch lens cameras, one in each dummy 50-gallon drop tank, for low-level photography.

47 Each of the early PR.Is was named after a different variety of strong liquor, W4055 being

christened *Benedictine* and others *Whiskey* and *Vodka, Drambuie, Cointreau* and *Creme de Menthe*.

48 Rupert Clerke had been a flight commander in 79 Squadron in 1940 flying Hurricane I fighters. He was awarded a one third share in downing a He 111 off Sunderland on 9 August and a one fifth share for a Bf 110 and a Do 17 'probable' over the North Sea on 15 August. On 28 August he scored his first outright victory when he destroyed a He 59 and he was also awarded a Bf 109E 'probable'. He returned to fighters early in 1942 and became a flight commander in 157 Squadron flying the Mosquito II. His second outright victory followed on 30 September when he destroyed a Ju 88A-4 of I/KG6 off the Dutch coast. Two more victories followed in 1943 when he was CO of 125 Squadron.

49 W4051, W4055, W4059 and W4061.

50 Two days earlier a PR.I was sent out to Malta for trials in the Mediterranean. However, the aircraft piloted by Flying Officer Kelly was written off in a crash-landing on arrival at Luqa. A second Mosquito, piloted by Pilot Officer Walker arrived safely on Malta on 17 January and after a series of sorties over Italy, it was lost on 31 March after a mission to Sicily. Badly shot up by Bf 109s, Pilot Officer Kelly and Sergeant Pike nursed the ailing Mosquito to Hal Far, where it crashed and burnt out. Both crew survived.

51 In a talk to de Havilland workers at Hatfield on 11 March.

52 Production was halted for 4 weeks and final repairs were not completed for several months. A post-war American estimate said that the production loss was almost 2,300 vehicles. Just 1 aircraft (a Wellington) was lost but 367 French people were killed, 341 were badly injured and 9,250 people lost their homes.

53 On 3 April 1942 W4056 was shot down over Stavanger and the two crew taken prisoner.

54 DD615, 620, 659 and W4089 and DK284 and 311 respectively.

55 *Maschinenfabrik Augsburg Nürnberg Aktiengesellschaft.*

56 *Above All Unseen* by Edward Leaf. PSL. 1997.

57 W4060 was subsequently repaired and was lost with David O'Neill and David Lockyer on 20 February 1943 when it was badly hit by flak and crashed at Loddefjord.

58 *The New Wooden Walls in Bombers Fly East* by Bruce Sanders, (Herbert Jenkins Ltd 1943).

59 At this time 1 PRU was responsible direct to Headquarters Coastal Command.

60 *The New Wooden Walls in Bombers Fly East* by Bruce Sanders, (Herbert Jenkins Ltd 1943).

61 In reality PRU aircrew who arrived at Vaenga some weeks later found that the accommodation, half barrack block and half country house, quickly christened the 'Kremlin', was not only infested with mice but that it was also the target of numerous air raids. The Russians therefore lived in underground shelters. When the PRU detachment moved into its own shelter they later found that it was the morgue! See *Above All Unseen* by Edward Leaf. (PSL. 1997).

62 The unit disbanded on 18 October and the personnel sailed for Scotland five days later.

63 DK310 was retained by the Swiss, who later used it as a turbine test bed aircraft. Wooll returned to flying, as a test pilot for de Havilland in Canada.

64 Three of them were equipped with Spitfires, while H and L Flights at Leuchars were merged to form 540 (Mosquito) Squadron, under the command of Squadron Leader M. J. B. Young DFC. 544 Squadron (which was equipped mostly with Wellingtons and Spitfires, but eventually replaced these in March 1943 with PR IV and PR IX Mosquitoes) was formed under the command of Squadron Leader W. R. Alcott DFC. In December 1942 two PR IVs (DZ411 and 419) joined 540 Squadron, followed, during the first three months of 1943, by a further 27 PR IVs - all conversions of existing B IVs. PRU training unit, 8(PR) OTU was also established at Fraserburgh, Aberdeenshire. Squadron Leader Lord David Douglas Hamilton OBE, son of Wing Commander the Duke of Hamilton, who Rudolf Hess flew to Scotland to visit in May 1941, was its CO. David Douglas Hamilton was lost with Phil Gatehouse not long after D-Day.

65 The famous daylight raid was led by Wing Commander L. C. Slee of 49 Squadron. Some 88 Lancasters made a direct attack on the factory and the other 8 bombing a nearby transformer station, which supplied the plant with electricity. The route was flown at tree top level with four aircraft being damaged by birds. Bombing was carried out from 7,500 to 2,500ft and 140 tons of bombs were dropped.

66 The factory was bombed again by 290 Halifaxes, Stirlings and Lancasters of 3, 4, 6 and 8 Groups on 19/20 June 1943.

67 *The New Wooden Walls* in *Bombers Fly East* by Bruce Sanders, (Herbert Jenkins Ltd 1943).

68 Dédeé' and her father Frédéric had formed the Comet line in 1941. 15 January would have been her 19th crossing to Spain.

69 During the 'Wooden Horse' epic escape on 29 October 1943, as the lightest man in the camp Mac McKay was chosen to be carried out to the horse as third man. His duty was to cover up the tunnel entrance on the parade ground while the two escapers went down the tunnel. The third escaper was already in the tunnel to dig out the last few feet before breaking through outside the wire. Mac covered up the tunnel entrance and was carried back in the horse to the hut where it was kept. As a result of this daring plan, Michael Codner, Eric 'Bill' Williams and Oliver Philpot escaped to freedom via Sweden, eventually returning to the UK.

70 Which began as B IV Series II aircraft, with 1,565hp two-stage- supercharged Merlin 61 engines in place of the 21/22. The PR.VIII had a greatly improved ceiling, which allowed PR Mosquitoes to operate at high altitude for the first time. DK324, which first flew on 20 October 1942, was a prototype for the Mk.VIII version, and it reached 540 for testing on 28 November 1942. DZ342 arrived on 15 December 1942, followed in 1943 by DZ364 on 22 January, DZ404 on 4 February and DZ424 on 28 March.

71 This aircraft was subsequently lost, along with Flight Sergeant M. Custance and his navigator, on 18 March 1943.

72 *Above All Unseen* by Edward Leaf. PSL. 1997.

73 Raids continued against secret weapons' sites in France, including the V-2 preparation and launch site at Watten, which was bombed by over 180 bombers of the USAAF on 27 August. A PRU sortie three days later revealed that the target was not completely destroyed. A follow-up raid was flown on 7 September, which devastated the complex and forced the Germans to concentrate development at Wizernes. On 17 July 1944 16 Lancasters of 617 Dam Busters Squadron (with a Mosquito and a Mustang as marker aircraft) aimed 12,000lb *Tallboy* earthquake bombs with 11-second delay on the huge concrete dome, 20ft thick. It lay on the edge of a chalk quarry protecting rocket stores and launching tunnels that led out of the face of the quarry pointing towards London. One *Tallboy* that apparently burst at the side of the dome exploded beneath it, knocking it askew. Another caused part of the chalk cliff to collapse, undermining the dome, with part of the resulting landslide also blocking four tunnel entrances, including the two that were intended for the erected V-2s. Ironically, though the construction was not hit the whole area around was so badly 'churned up' that it was unapproachable and the bunker jeopardised from underneath. The Germans abandoned the site and the V-2s were pulled back to The Hague in Holland where, in September they began firing them from mobile launchers.

74 PR Mosquito production was also at last beginning to take precedence over the bomber variant, with 90 PR.IX models being ordered compared with just 54 of the B.IX. The PR IX was powered by two 1,680hp Merlin 72/73s or 76/77s, and had a fuel capacity of 860 gallons, including two 50-gallon drop tanks under the wings. When it carried two 200-gallon tanks, its total fuel capacity was just over 1,000 gallons. Range with underwing tanks was 2,450 miles at a cruising speed of 250 mph.

75 Early in November 1943, Bill White and Ron Prescott were detailed to photo map the Azores, which belonged to neutral Portugal. They were on their way home by 8 December. Their photos of the Azores were good and after one more op, to Norway, Bill and Ron were transferred to the Photo Recce OTU at Dyce. They had made 63 daylight operational flights and had been honoured by the King, Ron being awarded the DFM and Bill the DFC.

76 See *The Mosquito Log* by Alexander McKee. Souvenir Press. 1988. Eighteen months later on his from to England Aston got straight into a Mosquito and flew it without any refresher training whatsoever. He continued to fly Mosquitoes on and off up to the end of 1949 when he graduated from the Empire Test Pilot School and he began a new career as an airline pilot.

77 Production of PR.XVIs began in November 1943 and 435 were eventually built. The XVI had a pressure cabin, which maximised to a pressure differential of 2lbs per square inch, which gave a useful reduction in the cabin altitude, especially since this model could cruise quite comfortably at 35,000ft thanks to its two-speed, two-stage superchargers and paddle blade propellers. With 100-gallon drop tanks, the PR XVI had a range of 2,000 miles. A pair of split F52/36-inch lens cameras were installed in the rear fuselage, split from vertical to increase the lateral coverage and controlled by a Type 35 control in the bomb aimer's nose position so that the cameras would turn over at pre-set intervals. This

ensured 60 per cent overlap between succeeding exposures and therefore gave a stereo-pair of photographs. In the forward end of the bomb bay was another camera with a 6-inch lens, which gave a series of small-scale photographs to assist the interpreters in plotting the large-scale 36-inch photographs. When in the Target area the navigator went down into the bomb-aimer's position in the nose to give the pilot the usual directions onto target and switched on the cameras accordingly. The first PR XVI to reach the Middle East was MM292 at the end of January 1944 and on 17 February the first of nine PR.XVIs for 680 Squadron arrived at Matariya, Cairo. 24 hours earlier, the unit had received its first PR.IX (LR444). On 7 May 680 flew its first Mosquito PR sortie when MM333 and Flight Lieutenant A. M. Yelland covered ports and airfields in Crete and the Cyclades. Apart from three PR.IXs detached from 540 Squadron to the Mediterranean in the summer of 1943, only a few PR Mosquitoes operated in this theatre. 'B' Flight in 680 Squadron mostly covered Greece and the Balkans and, later, central and southern Europe, whilst B Flight of 60 SAAF Squadron made deep penetration sorties over southern Europe and Poland.

78 MM258, a converted. B.XVI.

79 Bill Hampson's and Bill Newby's operational life on Mosquitoes came to an abrupt end over the Eastern end of the Baltic on 18 July when Me 262s blew their nose of their Mosquito off, hit both engines and put cannon shells in the cabin behind the pilot's armour-plate. They evacuated the Mosquito in 'quick time', were captured and transported independently to Dulag Luft. They were subsequently incarcerated in Stalag Luft I at Barth in Pomerania.

80 *Above All Unseen* by Edward Leaf. PSL. 1997.

81 In PR.XVI NS504.

82 For this outstanding operation Flight Lieutenant (later AVM) Dodd was awarded an immediate DSO. In September, Flight Sergeant (later Flying Officer) Hill was awarded the DFM. Hill was later commissioned and awarded the DFC (27 July 1945) for 'gallantry and devotion to duty in the execution of air operations'.

83 The Heinkel He 280 was a twin tailed mid wing monoplane powered by two turbojets attached to the undersides of the wing and first flew on 2 April 1941. A few test models were built but the aircraft did not enter production. On 29 September a He 280 was flown with V-type tail in place of the previous twin fin and rudder assembly.

84 Kenneth Watson, who was awarded the DFC, rejoined the RAF after the war and was posted to a RAF PR Squadron at Wyton flying Canberras. On 3 June 1954 he and his navigator took off for Cuxhaven to test a Night Photography Flash Bomb. The bomb exploded in the bomb bay and the aircraft was set on fire. Watson managed to land but both he and his navigator were killed.

85 *The Mossie*, MAA Vol.12 January 1996/*Otago Daily Times*, Dunedin, NZ. See also, *Focus on Europe* by Ron Foster DFC CdG, Crowood Press (2005).

86 On 29 October 1944 47 Lancasters attacked the *Tirpitz* but no direct hits were scored. On 12 November 30 Lancasters of 9 and 617 Squadrons attacked the *Tirpitz* again and at least two *Tallboys* hit the ship, which capsized to remain bottom upwards. Some 1,128 of the 1,900 men on board were killed or injured. About one-and-a-half hours later Flight Lieutenant A. R. Cussons and Flight Sergeant Ken Ellis from 540 Squadron took photos, which showed the ship had indeed 'turned turtle'.

87 Daniels and Baylis joined B Flight of 544 Squadron at Benson and flew their first squadron operation on New Year's Day to Denmark.

88 NS587 had been tested thoroughly in November, during which time it had earned a bad reputation due to engine overheating and myriad other problems manifesting themselves. In the event, this aircraft became the only PR 32 allotted to 544 Squadron:

89 'Lofty' South and his pilot, Flying Officer R. M. Hays later had a harrowing flight in PR XVI N5795 on 16 March 1945 when, over Leipzig, they were intercepted by three Me 163 rocket-powered fighters. Hays managed to throw them off by putting the Mosquito into a 480-mph dive, during which the starboard engine caught fire. After feathering the propeller the fire went out, so they decided to set course for the Allied lines. Flying through violent frontal conditions, they were then jumped by a Bf 109, which Hays threw off once again by putting the nose down and diving for He ground, before pulling up. NS795 eventually landed at Lille, still on one engine. For this exploit, Hays was awarded an immediate DFC. Two weeks later, on 30 March, Hays and South were killed when they lost an engine on take-off from Benson.

90   On 22 March 1945 Eric Hill and Frank Dodd left Benson for a last look at the *Tirpitz*. They refuelled at Sumburgh and then flew to Tromsø, where they took some magnificent obliques of the partly submerged battleship from zero feet. After a 10¹/₂ flight they landed back at Benson having completed the longest PR sortie of the war. Hill, a tall, upright batsman, made his debut for Somerset in 1947 as an amateur in a famous game at Lords, which Somerset won by one wicket. Turning professional the following year, he played for Somerset for four seasons. After retirement he became a journalist with the *Somerset County Gazette* and later a freelance on cricket and Rugby.

Chapter 3

91   *Oboe* was the code name for a high-level blind bombing aid, which took its name from a radar-type pulse, which sounded rather like the musical instrument. (All non *Oboe*-equipped squadrons in 8 Group were termed 'non-musical'!) Mainly because of this device, Bennett's force was able to conduct *eine kleine nacht musik* almost every night over Germany. Pulses were transmitted by Type 9000 ground stations at Hawkshill Down (Walmer), Kent, Trimingham near Cromer and Winterton both in Norfolk, Sennen and Treenin Cornwall, Worthy Matravers and Tilly Whim (Swanage), Beachy Head and Cleadon (Newcastle). A high-flying *Oboe*-equipped aircraft up to 280 miles distant could receive them. The 'cat' station sent the pilot and navigator a steady sequence of signals describing an arc passing through the target, with dots to port and dashes to starboard. If inside the correct line, dots were heard; if outside the line, dashes. A steady note indicated that the aircraft was on track. The 'mouse' station indicated distance from target, and was monitored by the navigator only. Flying the beam made considerable demands on the *Oboe* pilot, who for 15-20 minutes had to maintain constant airspeed, altitude and rate of change of heading. The navigator monitored the aircraft's position along the arc, and only he received the release signal, from the 'mouse' station, when the aircraft reached the computed bomb-release point. Ten minutes away he received in Morse, four 'A's; four 'B's at 8 minutes; four 'C's at 6 minutes and four 'D's at approximately 4 minutes. The bomb doors were then opened. Next was heard the release signal, which consisted of five dots and a 2¹/₂-second dash, at the end of which the navigator released the markers or bombs. The jettison bars were operated and the bomb doors closed. As the pilot could not hear the 'mouse' signals, the navigator indicated to him the stage reached by tracing with his finger on the windscreen in front of him, the 'A's, 'B's and 'C's etc. When the release signal came through, the navigator held his hand in front of the pilot's face. Permitted limits were strict - up to 200 yards off aiming point and crews were expected to be at the target within a 4-minute time span, from 2 minutes early to 2 minutes late. Sixty seconds off time on release point were acceptable. Failure to meet these criteria and the crew were off the squadron! *Oboe* was to become the most accurate form of blind bombing used in WWII and in practice, an average error of only 30 seconds was achieved.

In April 1942 109 Squadron was established at Stradishall, Suffolk to bring *Oboe* into full operational service as a navigation aid for Bomber Command before moving to Wyton in August, where at the end of the year, it received the first *Oboe* equipped Mosquito B.IVs. *Oboe* was first used on 20/21 December 1942 when the CO, Squadron Leader H. E. 'Hal' Bufton and his navigator, Flight Lieutenant E. L. Ifould and 2 other crews, bombed a power station at Lutterade in Holland. On 31 December.1942/1 January 1943, on a raid on Düsseldorf, sky-marking using *Oboe* was tried for the first time when 2 Mosquitoes of 109 Squadron provided the sky-markers for 8 Lancasters of the Path Finder Force. 'Sky markers' were parachute flares to mark a spot in the sky if it was cloudy. The PFF markers' job was to 'illuminate' and 'mark' targets with coloured TI's (target indicators) for the Main Force and other 8 Group Mosquitoes. The Path Finder Force achieved Group status on 13 January 1943 and 109 Squadron became the premier marking squadron in the RAF, carrying out the most raids and flying the most sorties in 8 Group, which it joined on 1 June 1943. On 10 December 109 Squadron at Marham received the first B.XVI for the RAF, although 692 Squadron were the first to use it operationally, on 5 March 1944. In addition to its flare marking duties for the heavies, 109 Squadron's Mosquitoes carried bombs.

92   Three types of marking, using names selected by Bennett from the hometowns of three of his staff, were later employed. *Parramatta* in New Zealand gave its name to the blind ground marking technique, which used only H₂S in bad visibility or broken cloud. *Newhaven* was ground marking by visual methods when crews simply aimed at the TIs on the ground and *Wanganui* in Australia lent its name to pure 'sky marking'. The TIs themselves were made in various plain colours and used vivid star-

bursts of the same or a different colour to prevented the enemy from copying them at their many decoy sites near major cities.

93 Later Group Captain DFC* AFC AE.

94 Wing Commander Roy Pryce Elliott DSO DFC, who had been awarded the DSO and DFC in 1942 while flying Lancasters on 83 Squadron was on his third tour. He commanded 627 Squadron until 3 June 1944, having flown a total of 81 operations. A bar to his DFC followed on 15 September 1944.

95 On 3 November Air Chief Marshal Harris had told Churchill. 'We can wreck Berlin from end to end if the USAAF will come in on it. It may cost us 400-500 aircraft. It will cost Germany the war.'

96 Squadron Leader Edward Inkerman J. Bell DFC and Flying Officer J. G. R. Battle, who were shot down on 8 January 1944. On 13 January both were reported PoWs in Stalag Luft III.

97 Simpson and Walker came down near le Beny Bocage in the Calvados region of France and they were taken in by the French Resistance. On 24 February 1944 both men crossed safely into Switzerland. See *At First Sight; A Factual and anecdotal account of No.627 Squadron RAF*. Researched and compiled by Alan B. Webb. 1991.

98 Lancaster III JA686 blew up at Wyton on 26 November 1943 killing five ground crew and three men aboard the airraft.

99 *At First Sight; A Factual and anecdotal account of No.627 Squadron RAF*. Researched and compiled by Alan B. Webb. 1991.

100 On 7 April 1944 571 Squadron was formed at Downham Market. A shortage of Mosquitoes meant that 571 had to operate at half-strength for a time. On the night of 13/14 April two crews from 571 and six Mosquitoes from 692 attacked Berlin for the first time carrying two 50-gallon drop tanks and a 4,000lb bomb. On 1 August 1944 608 Squadron at Downham Market joined LNSF. On 25 October 142 Squadron re-formed at Gransden Lodge and that same night they flew their first operation when their only two B.XXVs were despatched to Cologne. On 18 December 162 Squadron re-formed at Bourn with B.XXVs and soon accompanied the veteran 139 Squadron on target-marking duties. 163 Squadron, the 11th and final Mosquito unit in 8 Group, reformed at Wyton on 25 January 1945 on B.XXVs. it was commanded by Wing Commander (later Air Marshal Sir Ivor, KCB CBE DSO DFC** AFC) Broom DFC. The squadron flew its first LNSF operation just four days later when four Mosquitoes dropped 'Window' at Mainz ahead of the PFF force.

101 The navigator worked out the flight plan and calculated the time to set course in order to reach the target at the correct time. On marking sorties it was important that TIs were dropped at the correct time in order not to compromise the Main Force. Having worked out the time to set course, navigators actually did this with six minutes in hand to allow for any errors in the forecast wind, etc. Having settled into the flight and arrived at the ETA for the waiting point, crews usually had to make some sort of correction. If the full 6 minutes had to be lost, the pilot did a 360° orbit and most pilots became expert in achieving this in the 6 minutes. Lesser times to be lost were accomplished by making a dog leg.'

102 Eaton was awarded an immediate DFC for this operation and went on to complete ninety operations by 18 March 1945. On 10 July1944 he and Jack Fox took off on their first daylight operation when the port engine blew up as they reached the end of the runway, an event that was usually fatal. Eaton somehow flew a circuit and landed safely on one engine but when Fox dropped prematurely through the escape hatch the propeller killed him.

103 Weather over Belgium and eastern France was 0/10ths to 4/10ths thin cloud while Holland and the Ruhr were cloudless.

104 Mosquito spoof attacks on Cologne, Frankfurt and Kassel were identified for what they were because to the German defences they were apparently flying without H.S. As the bomber stream was clearly recognised from the start, 246 twin- and single- engined night fighters were sent up to engage the heavies. British jamming of the first interception of the bomber stream in the area south of Bonn was successful but from there on in the bomber stream was hit repeatedly and the majority of the losses occurred in the Giessen-Fulda-Bamberg area. A staggering 82 bombers were lost en route to and near the target.

105 At Nürnburg there was 10/10ths cloud at 1,600 to 12,000ft but the cloud veiled at 16,000ft with generally good altitude visibility.

106 See *At First Sight; A Factual and anecdotal account of No.627 Squadron RAF*. Researched and compiled by Alan B. Webb. 1991. Sixty-four Lancasters and 31 Halifaxes (11.9 per cent of the force

dispatched) were lost (and ten bombers crash-landed in England); the worst Bomber Command loss of the war. Marshallsay and Ranshaw were promoted to Pilot Officers in May 1944 and they were both awarded the DFC in October 1944.

107   See *At First Sight; A Factual and anecdotal account of No.627 Squadron RAF.* Researched and compiled by Alan B. Webb. 1991.

108   22 Mosquitoes of 5 and 8 Groups were despatched. Some 196 aircraft of 4 and 8 Group meanwhile, attacked rail yards at Ottignies in Belgium.

109   When 627 Squadron flew four early 'Window' and five marking sorties. The first visual marker, Squadron Leader E. F. 'Rocky' Nelles, dived DZ477/K from 5,000 to 400ft to mark the target.

110   The Brunswick raid was not successful. The initial marking by 617 Squadron Mosquitoes was accurate but many of the main force of Lancasters did not bomb these, partly because of a thin layer of cloud, which hampered visibility, and partly because of faulty communications between the various bomber controllers. Many bombs were dropped in the centre of the city but the rest of the force bombed reserve H2S-aimed TIs, which were well to the south. Damage caused was not extensive. Sir Arthur Harris had sanctioned the release of the Mosquitoes to 617 Squadron and insisted they could be retained only if Munich was hit heavily on 24/25 April. Bombing by the 234 Lancasters and the marking plan by the Mosquitoes went well and accurate bombing fell in the centre of Munich. While no award of the Victoria Cross was ever made for a Mosquito sortie, Leonard Cheshire's contribution to the success of the Munich operation, when he led four Mosquitoes of the Marking Force in 5 Group, was mentioned in his VC citation on 8 September 1944. The crews who took part were: Cheshire and Pat Kelly; Squadron Leader Dave Shannon DSO and Len Sumpter; Flight Lieutenant Terry Kearns and Flight Lieutenant Hone Barclay, and Flight Lieutenant Gerry Fawke and Flight Lieutenant Tom Bennett. The four aircraft flew to Manston on the Kent coast to begin the operation. Once over the target they proved highly successful, Cheshire diving from 12,000 to 3,000ft and then flying repeatedly over the city at little more than 700ft, coming under fire for 12 minutes before leaving the area. Shannon dived from 15,000 to 4,000ft but his markers hung up, while the fourth Mosquito got four spot flares away.

111   During the week in which these early low-level marking efforts against German targets were taking place, Bill Hickox and 'Benny' Goodman were suddenly called to the CO's office. They were trying desperately to fathom what they could have done wrong when they were ushered in to Roy Elliott's presence. He got up from his chair, grinned broadly and announced that they had each been awarded the DFC. This was a proud moment for them, particularly since these were the first DFCs awarded to members of 627 Squadron.

112   'Benny' Goodman and Bill Hickox were awarded the DFC on 21 April 1944 and bars to their DFC followed on 13 October 1944.

113   Saint-Smith and Heath were on their second tours after flying together on 460 Squadron, during which they each received the DFM.

114   See *At First Sight; A Factual and anecdotal account of No.627 Squadron RAF.* Researched and compiled by Alan B. Webb. 1991.

115   Mailly actually accommodated a *Panzer* regiment HQ, 3 *Panzer* battalions belonging to regiments on the Eastern Front and elements of two more as well as the permanent training school staff.

116   No.5 Group, which supplied nearly all the marker aircraft and the entire first wave, lost 14 of its 173 Lancasters. No.1 Group, which dispatched 173 Lancasters also, in the second wave of the attack and which were subjected to the greatest delay at Mailly, lost 28 bombers, including five out of 17 crews from 460 Squadron RAAF from Binbrook. Nos 12, 50 and 101 Squadrons each lost four crews. One Mosquito *Intruder* and one RCM Halifax were also shot down. Approximately 1,500 tons of bombs were dropped on Mailly and 114 barrack buildings, 47 transport sheds and workshops and some ammunition stores were hit. 218 Germans were killed or missing and 156 were wounded. 102 vehicles were destroyed, including 37 tanks. Damage to the buildings was German assessed as '80% destroyed, 20% worth repairing'. The only French civilian casualties in the village of Mailly nearby occurred when a Lancaster crashed into the house.

117   Both men were posthumously awarded the DFC on 15 August 1944.

118   Hugh Hay, who after three tours as a navigator, qualified as a pilot with the RCAF at the age of 29.

119   Bill Hickox has written that when the shattering news that their beloved leader, Roy Elliott, was

being replaced, it was not by one of their own Flight Commanders, but by a stranger from HQ 5 Group, Wing Commander George W. Curry DFC. (Wing Commander Curry DSO* DFC* met his death during a Battle of Britain display some time after the war). Hickox's loyalty was still with Don Bennett and 8 Group, so he was unhappy with this final take-over by 5 Group. Consequently, he took the opportunity of completing his second tour with a grand total of 81 operations and returned to 8 Group with a posting to the Mosquito Training Unit at Warboys. See *At First Sight; A Factual and anecdotal account of No.627 Squadron RAF.* Researched and compiled by Alan B. Webb. 1991.

120   The target was found by Flight Lieutenant Ronald Bartley DFC who after dropping his red spot fire 50-60 yards 245° from the Marking Point was followed by 'Benny' Goodman, who laid two further reds, which fell 200 yards 360° and could not easily be seen as they landed on the edge of a wood near the gun battery. Flight Lieutenant Douglas Peck DFC then backed up the original marker with two red spots, which were assessed as being 100 yards 240°. Finally, Flight Lieutenant John Thomson DFC RNZAF laid a green TI on the reds and this was assessed as being 300 yards 240° from the Marking Point. See *At First Sight; A Factual and anecdotal account of No.627 Squadron RAF.* Researched and compiled by Alan B. Webb. 1991.

Chapter 4

121   From June 1944 Mosquito night-fighters also used nitrous oxide injected with petrol, to give their engines added power to catch V-1s. During the first 10 days of operations in June 1943 with I./NJG1, which operated from Venlo and Münster, the He 219A-2 proved the only Luftwaffe piston-engined night-fighter capable of taking on the Mosquito on equal terms, the unit claiming 6 Mosquitoes destroyed (+ claims for 25 4-engined bombers). On the night of 12/13 December 1943 when the Krupp Works at Essen was the target and I./NJG1 claimed four aircraft destroyed. One of them was DZ354/D, a 105 Squadron Mosquito flown by Flying Officer Benjamin Frank Reynolds and Flying Officer John Douglas Phillips, which crashed near Herwijnen in Holland on the North bank of the Waal River. Both crew were later buried in the Herwijnen General cemetery. They were shot down and killed by Hauptmann Manfred Meurer flying a Uhu. On 21/22 January 1944 *Eichenlaubträger* Hauptmann Manfred Meurer, Kommandeur I/NJG1 and his *Funker, Ritterkreuzträger* Oberfeldwebel Gerhard Scheibe were killed when their He 219A-0 'Owl' was hit by debris from their 2nd victim and they crashed to their deaths 20 km E of Magdeburg. In less than two years Meurer had claimed 65 night victories, including 40 heavy bombers and two Mosquitoes in 130 sorties. Only 268 *Uhus* were built, 195 of which were delivered to operational units between mid-1943 and late 1944. The majority went to I./NJG1 at Venlo and to NJGr10, a specialist anti-*Moskito Gruppe* at Werneuchen near Berlin.

122   DZ608.

123   Downey had enlisted in the RAFVR in November 1938 and when war had broken out he was called up in December 1939. Qualifying as a bomber pilot at 16 OTU he was posted to 83 Squadron, which was flying Hampdens at Finningley, Yorkshire. During December 1940-July 1941 he completed 32 ops before he was posted to instruct at 16 OTU (where he volunteered for 2 ops whilst with the unit). In 1941 he was awarded the DFM for saving his crew and his aircraft when his Hampden suffered an engine failure on take off. Joe married LACW Margaret Mary Monk in 1941 and in 1943 they had a son, Patrick. In 1942 Joe had volunteered for another tour and was posted to 218 Squadron, which was flying Stirlings and during November 1942-April 1943 he completed a further 23 ops.

124   Downey and Wellington's Mosquito (MM125) was shot down at about 00.55 hours (continental time). Wellington was taken prisoner. On 23/24 September Modrow, now a *Ritterkreuzträger* and promoted to Hauptmann, the Staffelkapitän destroyed two heavies flying a He 219 *Uhu* for his 30th and 31st victories. On 21/22 June 1944 Modrow destroyed four Lancasters flying a He 219 *Uhu*. His final tally was 34 combat victories in 109 sorties.

125   Nabrich, Staffelkapitän of 3./NJG1, was killed in his vehicle during a strafing attack by RAF fighter-bombers on *Eichstrasse 54* from Handorf to Telgte on 27 November 1944, afterwhich Habicht crewed up with Hauptmann Alexander Graf Rességuier de Miremont. Feldwebel Fritz Habicht was WIA on 3/4 February 1945 when he and de Miremont baled out of He 219A-2 290070 G9+CH. Over the Ruhr they were pursuing a Lancaster coned by four searchlights but as they went to attack two of the searchlights suddenly moved and illuminated the *Uhu*. The Lancaster gunners set the He 219A-2 on fire while the nightfighter crew's fire caused the Lancaster to go down near Roermond. Habicht

jettisoned his canopy and his pilot ejected. Habicht's ejection seat handle had been shot off in the attack but he nevertheless managed to get free of the aircraft and immediately pull the ripcord of his parachute. He had been hit in the shoulder and chest in the attack and he suffered worse injuries when he hit some tall trees. Habicht survived although his operational flying was over. He had been involved in 17 victories.

126 *The Mosquito Log* by Alexander McKee. Souvenir Press. 1988.

127 Cassels and Woollard were later repatriated to Britain in a BOAC Mosquito from Bromma airport near Stockholm, on 28 September.

128 13 *Tame Boar* crews were credited with 21 four-engined bomber kills.

129 in ML960.

130 After a week or so in the station hospital Russell was given leave and returned to Little Staughton. Having suffered quite severe burns to his wrists on leaving the aircraft, Barker was grounded until on 4/5 October, when on only their second trip together after the 28/29 June incident, Russell and Barker's Mosquito was hit by flak North of Luxembourg returning from an attack on a precision tool shop at Heilbronn. MM153 was beyond control, pitching and going down in a spin. Both men baled out over liberated Belgium near Verviers and they returned to 109 Squadron. Russell was then attached to the Mosquito Service Unit at Upwood, which brought his operational flying to an end.

131 To try to overcome the crisis caused by 'Window' in early July 1943 free-lance single-engined night-fighting was hastily introduced into *Nachtjagd* under the command of *Ritterkreuzträger* Oberst Hans-Joachim 'Hajo' Herrmann. *Geschwader Herrmann* was equipped with Fw 190s and Bf 109s thrown into the fray in *Wilde Sau* operations, a primitive form of night fighting in which the pilots tried to intercept and destroy the bombers over the target with the aid of searchlights and in the glare of fires burning below.

132 Müller took his score to 23 kills with four victories while in command of I./NJGr10.

133 On one occasion, at 0120 hours on 11 July, Krause received a severe hit and he was only able to save himself by baling out.

134 B.XVI MM147 of 692 Squadron, which crashed West of Granzow, 9 km NNW of Kyritz at 01.55 hours. Flight Lieutenant Burley DFC (KIA). Flight Lieutenant E. V. Saunders DFC baled out (PoW).

135 *The Mosquito Log* by Alexander McKee. Souvenir Press. 1988. Krause, later *Kommandeur* of III./NJG11, claimed a Lancaster shot down on 4/5 November 1944 during a Bomber Command raid on Bochum. He survived the war despite three parachute jumps.

136 Unteroffizier Wittmann of 1./NJG10 claimed a Mosquito at Gardelegen-Berlin at about the same time as Strüning. It could be that both claims were for the same Mosquito, as only one FTR from the Berlin raid and no others were lost this night. The Germans buried Doddy Dodwell in the small cemetery at Laudin and later removed and reburied him in the cemetery at Heerstrasse in Berlin.

137 Squadron Leader C. R. Barrett DFC and Flying Officer E. S. Fogden of 608 Squadron (KIA) and Pilot Officer G. R. Thomas and Flying Officer J. H. Rosbottom of 692 Squadron (KIA) both crashed near Nauen.

138 KB239 6T-G, which crashed into the railway station at Rangsdorf at 02.30 hours. Flight Lieutenant B. H. Smith RCAF and Sergeant L. E. Pegg both perished. They were buried in a joint grave at the Berlin 1939-1945 War Cemetery. Three Mosquitoes and a Stirling of 199 Squadron in 100 Group were lost on Bomber Support. Leutnant Kurt Welter claimed two of the Mosquitoes, one south of Berlin and the other north of Aachmer and Feldwebel Reichenbach of 10./JG300 one other northwest of Wittenburg. One of Welter's victims was a 515 Squadron FB.VI in 100 Group flown by Squadron Leader C. Best DFC and Flight Sergeant H. Dickinson (KIA). Squadron Leader J. H. McK Chisholm and Flight Lieutenant E. L. Wilde of 157 Squadron disappeared w/o trace. Reichenbach's victim was a FB.VI of 239 Squadron flown by Flying Officer E. W. Osborne and Pilot Officer G. V. Acheson (KIA). Welter claimed another Mosquito North of Wittenberg on 18/19 September (B.XV DZ635 of 627 Squadron, which crashed at Schiffdorf in the eastern outskirts of Bremerhaven. Flight Lieutenant N. B. Rutherford AFC (31) and Pilot Officer F. H. Stanbury (27) were KIA).

139 B.XX KB267/E.

140 See *At First Sight; A Factual and anecdotal account of No.627 Squadron RAF*. Researched and compiled by Alan B. Webb. 1991.

141 Guy Penrose Gibson, born in Simla, India in 1918, joined the RAF in 1936 after leaving St.

Edward's School, Oxford. At the outbreak of war he held the rank of Flying Officer and in August 1940 he completed his first tour as a Hampden bomber pilot on 83 Squadron. He was promoted to Flight Lieutenant and won his first DFC (he was awarded a bar the following year). He was posted to instruct at an OTU before transferring to Fighter Command and a posting to 29 Squadron equipped with Beaufighters. In 99 operational sorties he claimed 4 e/a destroyed and was promoted to Squadron Leader. A bar to his DFC followed on completion of his second tour in December 1941. In March 1942 he returned to Bomber Command, was promoted Wing Commander and posted to take command of 106 Squadron. He was awarded the DSO with a bar in 1943. On 16/17 May 1943 he led 617 Squadron's 19 Lancasters in the famous operation against the Ruhr dams. Gibson awarded the Victoria Cross for his leadership on the raid. Later sent to America as an air attaché but he begged the Air Ministry to allow him to return to operations.

142   Flying Officer H. E. Brown RCAF (29) and Flight Lieutenant H. W. Cowan (29) crashed about 600 yards northwest of the target. Both men were later buried at Rheinberg war Cemetery.

143   See *At First Sight; A Factual and anecdotal account of No.627 Squadron RAF.* Researched and compiled by Alan B. Webb. 1991.

144   On 7 October 627 Squadron had lost a Mosquito crewed by Flight Lieutenant Geoffrey Bray and Flight Lieutenant P. N. G. Herbert which FTR from a reconnaissance of Walcheren flown two hours after the other aircraft had marked the targets on the island. On 19 October another 627 Squadron Mosquito crashed during practice dive bombing at the Wainfleet range when a practice bomb exploded in the bomb bay. The pilot managed to bale out but the navigator became wedged in the escape hatch and as killed on impact.

145   Mosquito XXV KB426 was a complete write-off.

146   Two of the three formations of Mosquitoes failed to link up with their *Oboe* leaders and bombed on timed runs from the docks south of Duisburg. 'Sky markers' defeated the solid cloud cover and smoke seen rising to 10,000ft seemed testimony to the bombing accuracy but most of the bombs were believed to have fallen beyond the plant. The Mosquitoes returned without loss.

147   XVI MM190 of 128 Squadron. Flight Lieutenant R. C. Onley and Flying Officer G. B. Collins RAAF KIA.

148   The only Mosquito lost was a NF.XXX that was hit by a V-2 in mid air during an *Intruder* patrol!

149   Acting Squadron Leader Robert Anthony Maurice DFC RAFVR, on his 110th operation of the war, was awarded a posthumous Victoria Cross. His body is buried in the Rheinberg War Cemetery with the other men who died aboard the Lancaster. Only the tail gunner escaped death, by taking to his parachute. On 21 April 1945 109 Squadron dropped the last bombs to fall on Berlin in WW2.

150   Squadron Leader Ron Churcher DFC* RAFVR had completed a tour of operations with 106 Squadron at Coningsby flying Hampdens, Manchesters and Lancasters. His second tour was with 619 Squadron at Woodhall Spa and this was completed in January 1944. Soon afterwards he was posted to the Operations Staff at 5 Group HQ, Morton Hall near Swinderby. In July 1944 he had joined 627 Squadron. His last trip was to Oslo Fjord on 13 December 1944. He was awarded the DSO on 13 April 1945.

151   Wing Commander Curry dive bombed from 1,300ft and hit the Northeast corner of the buildings. Two of the other Mosquitoes dive bombed and released their 2 x 1,000 MC bombs and the two others dived from 1,300 to 1,000ft and dropped their loads of 4 x 500 pounders, some of which fell on the southern building.

152   See *At First Sight; A Factual and anecdotal account of No.627 Squadron RAF.* Researched and compiled by Alan B. Webb. 1991.

153   There was too much smoke and Mallender jettisoned his bombs. Three others returned with their bomb loads while one Mosquito bombed the North building, which was completely wrecked. The sixth and final Mosquito in the second wave attacked the North West building at 1,300ft but it was already damaged so the pilot undershot on target.

154   Peter Mallender was awarded the DFC on 1 January 1945 and promoted squadron Leader to command A Flight on 8 February 1945. It was 45 years before he learned that dear old 'D-Dog' was repaired and lived to a 'ripe old age'. Flying Officer Bob Boyden concludes. 'The trip back to Peterhead was uneventful. Those Mosquitoes were really smooth and reliable and much credit must go to the manufacturers and, of course, our aircraft mechanics who worked hard to keep them flying. All

aircraft returned to Peterhead and all had some flak damage. Mine also had a cracked landing light cover, which they said had been caused by the concussion of the bombs. The next morning we did a fly-past in front of the control tower as we headed back to base. A few officers of high rank met us and shook hands and said a few words. I received the DFC for this trip and years later, when I read the citations, I felt proud to have taken part in this once in a lifetime adventure.' Bob Boyden was awarded the DFC on 2 March 1945 and a bar followed on 17 July 1945. See *At First Sight; A Factual and anecdotal account of No.627 Squadron RAF.* Researched and compiled by Alan B. Webb. 1991.

155 HM409

156 *K for King* came to an untimely end on 2 February 1945 when, returning from a Berlin sortie it was diverted in bad weather to Rougham, an airfield operated by the USAAF and home of the 94th Bomb Group flying B 17s. The aircraft overshot the runway and collided with a civilian car; no one was hurt. The crew were Flying Officer Phillip Back and Flying Officer Derek Smith.

Chapter 5

157 A 128 Squadron Mosquito crashed on take-off, killing the crew. A record of the bombing was to be made using cameras mounted in the front and rear of the Mosquitoes to record explosions at the entrance and exit of each tunnel.

158 Twelve tunnels were blocked in the Eifel and Ardennes area, holding up German lines of communication. Six out of seven Mosquitoes of 692 Squadron bombed tunnels near Mayen, losing Flight Lieutenant George Nairn and his navigator Sergeant Danny Lunn to light flak.

159 Five Mosquitoes from the Berlin raid crashed in England and three crashed in Belgium.

160 Later Air Marshal Sir Ivor, KSB CBE DSO DFC AFC.

161 'The story then died for 50 years until we were invited to attend the launch of Martin Bowman's book '*The Men Who Flew the Mosquito*' at Swanton Morley on 2 February 1995. Philip still had his licence so we flew in together from his home at Sisland, east of Norwich in his part-owned Cessna 172. Of course, this created considerable interest, especially as it was exactly 50 yrs on from our Rougham experience. After the launch, we were interviewed by Anglia Television and the *Eastern Daily Press* with the interview appearing on 'Anglia Tonight' that evening. This item was seen by Dick and Sybil Rayner, two occupants of the car, living at Holland-on-Sea, who got in touch with Anglia, who wanted to get us all together. I had returned home to Oxfordshire that night but Philip met them on 3 February at the 'Flying Fortress' pub at Rougham where Martin Bowman had first discovered details of the event during his researches. This get-together was again featured on 'Anglia Tonight' and the Rayners were able to give us copies of press cuttings and pictures which had been taken by the Americans.' (On 12 March 1945 Derek Smith completed his tour of 50 ops as a navigator on Mosquitoes and he was awarded a bar to his DFC. On 14 March Philip Back and Alex 'Sandy' Galbraith RNZAF, Joe Northrop's navigator, were posted to 139 Squadron. Philip Back flew his 51st op on 25 March and flew nine more before the war's end).

162 See *At First Sight; A Factual and anecdotal account of No.627 Squadron RAF.* Researched and compiled by Alan B. Webb. 1991.

163 Dresden had been targeted as part of a series of particualy heavy raids on German cities in Operation *Thunderclap* with a view to causing as much destruction, confusion and mayhem as possible The other cities were Berlin, Chemnitz and Leipzig, which like Dresden, were vital communications and supply centres for the Eastern Front. *Thunderclap* had been under consideration for several months and was to be implemented only when the military situation in Germany was critical. The campaign was to have started with an American raid on Dresden on 13 February but bad weather over Europe prevented any US involvement until the 14th.

164 In addition the US 8th Air Force despatched 450 B-17s of which 316 attacked Dresden shortly after 12 noon on 14 February.

165 In the case of the 5 Group attack the outward route consisted of no less than eight legs with feints towards the Ruhr, Kassel, Magdeburg and Berlin using *Window* at the same time. To assist the night operations of Bomber Command various 'spoof' attacks were made by Mosquitoes on Dortmund, Magdeburg and Hanover and 344 Halifaxes attacked an oil plant at Böhlen near Leipzig at the same time as the first attack. In addition to the above the routing and. feints carried out by the Main Forces involved caused night fighter reaction to be minimal. An indication of the effectiveness of these

operations was that out of over 1,000 aircraft taking part against Dresden only six were lost. Two more Lancasters crashed in France and one in England.

166 Winston Churchill later tried to distance himself from Dresden and declared that, 'The destruction of Dresden remains a serious query against the conduct of Allied bombing.' This was the same Winston S. Churchill who on 22 June 1941 had said. 'We shall bomb Germany by day as well as night in ever-increasing measure, casting upon them month by month a heavier discharge of bombs and making the German people taste and gulp each month a sharper dose of the miseries they have showered upon mankind.'

167 XXV KB409 powered by Packard Merlins. More than a few crews preferred the Mosquito IV aircraft with Rolls Royce engines. They had a smoother purr than the Packards and did not cut out as the Packards did when going into a dive due to the design of the Stromberg carburettor.

168 *At First Sight; A Factual and anecdotal account of No.627 Squadron RAF*. Researched and compiled by Alan B. Webb. 1991.

169 William Topper was awarded the DFC on 9 March 1945. Flight Lieutenant Garth Davies was awarded the DFC on 21 September 1945.

170 Hallows had passed through Sandhurst and took a commission in the King's Liverpool Regiment, which he later relinquished to take up civilian flying. He joined the RAF Reserve and was called up on the outbreak of war. As a bomber pilot on 97 'Straits Settlements' Squadron he was known as 'Darkie', not for his jet black hair and full moustache but for an episode when he got lost and invoked the R/T get-you-home service of those early days: *'Darkie, Darkie'*. Receiving no response, he had tried again but still no reply. Once more he had transmitted to the void: *'Darkie, Darkie...where are you, you little black bastard?* Hallows flew 4 trips on Manchesters before the Squadron re-equipped with Lancaster Is. Flying Officer Hallows was one of the pilots who took part in the disastrous daylight raid on the U-boat engine works at Augsburg on 17 April 1942. Hallows returned safely and was one of eight officers to be awarded the DFC for his part in the raid.

171 165 Lancasters took part in the raid and nine were lost and 4 crashed in France and Holland; 7.89% of the Lancaster force. On 21/22 February also another 77 Mosquitoes in 8 Group went to Berlin. No aircraft were lost. On the following night, 73 Mosquitoes went to the 'Big City' without loss, although one of four Mosquitoes was lost on a raid on Erfurt. Hallows' tenure of 627 Squadron was cut short by illness and he relinquished command on 17 March 1945. Wing Commander R. Kingsford-Smith DSO DFC RAAF, a nephew of Sir Charles Kingsford-Smith assumed command on 10 April.

172 See *At First Sight; A Factual and anecdotal account of No.627 Squadron RAF.* Researched and compiled by Alan B. Webb. 1991.

173 Some 248 Lancasters of 5 Group attacked the refinery. The target area was covered by cloud but some damage was caused to the refinery. Four Lancasters were lost. This same night 75 Mosquitoes visited Berlin, another 15 went to Gelsenkirchen and 36 attacked six other targets. Two Mosquitoes failed to return from the raid on Berlin and another was lost attacking Hallendorf.

174 In daylight on 6 March 48 Mosquitoes led by *Oboe*-equipped Mosquitoes of 109 Squadron to provide marking, bombed Wesel, which was believed to contain many German troops and vehicles. One Mosquito failed to return.

175 Edwards was flying B.XVI MM191. Twenty-eight of the 32 Lancasters dispatched carried *Tallboy* bombs and one from 617 Squadron dropped the first 22,000lb *Grand Slam* bomb.

176 Burke however, was picked to crew with William Worthington Topper to go out to Okinawa, in a Master Bomber role, for the attacks, which *Tiger Force* was to launch on the Japanese mainland and other Far East targets. Burke did not look forward to this, as he detested the thought of snakes, the jungle, the heat and the Japanese treatment of air crew prisoners but during a home visit to Preston the news broke of the dropping of the atomic bomb on Hiroshima.

177 An unusually high loss percentage, as the average losses usually only amounted to 0.99 % of the fast Berlin raiders.

178 *At First Sight; A Factual and anecdotal account of No.627 Squadron RAF.* Researched and compiled by Alan B. Webb. 1991. Barnett, bloodied and covered in deep yellow from the fluorescene in the Mae West life jacket and with a four day old beard, made it to a farmhouse on his hands and knees, where he scared an elderly lady half to death. Barnett was eventually apprehended and sent to

a PoW hospital at Schleswig. He finished the war in Stalag 20B. Johnny Day's body was never found.
179   Hudson, born in Kaponga, New Zealand on 16 November 1915, suffered from polio in early childhood, which affected both his legs but he overcame this and in High School played 1st Class cricket and rugby and participated in cross-country runs to build up his stamina. (*571 Mosquito Squadron History* by Barry Blunt).
180   Becker's victim was FB.VI MM131 XD-J of 139 Squadron, which had taken off from Upwood at 19.12 hours for Berlin. Squadron Leader H. A. Forbes DFC, the navigator/bomb aimer escaped and was taken prisoner but no trace has ever been found of his pilot, Flight Lieutenant André A. J. van Amsterdam, a Dutch escapee decorated with the DFC and the Dutch AFC.
181   Flight Lieutenant Kenneth Pudsey and Flying Officer John Reginald Dalton Morgan were on their 34th operation, to Magdeburg on 4/5 April when 31 Mosquitoes were despatched and they collided with a Mosquito of 571 Squadron over the Channel.

Chapter 6

182   *Highball* weighed 950lbs with a charge weight of about 600lbs and a diameter of 35in. Based on the *Upkeep* 'bouncing bomb', which 617's Lancasters had dropped on the German dams, *Highball* was significantly smaller and lighter (about 10 per cent of the weight of the larger weapon). Each modified Mosquito B.IV could carry two *Highballs*, launching them at low level with a back spin of approximately 500rpm from about 3⁄4 miles. On 28 February 1943 an Air Staff paper called for two squadrons of Mosquitoes and 250 *Highball* bombs and two squadrons of Lancasters and 100 *Upkeep* bombs.
183   618 spent much of 1943 perfecting the weapon and flying assimilation sorties. However, by 14 May, the day before Operation *Servant*, the intended strike on the *Tirpitz*, only six suitably modified B.IVs were available at Skitten and the strike was called off. (Twelve other Mk.IVs were at Hatfield for long-range tanks to be installed.) *Highball* trials continued but by September the Squadron had been reduced to a cadre at Benson. 618 Squadron was re-tasked for re-assignment to the Pacific so, in July 1944, it was brought up to full strength. Its mission now was to attack, with *Highball*, the Japanese fleet at Truk, which, because of the distance involved, meant that the Mosquitoes would have to operate from a carrier! Ten crews arrived from 143, 144, 235, 236, 248 and 254 Squadrons; while from 540 and 544 PR Squadrons came ten pilots and navigators whose task it would be to find the Japanese ships. They were attached to the Naval Air Torpedo School for carrier training using Barracuda II aircraft. After a series of aerodrome dummy deck landings (ADDLs) crews made a real deck landing and take-off from HMS *Implacable* using Mosquito IVs modified with arrestor hooks and four paddle-bladed props. On 31 October 24 Mk IVs and three PR.XVIs were ferried out to the Pacific on two escort carriers, HMS *Fencer* and HMS *Striker*. They docked in Melbourne, Australia on 23 December. In the meantime the Americans had sunk the ships at Truk. In January the aircraft were unloaded and on 7 February the detachment proceeded to Narromine in NSW and on to Darwin where a PR unit was stationed. On ANZAC Day, 25 April, nine crews flew a formation flypast of Mosquito IVs over Narromine and surrounding towns. The crews finally left Australia on VE Day on board the *Nieuw Amsterdam* and returned to England.
184   On 22 October 1943 two Mosquito FB.XVIIIs, which had a 57mm Molins cannon in place of the conventional four 20mm cannon, arrived at Predannack and were issued to 248 Squadron engaged in anti-shipping operations in the Atlantic. The squadron was equipped mainly with the Beaufighter, but earlier that October five Mosquito crews and 34 ground crew from 618 Squadron had been transferred to fly and service the new aircraft. The 618 Squadron crews were an ideal choice for maritime operations, two having commenced operations on XVIIIs two days earlier when Squadron Leader Rose DFC DFM and Flying Officer Al Bonnett RCAF attempted to track a *U-boat* in the Bay of Biscay.
185   The Molins was installed in the nose in place of the four 20mm cannon. An arc-shaped magazine, holding 24 rounds of 57mm armour-piercing HE shells capped with tracer, was positioned vertically about mid-ships, feeding into the breech block. The breech block was behind the crew, and the barrel extended below the floor of the cockpit, the muzzle protruding below the fairing of the nose. Two, sometimes four .303 inch machine guns were retained, however, for strafing and air combat. All these guns were sighted through one reflector sight, the firing buttons being on the control column. The Molins gun had a muzzle velocity of 2,950ft per second and the ideal range to open fire was

1,800-1,500 yards. The gun and its feed system were sensitive to sideways movement and attacking in a XVIII required a dive from about 5,000ft (at a 30° angle with the turn-and-bank indicator dead central. The slightest drift would cause the gun to jam.

186   On 22 October 1943 the first two Mk.XVIIIs arrived at Predannack for anti-shipping operations in the Atlantic. 248 Squadron was equipped mainly with Beaufighters but earlier that month, five Mosquito crews and 34 ground crew from Skitten were transferred in as the 618 Squadron Special Detachment, to fly and service the new Tsetses. Amid great secrecy three XVIIIs - HX902, 903 and 904 -were prepared for action. Operations commenced on 24 October with two XVIIIs flown by Squadron Leader Charlie Rose DFC DFM, who had been 'A' Flight commander at Skitten and Flight Sergeant Cowley, and Flying Officer Al Bonnett RCAF and Pilot Officer McD 'Pickles' McNicol but they returned empty-handed.

187   Rose and his navigator, Flight Sergeant Cowley were killed by return fire from a trawler in the second of two attacks on the vessel. Three days later, on 7 November, Flying Officer Al Bonnett scored hits on U-123, a Type IXB of 1,051 tons, which was returning on the surface to Brest at the end of her thirteenth war cruise. (The mine-swept channels off the French Atlantic coast leading to the U-boat bases at Brest, Lorient, St Nazaire, La Rochelle and Bordeaux, were ideal killing grounds because the water depth was too shallow to permit the U-boats to crash-dive if attacked). After the first dive Bonnett's cannon jammed and he was forced to strafe the U-boat with machine gun fire. As a result of this attack the *Kriegsmarine* was forced to provide escort vessels for its U-boats from now on.

188   Conversion from the Beaufighter moved on and by 1 January 1944 248 Squadron had XVIII Tsetse's and four FB.VIs available for fighter reconnaissance and support for anti-shipping operations in 19 Group, Coastal Command. On 20 February 248 Squadron flew their first interception and anti-shipping patrols in the Bay of Biscay. On 10 March four FB.VIs escorting two FB.XVIIIs tangled with four Luftwaffe Ju 88s flying top cover for a German naval convoy. One of the Ju 88s was shot down on fire and two 'probables' were claimed. Meanwhile the FB.XVIIIs went after the German ships. They damaged a destroyer and shot down one of the Ju 88s. Coastal Command Liberators waded in and continued the attack on the convoy.

189   Who had enlisted in the *Kriegsmarine* in October 1938 and had taken charge of U-960 on 26 January.

190   Altogether, the four minesweepers fired 45 88mm shells and 1,550 20mm shells and claimed one Mosquito 'definitely' shot down. Flight Sergeant C. R. Tomalin managed to put his FB.VI down at Portreath despite a large hole in the starboard mainplane. Flight Sergeant L. A. Compton and Sergeant Peters managed crash-landed also, with the hydraulics shot out. Aboard U-960 the conning tower, periscope and control room were badly damaged by Hilliard's 57mm shells. Ten men, including Heinrich, who was hit above the left knee by pieces of shrapnel, were wounded, some of them badly. U-960 managed to put into La Pallice for repairs. A year later she put to sea again and was sunk in the Mediterranean on 19 May by the combined efforts of four US destroyer and two squadrons of Venturas. In March 1996 surviving crewmembers of U-976 and U-960 and three French divers who had found the wreck of U-976 on the seabed where it had lain since the attack on 25 March 1944 when it was making its way to St. Nazaire, met at the Comet Hotel, Hatfield. Des Curtis, Hilly Hilliard, Jim Hoyle and two other members of the Mosquito Aircrew Association were there to greet them.

191   U-212 limped into St. Nazaire for repairs and when she put to sea again, was sunk by frigates in July.

192   U-155 was sufficiently damaged that it never saw action again.

193   Warrant Officer Lionel Douglas Stoddart and his navigator Warrant Officer Geoffrey Gordon Harker of 248 Squadron are buried in Le Verdon-sur-Mer communal cemetery.

194   Maurice Webb, returning after 50 years was shown the point where their Mosquito crashed and the spot where Harold Corbin landed. The high spot though was when he was taken to a farmhouse in Treguidel and re-united with the lady to whom he had given his parachute. At that time she was aged 20, as he had been and in 1945 she married and her mother made her wedding dress from the parachute silk. Remarkably she still retained the bodice of this dress, fifty years on and in a traumatic ceremony it was presented to Maurice Webb. He also met a member of the local unit of the Maquis who looked after him until he was reunited with Harold and then the Americans arrived.

195   235 and 248 Squadrons joined 333 Norwegian Squadron and 144 and 404 RCAF Beaufighter

Squadrons to form the Banff Strike Wing under Wing Commander Max Aitken DSO DFC. 333 Squadron had formed at Leuchars on 10 May 1943 from 1477 (Norwegian) Flight, and commenced its first Mk VI operations on 27 May.

196   On 19 January 1945 notification was received of the bar to Wing Commander Richard Ashley Atkinson's DFC. After continuous fighting for five years and two months (he had flown Catalinas in the South West Pacific and was awarded the DSO and DFC for his outstanding service in 1941-43) he was killed just six months before the end of hostilities. On 2 September 1944 his son William Ashley had been born in Redruth Hospital.

197   Both came from a farming background. Smith was just 18 years old in September 1939 and 'Reserved Occupation', working on his father's fruit farm. He was finally accepted for pilot training in 1941 but sent home on deferred service again until 1942. Peter McIntyre was also 'Reserved Occupation', coming from a farming background in Aberdeenshire and he had then done his flying training in Pensacola, Florida before injuring his back badly playing rugby.

198   U-804, U-843 and U-1065.

199   Squadron Leader Bert Gunnis DFC ordered the nine FB.VIs of 143 Squadron near the rear of the formation being led by Squadron Leader David Pritchard, to attack. The U-boats had not seen the Mosquitoes. Then they did, but it was too late. With the rest of the wing wheeling in behind, 143 Squadron attacked, their cannons blazing as they fired seventy RPs into the U-boats, now frantically trying to escape beneath the waves.

200   All three U-boats were sunk - one of them taking the photo-Mosquito with it in an explosion. In fact the Mosquitoes were so low, three suffered damaged engines when they were hit by flying debris and were forced to land in Sweden.

201   During McIntyre and Smith's internment the Mosquitoes sank a fourth U-boat, on 19 April and they would sink six more, including four on one day, 4 May, before the war ended. McIntyre and Smith returned to Leuchars aboard a BOAC DC-3 after internment at Falun. John Smith recalls. 'In Sweden I had changed about £25 into Swedish Krona and had bought silk stockings for our sisters and girlfriends. I also purchased an unabridged copy of *Lady Chatterley's Lover* (which was banned in Britain at this time). The book, printed in English made me so very popular back at Banff, until I was foolish enough to lend it to a WAAF who didn't return it! We were sent to the Air Ministry in London to be interrogated, then back to Banff to be re-kitted. On home leave we experienced VE-Day, 8 May 1945.'

202   Air Chief Marshal Sir Christopher Foxley-Norris GCB OBE DSO MA died on 28 September 2003.

Chapter 7

203   A modified PR.XVI could carry 12 M-46 PFBs, six in the forward half of the bomb bay and six ion the rear half. Extremely thin metal was used in the bomb's outer shell. The nose fuse had. Among its safety and firing features, a timing mechanism and three safety blocks that fell away when a small propeller had rotated a set number of revolutions. The nose fuse then detonated the flash bomb when the timer had counted down to zero.

204   The first was flown on 21 June by 114 B-17s, which bombed an oil refinery near Berlin before flying on to landing fields at Poltava and Mirgorod in the Ukraine. On 21/22 June, 47 B-17s were lost and 29 were damaged in a German air raid on Poltava. On 26 June 72 Fortresses flew home, bombing a target in Poland and staging through Italy, then bombing a target in France en route to England on 5 July. The entire tour covered 6,000 miles, ten countries and 29$\frac{1}{4}$ hours of operational flying.

205   *Aerial Intelligence of the 8th Air Force 1944-45.* George R. Sesler. 1996.

206   They placed him on a mattress and carried him to their battery office. They called a doctor, who arrived after two hours, set Cannon's leg and bandaged it. The next day Cannon was shipped to a PoW hospital at a prison camp in Eberbach. The doctors at this PoW hospital were Allied prisoners who cared for Cannon thereafter.

207   Because of Soviet advances he and fellow prisoners were marched in February 1945, to Stalag VIIA in Moosburg. Less than two months later, in April, Patton's 3rd Army liberated Stalag VIIA. For three weeks after his liberation Chipman was attached to the 254th Field Artillery where he flew observation aircraft. His duties were to locate targets for the artillery. He was later sent to Reims, France, inoculated, hospitalised and he finally returned to the 25th Bomb Group. See *Aerial*

Intelligence of the 8th Air Force 1944-45. George R. Sesler. 1996.
208   Pete Dustman flew a compiled total of 54 missions in the Marauder, Mitchell and Mosquito aircraft and completed the tour without a hole in an aircraft or having to land with an engine shut down. Of the 23 aircrew forming 654 Squadron he was the third and last to finish a tour of duty and the last of the original crews.
209   Who assumed command of the 25th Bomb Group on 23 September 1944.
210   Ralph Fisher was reported MIA one week later, 21 January 1945, on another *"Bluestocking"* meteorological mission. His pilot, 2nd Lieutenant Jerry M. Roberts was also lost.
211   Major John W. Walch was one of three crew killed on 19 March 1945 when their A-26 crashed near Bramsche, Germany during an OSS mission to Münster.
212   See *Aerial Intelligence of the 8th Air Force 1944-45.* George R. Sesler. 1996.

Chapter 8
213   Early in 1944 85 (Base) Group was formed for the purpose of providing fighter cover over the continent leading up to and after, D-Day by the transfer from Fighter Command to 2nd TAF of 29, 264, 409 'Nighthawk' (RCAF), 410 'Cougar' (RCAF), 488 RNZAF and 604 Squadrons. In January 1944 the first to transfer to 85 Group was 264 Squadron, which went to 141 Wing. The last, 219 Squadron would transfer from Fighter Command to 147 Wing on 26 August. In November 1944 418 'City of Edmonton' Squadron RCAF and 605 Squadron, transferred to 136 Wing, 2nd TAF. Though V-1 patrols had occupied most of 418 Squadron's time in July and August they were interspersed with other types of activity, 418 reverting, in September, to *Rangers* and abortive *Big Ben* patrols (trying in vain to 'jam' V-2 rockets). 418 finished the war with the distinction of destroying more enemy aircraft both in the air and on the ground, than any other Canadian squadron, in both night and daylight operations. See *Moskitopanik!* by Martin W. Bowman. (Pen & Sword. 2004).
214   Oberfeldwebel Mayer claimed his 26th and 27th victories on 19 November 1944 when he shot down two Spitfires of 412 'Falcon' Squadron RCAF on 4 January 1945 Leutnant Mayer was KIA when he was shot down by a Spitfire of 442 'Caribou' Squadron RCAF. (*The JG26 War Diary,* Vol.2 1943-45, Donald Caldwell (Grub Street 1998).
215   Ian McRitchie had obtained a Pilot's Licence in 1937 and after being considered reserved occupation, in 1940 he 'ran away to war', jumping ship in Adelaide for Britain to enlist in the RAF. On the ship he was greaser in the engine room, paid threepence a week. He arrived in Bristol in October 1940 after a ten-week voyage. He joined the RAF and as a Flying Officer on Mosquito NF.IIs of 151 Squadron in 1942 he destroyed two Dornier bombers that were attacking England. On 29/30 July he destroyed a Do 217E-4 of II/KG2 and on 8/9 September he got a second Dornier Do 217E-4 when the Luftwaffe attacked Bedford. (See *Moskitopanik!* by Martin W. Bowman. (Pen & Sword. 2004).) In 1944 he had joined 464 squadron and had been promoted to squadron leader. After being shot down on the Amiens raid McRitchie was incarcerated in Stalag Luft I, Barth until the end of the European war and he returned to England to receive the DFC.
216   A cousin of Wing Commander Bell-Irving.
217   The Honorable Michael J. Wedgwood-Benn DFC, at 22, was the eldest of three sons of William Wedgwood Benn DSO DFC Ld-H (*Legion d'Honneur*) and CdG (*Croix de Guerre*), a WWI veteran pilot and prominent politician who was created Viscount Stansgate on 22.12.40.
218   One of the great RAF navigators in WWII, after fighting in the French 61st Regiment of Artillery in WWI and at the beginning of WWII Livry-Level DSO DFC* CdG* DFC (USA) did at least four tours of operational flying in Coastal Command, on special duties and in 2 Group Mosquitoes. He could not be persuaded to have a break from operational flying. On 31 August 1944 'Buck' Taylor and his navigator, Flight Lieutenant Johnson were shot down on a *Night Intruder* to Strasbourg-Sarreborg when they attacked a train. Flak set fire to their port engine and the wing collapsed. They baled out and evaded capture, returning to England on 29 September 1944. Taylor rejoined 21 Squadron on 28 October after a spell in the RAF Hospital, Swindon. By January 1945 Squadron Leader Taylor DFC* Ld-H CdG* MID had flown a total of 48 low level day and night bombing sorties.
219   *Bommen Vielen Op Hengelo* by Henk F. van Baaren, translated into English in The Mossie Vol. 16 April 1997.

220   On 28 June Wing Commander 'Daddy' Dale and other squadron personnel attended Mike Benn's funeral. As soon as he heard the news, William Wedgwood Benn, who was also in the RAF at that time with the Allied Control Commission in Italy, returned home. Mike's younger brother Anthony who was training as a pilot in Rhodesia at the time received a telegram reporting his brother's death. Tony Benn became a Sub-lieutenant in the RNVR but the war ended before he could see action. De-mobbed in 1946, he became Viscount Stansgate upon the death of his father but later renounced the title to become the well-known Labour politician.

221   In fact, the soldiers clubbed to death were a reconnaissance party of the SAS, code-named '*Bulbasket*', who were dropped south-west of Châteauroux on 5 June to harass the *2nd SS Panzer Division* on its move from Toulouse to Normandy. The main party was dropped on 11/12 June and joined up with the Maquis. On 3 July their main camp in the Foret de Verrieres was attacked by German troops. Nine SAS members got away but 31 SAS and Lieutenant Tom Stevens, a USAAF evader who had joined them, were taken prisoner. One officer was wounded before capture and was tied to a tree and publicly beaten to death in Verrieres. Three SAS prisoners were also wounded and taken to hospital in Poitiers, where they were given lethal injections. The remainder, including the American and two other SAS captured previous to this engagement, were shot in the Foret de Saint Sauvant near the village of Rom. The German unit responsible for this atrocity was believed to be the 158th Security Regiment from Poitiers. The SAS survivors signalled the UK with the information of their disaster and that the unit responsible was billeted at Bonneuil Matours.

222   2nd TAF decided that rather than have all its fighter units flying tactical reconnaissance, its three recce Wings should each contain a PR unit. B Flight of 4 Squadron in 35 Wing (84 Group) and A Flight of 400 Squadron RCAF in 39 Wing (83 Group) therefore received PR XVIs for the role. At the end of May 1944 both flights reverted back to Spitfire IXs. 140 Squadron, operating in 34 PR Wing (HQ), retained all its PR XVIs, which they had equipped with Gee and Rebecca so as to fly long-range blind night photography operations, first from Northolt, and later, the continent.

223   140 Squadron provided photo coverage throughout the winter of 1944-45, moving to France in September to keep in touch with the action. In January 1945 Flight Lieutenant Kirk got a new navigator, Flight Lieutenant Anthony Guy Humphryes, who was the unit's navigation leader. Kirk recalls. 'We did 17 operations together. Our best joint effort was on the night of 24 February, when were sent to photograph the railway sidings at Mönchengladbach. We approached the target three times. Each time, just as we were set to release the flashes, the "natives" were decidedly hostile. Lots of little red balls kept coming up at us, starring off apparently quite slowly, then, as they got nearer, whizzing very rapidly by. I didn't think we'd get very good pictures while all this was going on. We had a moment's consultation as to how best to cope with the situation. 'I decided to do the run in reverse. I asked Tony to navigate us to the far end of the run and give me a reciprocal course to steer. He put his skills to work, and at the correct moment we turned onto the target, straightened up, and raced over the marshalling yard. Down went the flashes one after another, going off like bolts of summer lightning. We didn't mind the gunners shooting at our tail as we left. Perhaps the million candlepower flashes put them off a bit! Next morning, the photos delighted the interpreters, as well as Tony and I. This night, added to our other efforts, earned us a DFC each.'

224   Wellings was returning to ops on Mosquitoes with 107 Squadron and did not have a navigator so he asked Hemmings if he would fly with him? Hemmings readily agreed and his transfer to 138 Wing at Lasham was arranged. On 13 August 1940 Wellings had gained an eleventh hour reprieve when, taxiing out for the suicidal trip to Aalborg airfield in Denmark, he and his crew were recalled because their posting had just come through. Wellings, who had a son named James and was married to Stella who lived about twenty miles from Lasham, often rode home on his motorbike on stand down nights to 'spend a night between the sheets' as he called it, as at Lasham they were living under canvas tents with blankets only with a view to moving into France wherever airfields could be cleared.

225   Of over 10,200 British airborne troops landed in the Arnhem area, 1,440 were killed or died of their wounds. 3,000 were wounded and taken prisoner and 400 medical personnel and chaplains remained behind with the wounded and about 2,500 uninjured troops also became PoWs. There were also 225 prisoners from the 4th Battalion, the Dorsetshire Regiment. About 450 Dutch civilians were killed. The operation also cost 160 RAF and Dominions aircrew, twenty-seven USAAF aircrew and 79 Royal Army Service Corps dispatchers were killed and 127 taken prisoner. A total of 55 Albemarle,

Stirling, Halifax and Dakota aircraft of 38 and 46 Groups failed to return and a further 320 damaged by flak and seven by fighters while 105 Allied fighter aircraft were lost.

226   Later Air Marshal Sir Peter Wykeham KCB DSO OBE DFC AFC.

227   The Jutland resistance organisation hid Sandbäk until he was well enough to travel and, six weeks later, having read with some interest his obituary in the Danish papers and the German announcements of his death Sandbäk and his wife escaped to London via Sweden. Their children were safely hidden until the liberation. *The Sixth Floor* by Robin Reilly. (Leslie Frewin 1969).

228   On 29 October 47 Lancasters – 18 from 9 Squadron and 18 from 617 Squadron, attacked the *Tirpitz* which was moored near the Norwegian port of Tromsø. 32 Lancasters dropped *Tallboy* bombs on estimated position of the capital ship (30 seconds before the attack a bank of cloud came in to cover the ship) but no direct hits were scored. One of 617 Squadron's Lancasters, which was damaged by flak, crash-landed in Sweden and its crew were later returned to Britain. On 12 November 30 Lancasters of 9 and 617 Squadrons attacked the *Tirpitz* again and at least two *Tallboys* hit the ship, which capsized to remain bottom upwards. Approximately 1,000 of the 1,900 men on board were killed or injured. One Lancaster, of 9 Squadron, was severely damaged by flak and landed safely in Sweden with its crew unhurt.

229   'Peter and I did have one interesting Interlude in Stockholm, where we chanced to meet the farmer and-his wife who had-received-us-so warmly upon our unceremonious arrival at Harplinge and we tried to return the compliment. After this we did not fly together again, going our separate ways. Mine led to Transport Command and the Far East. After the war all who participated in these raids received commemorative cufflinks from the Danish government.'

230   'Ed had done the requisite fifty trips and I'd managed 52 because Ed had an argument with a motor cycle early in our tour and finished up in hospital. While he was in there I did two trips with an Irishman, Flying Officer Smith. Ed and I went on two weeks leave and I expected that we would be sent on rest to an OTU but I was in for an unpleasant surprise when I returned to pick up my kit and move on. While I was away 2 Group had moved the goal posts. A tour was now 85 ops with a month's leave around the halfway mark, 200 operational hours or twelve months on the squadron, whichever came first. I was told to take another fortnight's leave and come back for another 35 trips. It was rather like being given the death sentence. Having survived 52 ops I couldn't believe that my luck would last for another 35. I never saw Ed McQuarrie again and it is only in recent years that I learned that the RCAF would not go along with the extended tour and Ed was shipped back to Canada.'

231   138 and 140 Wings lost nine Mosquitoes and many more were damaged. 2 Group lost a total of 21 Mosquitoes with 40 damaged. Les Bulmer concludes: '21 Squadron lost 1 aircraft (Hugh Henry 'Fiji' Fielding-Johnson and Flying Officer L. C. Harbord), 464 two and 487 Squadron took a hammering, losing 5 aircraft. This was a pretty high price to pay and it was never repeated.'

Chapter 9

232   Other neighbouring buildings were also taken over, including the offices of the Association of Engineers (Ingeniorhuset), which formed the northern continuation of the east wing of the *Shellhaus*. Its longest facade faced south along Kampmannsgade and there were two shorter wings, one facing west on Nyropsgade and the other facing east on Vester Farimagsgade. On each of the corners on Kampmannsgade there were two huge glass windows giving light to the main staircase.

233 and 234 Assisted by experts of specialist departments and a large staff the *Gestapo* began to assemble files about the resistance movement. Card index systems were used to store names, descriptions, and photographs. aliases and every other known detail of all Danes suspected or wanted by the *Gestapo*. Prisoners were kept in cells in the Vestre Fængsel (Western Prison) and brought to the *Shellhaus* for interrogation. At first the cellars were used to torture uncooperative captives so that their screams would not disturb the staff working above but later interrogations and torture were carried out on the fourth and fifth floors. A number of Danish *Nazis* assisted the *Gestapo* and others received training at the *Shellhaus* to infiltrate the resistance and inform against their compatriots. Not many prisoners passed through *Gestapo* hands without being tortured. The underground operated on the rule that if a member was arrested all code-names, addresses and meeting places were immediately changed. Consequently. the interrogations were usually most severe in the first 48 hours after capture because any information obtained later would most likely be out of date. *The Shell House Raid* by Douglas Hinton. *After The Battle*, No.13. 2001.

235 *The Shell House Raid* by Douglas Hinton. *After The Battle,* No.13. 2001.
236 The *Sickerkeitsdienst des Reicksführers Schutzstaffeln* or SD, was an espionage organisation both for the Nazi party and for the State, which also assisted in the work of the security police (*Sickerheitspolizei*). Recruitment to the SD was secret and members did not wear uniform. The *Sickerheitspolizei* included the criminal police and the *Gestapo* (*Geheime Staatspolizei*). *The Sixth Floor* by Robin Reilly. (Leslie Frewin 1969).
237 On 2 February 'Daddy' Dale and Hackett, his navigator, went missing on a night patrol. On 6 February the squadron transferred to Rosières-en-Santerre and shortly afterwards Wing Commander Victor R. Oates took over command. He and his navigator F. C. Gubbings failed to return from a sortie on 12 March and Peter Kleboe arrived to take over the squadron.
238 *Operation Carthage* by Kjeld Sasbye. Denmark 1994.
239 Altogether, evidence of at least 11 bomb explosions was found after the raid in the Frederiksberg Allé-Maglekildevei area just behind the northwestern corner of the school. *The Shell House Raid* by Douglas Hinton. *After The Battle*, No.13. 2001.
240 *The Shell House Raid* by Douglas Hinton. *After The Battle*, No.13. 2001.
241 Aage Schoch became managing Editor of Denmark's leading Conservative newspaper. Mogens Fog became a member of Denmark's first port-war government and in 1967 he became Vice Chancellor and Rector of Copenhagen University.
242 *The Sixth Floor* by Robin Reilly. (Leslie Frewin 1969). Pøul Sørensen became chairman of the Danish Conservative Party and in 1967, Minister for Internal Affairs. Tiemroth retired from the army in the 1970s with the rank of major general. Professor Rehberg became chairman of Denmark's Atomic Energy Commission.
243 Becker's body was discovered in an unmarked grave on the Danish island of Samsø. Becker was Jewish and all his family were eradicated by the holocaust.
244 Coe was killed in a flying accident on 6 April 1945. Squadron Leader W. P. Kemp RNZAF and Flight Lieutenant R. Peel in PZ339 and New Zealanders' Flying Officers G. L. Peet and L. A. Graham in SZ985 returned safely. Flight Lieutenant R. J. Dempsey and Flight Sergeant E. J. Paige RAAF in PZ462 had one engine damaged by a single bullet in the coolant system over the west coast of Jutland and flew 400 miles home with the engine feathered.
245 Pattison broke R/T silence with the message "*Z-Zebra- Christmas*" the code for a forced landing in Sweden. The aircraft had been hit on the port engine, which began to burn fiercely. Flying towards the Oresound, with hopes of making it across the water to neutral Sweden, the aircraft lost height rapidly and control was difficult. The Mosquito was last seen as it ditched in Oresound 1 km ESE of the Swedish Hveen Island. The crew was spotted standing on the wing, but the weather conditions made it impossible to launch a rescue boat. Both men were posted as missing believed killed in action - no bodies were ever recovered. The wreck of the Mosquito has since been precisely located at a depth of 115ft.
246 Bob Bateson retired as an Air Vice Marshal in 1967. In May 1951 Ted Sismore qualified as a pilot and he retired as an Air Commodore in February 1971.

Chapter 10
247 The 'Flying Elephants' were commanded by Wing Commander James Brindley Nicolson, famous as the only Battle of Britain pilot to have been awarded the Victoria Cross, which he had gained for his actions on 17 August 1940. Despite terrible burns sustained in the action, Nicolson recovered and in 1942 he had been posted as station commander to Alipore, Calcutta. On 25 December he and Flying Officer Thompson made strafing attacks on Japanese railway targets. Nicolson flew 27 Squadron's final Mosquito operation on 9 March 1944: a reconnaissance of Japanese airfields. Later, as commander of training at SEAC, he spent some time with Liberator crews, studying the results of aircrew training operationally. On 1 May 1945 Nicolson was lost aboard a Liberator involved in a night raid on Rangoon.
248 This feat earned a commendation from Air Commander EAC, Major General George E. Stratemeyer and Flying Officer Winship later received a mention in dispatches. MAA archives as compiled and edited by Norman Maloyney of the West Canadian Air Museum.
249 This flight earned Newman the DFC and Smith the DFM.
250 In May Wing Commander A. C. Stumm, the Australian CO of 45 Squadron and Flight Lieutenant

McKerracher RAAF were killed at Amarda Road when their Mosquito broke up during a practice attack. On 13 September Flying Officer W. C. Tuproll and Flight Sergeant V. A. Boll of 82 Squadron died when their FB.VI crashed while making dummy attacks on another aircraft. Wing Commander L. V. Hudson, the CO, thought that a gluing fault had caused failure of the wing or tail. Then on 4 October the wing leading edge of a 45 Squadron FB.VI buckled in flight, but the pilot, Sergeant Bourke RAAF was able to land safely. On 10 October Flight Lieutenant Dick Campbell RCAF and Flight Lieutenant's Rimmel, 143 RSU's Chief Technical Officer, were killed in a crash near Bishnupur. Sergeant C. J. Cabot arrived from HQ Base Air Forces the following day to investigate the accidents. On 20 October two more Mosquitoes crashed. An 82 Squadron aircraft flown by Flying Officer A. E. Parker and Flying Officer M. D. Randall shed half its starboard wing during a practice bombing attack on Random Range and a 45 Squadron aircraft flown by Sergeant Edwards broke up when about to land at Kumbhirgram, Assam.

251   In the UK a series of fatal flying accidents among Mosquitoes of various marks (at the rate of two to four per month from January to June 1944) was attributed to failure of the wing structure. HQ 8 Group reported alarm over nine accidents in the 10 weeks 27 June-16 September, some caused by wing failure.

252   At first it seemed that the defects were restricted to the FB.VIs built at Canley by Standard Motors Ltd. Of 24 such aircraft inspected by 8 November, 23 had defects adjacent to Rib 12, located 6ft from the wingtips. But within four days, de Havilland at Hatfield had found similar faults in 16 Mosquitoes produced. An investigating team led by Major Hereward de Havilland arrived in India on 26 November and a week later reported that the accidents were not caused by deterioration of glue, but by extensive shrinkage of airframes during the monsoon season. However, an investigation by Cabot and Myers attributed the accidents definitively to faulty manufacture. Myers signalled: 'Defects not due to climatic conditions. The standard of glueing...leaves much to be desired.' Meanwhile, an inspection team at the Ministry of Aircraft Production at Defford found that six different marks of Mosquito, all built by de Havilland at Hatfield and Leavesden showed signs of similar defects. Yet none of the aircraft had been exposed to monsoon conditions, nor had termites attacked them! In 684 Squadron there was no uncertainty about the cause of the grounding of the Mosquitoes. The 12 November 1944 entry in the Operations Record Book says: 'Section of wing-tip splicing on some aircraft found to be defective due to inferior workmanship at the factories building these components.'

253   To cure the problem, a plywood strip was inserted along the span of the wing to seal the whole length of the skin joint along the main spar. Despite this remedy altering the aerofoil section of the wing, it seems that Mod 638, as it was called had no effect on performance. The modification was applied to all Mosquitoes in production in Australia, but few, if any, sets were sent to India, where Mosquitoes found to have skin defects were simply struck off charge. 84 Squadron Mosquitoes saw no action against Japan but they were used, along with 47, 82 and 110 Squadrons, in late 1945 against Indonesian separatists until more faulty wing-structures were discovered in some FB.VIs. The aircraft were again grounded briefly for inspection.

254   45 Squadron at 1672 MCU at Yelahanka, near Bangalore, had been the first to convert from the Vengeance to the Mosquito, in February 1944.

255   *The Mossie*, Magazine of the MAA, No.27 January 2001.

256   Offensive operation by fighter aircraft, which had originated in Europe where these operations were used as a means of tying down enemy aircraft in the west to prevent them being sent east to the Russian Front.

257   While awaiting posting to 684 Squadron Pridmore and Campbell had been posted to 143 RSU at Bishnupar as a test crew for repaired Mosquitoes. On 10 October Campbell was asked to test a Mosquito whose exhaust shrouds had been burnt out leaving no shield to the exhaust flames. Campbell, anticipating a fire risk, did not want to fly this aircraft but Flight Lieutenant Rimmel, the Chief Technical Officer of 143 RSU, persuaded him it was safe and to let him go in Pridmore's place. He was watching from the ground and saw the wing break off when the Mosquito was at about 8,000ft. The aircraft spun in to wild scrub away from the airfield. Subsequent investigation revealed blood and feathers at the point of impact where a large Kite Hawk had broken the plywood skin causing the main spar to separate at the joint.

258   *The Mossie*, Vol.11 August 1995.

259 *The Mossie,* MAA, Vol.17 August 1997.

260 Wing Commander D. B. Pearson of 681 Squadron had flown over Everest on 26 May in a Spitfire. He was the first pilot to do so since the Houston Expedition of 1933 and he had taken photos of the mountain and the Rongbuk Glacier.

261 They had teamed up in October 1941 when they joined 604 Squadron on Mosquito night fighters. Constable-Maxwell had gained the first of his three confirmed Mosquito victories on 30 March 1943 on 264 Squadron when he destroyed a He 111. His second victory in a Mosquito followed on 15/16 May 1944 when he destroyed a Ju 188 off the Isle of Wight. On 2/3 July 1944 Constable-Maxwell and John Quinton destroyed a Ju 88 and followed this on 8/9 July with the destruction of another Ju 88 over France. Constable-Maxwell returned to the UK in December 1947 and in April 1948 took leave of absence to go to Ampleforth Monastery as a novice, where he remained for the next four years. He returned to the RAF in November 1952, retiring from the service in June 1964. On 13 August 1951 while on a navigation course at 228 OCU at RAF Leeming in North Yorkshire John Quinton was on board a Wellington detailed for an airborne interception exercise with a Martinet. During the exercise the Martinet and Wellington collided over the hamlet of Hauxwell near Richmond. The force of the impact caused the Wellington to break up and go out of control. Quinton picked up the only parachute within reach and clipped it on to ATC Cadet Derek Coates' harness. Pointing to the ripcord Quinton indicated that the cadet should jump. A large hole then appeared in the side of the Wellington flinging the cadet clear. Coates was the only survivor from the six men aboard the Wellington and he survived to tell the story of Quinton's unselfish act of bravery. Both men in the Martinet also died. For his heroism John Quinton was awarded the George Cross. Each year the Quinton Cup is awarded to the most efficient ATC Squadron in the North West region. Derek Coates emigrated to Perth, Australia. John Quinton lies buried in Leeming village cemetery along with three other members of the Wellington crew.

262 On 10 July 1945 a fifth PR.34 (RG191/M) joined No 2 Detachment on the Cocos Islands but on the 14th, flying out on a sortie, the port engine began vibrating when 450 miles out. The pilot, Flight Lieutenant Edwards, feathered the propeller and jettisoned his wing-tanks, but the aircraft lost height and crashed in the sea on final approach. For several days the Mosquitoes' objectives over areas of western Malaya, in preparation for Operation *Zipper,* were cloud-covered but Squadron Leader Newman and Warrant Officer Reg Smith, in RG185/Z, obtained satisfactory cover of Jahote Bharu and Singapore Island on the 16th. On 22 July Flight Lieutenant D. Warwick and Flying Officer C. Jowles in RG186/C covered more airfield sites at Batu Pabat, Yong Peng and Kluang in Johore State, Malaya. Four days later Newman and Flight Sergeant Pateman in RG184/X obtained further airfield coverage of Aitmotek in Sumatra, of Changi on the coast, Singapore Island, Tebtati, Bato Pahat and Lumut (Sitiawan) on the west coast.

263 Two PR.34s were duly lost, PR XVI NS528 breaking its back as a result of a heavy landing at Alipore on 11 August and newly-arrived PR.34 RG213/O ditched into the sea at China Bay eight days later whilst attempting to land on one engine. The crews were unhurt but both aircraft were written off.

264 On 20 August Flight Lieutenant J. R. Manners and Warrant Officer F. A. Bodey in RG210/J photographed Penang Island and Taiping in northern Malaya during a return trip of 2,600 miles on a record 9 hour 5 minute flight.

INDEX